➤ ANALYTICAL STUDIES IN W

Analytical Studies in World Music

⊷ EDITED BY ⊶

Michael Tenzer

UNIVERSITY PRESS

2006

OXFORD
UNIVERSITY PRESS

Oxford University Press, Inc., publishes works that further
Oxford University's objective of excellence
in research, scholarship, and education.

Oxford   New York
Auckland   Cape Town   Dar es Salaam   Hong Kong   Karachi
Kuala Lumpur   Madrid   Melbourne   Mexico City   Nairobi
New Delhi   Shanghai   Taipei   Toronto

With offices in
Argentina   Austria   Brazil   Chile   Czech Republic   France   Greece
Guatemala   Hungary   Italy   Japan   Poland   Portugal   Singapore
South Korea   Switzerland   Thailand   Turkey   Ukraine   Vietnam

Published by Oxford University Press, Inc.
198 Madison Avenue, New York, New York 10016

www.oup.com

Oxford is a registered trademark of Oxford University Press

Library of Congress Cataloging-in-Publication Data
Analytical studies in world music / edited and with an introduction by Michael Tenzer.
    p.   cm.
Includes bibliographical references and index.
ISBN-13 978-0-19-517788-6; 978-0-19-517789-3 (pbk.)
ISBN 0-19-517788-6; 0-19-517789-4 (pbk.)
1. World music—Analysis, appreciation.   I. Tenzer, Michael.
MT90.A56 2006
780'.9—dc22   2005016398

The audio files on the referenced companion CD are available online at
www.oup.com/us/aswm. Access with username Music3 and password Book3234

Printed in the United States of America
on acid-free paper

When first imagining this book, I had something very colorful and diverse in mind, but also something suitably intense and challenging. Even a forgiving interpretation of what the book's title suggests raises fears of a cook's tour, a smorgasbord of technical information about music from everywhere, without enough of the insight that makes analysis musical. If the finished product allays those concerns at all, it is because of the excellence of the contributors. I thank them all for being so marvelous to work with. My gratitude extends to Kim Robinson at Oxford, whose enthusiastic and steadfast faith in the project from the beginning saw it through. At the end, Maisie Sum provided superb editorial assistance.

Traveling the world as a musician—literally or in the proverbial armchair—is often entrée to an experience of human connection through mutual appreciation of a culture's best creativity and ingenuity. Listening together with musicians anywhere leads to eyes widened, heads shaken in amazement, and shared admiration. In each of these chapters the reader should recognize some of that sense of wonder.

I owe my own attitudes toward music, travel, and experience to important mentors. There is my father, to begin with, and many musical polymaths I have thanked elsewhere. On this occasion I single out only Philippine composer-scholar José Maceda (as I write it is May 4, 2005, the first anniversary of his death) and Balinese musicians Gusti Madé Griya, Nyoman Rembang, and Wayan Sinti, artists of incomparable mastery, humility, breadth, depth, and curiosity, whose lives are models to aspire to. To all of these, *musician* is a single category, and life means rising to meet all of its challenges.

→ CONTENTS ←

CONTENTS

William Benjamin (w.benjamin@ubc.ca) received a Ph.D. in music from Princeton University in 1976 and has been a faculty member at the University of British Columbia since 1978. He began publishing in leading journals over thirty years ago, with studies of works by several twentieth-century composers, critiques of present-day analytical method, and contributions to the theories of harmony and meter. More recently, his scholarly work has shifted to the intersection of music theory, cognition, and aesthetics.

Stephen Blum teaches ethnomusicology at the City University of New York Graduate Center. He contributed to the volumes of *The Garland Encyclopedia of World Music* on the United States and Canada, the Middle East, and Europe. He is the author of the articles "Composition" and "Central Asia," and co-author of nine other entries in the second edition of *The New Grove Dictionary of Music*. Among his analytic writings are articles in *L'Homme, Studia Musicologica,* a chapter in *Ethnomusicology: An Introduction,* edited by Helen Myers, and others.

Donna A. Buchanan is associate professor of music and director of the Russian, East European, and Eurasian Center at the University of Illinois at Urbana-Champaign. She is the author of *Performing Democracy: Bulgarian Music and Musicians in Transition* (University of Chicago Press, 2006) and directs and performs with Balkanalia, the University of Illinois Balkan Music Ensemble.

Stuart Folse received his DMA in composition from the University of Texas at Austin in 1997. In 1998 he joined the faculty of Roosevelt University's

Chicago College of Performing Arts, where he is an associate professor of music theory.

Susanne Fürniss (furniss@vjf.cnrs.fr.) is ethnomusicologist at the Centre National de la Recherche Scientifique (France). She works on Pygmy music (Aka and Baka) and is particularly interested in musical systematics and in the articulation between musical categories and the socioreligious system of a given society.

Peter Manuel teaches ethnomusicology as a professor at John Jay College and the CUNY Graduate Center. He has researched and published extensively on traditional and contemporary musics of India, the Caribbean, and Spain.

Robin Moore is associate professor of music at the University of Texas. His awards include fellowships from the Rockefeller Foundation, the MacArthur Foundation, and the National Humanities Center. Among his publications are *Nationalizing Blackness: Afrocubanismo and Artistic Revolution in Havana, 1920–1940* (University of Pittsburgh Press, 1997) and numerous articles on Cuban music. His bands Areíto, Conjunto 23, and Crisol play frequently.

Robert Morris is professor of composition and affiliate member of the Theory and Musicology departments at the Eastman School of Music, University of Rochester. A well-known composer and author, he has written over 150 works, including computer and improvisational music. He also has been active as a music theorist and author of three books, and over forty scholarly articles and essays. Morris was the recipient of the Outstanding Publication Award of the Society for Music Theory in 1988 and 2002. He continues as co-editor of *Perspectives of New Music.*

John Roeder (j.roeder@ubc.ca) is a professor of music theory in the School of Music at the University of British Columbia. His research focuses on theories of rhythm and pitch in recent art music, and extends to computer applications, musical semiotics, and rhythm and form in earlier music.

Elizabeth Sayre (esayre@mindspring.com) is a Ph.D. candidate in ethnomusicology at Wesleyan University, and specializes in West African and Afro-Latin percussion. She has been active as a performer, writer, organizer, teacher, and consultant in the Philadelphia area since 1990 (Philadelphia Folklore Project, Asociación de Músicos Latino Americanos, Temple University, and Swarthmore College).

Jonathan P. J. Stock, coeditor of *The World of Music,* is professor in ethnomusicology at the University of Sheffield, UK. His books include *World Sound Matters: An Anthology of Music from around the World* (London, 1996), *Musical Creativity in Twentieth-Century China: Abing, His Music, and Its Changing Meanings* (Rochester, N.Y., 1996), and *Huju: Traditional Opera in Modern Shanghai* (Oxford, 2003).

R. Anderson Sutton is professor of music at the University of Wisconsin-Madison, where he teaches ethnomusicology, directs the Javanese gamelan ensemble, and is currently Director of the Center for Southeast Asian Studies. He has published three books and numerous articles on music in Indonesia (Java and South Sulawesi).

Michael Tenzer (mtenzer@interchange.ubc.ca; http://www.interchg.ubc .ca/mtenzer/) is professor of music at the University of British Columbia and director of Gamelan Gita Asmara in Vancouver. He is active as a teacher, author, composer, and performer. His *Gamelan Gong Kebyar* (University of Chicago, 2000) was awarded the 2001 Alan P. Merriam Prize for best book in Ethnomusicology and the 34th ASCAP-Deems Taylor Award.

Roger R. Vetter is an associate professor in the Music Department at Grinnell College, Iowa. He has studied the central Javanese gamelan tradition over the past thirty years. His publications on the subject have appeared in professional journals and edited volumes, as published field recordings, and on Web sites (e.g., http://web.grinnell.edu/courses/mus/gamelans/open.html).

Analysis, Categorization, and Theory
of Musics of the World

MICHAEL TENZER

A symphony is a musical epic . . . a journey leading through the boundless reaches of the external world," says the narrator in *The Book of Laughter and Forgetting*, Milan Kundera's fantasia-like novel of Czechoslovakia in the throes of mid-twentieth-century communism, but "the journey of the variation form leads to that second infinity, the infinity of internal variety concealed in all things." He is recalling what his father tenderly taught him as a child: that symphonies progress through a limitless musical field, whereas variations descend deep into a paradoxical space that is both bounded and infinite; and that the two archetypes encompass the eternal questions music poses.

In life we aspire to both kinds of journeys, accepting that we cannot literally travel as far as we might wish, but grateful that music evokes them. Music-knowledge is wisdom, and we require it in both of its contrasting manifestations. Kundera longs especially for the inner passage: "That the external infinity escapes us we accept with equanimity; the guilt over letting the second infinity escape follows us to the grave. While pondering the infinity of the stars, we ignore the infinity of our father."

Kundera's exemplars for these complementary sorts of musical explorations were Ludwig van Beethoven and other great European composers, whose compositions he contrasted with the Czech pop music "idiocy" of the era, mocked as "music minus memory." In his time and place this apparent choice, politically charged, was between art and mass-market music, and Kundera makes a clear claim of superiority for the former. But he and his father, thoughtful contemplators, also invoke spiritual qualities by comparing musical space and time,

3

motion and stasis, perspectives of musical macro and micro levels, as well as external and inner experience, all as dimensions of musical knowing. They submit that there are kinds or categories of musical journeys as well as magnitudes of scale on which to perceive them, and that sensitivity to the differences—what we call analysis—enriches the voyage.

A generation ago, a book on music analysis would not have questioned Kundera's repertoire preferences. Today things are different, but we still appreciate such choices in their historical (and especially in his case, political) context. But now the classical/popular or Western/non-Western divide is frozen in the past. People's taste and purview scan the world, and claims to monopoly on musical value are disenfranchised. European repertoire, in this book as in music scholarship and culture at large, seeks equal footing and inexorably interacts with other music. It is but one music tradition among many world traditions of specific local origins now best thought of as more or less historical phenomena that have coursed separately to a delta beyond which the fate of their identities is presently unknown. Ubiquitous recording media and computer technology accelerate this mixing and destabilize not just Western music's centrality but also the notational literacy associated with it (Taruskin 2004; Halle 2004). To sail with the boats on that rising tide, however, leads to a threshold this book stops short of crossing. Assembling musics of the world together and juxtaposing them via transcription in staff notation asserts the present and future value, Eurocentric or not, of notational literacy as a potent means of imagining, knowing, comparing, and emulating sounds and sound-structures. Computers, recordings, books, and scores are a mutually enhancing quartet.

This is a book by music scholars, teachers, composers, performers, and theorists offered to all musicians, but especially to students, who need models for resisting pressure to identify themselves exclusively as one kind of musician or other. Kundera's stirring metaphors of discovery inspire us to know many kinds of music in many ways. Here we inscribe and analyze musical structure to journey attentively into it, to experience each performance/piece/sound-world as a singular, textured, and refined event; an utterance shaped, both like and unlike language, from individual creativity and the collective resourcefulness and effort of the generations. It is as if a composition or performance tries to speak to us in carefully hewn gestures, nuanced like the behaviors of someone we know well communicating a particular message with heightened awareness on a particular day. We instinctively strive never to distort or trivialize it. Seeking both specific and broader meanings in each analysis is critical

> If we are to distinguish one experience from another, if we are to have an identifiable experience with some music—you name it—that differs from an identifiable experience with some other music. Entering

4

into, entrapping, enticing us; touching, moving, alienating, enraging; our thoughts concerning our music emanating out of our hearts and minds, our senses, our bodies; at times, our entire being; at times, just a part of us; at times, no part at all. Rather like experiences and relationships we have with individual persons throughout our lives. (Barkin 1992:229)

But is the metaphor of analysis-as-discovery valid for all music? Is it all right to analyze music independent of its political, geographical, or cultural distance from the analyst or reader? Shall we allow ourselves to become absorbed in music's sound, conceiving of it as if in isolation from the world? Polemics and traditions of debate surround these questions which we visit in a moment, but no clean resolution exists. The response proposed here is nonetheless that yes, it is valid to do so, and anticipation of pleasure and refinement to be had is sufficient rationalization. We are all creatures of culture and ideology, but there is a moment in analysis at which we must curtail our penchants for modernist universalism, postmodern irony, or other language-based responses in order to confront music as elementally as possible. We submit that analysis is a path to musical awareness and better musicianship. Our purpose is to make the diverse systems of musical thought under consideration available for creative musicians looking for an informed basis on which to know assimilate, model, or borrow from world musics. The authors are at pains to crystallize what is distinctive about the music they discuss at the level of their selection itself, in its cultural context, and in implicit relation to the chapters surrounding it.

The goal of the second half of this introduction, moreover, is to suggest a simple and unified perspective on music structure that may enable closer comparisons and the formulation of common principles. With any luck, such an encompassing perspective may rouse us to a vision of what we can aspire to as musicians in the decades to come. At the end there is time to reflect on how we might harness energy from the contemporary world's torrent of musical interactions and put it to work shaping our futures. Our best energies will be well spent if we try to conceive of how we can influence musical change. The potential is enormous: ethnomusicologist John Blacking seems to speak with Kundera and his father in saying that the most efficacious use of music is for

the education of human emotions, the attainment of ownership of the senses, and the expansion of consciousness and social relations . . . the whole point of understanding music *as* music is that we carry in our bodies the cognitive equipment to transcend cultural boundaries and resonate at the common level of humanity. (1983:15)

Analysis: Definition and Perspectives

The eleven contributors to this volume are indebted to traditions of music analysis that shape their approaches to music and what they view as analytically relevant. They were invited to provide basic background and context for their selections, leading to a close reading of a single recorded musical work/performance from the perspective most important to them. Here I will consider some general contexts of music-analytical thought before locating the chapters in relation to these currents.

Analysis in Modern Western Discourse

Analysis as we shall speak of it is the encounter between the hierarchy-seeking mind and the music-sound event, often (as here, but not necessarily) inscribed in some way so as to fix it for study.[1] The encounter consists of structural listening— listening with explicit attentiveness to musical design and architecture—followed by reflection and synthesis, and is supported by the analyst's musical skill and experience. It is important to emphasize the listener's individual prerogative and agency in music analysis: one can listen structurally because one chooses to, for other ways of listening are means to different ends. But as we define it, the central result of analysis is the identification and grouping of manifest sound patterns and their relationships to governing schema in a work, repertoire, or genre, and especially the compelling musical tension that results as the patterns become set off in relief from the schema.[2] A description of the immanent, underlying principles uniting diverse musics (however delineated) is best thought of as theory; analysis is the application of theory to reveal individuality within and between levels of structure.

Music analysis must be rigorous but it is essentially creative, with only tangential claims to being scientific.[3] Once observed, sound-patterns can be mo-

---

1. Musicians in many cultures preserve complex musical structures in their minds without notation as a reference and think theoretically or analytically about them. Analysis is made possible by musical memory.

2. The two never coincide as musical schema are Platonic concepts, not human realities.

3. Scientific knowledge, per epistemologist Karl Popper, involves the necessity of being able to disprove and discard earlier theories in favor of more powerful explanations. Music theory and analysis do not partake of that kind of progress: analyses are always interpretations that do not supplant, rather complement, other analyses. Other dimensions of this issue are explored in depth in Meyer 2000, ch. 1. Perlman (2004:5–7) demonstrates the subjective contingency of music theory especially well, implying that it and analysis are not fundamentally separate creatures, but rather two levels of the same quest to make

bilized for many purposes: to demonstrate or inspire compositional depth or ingenuity, to discover an archetypal sound-structure model on which a music or repertoire is based, to symbolize or reflect a philosophy, social value or belief (of the analyst, the composer(s), performer(s), or their society), to reveal a historical process of change, to unearth unsuspected connections to music elsewhere, to embody a mathematical principle. Good analysis demystifies by cracking sound codes, better enabling the ear to collaborate with the mind in search of richer experience.

In the West, analysis is allied with a conception of absolute music, music as escape-from-the-world, that has roots in nineteenth-century European romanticism and earlier. In describing music, Theodor Adorno emphasized the "truth value" that analysis reveals (1982:176), and although he, like Kundera, had only one kind of music in mind, we still know what he means. The "truth" is insight into how the hierarchic organization of music helps us tune into indispensable percepts different from those ordinarily gleaned from the world around us. This impels us to see what music provides as legitimate, even privileged, experience, which would otherwise be unknowable.[4] Through analysis, we also may have the opportunity to understand and acknowledge that musical structures—not unlike cultural or mythic narratives that shape us (and of which we may be equally unaware)—result from the time-tested efforts of successive forebears, and constitute a treasured inheritance, even as our generation adds to and modifies them.

Questioning the motivations for analysis and the validity of its results is always important. In the closing years of the twentieth century, analysis weathered an intellectual storm precipitated by the ascent of cultural relativism in the preceding decades. Relativism is more of a reaction than a perspective: it takes a critical view against Western enlightenment's claims to universal value, and wants to understand what other peoples and histories have to say (Krausz 1989). Wide-ranging debates over the value of analysis, especially in terms of its ideologies, have raged in music scholarship; here we want to be aware of these polemics without allowing them to paralyze us. Bear in mind that despite these debates, the experiential value of analysis—the extent to which it teaches the mind and ear—has rarely been at issue. In a discussion of transcription from

---

sense of music. Both rely not on autonomous principles or even necessarily agreed-on social conventions, but rather on individual theorists' and analysts' perspectives and their institutional and social circumstances.

4. This is quite different, as Leonard Meyer points out, from enriching our actual musical experience. An analysis, or a theory on which it is based, may enrich our understanding of how a music is made, but this is not to be confused with the phenomenon of the music itself, which is "ineffable" (2000:292).

recordings or performances (itself a very important kind of analysis since the act of notating music requires deciding how to represent virtually all music elements), ethnomusicologist Ter Ellingson wrote definitively that "one goal of transcription is the experience of transcription itself" (1992:147). It is a given that analysis—whether based on focused interior listening, working with a composer's score, or by making one's own transcription—is a worthy exercise because it brings us to a more intensive relationship with the particularities of sound. What arises next is the question of how we interpret and present our perceptions and decisions.

Adorno's truth has an implied aura of universality, and we should be mindful that his view seeks to fuse scientific-style inquiry with artistic sensibility in the name of the universalist legacy of European Enlightenment thought. Seeing art as *the* privileged domain of truth is an idea inherited from his nineteenth-century Romantic predecessors. In any event, we shall allow Adorno, in his established role as iconic musical thinker, to represent the modern West for current purposes. His is not the only perspective, but he has been both celebrated and critiqued extensively. To Adorno, music sound is a fixed autonomous object consisting of the composer's work, separated out even from words in song or opera. It is a container of quasi-sacred truth-knowledge to be revealed, and this powerful knowledge is analogous to the reach and might of the culture itself. Autonomy suggests abstraction and aloofness from the real world and is compelling in a religious way, too, like the tolling timelessness of dictum.

This is not an outrageous analogy to make, as Nettl's (1995) persuasive allegory of music conservatory-as-religious-system memorably illustrates. Dicta come from on high and regulate beliefs for the diverse world below; thus the more abstract analytical knowledge of Western music is, the more ostensibly authoritarian, and potentially condescending to other music systems and beliefs about music.[5] Scores of polemics since the 1970s have brought this realization home, making it essential to care about how we circumscribe the validity of our analyses, make appropriately modest claims for them, and account for them as interpretations rather than pronouncements about what is universally valuable (or, unworthy) in music.[6] The crux of the political critique of

5. Nettl explains the resemblance of the behaviors, beliefs, and institutions of the culture of Western art music to the legacy of Judeo-Christian religious practices. See also Small (1998: 87–93) on the perceived mythical character of great European composers.

6. In ethnomusicology, the debate between Kolinski and Herndon in the 1970s was especially dynamic and formative (Herndon 1974, 1976, and 1977; Kolinski 1974, 1976, 1977). Martin Stokes (2001:394) summed up the prevailing perspective in his depiction of recent ethnomusicology written for the *New Grove Dictionary:* scholars are "ambivalent about the application of western music-theoretical systems to non-western musics"; apply-

Western analysis has been to urge a cautionary "stop" to those who would adopt rhetoric like Adorno's uncritically, or who would not take into account (even implicitly) other kinds of musical value or complexity.

A different sort of critique, emerging from studies of music cognition and perception, considers the listener's point of view. Music analysts sometimes seem to be saying that one *must* listen structurally, the deeper and more abstractly the better. Yet should we? Listening is the most discrete and interior of activities as our ears do not visibly focus like our eyes and hence they reveal nothing about what they perceive to outside observers (Szendy 2001:29). Inside our own minds we may relate to music in many ways. Nicholas Cook claims that structural listening is not necessarily related to musical experience, and may be far less important than has been claimed (1990:15–21). Is it a chore, then, to even try? Adorno would have us *only* hear structurally but Cook would say to ease up and listen associatively for what music signifies to us personally, historically and culturally. Beyond either of these approaches, we often use music to evoke just a mood, which might be spoiled by too much attentiveness, so shall we just listen moment-to-moment, sensuously, or even distractedly, according to our whims?

The answer is that we choose the most appropriate listening mode depending on circumstance. Yet in defense of structural listening one can aver that structure, although abstract, has indispensable objective properties. For one thing, we need to know structure in order to grasp and admire the accomplishments of musicians as designers, builders, and inventors of ingenious frameworks for sound, itself an inspiring objective. Structure guides composition, enables performers to comprehend and interpret, and, as something anyone with suitably developed capacities can perceive, provides a basis for common understanding and appreciation. Music has many dimensions other than structure, but the sharing of its cultural and personal significance has limits without the basis structure provides. We need to hear structure to give our diverse personal interpretations a common orientation. Structural listening deepens specifically musical experience.

Is every analysis an expression of ideology? Yes, in that we are who we are. Rather than shirk from the supposed risks of subjectivity, and without insisting that one must *always* listen for structure, let us do what we can. Musicians need to create representations of music *as music* in order to embody it and teach it: but we also must be ideologically self-aware. Analysis may have been part of the problem, but, reconstructed, it also provides many good solutions.

---

ing theory and analysis amount to a "quasi-colonial form of ethnocentrism." In historical (Western) musicology Susan McClary's *Feminine Endings* (1991) and many associated publications in the early 1990s raised doubts about the supposed ideological neutrality of earlier analytical work.

Analysis and Musics of the World

The introspective autocritique summarized above is part of a Western culture in which doubt and self-questioning have been core values since Socrates. People in some cultures regard their musical knowledge as especially powerful and worthy of keeping secret; of course, this is a tenet one sensibly wants to treat with both common sense and respect (Berliner 1978:7; Nettl 1983:290–300). But in general there have not been voices from elsewhere accusing analysts of non-Western musics of pillaging; nor have other cultures weighed in to say that they think analysis is a bad idea. To the contrary, there have been what I would characterize as commonplace musical behaviors: interest and willingness to share. Perhaps only we analysts see the stakes as high enough to merit pondering our actions in terms of a moral or ethical quandary. In my own experiences in Bali and South India, whenever I had the chance to explain my enthusiasm for talking about music sound and structure, people were never negative; their responses ranged from respectful apathy to intense curiosity, to immediate and productive debate about musical details.

Recent scholars of African music have argued forcefully against many Western observers' "denial" of the potential for analysis to be enlightening in those repertoires. The claim is that this neglect has been a form of racism that "reduced [African music] to a functional status or endowed [it] with a magical or metaphysical essence that put it beyond analysis" (Agawu 2003:183). Writers such as Agawu or Scherzinger (2001) assert that to analyze African music is to welcome it into international musical discourse, and to empower African musicians to publish their own findings. Although the situation is different everywhere, when people cross borders to analyze others' music, it is usually motivated by respect and desire to understand. Few respond to that unkindly. Negative forms of such border-crossing appropriations are certainly possible, however, so inappropriate ones ought to be critiqued and questioned.

Throughout the twentieth century, via practices such as ethnomusicology and anthropology, a worldwide topography of musical practice, value, and meaning was under construction. Discourse in the arts and humanities evolved to accommodate a kaleidoscope of multiple voices. It is our common lot to look or move around the world for guiding ideas. We listen and become aware of our affinities. Focusing those affinities into an analytical gaze is intrinsically difficult, however, especially when transcription and the learning of a foreign musical language and culture is involved. First, one asks what sort of cultural perspective is appropriate. Then, one must learn the music, often through fieldwork and the establishment of extended relationships with foreign musicians. Finally, one must formulate a point of view about it. This usually takes many years. One needs the discernment to evaluate which musical features are relevant and which are not, and according to whom. Most musics are in fact flexibly structured (unlike typical Western scores), or rely to varying degrees on improvisation, lack clear beginnings or endings, or are inextricable from ritual, poetry, or liturgy. Often the idea of a "piece of music" seems like an old butterfly net, frayed and torn, from which delicate creatures easily escape and avoid even sympathetic scrutiny. Often one is better off thinking in terms of a particular *performance* of music to be isolated by recording, and transcribed. But still, what should one focus on therein? Each writer makes choices and must explain and justify them.

One may emphasize learning and analyzing the music of others using a mixture of local and the researcher's own terminology and techniques (most of this book tilts in that direction); or one may focus more on how others do their own kinds of analyses for their own purposes. Local analytical knowledge is often implicit, passive knowledge not formalized through writing or even oral means; in other cases, it is formalized orally but regionally varied within a culture; in still other cases encounters between Western researchers and the musicians they study have engendered new, hybrid streams of analytical thought. Here, ideological sensitivity amounts to recognizing that in representing another musical system to facilitate one's own learning, some distortion is inevitable. Of course, even within well-bounded cultures there is never uniformity of understanding. Now that knowledge and ideas about world music cultures have leapt into international awareness, local concepts fluctuate and exchange with cosmopolitan ones all the more. The music appears differently even to its own creators once outsiders value it.

The idea of autonomous music is strengthened, for better or for worse, by the ease of transforming music into commodifiable, infinitely replayable digital bytes. Yet even before the age of infinite accessibility "absolute music" was compatible with the spiritual dimension of music in many non-Western societies. If musicians worldwide read Adorno and could overlook his Eurocentrism, many might nod in approval of his notion of musical truth, understanding it in ways relevant to them. What have come to be called ethnotheories—indigenous conceptualizations about music—are, unsurprisingly, less grandiose than he was, however.[7] Some ethnotheories are identified as such because researchers discover vocabularies people use to describe and critique their own music. Feld's definitive 1981 study of Kaluli use of metaphors of water flows to classify melodic shapes demolished older, myopic notions denying such kinds of knowledge to non-literate peoples. The affirming idea is that water and its life-giving power are as much a truth to Kaluli as Enlightenment thought is to Adorno.

---

7. Nonetheless, in some cultures (e.g., Brahman or Vedic), cosmologies linking sound and music to the ultimate questions of existence reach at least as far as Adorno did.

In learning music of oral traditions one is often deeply moved by how the best teachers, often trained without notation, cultivate not only amazing memories for music but also an internal mastery that unites repertoire, practice, theory, analysis and broad cultural knowledge as inseparable components of an encompassing musicianship. When such musicians need verbal or written analysis—perhaps for the first time, and especially in late-twentieth-century contexts—it is often because circumstances demand that they classify, describe, and become aware of what they hear for some practical purpose. They may need to teach it in modern institutions, collaborate with outside researchers, or transmit to the next generations. Thus, in Central Africa, Simha Arom elicited the simplest, model-like realization of a complex improvised music when, after years of study and transcription, he at last thought to ask performers how they taught it to initiates (1991:370). This model was a kind of analysis that the musicians used to teach their own children, although they did not think of it as such nor identify it until Arom asked them the right questions (see also the chapter by Susanne Fürniss in this volume). In Java, some late-twentieth-century musicians sought to inquire deeply into their music's structure in response to a pressing need to help students, an increasing number of whom were Western researchers (Perlman 2004:127–128). Yet even before that they had been impelled, by nature of their own cultural values, to undertake solitary quests for enlightenment regarding their music's true nature.

The South Indian scholar Sambamoorthy's vast classificatory system was developed in the mid-twentieth century at the University of Madras, where it filled a formal pedagogical need. In 1989, my tutorials with his successor Karaikudi Subramaniam were centered around the latter's intense microanalyses of South Indian vocal ornaments (*gamaka*), which instantly deepened my hearing of South Indian vocal styles. Many of Subramaniam's own Madrasi (Chennai) students had to adjust to his penchant for pinpointing such details, as they were used to absorbing them aurally and intuitively. But to me it was like a rocket into the music. It was the kind of experience that makes one want to come home to share the insight of understanding, even if just a bit, something so finely and carefully wrought.

Choosing Perspectives for This Book

Let us set those issues aside for now; they will arise again in the chapters to come. This is a book of analyses, not a study of debates about analysis or an argument for a particular method, though it is important to understand this discursive background before proceeding. Merely using the English language and distributing the book through the academic arm of Oxford University

Press unifies and privileges the collection in important fundamental ways. But within this there is ample room for diversity. The present objective is to provide tools to listen and to enrich with recordings, notation, and other visual aids. All authors use indigenous terms and concepts, combining them in differing amounts with imported ones. They focus on clearly defined "pieces" of music to the extent appropriate in each case; where improvisation or a flexible concept of musical form is important the analysis may also focus on principles or strategies for shaping music, as realized in the performance included on the enclosed CD. Readers must be mindful of the wise ethnomusicological counsel, echoed throughout, that music's intense formative contexts embed layers of meaning and experience that structural analysis alone cannot penetrate.

William Benjamin's study of Mozart and John Roeder's of Elliott Carter (chapters 10 and 11) represent Western art music in this global context. Their chapters level the playing field, defamiliarize that repertoire for those who have not yet ventured far beyond it, and bring it to the attention of world music students and scholars who might not ordinarily encounter it so intensively. It is a refreshing experience to have Mozart unapologetically called a "genius," as does Benjamin, without also having to reflexively assume an outdated view of the European art tradition as a lone and embattled bastion of worthy musical values. Mozart, at least, is relieved of having to guard those boarded-up old gates anymore.

That the playing field might be leveled is, at this time, more of a wish than a possibility, it is true. Benjamin and Roeder have at their disposal authoritative scores and a range of preestablished vocabulary and concepts developed to discuss everything from minutiae to large-scale form. Their springboard is the history of ideas, debates, writing, and theorizing that led to the current state of Western music theory. In keeping with the tradition's specially individualized aesthetics, they have the luxury of being able to focus on qualities owing as much to Carter's or Mozart's personal compositional style as to general or historical musical characteristics of the genres. But here they set for themselves the tricky task of approaching their topics as if outsiders themselves. They build concepts from scratch, as if explaining a foreign music to someone from their own culture, and as if the Western notation they employ is a neutral tool not specifically evolved to convey the music they consider. (Roeder, acting the ethnomusicologist, even retranscribes the published score so as to render it in a way that better reflects what he hears and wants to explain.) It is virtually impossible for these authors to pull off assuming such a pose, of course, yet it is very much worth trying for. Whether or not close to Western repertoires, readers are encouraged to receive these chapters in the spirit of imagining Western music as if it is new to them.

The remaining nine chapters appeal for parallel reasons to those who have yet to consider non-Western musics closely as structures. As noted earlier, much non-Western music does not come packaged to us with the kind of knowledge and specificity developed for the European art tradition—it must be gradually assembled through fieldwork and is typically augmented and extended by the scholar's own expertise. Peter Manuel, writing here of *flamenco* (chapter 3), nevertheless rejects the imposition of too much Western theoretical apparatus. He asserts that "formal structures seeking development, climax, and closure are distinctively modern bourgeois creations, [while] flamenco, in its essentially additive, sequential structure, is thus typical of many premodern forms," thereby declining to examine the performance at a higher level of form than that suggested by those sequential units. This assertion importantly brings us up short, raising questions as to what flamenco musicians may actively or passively know about what they do, what they may wish or find worthwhile to know, and whether it is fair or appropriate for scholars to layer on analytical conclusions that do not originate with the culture under consideration. The remaining chapters are comfortable with that layering process to varying degrees; Manuel reminds us to weigh the ramifications.

Donna Buchanan and Stuart Folse's study of Bulgarian *horo* (chapter 2) hews to remarkable articulate commentary fortunately provided by their teachers, who "systematically outlined the [music's] structure and creative process" for them. Speaking of modes, modulations, cadences, and improvisational strategies, they partake of a vocabulary both they and their teachers understand. Later, pointing out the structural ambuiguities inherent in the song *Georgi le, lyubile,* they move beyond this dialogue and are able to "offer some clue" as to their teacher's unspoken perceptions. They thus go slightly further than Manuel in terms of integrating their own analysis techniques, but their teachers' enthusiasm for the venture rings out clearly in support.

Stephen Blum's chapter on Iranian poet/singers' renditions of verse (chapter 1), Robert Morris's on a South Indian *varnam* (chapter 9), and R. Anderson Sutton and Roger Vetter's study of Javanese gamelan (chapter 7) all rely on musicological discourse and terminology from these traditions. They extend and focus it gently to illuminate what might not be evident to untrained ears, or make observations that emerge from considering specific performances as fixed objects of contemplation—an approach not necessarily relevant for practicing musicians inside the culture. Blum works near the interstices of literate and oral tradition. One of the main fruits of his chapter is the demonstration of how singers cope with the strict demands of the former in the context of the latter's flexibility. His cosmopolitan analysis begins invoking Wagner's *Tristan und Isolde* as an example of how poetic meter and musical rhythm interact. Blum soon juxtaposes Wagner with Iranian bards, then continues on to show something the bards themselves may not be aware of: how competing poetic and musical norms shape their music and provide options at the level of rhythm, melodic pattern, and instrumental pattern.

Robert Morris's study of a performance of the South Indian composition *Valachi Vacchi* describes the music in accord with venerable Indian discourses of music structure and terminology. He enriches his analysis by integrating the commentary and demonstrations of noted Indian scholar S. Bhagyalekshmy (CD tracks 16 and 17) then takes a leap by applying contour theory, a technique developed in the 1980s for analysis of post-tonal European art music but portable enough to enable new insight into very different musics. This explicitly cross-cultural fusion of preexisting tools produces an analysis whose enforced hybridity is strengthed by the author's mastery of both intellectual traditions.

Theory of central Javanese music is not as copious or old as Indian theory, but Sutton and Vetter's chapter about the Javanese gamelan composition *Ladrang Pangkur* nevertheless has a mature body of mainly twentieth-century scholarship to engage with, some indigenous and some Western. Yet most earlier studies of Javanese music are concerned with performance "rules" and the generalized explanation of music concepts and process (such as *gendhing*, basic compositional form and structure; or *garap*, improvisational treatment of melodic elements). This is because practicing musicians have sought guidance bringing the minimal skeletal framework traditionally provided for each piece to life. This must be done in a different way for each performance. By contrast, this chapter may be the first to consider in detail a particular Javanese performance as a finished product. The performers' many bold pathways through the cyclic template used to define the *gendhing* reveal an inner world of detours, transformations and asymmetries, the result of infinite choices the performers made. This complex manifest structure falls within norms that are just as much a part of the tradition as the performance practice, however. But it is new to grasp *what* Javanese musicians create, which importantly counterbalances the normative focus on *how* they create.

Robin Moore and Elizabeth Sayre must be inventive to analyze Cuban *batá* drumming and song (chapter 4), as that music has rarely been conceived or discussed in the way they do. It helps that the music's West African roots allow them to situate their analysis and transcriptions within a lineage of scholarship about other African or African-derived traditions. It is nonetheless incumbent on them to rigorously explain performance norms and the conventional freedoms and limitations of ritual and musical contexts *before* they can venture into the particulars of the recorded performance at hand. Once trained there with a fine enough lens, it becomes possible to follow the nuances of altered standard patterns, long calls, and conversational responses from supporting drums. The texture of the music comes alive with potential and significance to the attentive listener.

African polyphonic vocal traditions are comparatively less studied than drum-centered musics such as batá or its African antecedents, so Susanne Fürniss needed, even more than Moore and Sayre, to deduce principles of Central African Aka polyphonies and find ways to categorize and describe them (chapter 5). Although based on Aka terminology, her analysis (and that of her mentor Simha Arom) is almost entirely produced through observation, fieldwork, and meticulous transcription and comparison of a vast stock of melodic fragments and their variations. The emphasis on discovering underlying typologies and implicit cognitive models locates this kind of analysis in the lineage of French structuralism indebted to the anthropology of Claude Lévi-Strauss.

In a related way, my chapter goes some distance toward identifying a typology of melodic variants in a mid-twentieth-century Balinese composition (chapter 6), and then organizes this information to show how minimal the underlying structure actually is. At the same time I demonstrate that the music is practically without repetition at the surface. By pushing beyond the culture's own analytical observations, I make rather unexpected claims about form and structure that I point out to the Balinese musicians I have known and worked with, much to their interest. Yet they and I know well that without the use of their terminology, categories, and discourse about composition and style I would be unable to say a thing. Jonathan Stock's essay about the Shanghai opera star Yang Feifei is comparable in that way (chapter 8). By explaining how Yang's radical transformation of standard musical forms leads to new kinds of structural elegance, his analysis uncovers a remarkable by-product of her more immediate concern for invigorated expression and drama. As Stock concludes, knowledgeable Chinese listeners—and Yang herself—may not be aware of her own architectonic accomplishments. But his analysis, he continues, also can be integrated into a feedback loop of interaction involving the scholar and performer in future fieldwork and research situations. When this kind of thinking ricochets back to the creators of the music that stimulated it the analyst feels the satisfaction of making a contribution that can fuel further interaction, exchange, and musical development. That kind of long-range collaboration is a fitting hope for, and often a proven consequence of, cross-cultural musical contact.

The genres represented between these covers were selected with several balances in mind. Geographical diversity was a factor, but not a paramount one; it was not possible to be comprehensive even at the level of continents (Oceania is not discussed and the Americas are represented by African- and European-derived genres). Existing traditions of theory and analysis played a role as these can enrich; hence some weight has been shifted toward "larger" art music forms and ensembles (Java, Bali, India, Europe). "Smaller" musics such as those representing Iran and Bulgaria are here, too, as intricacy and musical interest are by far not the provenance of large ensemble or storied "classi-cal" traditions alone. Each writer's strength as an analyst and sympathy for the project (not axiomatic in ethnomusicology) was a factor, as was including con-tributors from both Europe and North America. Popular or contemporary or fusion musics ought to be here, but the roll of the dice (and limits of space) did not favor them this time; also, they have begun to receive ample analytical attention elsewhere (e.g., Covach and Boone 1997).

The book as a whole models a repartitioning of the universe of music study, to encourage close analytical work in all kinds of contexts. But what we do not have—and may never have—are the likes of native Aka analyses of batá drumming, or Iranian perspectives on flamenco, that would catapult us to different revelations. From Bulgaria to Bali, few devote themselves as think-ers to other musics unless they have passed through a Western education sys-tem. The open tent of cross-cultural analytical research is inseparable from the acquisitive Western culture that cultivated it. That conclusion is impossible to avoid, however one may view it.

World Music as a Context for New Music

Humans are biologically predisposed to making music and it played an impor-tant role in human evolution (Blacking 1972; Cross 2003; Dissanayake 2000). Correspondingly, it is music's nature to fuse, recombine, and proliferate like genes. Musicians and composers, witting or unwitting, acting independently or constrained by beliefs and institutions, are the matchmakers in these repro-ductive sonic trysts. Music fusion is inexorable and something of an advance guard for actual genetic fusion: no human intolerance nor any reservations about propriety stopped Spanish melodies from eloping with West African rhythms to form rumba in racist, socially segregated, late-nineteenth-century Havana. One of ethnomusicology's most enduring contributions has been to show that such weddings take place whether the cultural parents approve of them or not (especially when they don't, it seems), and that they both prefigure and catalyze broad social changes.

The courtship that produced rumba was centuries long. Our accelerated era is wholly different from old Cuba's slow hotbed of West African and Span-ish entwinement. That pace seems if anything luxurious in today's landscape. By comparison, contemporary music fusions are often like quick and casual ar-rangements, mail order bride services, or Las Vegas honeymoons, any of which may or may not work out in the end. A jazz trio fronted by koto, Gambian kora with string quartet, an orchestral work modeled on North Indian musi-cal form, gamelan with electronica for *manga* soundtrack, the proverbial sitar in the rock band—these are all post-late-twentieth-century alchemies arching across histories and cultures and designed by peripatetic musical geneticists. We become inured to such juxtapositions and the resulting hybrids, until recently felt to be radically novel, are common.

These comments are by way of observation. They are not intended as critique of the creators, whose actions as fusionists may range from inspired pilfering based on brief acquaintance to careful planning supported by years of immersion and reflection.[8] Neither way guarantees better music: mishearing can be as creatively productive as intensive engagement, and it is unwise to argue for one or the other approach. Whether such activities fragment, unite, or simply reconfigure us as human participants and receptors of music is also an open question to save for another time. The key realization is that the proliferation proceeds apace with tremendous energy and it requires sympathetic consideration not just to try to understand it, but to participate. That is why, in addition to reimagining the domain of analysis as something that is not positioned in terms of a Western/non-Western split, this book also assumes that analyst and composer are two interacting sides of each musical self. It is addressed equally to the composer in each of us and takes a proactive stance against the way Western music education channels students to choose among identities such as composer, theorist, musicologist, performer, and so on. In this book, designs and blueprints are available that may potentially contribute to future fusions. As a book written by educators and directed at learners, we assert that knowledge of structure in a variety of musics is necessary for the contemporary musician.

In the recent past, "new music" had a special niche in Western culture in terms of its complex range of tonalities (or atonalities), the radical contextuality of each work, instrumental virtuosity, alliance with computer research and technology, and the prestige of certain educational and performing institutions. That scene's exclusive and faithful core audience is no longer exclusive nor faithful. This reflects the composers, who are off exploring and have subverted everything that new music used to stand for, including and especially merging it with popular musics. But new music is best seen neither as the pedigree descendant of the Western tradition nor the constantly renewing product of the music industry; it is now nothing if not equivalent to world music in its prismatic and hybridizing forms.[9] Conservatory trained composers in Seoul

8. Critiques and explorations of ethical, aesthetic, political, and historical aspects of music fusions, particularly those involving the West, have appeared elsewhere; see especially the varied essays grouped in Born and Hesmondhalgh (2000).

9. Philip Bohlman (2002:36–39) defines world music as something unpredictable and fundamentally shaped by encounter and creative misunderstanding between people

work out their ideas on Korean drums and present them as a performers' collective, or in collaboration with Austrian jazz players. The Bang On a Can ensemble, fronted by their guest Burmese musician Kyaw Kyaw Nang, performs transcriptions of his traditional repertoire in New York. Of the best musical minds of our time, it can safely be said that "only a few of them are writing symphonies" (Halle 2004).

As stated, there are many justifications and goals for analysis. But today one of them surely ought to be activism—the development and promotion of a relevant and timely musicianship in accord with the international and cross-cultural nature of contemporary music creation. Once all of this is recognized and accepted, the task of theory and analysis becomes a fully global affair. But now that we have asserted that the music of the whole world is the proper context for new music, how shall we organize the former to make it comprehensible to the latter?

Categorizing Music

"I want to live the whole world of music," the American composer Henry Cowell (1895–1965) famously remarked. For some he was the oracle of that irresistible spirit of inquisitiveness and passion, setting the tone for generations of musicians whose similar impulses to musically merge with others are now enshrined as a central aesthetic of our time. If we take Cowell at his word, no music should be excluded from our view, at least in concept. But it is mind-boggling to suggest that all of it—on a scale from Gustav Mahler's gargantuan Ninth Symphony to the intimate whispers of Rosa Salolosit, a girl singing a "private song" in her small room on Mentawai, an island isolated hundreds of miles off the west coast of Sumatra (Yampolsky 1999)—can be usefully considered under a sole capacious rubric like musical analysis.[10] Yet such a conception is in fact inevitable as the music is already all around us and cannot be made unavailable any more. When I play that young girl's song for my students

---

making music at cultural interstices, a formulation that admits a Self/Other distinction rather than an East/West one, and extends to what is conventionally called Western New Music.

10. There is no point, at the outset at least, in judging. Are all musics *worthy* of analysis? That depends on the analyst's needs; besides, it takes equal amounts of insight to say clearly why one disparages a certain music, or why one is aloof towards it but recognizes its significance, or why one values it. Bad music is not off limits (see Washburne and Derno 2004), though here our motivation is desire to deepen a sincere and nonironic aesthetic pleasure.

we always feel uncomfortable in our classroom like eavesdroppers on something too intimate for our ears, listening to her tiny voice across oceans and years. But, the liner notes tell us, she consented—in fact, insisted—that the recording be made, that her song be digitally transported, and she practiced diligently in preparation for the recording session. I know both the recording engineer and producer personally. I trust them and their ethics, their human sensitivity. I can focus on the powerful inkling that she has something to teach us, and from what we know of Mahler, he would do the same.

We may ultimately only be able to follow Cowell in spirit. Nevertheless, just to aspire to his vision we must sort and categorize all music in some way. It is much harder to propose a categorization now than when Cowell was alive because we have such a proliferation of nuanced perspectives on music, much more detail about its varieties, and endless access (not even a vague dream in his day). The amount of study needed to know even a few music cultures and repertoires further raises the magnitude of difficulty. We have more skepticism now, too, about the status of music as an objectifiable entity, and are more comfortable with the notion of music as something contingent, a process of producing organized sound subject to varied perception and interpretation by those who make and listen to it. Yet categorization remains a cognitive imperative prior to which meaningful learning is impossible. Our task is to choose a point of view best suited to the philosophy of this book, one also useful to future writers and capable of being further developed.

Shall we use criteria such as tuning system, mode, or rhythmic organization? What about ensemble size, age, musical instrument types, singing style, timbre, dance movement, or the use/absence of improvisation? We could stick with geography (what are West African musics like? or Central American ones?), an obvious choice that has driven much scholarship but misses the point in today's world of perpetual diaspora and transcontinental recombination. We could think in terms of broad historical categories—prehistoric, ancient, high civilization, or modern and postmodern (Wiora 1965). We might be drawn to base our categories on social concepts like culture, or its offshoots traditional/modern, local/global, high/low, cosmopolitan/rural, individual/collective, or others. What about trying to translate, cross-reference and compare already existing indigenous or ethnotheoretical music-categorization systems from around the world? (It is hard enough to make any two of these align, let alone a multitude of them!) Or something related to how people use music—for education, pleasure, refinement, ritual, governance, love, enculturation, capitalism? What of function, use, aesthetics, taste, value, durability, importance? This survey of choices is only the beginning and each threatens to reduce music to something far less than the sum of its parts.

One thing is clear: when we categorize according to a certain criterion, the results will disperse other criteria. For example, if we group musics by social function (e.g., dance music or work songs), we will not have separated them in terms of musical structure (e.g., tempo, or pitch content), and knowledge of the latter will remain elusive until we train our lens differently. It is thus imperative to choose wisely according to our needs.[11]

Many music categorizations have been proposed in the last century or so, and not a few before then. Among early comparative musicologists Alexander Ellis (1885) measured and sorted scales and tuning systems, whereas Curt Sachs (1943), who contributed many seminal works, grouped "primitive" singing styles and melody types according their origin in textual/liturgical or dance/celebratory contexts. Béla Bartók (1921, 1933, etc.) most influential of many musical forklorists active before 1950, grouped Hungarian (and several other nationalities') songs into age-stratified layers. Later, Mieczyslaw Kolinski copiously categorized pitch and rhythm varieties (1965, 1973, and others). Alan Lomax's *cantometrics,* a vast typology of world musics painstakingly coded according to thirty-seven criteria, was not well received when unveiled in 1976, at least partly because ethnomusicology was by then firmly committed to separate, relativistic studies of discrete cultural systems.[12] David Reck's memorable *Music of the Whole Earth* (1977), an inspiration for the present book, proposed division according to ensemble size, from solos ("alones," as he called them) to large ensembles ("togethers").

Music theorists offered not classifications, but techniques, or rubrics, through which one could view all music: in the early 1970s, Benjamin Boretz published his phenomenological *MetaVariations,* and in the 1980s James Tenney brought out *MetaHodos,* originally written in the '60s. Rober Cogan's *New Images of Musical Sound* and his many publications with Pozzi Escot in the journal *Sonus,* and Jay Rahn's *Theory for All Music* (1985) also appeared around this time. Cogan offered graphic acoustical snapshots, and Tenney was concerned with describing varieties of *klang,* or sound complex. Rahn, following Boretz, promulgated analysis based on strict adherence to empiricals, that is, solely what was written in the score or transcription. What Rahn called "men-

11. An incisive theoretical approach to the study of musical categorization is found in Arom et al. (2005). An earlier, incomplete version of the same research was Olivier and Riviere (2001).

12. Blum (1992) is an invaluable study of analytical classification schemes in the history of ethnomusicology. Slobin (1992) was a remarkable categorization not of music itself but a vast array of cultural formations and perspectives; ethnomusicologists were so hungry for such a document that it achieved "classic" status almost instantly.

talism," that is, anything attempting to account for people's perceptions or ideas about music, was deemed subjective and unknowable, hence off-limits.[13]

The failure of such comparative or culture-blind perspectives to exert sustained influence is commensurate with thte twentieth century's grand march toward knowledge specialization in all fields. Ethnomusicologically speaking, the aim has been to describe music cultures everywhere as particular phenomena so as to know them on their own terms, obviously an inestimably valuable collective venture. Here we avail ourselves of some of that knowledge to categorize with a different purpose: to abet the *activist use* of world music, to sort the music, as it were, into the drawers and compartments of a toolbox. This feels natural enough, as most of us are generalists or comparativists in our everyday experience. We hear music from all over, take or teach "world music" courses, and read encyclopedic music books from *Grove's Dictionary* to the *Rough Guide*. The question thus becomes: which criteria are most useful for the creative musician? Posing this is possible only if one accepts the utility of broad perspectives and is ready to live with their shortcomings. Standing on the shoulders of the many hoary debates about representation and discourse in music analysis glimpsed in the foregoing, we focus on *efficacy*. What can we put to productive use?

Periodicity and the Composer's Toolbox

For our categorization criterion, we turn to *periodicity,* a term from mathematics and physics referring to regular recurrence of waveforms, functions, or phenomena (e.g., orbits). In music, periodicity has long signified repetition or restatement, literal or transformed, of all kinds—of beats, rhythms, motives, melodies, structures, timbres: virtually any musical element can create a sense of stability through return or constancy, and such stability will always be in dynamic dialog with change. The potential for change and transformation within a higher-order framework of repetition is suggested by the related but distinct use of the word *period* to name time scales as long as historical eras: we understand Western music history, for example, in terms of transitions from, say, baroque to classic periods, while acknowledging that the fact of such change is both predictable and takes place in characteristic ways (a period of innovation followed by consolidation, and so on). For periods of all kinds, *plus ça change, plus c'est la même chose.*

Music is nothing if not iteration and pattern; periodicity is music's ultimate organizer on many levels. It is multidimensional and its range of quali-

13. In the 1960s, ethnomusicologists tried something similar, devising mechanical transcription devices such as the Seeger melograph.

ties should not be conceived along any single complexity scale. Periodicity is time line, cycle, riff, ostinato, passacaglia, song form, sentence form, meter, drum pattern, call-and-response, twelve-bar blues progression, tala (India), usul (Turkish), iqa'at (several Arabic), ban (China), gongan (Java and Bali), changdan (Korea), clave (much Caribbean), aksak (Eastern Europe),[14] hayayahyoshi (ancient Japanese court) and on ad infinitum, with many ideas, terms, and manifestations both within each music culture and suggested by outside scholars. The absence of periodicity in *any* music is a challenge to imagine. Even if one could invent such music algorithmically, we, as aware listeners, would impose or construct pattern, as that is the nature of mind relating to world.

For over a century extinguishing periodicity by creating continuous variation (Johannes Brahms, Arnold Schoenberg, Anton Webern) or types of hypercomplexity, or indeterminacy (Pierre Boulex, John Cage, Iannis Xenakis) was a major preoccupation among Western composers, and continues to be for some (Brian Ferneyhough).[15] The effort to comprehend such music's structure, especially in contrast to the highly ordered periodicities of earlier tonal music, has been a core goal for theorists and analysts of Western music. That is, it is understood that composers attempted a fundamental break with the past of periodic tonal rhythms and underlying regularities, so analysts and theorists need to discern and describe other systems of coherence. Such twentieth-century music loomed large as a cultural jettisoning of the past, a powerful trope on the archetypal, intensifying individuality of Western humanity. "Liberated" from the periodic rhythms that bounded the Western tradition together in an earlier time, modern music sought to transcend this and approach an imagined "objective" state of perpetually renewing nature (Tenzer 2003:117). Zooming out to a worldwide perspective, however, the swansong efforts of modern composers can realistically be seen as significant only within the culture that produced it. When accounted for as a world music genre, the trend must instead take its place as a rare star in the galaxy of world musics—a small but vital exception proving the towering rule that periodicity is the stuff of music everywhere.

Periodicity is really a universal, inseparable from a conception of music. This justifies choosing it as a framework, but does not provide focus as virtu-

14. A term developed by the ethnomusicologist Constantin Brailoiu for metric types built from combinations of duple and ternary units (see Blum 1992: 176–177).

15. Even in such extreme cases, however, periodicity remains a crucial factor from virtually all perspectives except that of the composer's score. Although repetition may be sedulously avoided, inhere only minimally or be dispersed to the point of disappearance in the music *per se,* no such work is conceivable without the "slightly" extramusical factors of performers' repetition through preparation and rehearsal, and repetition as experienced through multiple performances, recordings, or listening.

ally nothing is excluded. For this we must subcategorize. Periodicity structures and measures musical time, so we shall be concerned especially with *types* of periodicities: essentially rhythmic, hierarchial structures that enable us to perceive entities labeled, in tonal European art music, with terms such as measure, meter, measure-group, hypermeasure, sentence, formal section, and the word period itself. The South Indian analogue to meter is *tala,* whereas other kinds of rhythmic groupings such as *mora* build rhythmic groups at higher levels. In Moore and Sayre's depiction of bata drumming, a basic metric periodicity is expressed through the repeating (literally stated or implied) *clave* pattern, whereas larger grouping structures emerge through the varied repetition of drum patterns (toques) and songs. Periodicities are *cyclic* or *metric* in that something equivalent to hierarchic beat or meter organizes them; higher-level periodicities constructed from groups of events are heard in relation to cycle and meter.

Some music (compositions for the Japanese bamboo flute *shakuhachi,* many kinds of chant, recent Western open form works, the pulse-less *alap* of Indian classical music) is, in terms of strict rhythm, *nonperiodic;* that is, unmeasured with steady beats or cycles. Yet any number of musical behaviors impel us to perceive regularized pattern in them nevertheless, with the result that we may legitimately listen to such musics *as if* they approximate periodic ones, because even without the framework of steady pulsation we may group events such as returning motives patterns or a series of agogic accents into period-like components (see Widdess 1994:62–68 for an interesting example of this). In the next section, I implicitly encompass such music when I sketch subcategories of periodicity types. Admitting such music into a categorization scheme founded on strict periodicity requires us to immediately relax our definition to accommodate what may not literally recur in either clock or rhythmically counted time, yet exhibit behaviors closely enough related to make the analogy plausible.[16] In this book, however, such music only appears *passim* in Stephen Blum's Iranian selection and Jonathan Stock's Chinese one; readers may decide for themselves whether passages in the Elliott Carter work John Roeder considers are so complex that periodicity is neutralized.

Why all these architectural perspectives? Because the way periodicities are laid out generates musical form, perhaps the most fundamental compositional concern. When one grasps how periodicity drives music one thinks and understands more compositionally than when one deals with a less malleable, more static element such as scale or mode. This means that, given a perspective as broad as ours, rhythms and formal structure are prior in importance to pitch and other parameters. In a manner of speaking periodicity *is* form, and content—what fills and to greater or lesser degrees generates form—is to be heard in re-

---

16. I develop and rationalize this analogy for Balinese music in Tenzer (2000:334).

lation to it and supported by it. Return to Kundera's archetypes and to how he reserved special awe for the inner voyage suggested by variation form—which we can now understand to mean the spiraling into periodicity, repetition, the simultaneity of change and constancy in a fixed, hierarchial formal frame. When we defined analysis earlier as a search for the ways sound patterns create tensions in relation to governing schema in music, the "governing schema" are the periodicities to which we now refer; the "sound patterns" are the musical materials, the content.[17] These interact and shape each other in as many ways as there are musics. Periodicity may be relatively static or dynamically entwined with process.

Periodicity orients us in music and a much larger hierarchy of time that connects to experience both at and beyond the scale of human lives. Lewis Rowell wrote memorably:

> The experience of human temporality in music arises as a result of our perception of time as an immense hierarchy, a hierarchy that extends from the smallest rhythmic units (individual tones, durations, accents, and pulsations) to intermediate levels of structure (patterns, phrases, poetic lines) to the larger, deeper structural levels (formal sections, entire compositions and performances). In the case of Indian music it seems particularly important to recognize and emphasize those aspects of the temporal hierarchy that outlast the duration of the individual musical event: musical seasons, creative lifetimes, the understandings that are handed down from teacher to student, . . . and the glacial evolution of musical practice and its theory over many centuries. (1992:181)

Given the venerable age of the Indian tradition he describes, it would be presumptuous not to grant Rowell his emphases, yet what he says is true for any time-tested music, else it would likely not survive.

Qualities of Periodicitiy

Periodicity is an implicit concern of every author in this book. Whether focusing on melody, rhythm, or some other element, in order to analyze their selection each must come to terms with this aspect of it. Looking forward to some future integrated, comprehensive categorization of the world's musical

---

17. Schema and content are fused in non-periodic contexts such that one must deduce which musical events (e.g., longer agogic accents, motivic rebeginnings, sudden contrasts) qualify for higher-level positions in an implied hierarchy.

periodicities, here we propose a beginning, a blueprint for organization, a grouping of architectural types as reflected in the ordering of the chapters and rationalized in what follows.

To begin, resist any easy intuition that music could be arranged along a two-dimensional continuum with some bare and unchanging heartbeat of an ancient ritual rhythm at one end and the ultimate aperiodic modern Western music at the other. World periodicities have infinitely distinctive qualities, unpredictable similarities, and extended family resemblances that demolish a linear logic; besides, a line-continuum with aperiodicity at one end smacks of an archaic Darwinism placing Western music at the culmination of world musical development. (Were such a line even possible the idea of direction or progress would still be an illusory byproduct of the visual metaphor "line": only diversity, not purpose as in a strict Darwinian view, would be represented there.) By contrast, a point of orientation is of course essential, and common sense leads us to try to find something straightforward to fill that need, something that can be directly compared to as many other things as possible. Perhaps economical is a better term, for simple periodicities need not correlate with simple music.

Rather than a line, let our model be a constellation in motion around a hub of *isoperiodicity* (figure I.1). Seen from the perspective of their periodicities the most economical musics are those that are *isoperiodic:* constructed from the uninterrupted reiteration of a single, bounded musical time cycle. In this book, isoperiodicity is offered not as a beginning but as a focal point—in part II—for other musics to congregate around; and it is discussed first below. I discuss it first because it is particularly essential to the book's organization; but I place the actual chapters about isoperiodic music second so that they appear in the middle or center of the book, as they do in the constellation "model." The realization of the book's concepts in these contrasting configurations illustrates that music's organizing principles cannot be ordered or compared in any single way. The dotted-line rings in the figure are intended to be merely suggestive of the many other possible ways to group and interrelate the chapters.

In part I, described after part II, tensions between contrasting periodicities coexist sequentially within individual musical works or performances. These may be restricted to a small number of culturally authoritative musical states that recur in some conventional order. In other cases, the logic is not one of return but of succession, where different states follow each other, medleylike, without necessarily ever looking back. The musics in part I might be described as having a series of discrete isoperiodicites, including both cyclic and unmeasured structures. In part III, described last, a music's grounded, fundamental periodicity cedes some control as it meets an overarching compositional logic

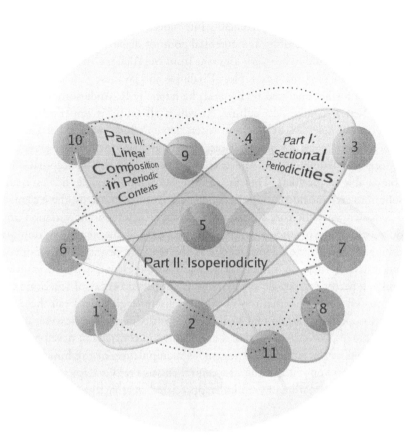

Figure I.1. *A constellation model for the book's chapters. Graphics realized by Adriana Dawes.*

binding it over longer spans to other processes, be they melodic, harmonic, or indeed other periodicities layered on simultaneously. Here periodicity is malleable, extendable, and adaptable to the expressive needs of the moment.

Part II: Strict and Discursive Isoperiodicity

In the essential musical state of isoperiodicity, variation is the procedural mandate. The strictest isoperiodic music discussed in this book is that of the Aka pygmies, chapter 5. In the song analyzed by Susanne Fürniss, Aka singers build an elaborate polyphony working within a rigorous and unchanging cycle of twelve ternary beats (thirty-six subdivisional positions). Their concept of a four-part melodic space in which the modelised constituent parts are both continually varied and unpredictably interwoven is both dazzling as an aural experience and compelling as a potential point of departure for a composer.[18]

Also isoperiodic, but very different from the Aka, are the geographically and culturally proximate examples of Balinese and Javanese gamelan (chapters 6–7), the former analyzed by me and the latter by R. Anderson Sutton and Roger Vetter. Unlike Aka culture, in which all music is isoperiodic, these gamelan examples are drawn from repertoires in which many other kinds of structural strategies are also available. But these thrity-two-beat Javanese and sixteen-beat Balinese cycles are strict and unchanging in a conceptual sense comparable to the Aka's. They are in other ways more flexible, however, and submit to extreme fluctuations in tempo and temporality. Across these changes a consistent melodic core supports rich layers of heterophonic variation produced in a range of idioms. Meanwhile, processes of augmentation, diminution, and transposition coordinate with the tempo topography to produce a musical form that, in important ways, is through-composed. In gamelan music, it becomes especially evident how even strict processes of repetition can be molded into forms that transform radically through time. I call these *discursive* isoperiodicities, in that a single cyclic entity narrates, as it were, a journey through processes of temporal expansion and contraction developed and sanctioned by the culture. The ingenious manipulation of rhythmic motion, density, and tempo in gamelan is a central creative resource for gamelan musicians and, internationally, an underappreciated creative legacy.

Part I: Sectional Periodicities: Poetry, Strophe and Song

In gamelan and with the Aka, periodicity and the basic melodic conception are coextensive, hand-in-glove. But in other musics arrayed around our isoperiodic point of reference they decouple. In this cluster of types isoperiodicity is in dialog with the demands made by a variety of forces such as poetic meter, call and response, strophe and refrain, or a ritual's progress. At the highest level there is kind of binariness to such music: either it is in or out of pulse; or it toggles from one kind of rhythmis cycle to another, or it juxtaposes contrasting elements within an otherwise isoperiodic framework. Formal elements are discrete and change from one to another is decisive, not blurred.

When setting text to music it is impossible, as Stephen Blum says of Iranian *Navā'i,* for poetic and musical meter not to come into some sort of relation-

18. The central position of the Aka in the book is also partly motivated by the likelihood that Aka music is particularly ancient and has changed but little over a long span of time (Olivier and Fürniss 1999).

ship of juxtaposition and tension. In his example, the two parry, switching in and out of prominence according to a roster of stylistic considerations, for the performer is "not constrained by any obligation to maintain the pulse." But when a constant pulse is absent, a language-based periodicity, based on conventions such as syllable counts, is still implied since "the quantitative poetic meter may serve as a framework for interpreting the temporal flow of a performance."

The "spinning" metaphors *horo* players use to describe the progression of musical elements stem from what Donna Buchanan and Stuart Folse describe as "the organic development . . . inherent in a *horo*'s structure." At the level of periodicity, however, the spinning takes place within one of two contrasting frameworks: songs of varying lengths and shorter, squarer, transition-like *otsvir*. Subsequent improvisation is often conceived within symmetrically arranged periods called *kolena* that can be inspired by either the song or the otsvir. As musicians move among these contexts, they enrich the juxtapositions with motivic, modal, registral, and ornamental dimensions. Similarly, as Manuel describes flamenco, the *compás*—the period—is an unwavering twelve-pulse cycle, but there are sharp contrasts of length and musical elements between the song forms (*copla*) and the guitar interludes (*falseta*) that overlay it.

In the succession of songs layered over drumming in Cuban batá performance there is constant change at various levels: melodies of different lengths, call and response, and rhythmic enhancement through controlled improvisation. But as Moore and Sayre point out, moments of true structural shift between *toques* (precomposed interlocking drum patterns), signaled by the mother drum *iyá*, constitute clear dividing points for aware listeners and are linked to ritual time. Musics with sectional periodicities such as those addressed here offer a range of models for the creative musician wishing to create strong and definitive contrasts, and the potential for masking or complicating those contrasts with a range of layering techniques.

Part III: Linear Composition in Periodic Contexts

In some cases, periodicity's strength as a foregrounded, controlling element partially recedes in deference to a more linear kind of thought. A great counterpart to periodic structure is gradual change in melodic, harmonic, or some other dimension. The sustained development of a musical idea, one that need not necessarily return precisely "home" each time the period does, forces the periodicity to be heard as a more neutral, background calibrator. Here is where periodicity itself may stretch, contract, dissolve, or otherwise distort to accommodate the needs of the rest of the music. We are challenged to perceive local irregularities as regular at a higher level, much as we measure different kinds of patterns in nature when observations are scaled at different orders of magnitude.

In Jonathan Stock's analysis of Shanghai opera scene, the singer Yang Feifei moves in and out of meter, constantly varies phrase length, and holds forth with extended melody, building long sections that are internally varied and often rhythmically irregular. Overall periodicity and symmetry is apparent when the whole is considered from a bird's-eye view; otherwise local patterns of repetition dissolve in flux. In the South Indian *varnam* ("etude") explained by Robert Morris a cycle of eight slow beats is a constant, and an insistent drum rhythm ($\mathcal{L}$ $\flat$) persists with minimal variation throughout. For the first two sections, the *pallavi* and *anupallavi*, tala cycles are linked in tidy groups of two (each repeated with subtle changes of melodic ornament, for a total of four). Beyond this tala groupings change a bit (see the second row of Morris's figure 10), but, far more significantly, the melody, always mutating in pitch content, ornament and range, follows an arching, one-way, serpentine trajectory. This subdues the *tala*, making it a reference for correct rhythmic placement rather than a force explicitly dominating the music. The melodic curve etched in Morris's transcriptions opens a window to a world of refined compositional sensibility.

Harmonic rhythm and textural change, with their variable speed, multiply layered trajectories, are but two possible enrichments to periodicity in Western tonal music. In the detail of Benjamin's figure 2 we see the myriad linkages, elisions, extensions, and contractions that wreak havoc on regularity in Mozart's K. 453, yet a sense of regularity at several levels persists. Similarly, the ingenious working out of the basic triumvirate of tonic, dominant, and subdominant harmonic functions transforms their simple, balanced impulse into an omnibus set of interrelations. In Elliott Carter's *Enchanted Preludes,* we may be hard-pressed to hold on to a sense of grounded regularity, as periodicity is often cast in simultaneous different tempi or groupings that do not relate by simple ratios (such as the use of five against seven). Yet John Roeder identifies instrumental behaviors, patterns, and relationships that foster cooperation, hence support pattern and form. One feels in Carter's music a confidence and rhythmic freedom that is characteristically bold and individual: his ultracomplexity takes the music to the brink of aperiodicity.

Aperiodicity recalls nonperiodicity through the dissolution of perceivable steady pulsations. Thus, we are led back from Carter, as if returning to an origin along a Möbius strip, to Hasan Yazdani and Moxtār Zambilbāf, the Iranian bards introduced by Stephen Blum in chapter 1. Carter's quest to "speak" naturally and musically through rhythmic design, to make an utterance lifelike in contexts with only one or a few performers, serves as a worthy nexus of contemplation among these distant musical cousins. It takes a leap through a chasm of imagination to do so, but this is what composers do. Besides, such distances are in other ways no farther apart than the tracks on a CD.[19]

Overlaps, Exchanges, and Contingencies

Viewed differently, many of the chapters could be reclassified. Reaching behind part II for an occasional handshake, the musics in parts I and III, as they are not strictly isoperiodic, partake of various kinds of structural contrasts that link them, however conceptually, with the symphonic half of Kundera's great musical divide. Although Stock emphasized the directed dramatic progression shaping Yang Feifei's performance, for example, one also could think of its structure as a succession of separate periodicities, which would tend to ally it with the musics in part I. In Cuban batá, the sectional basic drum patterns and song melodies could be heard as secondary to the incremental rise in drumming intricacy, which would be an argument for placing this music in part III.

Going from part I to part II, if we downplay the structural contrasts between copla and falseta in flamenco, for example, we might be able to hear the unchanging twelve-beat compás as providing a strict isoperiodic framework. Reinterpreting music in part II, perhaps the through-composed aspects of Balinese and Javanese gamelan qualify them to shift into part III, where their "unfoldingness" would be prioritized. Yet, as Benjamin shows in part III, it is profound and revelatory to think deeply enough into a developmental music like Mozart's to recognize its ultimate allegiance to an isoperiod.

It is as difficult to disentangle the properties of diverse musical structures as it is to essentialize cultural or ethnic traits. In this regard, remember that all of the examples categorized here represent their cultures of origin as *individual utterances*. Not all music in these traditions could be described or categorized in the same ways, although of course analysis of local styles, repertories, and social formations would reveal many strong intracultural commonalities. For these and other reasons, it requires force of imagination to make our analyses hold their places in the cross-cultural periodicity schema devised for them. That our constellation of musics is in multidimensional motion is a boon for human expression, but it makes the categorization unstable. At a higher level, the relation of chapters to categorization is rather like that of content to form in each music analyzed; and it is right to conclude that, at both levels, other in-

---

19. There are many cases of such seemingly haphazard connections being put to productive use. A great deal of Filipino composer José Maceda's (1917–2004) creative work, for example, sprang from the unlikely relation he perceived between the ultracomplex music of Greek composer Iannis Xenakis and the precolonial indigenous music of the Philippines (Tenzer 2003).

terpretations are possible. By committing our selections to their places in the constellation here we do not impede their movement, but we capture and depict certain useful and characteristic positions in the musical universe according to the view taken at the particular moment of this book.

Universals and a Future Music Theory

If we accept periodicity as one universal we ought to consider others, too.[20] In his remarkable 2001 *Musique au Singulier* (*Music in the Singular*) Francois-Bernard Mâche meditates on what all musics of all places and times has in common. A composer-scholar closely connected with ethnomusicology in France since the late 1950s, his research and writing is motivated by a lifetime of considered responses to music he has encountered from all over the world. His drive to think beyond immediate creative concerns reflects a belief that

> . . . within each true musician is also a philosopher of sounds, whose aesthetic conceptions take them beyond simple considerations of craft or emotion. In music, to ask what is universal is to ask what is true or important for all. Every musician who can see farther than ego or the public has experienced this problem, even if he keeps his questions and conclusions to himself. (15, my translations here and below)

Each of the book's twenty-four essays identifies either a universal (e.g., variation, repetition, fixed forms, ostinato, litany), a formal category in which to describe them (archetype, genotype, phenotype, model), or explores practices and phenomena that link with all music (myth, animal sounds, language, ritual, play) He is careful, as we also must be, to situate the venture in terms of the powerful cultural forces of modernism:

> Modernism very quickly drew its own radical conclusions with regard to awareness of musical *others*. Just as the discoveries of Japan, Oceania, Africa, etc. threw painters from Van Gogh and Gaugin to Picasso into upheaval, the discoveries of India, ancient Japan, Java and Bali have bit by bit had the same effect on the musical world. The appetite for exoticism was the most superficial reaction. Soon Debussy, Bartók, Milhaud, Varèse, etc. had intuitively or systematically applied logic as they wished. Since musical systems around the world exhibited

20. The study of universals is of importance to ethnomusicologists, but sustained interest has been dormant for some time. Volume 15/3 (1971) of *Ethnomusicology* is devoted to the topic.

such diversity, and had led to such accomplishments, nothing prohibited composers from inventing new, equally viable systems despite their rejection of traditional norms. The relativity of musical cultures would serve as new justification of new aesthetic systems. If, by obvious paradox, relativity truly was universal, then the aspiration to universal value could occur through the elaboration of a new system, however relative it was. (16)

The central paradox of the *universality of relativism*—the independent structures and meanings of *all* musical systems—is what drives Mâche to search for supracultural connections. As a listening musician, he is confident that his ears and mind are experiencing a single kind of "truth" when hearing even strange or distant musics. Searching for unifying elements, he is ultimately compelled to reach beyond culture and even humanity, blurring what for many are sacrosanct distinctions between music and nonmusic, culture and nature, or human and beast. Asserting that the instinctive, mythic aspect of music is "situated at the deepest level of psychic life, more archaic than that of language" (p. 169), or that there are "important preliminary signs of musical thought in animals, enough to lead to subsuming them with humanity under a common natural law" (p. 24) is an appeal to our fullest appreciation of the role music plays in world history.

Contemplation of these issues, one gleans, is also a further step along modernism's path toward future music informed by our cultural cosmopolitanism and sensitive to our natures and needs as a species. As a composer like Debussy and his other forebears, Mâche's wish is to fuse modernist freedom of style and syntax with broad global awareness to transcend both. But where the modernists consciously developed "systems" in response to historical change, or to awareness of parallel other cultures, Mâche looks beyond the relativism of systems to locate music's essence in our collective unconscious.

Inspiring and original though it is, perhaps his vision is too abstract for our present situation. One thing Mâche has undeniably put his finger on, though, is the *need* for a vision. In quotidian musical life, we hear so many things and respond to them routinely, as does he, with a diminishing sense that cultural boundaries are the obstacle they used to appear to be. We feel a growing confidence with musical diversity, nurtured by the intense variety we encounter from childhood on. But how shall we harness these new energies?

In coming years it is conceivable that we will want a *world music theory*. Unlike either Mâche's style of philosophy or the kinds of separate studies of isolated examples presented herein, it would have to be an umbrella set of practical concepts for teaching. In this book, the use of periodicity as a guide may be taken as a tentative suggestion as to what this could be like. The purpose of such a theory would be in the first place to start making sense of our complex cross-cultural musical selves and perceptions. We are often told of the world's vast and rapid changes but rarely advised on how to make sense of them *as musicians.* A world music theory would be a response to economic and cultural transformation making it desirable for musicians to acquire competence not just passively hearing, but contemplating and integrating any music. The well-established ethnomusicological model of bi- or trimusicality is inadequate to describe us anymore; we are approaching multi- or a virtual panmusicality. For many this is already a fact of life, and not just for composers: trumpet players do salsa, Corelli, free jazz, and mariachi all in the same week, and the iPod shuffle mode compresses infinite musics, cultures, eras, and locales for listeners with consummate effortlessness.

Yet real musicality actually comes from prolonged exposure to deep details which we learn to experience cognitively and feel bodily. That takes years of focused study. To suggest world music theory implies a comparative perspective so diffuse that it would seem to preclude such closeness. Before any implementation, music education would have to change more radically and rapidly than institutions that provide it tend to do. Could such a course coexist with the need for students to master particular instruments and traditions? How could the unwieldy breadth of world music theory not stretch it too thin? And who will have the mastery to teach it? The questions are discouraging, yet the problem remains. Music theory in Europe and North America, oriented so heavily toward Western art music, fails to address the needs, selves, and likely life trajectories of more and more musicians.

Proponents of the status quo might aver that the point is not to reflect the world, but to (re)create it. In any tradition, theory (in whatever form it takes) is an aid to transmission, and is emblematic of the need to sustain and protect the tradition itself and its distinctive identity. From that perspective the current system is hegemonic, but necessarily and effectively so: it sustains Western art music. Any tradition would do the same in its own interest.

These issues mirror characteristic unresolved twenty-first-century tensions between the local and the global at the highest levels of political and social life. The tense dyad of local hegemony versus global perspective is a familiar one that we encounter all over: we are concerned about balancing the effects of local versus international media information, production and trade, politics, belief systems, and on *ad infinitum.* It seems inevitable that even an institution as venerable as the nation-state is itself fated to respond to these tensions. Anthropologist Arjun Appadurai, scanning the destruction wrought by nationalism worldwide, writes of his hunch that the nation-state "is on its last legs" and asks what might substitute for the way it "distributes democratic rights and allows for the possibility of the growth of civil society." He answers himself, saying that "I do not know [what will replace the nation-state], but this admission is hardly an ethical recommendation for a system that seems plagued by endemic disease" (1996:19). Correspondingly, a music theory paradigm continuing to valorize the Western art tradition in the face of evidence that it only partly corresponds with the needs or experiences of musicians can equally be said to need reform. Like Appadurai, I am for the present content to acknowledge the quandary without prescribing answers, for saying that the existing paradigm is anachronistic is not at all the same as saying that a proper substitute is at hand.

Yet glimmers of solutions to Appadurai's dilemma exist or are developing. Nonsovereign models of international cooperation such as the European Union, or even the humble international postal service (not to mention the internet) are excellent examples (Cranston 2004:49–68). In all of these arenas, people put faith in global entities independent of their ethnicity, nationality, or other conventional mark of identity. Appadurai's best hope would be a future balanced integration of local self-determination and international cooperation along these lines.

Music's situation is bound up with this and analogous to it. Organizations such as UNESCO and the International Council for Traditional Music (ICTM) work to protect and recognize distinctive local musics needing assistance; and governments and cultures everywhere—including the superculture West—strive to strengthen their own identities. But in counterbalance, musics mix freely and internationally, carried via media or diaspora. When we transmit musical values and skills to coming generations, how shall we reflect this tangled nexus? Should musicians specifically be educated to nurture the growing reality of musical interdependency? Within teaching institutions ethnomusicology's importance may be uncontested, but its predominant status as an enrichment, a humanistic discipline at some remove from the core mission of training musicians to master musical materials, has barely been problematized. We may ask ourselves if our commitment to preserve the historical Western tradition can, in its own best interest, cede some hegemony to the unbounded, cosmopolitan vitality of the whole world of music, including new music and the gamut of traditional and other globalizing forms.

Such a situation looms as a possibility—tantalizingly or ominously, depending on one's predilections. But our first approach to any action must come through comparative analysis and understanding of the variety of musical structures that would ultimately have a voice in it. Analysis will not tame music, nor neutralize its mysteries, but it will gradually enlighten us. There is still much listening and reflecting to do, and that is purpose enough for this volume.

References

Agawu, Kofi. 2002. *Representing African Music.* London: Routledge.

Adorno, Theodor W. 1982 [1969]. (Max Paddison, trans. and ed.) "On the Problem of Musical Analysis." *Music Analysis* 1/2:169–187.

Arom, Simha. 1991. *African Polyphony and Polyrhythm.* Cambridge: Cambridge University Press.

Arom, Simha, Nathalie Fernando, Susanne Fürniss, Sylvie Le Bomin, Fabrice Marandola, and Jean Molino. *La Categorisation des Patrimoines Musicaux dans les Sociétés de Tradition Orale* (in press).

Barkin, Elaine. 1992. "Either/Other." *Perspectives of New Music* 30/2:206–233.

Bartók, Béla. 1921. *Hungarian Folk Music.* London: Oxford University Press; repr. in Bartók 1976, 58.

———. 1933. *"Hungarian Peasant Music." Musical Quarterly 19;* repr. in Bartók 1976, 80.

———. 1976. *Béla Bartók Essays.* (Benjamin Suchoff, ed.). Lincoln: University of Nebraska Press.

Blacking, John. 1983. "New Babel or New Jerusalem: Cosmic Consciousness or Cultural Apartheid?" *Studies in Music* 17:9–22.

Blum, Stephen. 1992. "Theory and Method: Analysis of Musical Style." In *Ethnomusicology: An Introduction.* Helen Myers, ed. New York: W.W. Norton, 165–218.

Bohlman, Philip. 2002. *World Music: A Very Short Introduction.* New York: Oxford University Press.

Boretz, Benjamin. 1969–70. "MetaVariations." *Perspectives of New Music* 8/1:1–74; 8/2:49–111; 9/1:23–42.

Born, Georgina, and David Hesmondhalgh. 2000. *Western Music and its Others: Difference, Representation, and Appropriation in Music.* Berkeley: University of California Press.

Cogan, Robert. 1984, *New Images of Musical Sound.* Cambridge, Mass.: Harvard University Press.

Cook, Nicholas. 1990. *Music, Imagination, and Culture.* New York: Oxford University Press.

Covach, John, and Graeme M. Boone, eds. 1997. *Understanding Rock: Essays in Musical Analysis.* New York: Oxford University Press.

Cranston, Alan. 2004. *The Sovereignty Revolution.* Stanford: Stanford University Press.

Dissanayake, Ellen, 2000. *Art and Intimacy: How the Arts Began.* Seattle: University of Washington Press.

Ellingson, Ter. 1992. "Theory and Method: Transcription." In *Ethnomusicology: An Introduction.* Helen Myers, ed. New York: W.W. Norton, 110–52.

Ellis, Alexander J. 1885. "On the Musical Scales of Various Nations." *Journal of the Society of Arts* 33:485–527.

Feld, Steven. 1981. "'Flow Like a Waterfall': The Metaphors of Kaluli Musical Theory." *Yearbook for Traditional Music* 13:22–47.

Halle, John. 2004. *Meditations on a Post-Literate Musical Future.* New Music Box: http://www.newmusicbox.org/page.nmbx?id= 64vwo1.

Herndon, Marcia. 1974. "Analysis: The Herding of Sacred Cows?" *Ethnomusicology* 18: 219–262.

———. 1976. "Reply to Kolinski: Taurus Omicida." *Ethnomusicology* 20:217–231.

———. 1977. "A Clarification." *Ethnomusicology* 21:463.

Kolinski, Mieczyslaw. 1965. "The General Direction of Melodic Movement." *Ethnomusicology* 9:240–264.

———. 1973. "A Cross-Cultural Approach to Metro-Rhythmic Patterns." *Ethnomusicology* 17:494–506.

———. 1976. "Herndon's Verdict on Analysis: Tabula Rasa." *Ethnomusicology* 20:1–22.

———. 1977. "Final Reply to Herndon." *Ethnomusicology* 21:75–83.

Krausz, Michael, ed. 1989. *Relativism: Interpretation and Confrontation.* Notre Dame, Ind.: University of Notre Dame Press.

Kundera, Milan. 1980 [1979]. *The Book of Laughter and Forgetting.* New York: Alfred A. Knopf.

Lomax, Alan. 1976. *Cantometrics.* Berkeley: University of California Press.

Mâche, François-Bernard. 2001. *Musique Au Singulier.* Paris: Éditions Odile Jacob.

McClary, Susan. 1991. *Feminine Endings.* Minneapolis: University of Minnesota Press.

Meyer, Leonard. 2000. *The Spheres of Music.* Chicago: University of Chicago Press.

Nettl, Bruno. 1983. *The Study of Ethnomusicality: Twenty-Nine Issues and Concepts.* Urbana: University of Illinois Press.

———. 1995. *Heartland Excursions.* Urbana: Elephant and Cat.

Olivier, Emmanuelle, and Susanne Fürniss, 1999. "Pygmy and Bushman Music: A new Comparative Study." In *Central African Hunter-Gatherers in a Multidisciplinary Perspective: Challenging Elusiveness.* K. Biesbrouck, S. Elders & G. Rossel, eds, Leiden: CNWS, 117–132.

Olivier, Emmanuelle, and Hervé Rivière. 2001. "Reflections on Musical Categorization." *Ethnomusicology* 45/3:480–488.

Perlman, Marc. 2004. *Unplayed Melodies: Javanese Gamelan and the Genesis of Music Theory.* Berkeley: University of California Press.

Rahn, Jay. 1983. *A Theory for All Music.* Toronto: University of Toronto Press.

Reck, David. 1977. *Music of the Whole Earth.* New York: Charles Scribner's Sons.

Rowell, Lewis. 1992. *Music and Musical Thought in Early India.* Chicago: University of Chicago Press.

Sachs, Curt. 1943. *The Rise of Music in the Ancient World.* New York: Norton.

Scherzinger, Martin. 2001. "Negotiating the Music-Theory/African Music Nexus: A Political Critique of Ethnomusicological Anti-Formalism and a Strategic Analysis of the Harmonic Patterning of the Shona Mbira Song *Nyamaropa*." *Perspectives of New Music* 39/1:5–118.

Small, Christopher. 1998. *Musicking: The Meanings of Performing and Listening.* Middletown: Wesleyan University Press.

Stokes, Martin. 2001. "Ethnomusicology, IV. Current Trends, 10. Theoretical." In *The New Grove Dictionary of Music and Musicians,* second ed. London: Macmillan, 8:386–395.

Szendy, Peter. 2001. *Écoute: Une Histoire de Nos Oreilles*. Paris: Les Éditions de Minuit.

Taruskin, Richard. 2004. *The Oxford History of Western Music*. New York: Oxford University Press.

Tenney, James. 1986 (1966). *Meta + hodos: A Phonomenology of 20th-Century Musical Materials and an Approach to the Study of Form*. Oakland, Calif.: Frog Peak Music.

Tenzer, Michael. 2003. "José Maceda and the Paradoxes of Modern Composition in Southeast Asia." *Ethnomusicology* 47/1:93–120.

———. 2000. *Gamelan Gong Kebyar: The Art of Twentieth Century Balinese Music*. Chicago: University of Chicago Press.

Washburne, Christopher, and Maiken Derno, eds. 2004. *Bad Music: The Music We Love to Hate*. London: Routledge.

Widdess, Richard. 1994. "Involving the Performers in Transcription and Analysis: A Collaborative Approach to *Dhrupad*." *Ethnomusicology* 38(1):59–80.

Wiora, Walter. 1965. *The Four Ages of Music*. New York: W.W. Norton.

Yampolsky, Philip, prod. 1999. *Music of Indonesia 7: Music from the Forests of Riau and Mentawai*. Smithsonian Folkways CD 40423. ("Private Songs" tracks 11–12.)

→→ PART I ←←
Sectional Periodicities

Poetry, Song, Ritual

CHAPTER 1

Navā'i, A Musical Genre of Northeastern Iran

STEPHEN BLUM

Templates for Sung Poetry

A question commonly addressed in analyses of sung poetry is how, or to what extent, the musical treatment of the verses complements, amplifies, or violates the meter and rhythms of the poem as it might be spoken. A composer or singer can never "translate" a sequence of spoken syllables into a sequence of sung syllables that fully preserves the structure of the spoken sequence without creating additional levels of structure.

It often happens that patterns played on instruments prepare singers and listeners for the rhythms to which words will be sung. As we listen to the chord played by two oboes, two clarinets, an English horn, and two bassoons in the second bar of the prelude to Wagner's *Tristan und Isolde* (figure 1.1), we recognize it as a dissonance that requires resolution, and we may also recognize in the four-note melody played by the first oboe a template for poetry: a grouping of four syllables in which the first and third are stressed (a "double trochee"). As the work continues, this template looms large, in sequences that may substitute three- or five-syllable groups for the four-syllable pattern while retaining the stress on all odd-numbered syllables. At measure 310 in the first act, Isolde extends the initial four-note melody through the entire chromatic scale (figure 1.2), and in the *Liebestod* that concludes the opera (beginning "Mild und leise," at m. 1621) she sings sixty small groups of syllables (printed in libretti as "lines") of which thirty-six are double trochees and thirteen have the shortened, three-syllable form of the pattern.

FIGURE 1.1. *Wagner,* Tristan und Isolde,
Prelude, mm. 2–3.

FIGURE 1.2. Tristan, *Act I, mm. 310–317.*

FIGURE 1.3. Tristan, *Prelude, mm. 1–2.*
cello line.

The prominence of these trochaic feet at key moments in the drama contributes to the unique sonic universe of Wagner's *Tristan.* Iambic feet, not trochaic, were the norm in his earlier operas, as in those of his contemporaries. Beginning with the initial cello line (figure 1.3), *Tristan* as well has far more iambic than trochaic feet, causing the latter to stand out against the norm.

In the traditional music of Iran and Central Asia, instruments also play rhythmic patterns that evoke conventional poetic meters. Here the meters are often quantitative, like those of ancient Greek poetry for which such terms as *trochee* and *iamb* were first devised. For an ancient Greek poet, the basic trochaic foot was the sequence long-short-long-short. The quantitative meters used in Persian poetry are different from those used in ancient Greek or, for that matter,

Moxtār performing on the dotār. Photo by Jean During.

in classical Arabic poetry.[1] The Persian meters were adapted by court poets who composed verses in Turkic languages, such as Çağatay, Ottoman Turkish, and Azerbaijani, and for that reason the same musical resources could be used for singing poetry in any of these languages.

A system of syllables devised by Arabic prosodists for representing quantitative meters was successfully applied to Persian and Turkic poetry, and music theorists writing in Arabic developed a second system of syllables to represent musical rhythms. Figure 1.4 shows the same rhythm in (a) the syllables of prosodists, (b) the syllables of music theorists, and (c) conventional Western notation. Vocal and instrumental rhythms are sometimes direct translations of a poetic meter; in other words 4(a) may be sung or played as 4(b) or 4(c). Far more

---

1. The respects in which Persian meters differ from those of classical Arabic verse are well discussed by Elwell-Sutton (1976, 1987).

43

FIGURE 1.4. *Three representations of one rhythm.*

(a) fa - 'i - la - tun

(b) tan   ta - nan   tan

(c)  ♩ ♪ ♩ ♩

often than not, however, vocal and instrumental rhythms create what we might call "rhythmic counterpoint" when heard with reference to the poetic meter.[2] By continually altering the durational relationships and varieties of accent in a succession of sung syllables, singers can elicit the close attention of listeners. The alternative, performing a sequence of verses to a constant rhythm that translates the poetic meter just as 4(b) translates 4(a), creates a groove that listeners can enter; it is especially appropriate at certain points in religious ceremonies. (see figure 1.4)

Many types of solo performance in Iran and Central Asia center on the performer's ability to effectively coordinate verse structures, instrumental patterns, and vocal melodies. One such performance is the subject of this chapter: eight verses from a poem in the genre *sāqi-nāme,* performed to the musical scheme called *Navā'i,* by one of the bards who are called *baxşi* in Xorasan, the northeasternmost province of Iran.[3]

The Baxşi's Musical Resources

The baxşi of northern Xorasan is a singer who has memorized a great many verses in three languages—Xorasani Turkish, Kormanji Kurdish, and Persian—and, in addition, has created new verses in one or more of these languages. That, at least, is the strongest sense of the term, although it is commonly applied as well to performers who have not composed verses of their own. A baxşi accompanies himself on the *dotār,* a long-necked lute with two strings and eleven or twelve frets. His performances animate the festive gatherings known as *toy* in

2. In some practices, such as the Tajik-Uzbek *şaşmaqom,* the rhythmic counterpoint is based on the relationship between poetic meter (*vazn*) and a constant rhythmic cycle (*usul*); for examples, see Levin and Sultanova (2002:914–915).

3. Baxşi is but one of the terms used in Turkic languages for a singer of tales. Cousins of the Xorasani baxşi include, among others, the Uzbek baxşi, the Türkmen bagsy, the Qaraqalpaq žiraw, and the aşıq of Azerbaijan and Anatolia (see Reichl 1992).

Turkic languages,[4] and in recent years his repertoire has been seen as a significant portion of Iran's cultural heritage (*mirās-e farhangi*) and featured at festivals of "traditional" (*sonnati*) performing arts. The repertoire includes lengthy prose narratives that are recited in performance to provide a context for the sung poetry, which represents words exchanged by the protagonists.

Baxşis master the available musical resources as they learn through experience which dotār patterns and which vocal melodies are the most effective vehicles for performing verses on a given topic, or verses in a specific poetic meter. The name of a musical or poetic genre serves as a convenient handle for a bundle of features, possibly including the appropriate topics, poetic meters, musical rhythms, melodies, vocal and instrumental techniques, performance occasions, behavior expected of participants, and associated stories. Even within one region, and all the more so in different regions, performers are likely to have acquired somewhat different conceptions of the makeup of these bundles. That is certainly true of the genres with which this chapter is concerned, the musical scheme(s) known as *Navā'i* and the poetic genre called *sāqi-nāme*.

The verses of a sāqi-nāme are addressed to a cup-bearer (*sāqi*) by a man who wishes to drink wine. His desires and thoughts, as they change from the effects of the wine, commonly fuse love for a woman or a boy (perhaps the cupbearer himself) with love of the divine. The most famous such poem is the sāqi-nāme of Hāfez, greatest of all Persian poets. Figure 1.5 shows the first line of that poem beneath (a) a simplified notation of the rhythm to which it is commonly sung in Persian classical music, and (b) the syllables that are conventionally used to represent the quantitative meter of the verse. The two halves of the line share a common rhyme, -*āl*, which is followed in both halves by the same word, *avārad* (the technical term for a word or words placed after the rhyming syllable is *radif* "row"). One musical strategy for presenting such a line is to sing each half to exactly the same rhythm and the same tune. A singer who adopts that strategy for the first line of a poem may then proceed to create rhythmic and melodic contrasts between the two halves of each succeeding line.[5] Poetry in which each line is divided into two equal parts pro-

---

4. For more information on the Central Asian toy with reference to the Türkmen bagşy and the Uzbek baxşi see, respectively, Zeranska-Kominek (2002:968–969) and Levin (1996:146–148).

5. Persian classical music is performed according to repertoires of models known as *radif* "row" (the same term that is used for the syllables following a rhyme). Most radifs include melody-types for singing any sāqi-nāme composed in the meter used by Hāfez. *Sāqi-nāme* is also the name of a musical genre in the Tajik-Uzbek şaşmaqom, which is associated with poems in that meter and a few others.

Figure 1.5. *Initial line of Hafez,* Saqi-name.

(a)

(b)

˘	—		—	˘	—		—	˘	—		—
fa - 'ū	-	lon	fa	-	'ū	-	lon	fa	-	'ū	-
bi - yā		sā	-	qī		ān		mey	ke	hāl	
ka - rā	-	mat	fa	-	zā	-	yad	ka	-	māl	

vides a foundation on which singers can create a rich variety of relationships among the melodies and rhythms they select for the two halves of each line.

The sāqi-nāme discussed here is the work of the Azerbaijani poet Qomrı (1819–1891) and uses a different meter, built from the four-syllable pattern shown in figure 1.4. A full line contains thirty syllables, each half-line or "hemistich" fifteen (figure 1.6). After the initial line, both halves of which end with the rhyming syllables *-ani* (always followed, as in the Hāfez example, by the radif, gə-tır *"bring"*), the rhyme is heard only at the end of every full line. This is the rhyme scheme of the Persian (and Azerbaijani) *ğazal,* the poetic genre that is central to the performance practice of Persian (and Azerbaijani) classical music.

Because the Turkic dialects of Xorasan differ in a number of ways from Azerbaijani Turkish, baxşis are sometimes uncertain of how to pronounce Azerbaijani verses as they read them from printed or manuscript texts in the Arabic script (which omits most Turkish vowels), and this uncertainty may also affect their rhythmic choices.[6] They do not always articulate fifteen syllables in each half-line of Qomrı's text, either because of errors or poetic license on Qomrı's part or to the baxşi's having read or memorized certain lines incorrectly.

Whereas *sāqi-nāme* designates a poetic genre and by extension certain musical frameworks to which such poems can be sung, *Navā'i* is a name applied to three related but distinct musical schemes (called *maqām* or *āhang* in Persian), which are played, respectively, on three different varieties of dotār: those of eastern Xorasan, northern Xorasan (discussed here), and the Türkmen of Iran and Turkmenistan.[7] *Navā'i* is also the title of a composition derived from

6. The phonology, grammar, and lexicon of five dialects of Khorasani Turkish, as spoken in twenty-three localities, are described in Doerfer and Hesche (1993). Singers in Iranian Azerbaijan would presumably find it easier than Xorasani baxşis to read the editions of Qomrı's book *Kenz ül-məs'əb* that were printed in Arabic script. On a visit to the Republic of Azerbaijan, I was unable to locate a copy of the book in Cyrillic or Latin characters, which would have clarified for me the proper vocalization of the *sāqi-nāme.*

7. For excellent descriptions of these three varieties of dotār, which include measurements in cents of the intervals made available by the freting of specific instruments, see Darvişi (2001:123–184). Notations of eastern Xorasani and Türkmen performances of *Navā'i* are available in Mas'udiye (1980:104–111; 1992:387–389; and 2000:99–101).

FIGURE 1.6. *Scansion of the seventh line of Qomri's* Sáqi-nāme
(as sung by Moxtār Zambilbāf).

rū- yā- tē   fēk-rīm ō-lūb-[ə]   hər tər- ə- fəh şə -qə go-şa

bīr də-mə təb- 'ə   rə- vūn   ba şım- ə   sev-da- nī gə-tır

the eastern Xorasani scheme, and it is the name given by some baxşis to the
twelfth fret on the dotār neck, used only in playing *Navā'i*.[8] Some Xorasani
performers associate the musical schemes with the fifteenth-century poet and
statesman Mir 'Ali-şir Navā'i (1441–1501), who was born and died in Herāt, the
main city of Afghan Xorasan. Navā'i's verses in Çağatay Turkish are often sung
in performances of the Tajik-Uzbek *şaşmaqom,* but they are virtually unknown
to Xorasani singers.[9]

Most of the verses sung by baxşis are organized as quatrains, generally
containing three lines of eight or eleven syllables plus a final refrain line which
is shared by several quatrains in a sequence. With a few exceptions, the meters
are defined by the number of syllables in each line rather than by the distribution of long and short syllables; hence the poetic meters are called "syllabic"
(*hejā'i* in Persian) rather than quantitative. The maqāms designed for singing
quatrains allow the baxşi both to repeat any line once or twice and to interpo-
late vocables (syllables that do not belong to the poem) before, in the middle,
or at the end of any line. Vocables, which may or may not carry lexical meanings, are essential to the act of musical communication, serving both to solicit
the attention of listeners and to express the singer's emotions, or those of the
characters he portrays.

Maqāms used for singing quatrains include one phrase to which the third
line—and often the second, sometimes the first, but only rarely the last line—
can be sung. Differences among maqāms are more striking in these "medial"
phrases than in the initial phrases. Repetitions of a medial phrase increase one's
anticipation of a final phrase that will effect a melodic descent, or will complete a descent initiated in the medial phrase. In performance, a baxşi normally
plays instrumental versions of the full melody type in alternation with the sung
quatrains. In *Navā'i,* however, the instrumental sections present additional
facets of the maqām, without repeating the vocal melody. The difficulty of the
instrumental passages has led baxşis to describe *Navā'i* as *harif-koş,* "slayer of

8. For a diagram showing the frets of the northern Xorasani dotār, see Youssefzadeh
(2002:83–84, 214).

9. Moxtār, the baxşi whose performance is analyzed here, had acquired a book of
Navā'i's poetry printed in 1901 in Tashkent, but finding it difficult to read he offered it to me
as a gift. See also the remark under *Musiqi-ye şomāl-e Xorāsān (Qučān)* in the discography.

one's competitors." This maqām is also exceptional in being used for singing verses drawn from ṣazals (in the quantitative meter shown in figure 1.6) as well as quatrains in the same meter. Verses in that meter, sung to *Navā'i* or *ṣāh Xatā'i*, often serve to introduce a performance of one of the Turkic narratives.[10]

Three Singers of Bojnurd

My first exposure to the art of the Xorasani baxṣi came in the winter of 1969 during a visit to the city of Bojnurd, where many residents speak Xorasani Turkish. Two men, Hasan Yazdāni and Moxtār Zambilbāf, were performing nightly in tea houses located in the bazaar. I interviewed both and made my first recordings of Turkic narratives. Three years later I arranged to spend several days in Bojnurd in order to speak with Moxtār at length and record substantial portions of his repertoire, which also included verses on religious subjects in Xorasani and Azerbaijani Turkish and in Kormanji Kurdish. My tape recorder, an Uher 4000-Report-L, balked at recording our long sessions and from time to time declined to capture the sounds that were being fed to it; one such break of two seconds occurs on the recording discussed here.

Moxtār was born in a village near Esfarāyen, south of Bojnurd, where his Kurdish ancestors were shoemakers, some of whom had married Turkish women. He had moved to Bojnurd in the early 1960s and found it a better place to work as a baxṣi, performing in tea-houses during the winters, traveling to celebrations in late summer and autumn, and repairing shoes when invitations to sing were scarce. He took great pride in his literacy and was able to refresh his well-stocked memory by consulting notebooks in which he had notated verses in a coded script, to prevent others from stealing the notebooks.

During four of our sessions Moxtār sang verses from Qomri's sāqi-nāme. He sang the first four lines to introduce a performance of the Turkic narrative *Hamrā Huri Laqā* and, later the same day, as a prelude to a sequence of strophes belonging to the story *Bābā Rowṣān*. He performed the entire the sāqi-nāme, omitting only the last of its thirty-one lines, before singing a series of Turkic verses on the creation of humankind. The recorded performance discussed in this chapter (CD track 2; figures 1.10b and 1.12) includes lines 7–14 of Qomri's poem and was followed by a performance of the Turkic story *'Ajam* lasting an hour and thirty-five minutes.[11] This is the only performance in which I heard Moxtār sing Qomri's verses to the *Navā'i* maqām; in the others he used

10. An excellent example is the recording of an entire dāstān as performed by Rowṣān Golafruz, which is introduced with Navā'i (see discography).

11. Moxtār began this performance with the first six lines, but my tape recorder functioned only for lines 7 through 14.

the *Šāh Xatā'i* maqām, to which he often performed verses in this fifteen-syllable meter. In Xorasan, Qomri's poem is generally sung to one or the other of these maqāms, both of which allow numerous rhythmic options that are appropriate to the meter.

A compact disc compiled by Jean During as a survey of several types of dotār in Iran and Central Asia includes a performance of *Navā'i* by Hasan Yazdāni in which he sings the first two lines of Qomri's sāqi-nāme. I will compare aspects of Moxtār's performance both with Hasan's recording and with a performance I recorded in Bojnurd from an amateur singer who made his living selling ice in the bazaar (CD track 1; figures 1.10b and 1.11). This man, Hoseyn Na'imi, was quick to admit that he was unable to play *Navā'i* "correctly" and, being illiterate, he had no occasion to perform it as an introduction to one of the Turkic narratives that baxšis learn from books and manuscripts.

Stable Tonality and Variable Rhythm

What is most stable in any performance of a Xorasani maqām is the tone-system appropriate to that maqām and the interrelationships of initial, medial, and terminal phrases as defined within that tone-system. Figure 1.7a shows the tone-system used for the vocal sections of *Navā'i*. The lower-pitched string of the dotār (called *bam* "upper" because of its location) supports the voice with a constant drone (treated in figure 1.7 as scale-degree 1), perhaps inflected every so often by its upper neighbor (degree 2). The lower string becomes more active in the purely instrumental sections (see figure 1.7b), sometimes playing a flat scale-degree 3 as flat scale-degree 6 is produced on the higher-pitched string (called *zir* "lower"). Vocal lines are always directed toward degree 5, often through a stepwise descent from the second scale-degree in the upper octave, numbered "9" for convenience. The two conjunct fifths formed by degrees 1 to 5 and 5 to 9 constitute the framework of the *Navā'i* tone-system, distinguishing it from the more common Xorasani systems which are built around two conjunct fourths. A baxši who has tuned the two strings of his instrument

FIGURE 1.7. *Tone-system of Navā'i (northern Xorasan).*

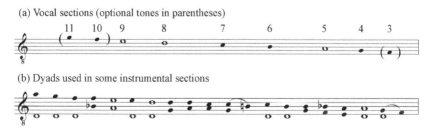

(a) Vocal sections (optional tones in parentheses)

(b) Dyads used in some instrumental sections

a perfect fourth apart is apt to begin a performance of *Navā'i* by striking the open strings together, then shortening the higher-pitched string at the second fret to produce scale-degree 5. Such a performance will close with the reverse progression, from the fifth formed by degrees 1 and 5 back to the fourth formed by degrees 1 and 4.

Before presenting the first line of verse, a baxşi sings vocables that usually ornament the progression from degree 4 to degree 5 which has already been heard on the dotār (figure 1.8). Likewise, subsequent vocal entries are clearly located within the *Navā'i* tone-system as established on the dotār. The singer's rhythmic choices, however, are not constrained by any obligation to maintain the pulse, if any, that he may have adopted in the dotār introduction or interludes.

In the event that a regular pulse is momentarily maintained on the dotār, the next vocal entry may change the tempo or abandon the pulse altogether. Figure 1.9 illustrates a smooth connection made by Hasan Yazdāni between the concluding rhythm of an instrumental introduction and the opening of Qomri's poem. The dotār plays the rhythm shown in figure 1.4, which as already noted is equivalent to the four-syllable pattern that forms the basis of the poetic meter. Hasan retains this rhythm as he begins to sing the first hemistich, but he makes the line more fluid by declining to strictly maintain the rhythm all the way through. Unmodified repetition of a rhythmic figure is far more com-

FIGURE 1.8. *Introductory vocables in three performances of Navā'i.*

(a) Rowşan Golafruz

pulse marked on dotār ♩ = ca. 88

he - - - ey ya-rey - - - - - .

(b) Hoseyn Na'imi

dotār tacet, ♩ = ca. 100

hey gəl ey   ca - - - an, e   gəl oy   gəl

(c) Hasan Yazdani (tone-system transposed up a fourth)

vocables sung ca. ♩ = 108, strumming on dotār ca. ♩ = ca. 120

ey yar yar   ya ya ya ya ya yar   yar ya - rey

FIGURE 1.9. *Connection of dotar rhythms and initial hemistich in Yazdani's recording.*

mon in dotār interludes than in the vocal sections. Against the background of the poetic meter, singers tend to articulate the syllables in groups of two or three, often with a slight stress on the first syllable of each group. Such stresses may or may not occur at relatively equal, hence predictable, intervals of time.

Baxşis create forward momentum or abrupt changes of pace by introducing or abandoning a regular pulse as they strike the dotār strings or tap on the instrument's belly or articulate the syllables of the poem. They may or may not strum on the dotār as they sing and may or may not highlight certain syllables with a series of taps, as Moxtār liked to do. Once initiated (perhaps at a predictable moment), the taps, even more than the syllables, are apt to come at unpredictable intervals of time. The rhythmic counterpoint produced by the actions of a baxşi's tongue and fingers is not controlled by a constant pulse, making it difficult to devise appropriate notations. In the absence of a pulse, or of a basic reference duration for short syllables (called a *mora* in Cooke 1970), the quantitative poetic meter may serve as a framework for interpreting the temporal flow of a performance. When each hemistich provides the same number of positions for sung syllables (fifteen in our examples), the singer's melodic choices at one moment become meaningful through comparison with the pitches chosen for the same position in earlier lines. Even when lines have too few or too many syllables with reference to the norm, performers and listeners can still compare what they hear at a particular moment with what they remember hearing in analogous segments of earlier lines.

The diagrams provided for use with the recordings of Navā'i by Hoseyn and Moxtār (CD tracks 1–2) focus on two aspects of rhythm. The relative proportions of the dotār interludes and the vocal sections are indicated in figure 1.10, and the ways in which pitch choices differentiate equivalent positions in the quantitative meter are shown in figures 1.11 and 1.12 (with vocables enclosed in brackets). Richard Widdess supported his analysis of two examples of North Indian *ālāp* (1985:149–155) with figures that align the climactic scale-degrees of the successive phrases in a central column, thus facilitating comparison of the melodic progressions that lead up to and that follow each climax. My figures 1.11 and 1.12 likewise enable comparison of the distribution of scale-degrees in the first and second halves of each line, and in larger groupings (each pair of lines; all first halves; and all second halves).

The topic of the quatrain that concludes Hoseyn's performance of *Navā'i* (figures 1.10a and 1.11) is "the Major Festival" of Muslims, 'Eyd-e Qorbān, marking the day when Abraham was commanded to sacrifice his son, Ismā'il (not Isaac, as in the Torah). The radif, *şu gün* "that day," also can mean "today" in at least one dialect of Xorasani Turkish (Doerfer and Hesche 1993:174). Two melodic phrases, the first with a higher tessitura than the second, are all that Hoseyn requires for singing the quatrain (figure 1.11). The first line is sung twice, to an initial phrase centered on scale-degree 9 and its lower neighbor, 8. The medial phrase, to which the second and third lines are sung, begins with a turn, approaching degree 9 from 7 before reversing direction. In the second

FIGURE 1.10. *Structure of two recorded performances.*

(a) Final quatrain sung to *Navā'i* by Hoseyn (CD, track 1)

D = dotār interlude
V = vocables
L = line of verse

approximate
time in

seconds:	22	4	5	5	7	5	4	5	4	5	17 = 1'23"
	D	V	D	L1	D	L1	L2	D	L3	L4	D

(b) Moxtār's performance of lines from Qomri's Sāqi-nāme (CD, track 2)

approximate
time in

seconds:	17	12	7	22	22	13	16	19	16
	D	L7	D	L8+V	D	L9	D	L10+V	D
	12		18	21	13	7	18	7 = 4'00"	
	L11		L12+V	D	L13	D	L14+V	D	

FIGURE 1.11. *Quatrain on the Feast of the Sacrifice sung by Hoseyn Na'imi, 1969 (CD track 1).*

```
 9   8   9    10 98767
[ey gəl ey,    can]

 9  ·  ·  ·̄  ·̆  ·̄  ·  8       ·̄  ·  ·̆  · 9̄   8̄   9̆   ·  8̄   7̄   6̆   7̄
[ay dey bi-lə] İs-ma-'il [ey] Eb  -ra-him o-ğlı Haq-qə qur-ban-dır şu gün

     9  ·  ·  ·  ·  ·  8         ·  ·  · 9   8   9   7   8   7   6   7
    [dey bi-lə] İs-ma-'il [ey] Eb  -ra-him o-ğlı Haq-qə qur-ban-dır şu gün

           7  ·  ·      9   8  7  ·  6  7   6   8  7  6  5  ·  675
           u mə- lək-   lər [ey] u xə -la-yık cüm-lə gir-yan-də şu gün

           7  ·  ·      ·  ·  ·  ·  ·  ·  · 9  ·  8  · 76 7
           ha-cı- lar   beyt -ül-hə-rəm-də Haq-qə mey-man-dır şu gün

           7 · 9     8 · 7  ·  ·  ·
           ha-cı- lar   zekr e-di-lər [ey can],

                           ·  ·  ·  ·  ·  ·  ·  · 6 75
                           sur- e   sub-han-dır şu gün [ya Cə-lil!]
```

Translation
On that day Isma'il, Abraham's son, was sacrificed to God (2)
On that day angels and [God's] creatures gathered round
On that day the pilgrims are guests of God in the Beyt-ul-Haram
On that day the pilgrims perform zekr and [the litany] Subhan

line, the melodic figure to which the first eight syllables are sung is transposed down a step for the next six syllables, and on the final syllable the fifth scale-degree is ornamented with two upper neighbors. In the third line, the melodic figure that accomodated eight syllables in the previous line is stretched out to accommodate all fifteen syllables, and the approach to degree 9 from 7 is delayed until the tenth syllable. All fifteen syllables of the final line are likewise sung to a variant of the same figure, now arriving much sooner on 9, then lingering on 7 before arriving on 5 via the same ornament that concluded the second line. To some extent, the prolongation of 7 transforms the medial phrase into a final phrase, but the difference between these is small, as is often the case in performances of *Navā'i.*

In singing eight lines from Qomri's sāqi-nāme (figures 1.10b and 1.12), Moxtār treats every pair of lines (comprising four half-lines) as a quatrain; in other words, the presentation of odd-numbered lines differs from that of even-numbered lines. For convenience I will refer to the half-lines as 7a, 7b, and so on. Moxtār sings the first half-line of each pair (7a, 9a, 11a, and 13a) to a version of the same initial phrase used by Hoseyn. After the final half-line of each

FIGURE 1.12. *Eight lines from the Sāqi-nāme of Qomri as sung by Moxtār Zambilbāf. (A dot indicates that the scale-degree has not changed; "T" marks the onset of a series of taps on the belly of the dotār)*

<pre>
     9 ⁻ ̆8 9̄ ⁻ ⁻ ̆ : ⁻ ·   ⁻ 8̄ : ⁻ ⁻ 7̄ : ⁻ ⁻
7a. [ey] ru-ya -te fekr-im o-lub-[ə] hər tər-əf-ə şəq-ə go-şa

        9   8   · 7 · · · · · · 78 65
7b.   bir dəm-ə təb-'ə rə-vun ba-şım-ə su-da-ni gə - tır
                                                      T

   7678 8 · · · · 9   · 8 7 · 6 7 ·
8a. [ey] bal-e zər-rin gət-ı- rub   iç-ma-qa şa-hin mə-qal

        9   8   · 7 · · · · · · · · 6 78 6565 7 · 765   8
8b.   dur qa-lıx-maq-lıq ü-çün 'a-ləm-e ba-la-ni gə-tır [ə - ziz, ey can, ey, həqq]
                                                      T

      9 89 ·   8 9   · 8 9 · 8 · 7
9a. [ey] ul ey-la   gəz-ər   mum-lə-kət-i Şir-va-ni

        9 8 · 7 · ·   · · · · · 78 65 6
9b.   nəzm-i-də fur-qə'i şa - 'er-ler-ə xa-qa-ni gə- tır
                                                      T

      9 · 8 9 · 8 86   7 · _ ·
10a. [ey] söy-lə   Xa-qan-e Çin   su-xan xa-qan

       7 · 9   · · 8 ·   7 · · · · · · · 78 65 7657 7 8 65
10b. ar-mə-ğun ol - dı du-tub nəzm-ə dər af-şa-ni gə-tır ['ə - ziz, ey, gəl 'ə-ziz]
                                                      T

       9 · 89 ·   8 9   8 9 · 8 · 7 · ·
11a. [ey] qil xə-bər-dar Nə-va - 'i kim-i sa-heb ho-nə-ri

         9 · · 8 · 7 · · · · · · · · 6
11b.   de-yi t'ma-şa - yə təm -um əf-sə Tu-ra-ni gə-tır

       7 9 8 · 7 · · · · · · · · · 8 65
12a. Ən-və- ri ney-yir [ki-mi] 'ə-zəm kim-i nəzm-un-də mu-nir

       7 · · · · · · · · · 78 65 7678765 7
12b. [ey] dur nə-şar eyl-ma-qa 'ıqd-ı   sur-ya-ni gə-tır [ə - ziz, ey,   gəl!]
                  T   T

      9 · 89 · · 89 9 8 · 7 · · · ·
13a. [ey] cam-e vah-dat-dan i-çin cam-e Cəm-ə cam-e-ye di-vun

        7 · 9 · 8 · 7 · · · · · · · 78 65
13b.   i-çi-bin-e durc-ə fəs-a-hət-e durr-e mər-ca-ni gə- tır
                                                      T
</pre>

FIGURE 1.12. *Continued*

```
      7    ·    ·    ·    ·    ·    ·    ·    ·        _·    ·
14a. [ey] Sə'-di-ya esm-e sə-nun tal-'e-ye mas-'ud mə-nom
```

```
          9  8  ·    ·  7  ·    ·    ·    ·    ·  6   78   6565  7678765   5    7
14b.      bərg-e bi bar u bus-tan u gu-les- ta- ni gə-tır ['ə  -    ziz,      ey     gəl, gəl!]
                                                    T
```

pair he elaborates the arrival on scale-degree 5 by adding a series of vocables, then marks the conclusion of the "quatrain" by playing a dotār interlude that begins with several repetitions of the rhythmic pattern shown in figure 1.4(c). Hoseyn played a similar interlude at the end of each of his quatrains.

Perhaps the most striking tonal contrast evident in Moxtār's performance is that between the two halves of each line. Scale-degree 9 is often a strong presence in the first half but never occurs after the fifth syllable in the second half; and the descent in the second half usually arrives at scale-degree 7 on the fourth, fifth, or sixth syllable (as in lines 7b, 8b, 9b, 11b, and 14b). Two exceptions are the phrases (10b and 13b) that begin, like Hoseyn's medial phrase, with a turn that approaches 9 from 7 before reversing direction and descending stepwise; the other exception (12b) places all fifteen syllables on scale-degree 7.

The relationship between any pair of half-lines is more vibrant and more enticing when the equivalent metrical positions are differentiated by the singer's pitch choices, as happens throughout Moxtār's performance with one exception: line 9b has exactly the same distribution of pitches as line 7b, and the final syllables of both lines are also marked by tapping on the dotār. A reprise of a fifteen-syllable melody is more appropriate in the second half of a line than in the first half; such repetition offers a further means, in addition to the melodic descent, of restoring the stability that was temporarily challenged or abandoned in the first half. Dotār interludes, such as those that follow the even-numbered lines in this performance, generally continue the process of stabilization until it is interrupted and suspended by a new vocal entry.

This chapter has attempted to sketch an approach to musical practices of Iran and Central Asia centered on the coordination of three kinds of sequence: a relatively invariant ordering of a given number of long and short syllables (i.e., a quantitative poetic meter), instrumental patterns that are often shorter than a half-line of verse, and melodic progressions to which one or more verses may be sung. Rhythms that make a performance compelling may emerge as specific moments in each type of sequence coincide. Performers may produce rhythms on a larger time-scale by retaining or altering the initial set of relationships among the three types of sequence, or by returning to that initial set after a series of departures.

References

Cooke, Peter. 1970. "Ganda Xylophone Music: Another Approach." *African Music* 4/4: 62–80.

Darvişi, Mohammad Rezā. 2001. *Dā'erat al-ma'āref-e sāz-hā-ye Irān, i: Sāz-hā-ye zehi mezrābi va ārşe'i navāhi-ye Irān* [Encyclopedia of the instruments of Iran, 1: Plucked and bowed string instruments of Iran's regions]. Tehran: Māhur.

Doerfer, Gerhard, and Wolfram Hesche. 1993. *Chorasantürkisch: Wörterlisten, Kurzgrammatiken, Indices.* Turcologica, 16. Wiesbaden: Harrassowitz.

Elwell-Sutton, L. P. 1976 *The Persian Metres.* Cambridge: Cambridge University Press.

——. 1987. "Arūż." *Encyclopaedia Iranica* 2:670–679.

Levin, Theodore, 1996. *The Hundred Thousand Fools of God: Musical Travels in Central Asia (and Queens, New York).* Bloomington: Indiana University Press.

Levin, Theodore, and Razia Sultanova. 2002. "The Classical Music of Uzbeks and Tajiks." In *The Garland Encyclopedia of World Music,* 6. *The Middle East,* ed. Virginia Danielson, Scott Marcus, and Dwight Reynolds. New York: Routledge, 909–920.

Mas'udiye, Mohammad Teqi.1980. *Musiqi-ye Torbat-e Jām* [The music of Torbat-e Jam]. Tehran: Soruş.

——. 1992. "Die Begriffe Maqām und Dastgāh in der turkmenischen Musik des Iran." In *Regionale maqām-Traditionen in Geschichte und Gegenwart,* ed. Jürgen Elsner and Gisa Jähnichen. Berlin: 377–397.

——. 2000. *Musiqi-e torkomani* [Türkmen music]. Tehran: Māhur.

Reichl, Karl. 1992. *Turkic Oral Epic Poetry: Traditions, Forms, Poetic Structure.* New York: Garland.

Widdess, Richard. 1981. "Aspects of Form in North Indian ālāp and dhrupad." In *Music and Tradition: Essays on Asian and Other Musics Presented to Laurence Picken,* ed. D. R. Widdess and R. F. Wolpert. Cambridge: Cambridge University Press, 143–169.

Youssefzadeh, Ameneh. 2002. *Les bardes du Khorassan iranien : le bakhshi et son répertoire.* Travaux et mémoires de l'Institut d'études iraniennes, 6. Leuven and Paris: Peeters. Includes compact disc, with a performance of *Navā'i* by Hāj Qorbā Soleymāni on track 1.

Slawomira, Zeranska-Kominek. 2002. "Music of Turkmenistan." In *The Garland Encyclopedia of World Music,* VI. *The Middle East,* ed. Virginia Danielson, Scott Marcus, and Dwight Reynolds. New York: Routledge, 965–977.

Discography

PERFORMANCES OF NAVĀ'I (NORTHERN XORASAN VERSION WITH THE THREE EXCEPTIONS NOTED)

Asie Centrale: Les maîtres du dotâr, comp. Jean During. Archives Internationales de Musique Populaire, AIMP 26. Lausanne: Disques VDE-Gallo, VDE CD-735, p1993.

Track 11, *Navā'i* performed by Hasan Yazdāni (begins at 3:00 and includes two lines of Qomri's Sāqi-nāme at 4:09).

Track 8, *Navā'i* of eastern Xorasan, performed by Abdollah Sarvar Ahmadi (4:56).

Iran: Bardes du Khorassan, rec. with notes by Ameneh Youssefzadeh. Paris: OCORA C
560136, p1998. Track 1, *Navā'i* performed by Rowşān Golafruz (7:35).

Iran—Khorassan: L'Histoire de Tâher et Zohre / Rowshan Golafruz, chant et dotâr, notes by
Ameneh Youssefzadeh. Paris: Maison des Cultures du Monde, Inédit W 260116, p2004.
Track 1 *Navā'i* (initial line of Qomrı's Sāqi-nāme at 2:10 concludes the performance).

Musiqi-ye şomāl-e Xorāsān (Qučān) / Hāj Qorbān Soleymāni. Tehran: Māhur, M.CD-6,
Track 1; although the verses are credited to the poet Navā'i, I doubt that the attri-
bution is correct. (Available via Web site, <http://www.mahoor.ir>).

Musiqi-ye şomāl-e Xorāsān / Ostād Mohammad Hoseyn Yegāne. Tehran: Māhur, M.CD-91,
Track 3. (Available via Web site, <http://www.mahoor.ir>).

Music from Northern Khorâsân: Bakhshi Olyâ-Gholi Yegâné, dotâr, rec. with notes by Fozié
Majd. Tehran: Māhur, M.CD-136, p2003. Track 3, Türkmen Navā'i (Available via
Web site, <http://www.mahoor.ir>).

Music from Northern Khorâsân: Mohammad-Hosseyn Yegâné. The Story of Zohré and Tâher,
rec. with notes by Fozié Majd. Tehran: Māhur, M.CD 154, p2003, Track 8 Available
via Web site, <http://www.mahoor.ir>).

The Instrumental Maghâms of Torbat-e Jâm: Nazar-Mohammad Soleymâni, dotâr, rec. with
notes by Fozié Majd. Tehran: Māhur M.CD 137, p2003, Track 5, *Navā'i* of eastern
Xorasan (Available via Web site, <http://www.mahoor.ir>).

CHAPTER 2

How to Spin a Good Horo

Melody, Mode, and Musicianship in the Composition

of Bulgarian Dance Tunes

DONNA A. BUCHANAN AND STUART FOLSE

For over two hundred years, improvised instrumental dance tunes called *hora* (sing. *horo*), together with the dance songs to which they are often closely linked, have comprised the cornerstone of Bulgarian celebrations.[1] Despite the impact of industrialization, urbanization and advanced technology, the principles guiding the creation of *hora*, like the songs and tunes themselves, have remained largely in oral tradition. In June 2002 we traveled to Sofia, Bulgaria's capital, to investigate the nature of *horo* composition. Did musicians have a compositional model in mind when they improvised such pieces? How did they know what to play? Was there a particular structural format or formal plan that they followed?

The hustle and bustle of Sofia's central market whizzed past the windows of the electronic trolley bus as it threaded its way through congested streets on the forty-minute ride to Lyulin, a sprawling residential complex of identical

Our sincere gratitude to Stoyan Velichkov and Georgi Andreev for their gracious assistance with this article. We also wish to thank the Roosevelt University Summer Grant Fund, and the University of Illinois Scholar's Travel Fund, European Union Center, Russian and East European Center, and School of Music, each of which funded various portions of our research.

1. The Bulgarian vowels "*o*" and "*a*" are pronounced similarly to their English "long" forms, as in the words "go" and "father." The Bulgarian vowel "*i*" is pronounced ë as in "see"; the Bulgarian vowel "*ŭ*" is pronounced as a short "u", as in the English "gut"; the Bulgarian vowel "*e*" is pronounced as a short "e," as in the English "let."

Stoyan Velichkov playing a bavna melo. Photo by Donna Buchanan.

concrete apartment blocks located on the city's northwestern outskirts. We were on our way to visit Stoyan Velichkov (b. 1931), one of the country's premier folk musicians. Stoyan had played *kaval,* an obliquely blown, keyless, eight-holed wooden flute, for over thirty years in a prestigious professional orchestra of indigenous instruments affiliated with the Bulgarian National Radio. Now retired and in frail health, he spent most days at home with his wife, Radka, in their small, sparsely furnished apartment, not far from the final stop on the trolley's route.

Our intention was to question Stoyan about *horo* composition, for he had been playing such music all of his life. Since at least the 1800s, musicians like Stoyan, whether as soloists or in small groups, had spontaneously improvised *hora* to accompany line and ring dances, also generically called *hora,* at community celebrations. During the 1930s and '40s, the years of Stoyan's youth, these events included life-cycle rites (such as christenings and weddings), village dances held Sunday afternoons after church (except during Lent), and myriad calendrical festivities related to agriculture and animal husbandry, the economic backbone of the small towns and villages in which most Bulgarians then lived. Music making was primarily an unpaid village pastime or semi-professional activity. Instrumentalists—virtually always men—rarely studied music formally. Rather, as young boys they began to learn by listening to and

FIGURE 2.1. *Map of Bulgaria. Courtesy of Perry Castañeda Online Map Library, University of Texas.*

emulating their older kinsmen or friends. As they grew more proficient, the best were invited by their relatives and neighbors to perform at family and public functions.

With the advent of socialism in 1944 came industrialization, urbanization, and the collectivization of agriculture, processes that induced many villagers to move to larger cities like Sofia, and which radically altered artistic life. By the 1950s, traditional music performance in urban areas had become a professional occupation. The size, shape, and tuning of traditional musical instruments like the *kaval* were standardized to facilitate collective playing in newly established folk orchestras. Such groups, modeled on the symphony orchestra, provided the instrumental component of larger, state-supported folk ensembles, which generally also included a choir of traditional women's voices and a dance troupe. Like the Bulgarian Radio Ensemble that employed Stoyan, the new professional groups were charged by the government with popularizing notated arrangements of traditional music written by conservatory-trained composers, but based on the songs and *hora* of individual ensemble members. Consequently, Stoyan and other musicians of his generation learned to read and write music notation in the workplace. By the 1970s the government founded two secondary schools and a collegiate-level academy to better train young musicians and dancers for ensemble performance careers. Hundreds of amateur groups arose in imitation of the professional groups. Thus, ensembles became the primary venue for traditional music performance from their inception through the demise of the socialist regime in 1989, when an uncertain economy caused many to disband.[2]

Our conversations with Stoyan concerned the music theory or logic informing *horo* composition, how he conceived the form of such pieces, their categorization, relationship to songs, and factors governing his choice of motives, rhythm, register, ornamentation, and mode as he improvised. We also wondered how this process had changed since Stoyan's childhood. Did musicians of different generations and training approach *horo* composition differently? Did notational literacy affect *horo* structure or content? Were the compositional techniques employed by musicians identical despite their choice of instrument? And what of place? Although a small country, Bulgaria possessed numerous ethnographic regions and subregions characterized by differences in musical texture, meter, instrumentation, and ornamentation. For example, Stoyan had grown up in the tiny village of Zidarovo, located outside the city of Burgas near the Turkish border, an area called Strandzha and a district of Thrace, the country's largest ethnographic region (figure 2.1). Did instrumentalists from different regions perceive *horo* composition in the same way?

To obtain a comparative perspective on these questions we also turned to thirty-three-year-old Georgi Andreev, a *gŭdulka* (bowed lute) player, composer, and conductor who is the current director of a second Sofia-based professional folk orchestra, that is affiliated with the highly acclaimed Kutev Ensemble.[3] Born in Haskovo, a small, southern Bulgarian city nestled in the eastern Rhodope Mountains, Georgi grew up in an area of southern Thrace that borders the Rhodope ethnographic region, or "Rodopa." He attended the Shiroka Lŭka folk music high school, in central Rodopa near Smolyan, in *gŭdulka* performance, later earning a Bachelor's and Master's degree in western art music composition from Sofia Conservatory. He was thus particularly fluent in the Rhodope and Thracian musical styles, in addition to classical music.

2. The information provided here represents only a thumbnail sketch of a much more complicated history. For more information about Bulgarian music and customs see Buchanan (2000, 2006); Forsyth (1996); Levy (1985); MacDermott (1998); and Rice (1994, 2000, 2004).

3. Founded in 1951 by its namesake, composer Philip Kutev (also spelled Phillip Koutev), the Kutev Ensemble was the first professional such organization. Over the years it has been known by several names, including the Ensemble of the Bulgarian Republic, the State Ensemble for Folk Songs and Dances—Philip Kutev, the National Ensemble for Folk Songs and Dances "Philip Kutev," and currently, the National Folkloric Ensemble "Philip Kutev." At present, the ensemble is directed by Kutev's daughter, Elena Kuteva.

Despite their diverse ages, training, and backgrounds, we found that both musicians spoke with remarkable similarity about the principles governing *horo* composition. Although Georgi's comments reflected his formal training, incorporating both indigenous expressions and the vocabulary of Western European art music analysis, he pointed to Stoyan as a master of the very techniques he described. We'll begin with a general survey of *horo* structure and categories, accompanied by a guided tour to the improvisation of major *horo* types provided by Georgi. Finally, we will compare and apply the principles learned to a *horo* created by Stoyan Velichkov.

The Horo *and* Horo *Categories*

According to Bulgarian organologist Ivan Kachulev (1967:48), villagers of the 1800s and early 1900s commended an instrumentalist gifted at the art of crafting dance melodies by saying, "He spins the tune very beautifully." "Spinning" referred to the act of improvising the melodic content and design of a *horo* line by line, in a succession of motivically linked, steadily evolving phrases. Musicians constructed these phrases by stringing together and improvising on brief, one- or two-measure melodic fragments called *zayavki,* derived from song motifs or their own personal instrumental creativity.[4] Each *zayavka* was typically repeated, with or without variation, any number of times to create a musical idea or phrase. Consequently, a *horo's* phrase structure was often irregular. The phrases themselves also typically repeated at least once, resulting in a sectional form.

Categorization by Social Function

Although *hora* can be categorized by region, meter, accompanying choreography, associated custom, or instrument, in regard to compositional process we can also classify them according to their social function and source material (see figure 2.2). In terms of the former, those *hora* composed for celebrations were (and are) usually improvised on the spot, during the course of dancing, their length determined by the demands of the occasion and those participating. Changes in the modality, tempo, and rhythm of a *horo* melody, such as the use of smaller, more vigorous note values, frequently mirrored and inspired new

---

4. Such melodic fragments are known by a variety of terms throughout the country. For clarity's sake, we have elected to introduce only one here. For a discussion of other pertinent terms, see Buchanan (2006); Levy (1985); and Rice (1994).

FIGURE 2.2. Horo *categories and types.*

Categorization by Source Material

Song-Based *Hora*

Type I: Song—*Otsvir*—Song—*Otsvir*

Type II: Song—Song-derived *Otsvir*—New Material (*Sitnezhi*) Developed from Song
and *Otsvir*

Hora Based on Instrumental Material

Type III: Song—Independent *Otsvir*—New Material (*Sitnezhi*) Developed from
Otsvir

Type IV: Motive/Fragment (*Zayavka*)—Musical Idea or Phrase (*Sitnezh/Kolyano*)
—New Material (in *Sitnezh* and/or *Kolyano* form)

Categorization by Social Function

Hora **for Dancing**

Usually improvised; sometimes worked out in advance

Hora **for Listening**

Generally worked out in advance, sometimes in musician's mind, sometimes on paper
with notation

May have more complicated structure and modal development

and more energetic choreography (Rice 1994:100, 105). At celebrations, then,
a *horo*'s shape developed symbiotically with the dancing.[5]

With the founding of Radio Sofia in 1929, however, instrumentalists began
creating *hora* not just to accompany dancing, but as listening entertainment
broadcast live from the Radio's transmitters. Local recording firms such as Arfa,
Balkan, and Orfei, in addition to larger foreign concerns—His Master's Voice,
Columbia Records, and Odeon—also released such music on 78 rpm records
(Brody 1998:2).[6] Once folk ensembles were established instrumentalists also
performed *hora* in concerts, whether as soloists or within a folk orchestra. These
developments inspired a new category of *hora* whose general form and content
were worked out by performers at least partially in advance, and whose duration was prescribed by the needs and limitations of the mass media or concert
stage. In these new performance contexts, musicians understood that they must
use their melodic resources strategically, to maximum aesthetic effect, within
the time frame allotted. As they gained fluency in music notation they there-

5. At contemporary events, notably weddings, this symbiosis is further facilitated
and invigorated by tips offered to the musicians by celebrants.

6. Early recordings of Bulgarian traditional music and an overview of their history
can be found on *Song of the Crooked Dance: Early Bulgarian Traditional Music, 1927–42*
(Yazoo 7016, 1998), produced by Lauren Brody.

fore began fixing their *horo* improvisations on paper. Although the principles guiding composition remained unchanged, once a *horo* was committed to notation, an instrumentalist could revise it as often as necessary to consciously fashion an ideal piece.[7] Notated *hora* frequently manifested a more complicated structure and modal development. They were designed to be appreciated by passive listeners as well as dancers. Although this chapter focuses exclusively on spontaneously improvised *hora,* both Stoyan and Georgi are adept at composing in both veins.

Categorization by Source Material

Categorizing *hora* according to their source material is more complicated. Most instrumentalists claim that everything they play, including dance tunes, begins with song, an illustration of the centrality of vocal music to traditional Bulgarian life (cf. Levy 1985:188–189). It is also an aesthetic remark—beautiful instrumental timbre is likened to a beautiful singing voice, whereas numerous song texts describe the ability of instrumentalists to "speak" through their playing. Contrary to these claims, we found that *hora* can be divided into two broad categories, some created from songs, and some not. This scheme can be broken down further into at least four major types of *hora,* distinguished primarily by their derivation, length, and complexity (figure 2.2). However, there are also many interrelationships between these subcategories, especially those described in figure 2.2 as Types II–IV. They utilize similar principles of motivic transformation and modal contrast, and exhibit a similar form, characterized by two or three larger sections, or phases of development.

Horo *Improvisation: Georgi Andreev's Guided Tour*

We learned of these four *horo* types through Georgi Andreev, with whom we met in one of the Kutev Ensemble's rehearsal rooms, following the daily work of the group's folk orchestra. Excited by our questions and eager to help, over the next several days he systematically outlined the structure and creative process characteristic of each. We then compared and interwove these findings with information gleaned from earlier scholarship and our consultations with Stoyan.

To reinforce our understanding Georgi illustrated his remarks with musical excerpts improvised on his *gŭdulka,* a fretless bowed lute generally made

---

7. During the socialist era, once the instrumentalist was satisfied with his *horo,* he might give it to a composer who would then arrange it for performance with folk orchestra. Today, many instrumentalists arrange their own material.

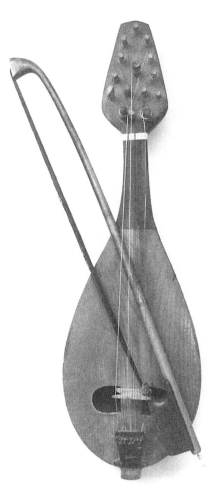

Three-stringed Bulgarian gŭdulka of the
Thracian variety with sympathetic strings.

from sycamore, walnut, or pear wood. The instrument is held vertically and stabilized by placing the squarish knob found on the lower end of its teardrop-shaped base in a belt slung horizontally across the torso. The bow is held in the right hand, whereas the three melody strings are fingered with the left. The strings are set quite high above the instrument's short neck, so that one need only touch the side of the fingernails to the strings to change pitches, rather than pressing them all the way down to the fingerboard, as on a violin or viola. The *gŭdulka's* resonance is enhanced by a dozen sympathetic strings, affixed below the melody strings. This is a versatile instrument on which players can execute numerous ornaments and techniques, including grace notes, trills, mordents, turns, glissandi, drone, pizzicato, double-stops, and harmonics.

Song-Based Hora

Type I

The most straightforward *horo* type resulted when an instrumental refrain, called an *otsvir*, was improvised between the verses of a song.[8] Through the early twentieth century, the Sunday afternoon village dance was typically accompanied by a pair or two groups of women's voices, who sang the lines or verses of a metered "dance song" antiphonally.[9] An accompanying musician might play his own rendition of the song tune alone or with the singers, improvising an instrumental break—an *otsvir*—between verses. For variety, an instrumentalist occasionally fashioned two different interludes, alternating each with the verses of the song. Such intermezzi permitted singers to rest and recall the lyrics of the next stanza. They also provided an opportunity for the instrumentalist to show off his virtuosity. The contrast between singing and instrumental music sometimes allowed for two kinds of dancing, more sedate as the girls concentrated on their singing, more vigorous as the instrumentalist took over (Rice 1994:104).

The *otsvir* took one of two forms: its content either derived from the song tune, or presented new and often contrasting material.[10] "The simplest type," Georgi told us, is when the instrumentalist "just continues with the last phrase of the song. If the song melody contains two phrases, for example, he'll repeat the last phrase."[11] Georgi then demonstrated by creating an *otsvir* from the

---

8. The term *otsvir* probably derives from *ot svirene*, "from the playing," or *ot svirnyata*, "from the *svirnya*." In its most general sense, *svirnya* means "instrumental tune" and is related to the verb *svirya*, or "to play an instrument." Thus, the content of an *otsvir*, or refrain, derives from the *svirnya*, or tune that it succeeds. A synonym for *otsvir*, *pripev*, likely derives from *pri pevitsa*, or music played "before a singer" enters to *pee* (sing) the *pesen* (song). Thus, *pripev* refers either to an introduction or refrain, depending on whether one is starting a song or between its verses. For more complete descriptions of these terms, see Buchanan (2006); Levy (1985:198–204); Rice (1994:104–109).

9. Songs appropriate for dancing are called exactly that—*horovodni pesni*—or, songs (*pesni*) to lead (*vodya*) the dance (*horo*).

10. In his study of bagpipe music in the Rhodopes, ethnomusicologist Mark Levy (1985:199) found that an *otsvir* may take any of five specific shapes, which are encompassed by Georgi's two categories: (1) "a fairly literal statement of the song melody"; (2) "a segment of the song melody"; (3) "an instrumental elaboration of the song melody"; (4) "an instrumental improvisation based on the melodic material of the song"; and (5) "entirely new, often contrasting, melodic material."

11. The instrumentalist also might repeat the entire song or its concluding two phrases, particularly if he wished to extend the *horo*'s duration.

FIGURE 2.3. Horo *Type I: Georgi's Dance Song with repetitive* Otsvir.

concluding five bars (mm. 6–10) of an unnamed dance song that came to mind as we spoke (figure 2.3; CD track 3).

Georgi told us that the phrasing of this tune, like that of most Bulgarian songs, reflects the rhythm of its text (not presented here). Irregular phrasing, regular phrasing with uneven numbers of bars, and phrases whose internal subdivision is asymmetrical or irregular all occur frequently in songs for this reason. Here, each of the melody's five-bar phrases contains a three- and two-measure subphrase. This phrasing is also reflected in the step pattern of the accompanying dance. Georgi's melody would be rendered as a *pravo horo* ("straight" horo): a duple-meter, moderate to fast tempo line dance that is the most widespread in the country. Participants hold each other by the hand or waistband, moving the dance chain to the right. The choreography varies, but always combines two "quick" steps (Q) to the right (a step on one foot and then the other on successive beats) followed by one or more "slow" steps (S). (A single slow step comprises a step to the right on beat 1, and suspension of movement—a "rest"—on beat 2. If a second slow step follows, it involves a rocking step backward or to the left on the downbeat, and a rest on beat 2.[12]) Where Georgi's song is concerned the choreography unfolds in accordance with the subphras-

12. In practice, these basic patterns were varied by better dancers to the delight of all involved. For other versions of the *pravo horo,* see Katsarova-Kukudova and Djenev (1976:21–22).

ing, in two related step patterns: QQSS (extending over the first subphrase of three measures, or six beats) and QQS (extending over the second subphrase of two measures, or four beats). Because the instrumentalist simply repeats the song's second phrase this same pattern holds for the refrain.[13]

The song's modal structure reflects the convergence of multiple modal systems in the Balkans over the centuries, and their influence on instrumental practice. These include the Byzantine and Eastern Orthodox church modes, those of Ottoman Turkish court and folk music, the Western European major-minor system and the medieval church modes that were its predecessor, as well as a variety of local modal practices specific to the region's folk music traditions.

The tune's tonal center is [E]. Its pitch content contains a variable fifth degree, which fluctuates between [Bb] and [B♮] (E F G A Bb/B♮C♯D). Such chromaticism is an integral feature of Bulgarian melodies. It is the likely result of modal mixing, vestiges of an older practice of employing untempered intervals or microtones, or the influence of Turkish modes, or *makamlar* (sing. *makam*), which use such microtones systematically. For example, it is possible that this melody was once rendered with a quarter tone on scale-degree 5 (a [Bb]) throughout, but as the influence of standard temperament spread during the 1800s, this practice fell into disuse. The chromatic fluctuation between [Bb] and [B♮] (the two tempered pitches on either side of the [Bb]) might have been substituted as a tempered alternative to the quarter tone itself, one that points to a neutral interval in between. Such microtones are not uncommon in songs sung in some circa pre-1950s styles; it is therefore quite possible that they also were part of the instrumental tradition.[14]

We also can perceive the song's pitch content as combining the lower pentachords of two modes, Lydian on G and Locrian on E, as illustrated in figure 2.4.[15] This interpretation is supported by the melody's phrase structure. The first subphrase (mm. 1–3) begins and ends on G, and clearly outlines the lower pentachord of a G Lydian scale. A shift to the lower pentachord of E

13. It is important to note that choreographic patterns and melodic phrase structure were not always so synchronized. Hypothetically, Georgi's illustration could also be danced using the QQSS pattern throughout, without disturbing the overall rhythmic flow of the piece. In such cases, the dancers concluded with an incomplete choreographic figure. Because *hora* were usually danced, played, and sung for an extended period (sometimes as long as an hour or more), it might be useful to think of the choreography and verse-refrain structure as two related, repetitive cycles that could intersect in an ever-changing manner, sometimes completely in sync, and sometimes not.

14. Hear, for example, Forsyth (1990:track 1); Lloyd (1994:track 3); Raim and Koenig (1988:track 15).

15. Although Locrian is uncommon in Western European modal music, it is not atypical of Bulgarian melodies.

68

FIGURE 2.4. *Modal mixture in Georgi's Dance Song.*

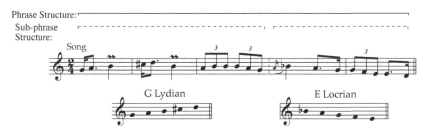

Locrian is initiated in the second subphrase (mm. 4–5) and continues to the end of the song. However, the distribution of [B♭] and [B♮] in the melody may relate more to an aspect of Turkish modal practice than to these overlapping pentachords.

It is not uncommon for a *makam* to employ different shades of the same scale degree. How high or low a pitch is taken can depend on the flavor of the mode and the melodic and registral environment within which the pitch appears. Thus, a particular *makam* might feature a higher variety of a scale degree (B♭, for example) in ascending passages, and a lower variety (such as B♭) in descending passages. (The melodic minor scale provides an analogue in Western European art music.) The distribution of [B♭]/[B♮] in Georgi's dance song resembles this practice. The [B♮] appears largely in the ascent, in passages dwelling on the lower, "major" sounding pentachord of G Lydian (G A B♮ C♯ D), whereas B♭ signals a seven-measure descent to the tonic through the lower pentachord of E Locrian, material that the *otsvir* repeats.

Type II

"Here's a song," said Stoyan. He played the twelve-bar melody to *Georgi le, lyubile* (Georgi, my love), which we will study later (figure 2.19). "Now, you can't bore everyone by playing just that. You begin with a melody that you like, and from it you should try to derive development. A good *horo* always demands development."

Stoyan alluded to a second type of *horo* composition, in which musicians use motives, contours, or intervals characteristic of a song to create new melodic material. Georgi underscored that this is an intuitive process. A musician doesn't consciously think about aspects of the melody he will use, he told us. Instead, he is thinking, "let the *otsvir* [and subsequent material] resemble the distinctive characteristics of the song."

The content of Georgi's dance song is motivically compact, deriving from just three motives, two of which are presented in its first measure. To illustrate his remarks he replayed the tune, following it with a potential *otsvir* whose content largely repeated, with little variation, whole measures of song material, but in a different order (figure 2.5; CD track 3, 0:17″). Measures 11–13 and 16–17 of the *otsvir* derive from mm. 4–5 of the song, whereas m. 15 of the *otsvir* originated as the song's second measure, the phrase's climactic point. Georgi concluded, "the instrumentalist creates something similar to the melody—a variation of the melody that preserves these elements." As stated earlier, this *otsvir* could be repeated between song verses for the latter's duration. However, once the song was concluded, the *otsvir* also could serve as the basis for further, idiomatically instrumental variations called *sitnezhi,* according to the principles of *horo* development discussed later in this chapter.

In addition to motivic features, the new *otsvir* retains the pitch content, range, and general contour of the song. In regard to modality, the logic behind the distribution of the chromatic variance remains the same: [B♭] signals a descent, through the lower pentachord of E Locrian, to the tonic, whereas [B♮] indicates an ascent, in the upper register, through the lower pentachord of G Lydian. The inclusion of [F♯] in the *otsvir* (m. 14) as part of this ascending passage results in a second chromatic fluctuation ([F♯]/[F♮]). It also triggers a momentary shift to a Dorian modal environment, retaining [E] as tonic, before the subsequent [B♭] again signifies a descent into E Locrian's lower depths. The motivic content of measure 14 is a transposed rhythmic variation of Motive B, which first appears in measure 1 of the song. The modal shift occurs through [F♯], which briefly transforms the *otsvir*'s pitch content into E Dorian (figure 2.6).

Significantly, the new *otsvir* also differs from the song in that its subphrases are organized proportionally in a pair of two-bar units, creating a four-bar phrase that contrasts with the song's five-measure lines.

The use of "square" phrasing reflects an important change in the history of *horo* composition. By the 1930s, urban Bulgarian musicianship had fallen increasingly under the influence of Western European trends. As *horo*s were harmonized and arranged, their phrase structure became increasingly predictable and symmetrical. Each *horo* phrase became known as a *kolyano,* meaning "knee" or "joint," in which one *kolyano* generally comprised two four-bar units. Musicologists and composers christened the *horo*'s overall compositional format *kolyano* form or *kolyano*-variation form. Like the older notion of "spinning," these metaphors aptly described the hinge-like or pivoting function of each line, as it connected preceding material with that which followed. It also characterized the organic development consequently inherent in a *horo*'s structure.[16]

16. On the *kolyano* and *kolyano*-variation form, see also Buchanan (2006); Levy (1985: 206); Rice (1994:192–194); and Todorov (1974).

FIGURE 2.5. Horo *Type II: Georgi's Dance Song with variational* Otsvir.

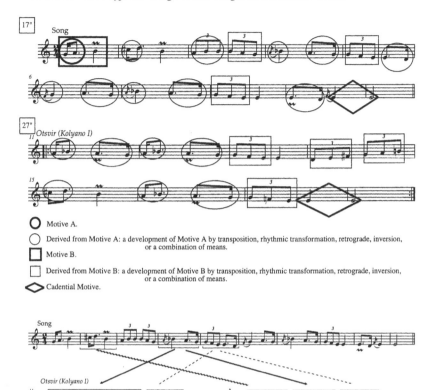

Entire measures are utilized from the song with little variation.

Thus, although each *horo* phrase might, as in the past, derive from *zayavki*, now these brief expository ideas were worked out in symmetrical constructions—in *kolena*. Significantly, Georgi noted that musicians call the stereotypical four-bar phrase improvisations "*chetvorki*," a term meaning "in fours" or "foursomes," and perceive the act of improvising as moving through them. This shows that musicians conceptualize *horos* as both spatial and temporal, and physically experience their performance as moving through and to particular places. "When improvising," Georgi told us, "in terms of musical logic it is always easier to move in *kvadratni*—in symmetrical structure—to think in even numbers of phrases and measures." Georgi's use of "*kvadratni*," a term meaning "squares" or "checks," as a synonym for *chetvorki* demonstrates that the latter are perceived as patterned symmetrical units comprising the building blocks of *kolena* and hence, of *hora*. It is "a sign of great mastery," he continued, "when an instru-

FIGURE 2.6. *Modal mixture in Georgi's Type II Otsvir.*

E Locrian	E F G A B♭	
G Lydian	G A B C♯D	
	E F♯G A	E Dorian

mentalist improvises lots of development in *chetvorki*—on the one hand, his phrases must be varied, on the other, structured in four-bar units (*chetvorki*)—not broken up measure by measure." For this reason he finds the second *horo* type the most difficult to create; within the *chetvorki* framework the instrumentalist is always constrained by the initial song material. At the same time, such *hora* manifest an economy of compositional means that affords them an inherent coherence. If *horo* phrases are viewed as spun out, like thread, from one or more tufts of musical wool, then this technique weaves them tightly together, bearing out assertions made by other musicians that the best *hora* use, at most, two or three basic melodic ideas, or even, as Georgi put it, "one idea that is developed brilliantly."[17]

Instrumental Horos

Type III

Over the years, certain instrumental refrains became fixed and attached to particular songs, whether through habit, or because they were especially well liked or well suited.[18] These *otsviri* became the basis of improvisation themselves, resulting in a third *horo* type. Typically, they comprised completely new melodic material, but at the same time retained something of the character, pitch content, contour, and sometimes, mode of the original melody, without resorting necessarily to song motifs. Georgi observed that this sort of refrain must "go with" or be "appropriate" to the song; it represents a complementary, instru-

---

17. Georgi noted that the most masterful *horo* artists employ a minimum of musical means to maximum effect. To illustrate, he pointed to a lengthy *rŭchenitsa* (dance tune in 7/16) by *gŭdular* Atanas Vŭlchev rooted in a single motive.

18. In some cases, a song and its refrain evolved together in oral tradition. Even when this was not the case, a particularly well-liked *otsvir* often came to signify the song to which it was attached. When such an *otsvir* was sounded audiences expected a particular song to follow. Conversely, when that song was sung, they expected musicians to supply the *otsvir* identified with it.

mental extension of it. "It's a 'plug in'!" he explained, using the language of computer technology:

> This is the most precise term. . . . With any given software you might have a number of 'plug in' programs that don't replace the original software but work together with it [to extend its capabilities]. This is a contemporary *horo* type and the most widespread, because it's both varied and not very difficult. It [also] puts the vocal and instrumental components on par with one another. In the first two variants [i.e., *horo* types], the instrumental part is in a subsidiary role to the vocal. . . . The second type . . . is homogeneous. But the song itself is a closed structure. It is encapsulated, delimited by the text, usually in an uneven [phrase] structure, and does not always lend itself well to variation. From here . . . the *otsvir* becomes the basis for *horo* development. Here . . . the instrumentalist begins, little by little, to *izliza* [to step out or emerge] with his own plan.

In Type III *horo*s, then, the independent *otsvir* becomes the springboard for improvisation—the basis for its own instrumental *horo,* one unrelated to the song. In contrast to the first two *horo* types, it is the *otsvir*'s material, rather than that of the song, which is spun through the rest of the work. With the *otsvir* the musician steps away from the song and into a complementary, instrumentally defined musical space whose structural principles or "plan," mandated jointly by tradition and the musician's own creative skill, were clarified as our discussion continued (see figure 2.12).

The song Georgi selected possesses just such a fixed *otsvir* which, in his words, has "absolutely nothing in common with the song" (figure 2.7; CD track 3 0:34″). The incorporation of an [F♯] and [C♮] shifts the *horo* into E Aeolian, creating a modal contrast, whereas its contour, a four-measure sequence of descending motives, also differs.

Georgi played the *otsvir* for us, following it with a second *kolyano* that further developed the refrain's material, a typical scenario (CD track 3, 0:41″). He took the *otsvir*'s motivic material (specifically mm. 13–14) and as he put it, "spun the [second] *kolyano* around it." In this respect, the *otsvir*'s motivic substance became like a spindle around which the thread of the successive *kolyano* was spun. The second *kolyano* remains in E Aeolian but for the first ending, whose [C♯] might be interpreted as a fleeting nod toward the Lydian quality of the song's second measure, or toward E Dorian, in the manner described above in figure 2.6.

A third *kolyano,* Georgi explained, might continue in the same vein or begin a new section of the *horo* with completely new material. Typically, however, the third or fourth *kolyano* captured the essence of the *otsvir* in a state-

FIGURE 2.7. Horo *Type III: Georgi's Dance Song with fixed* Otsvir *and subsequent development.*

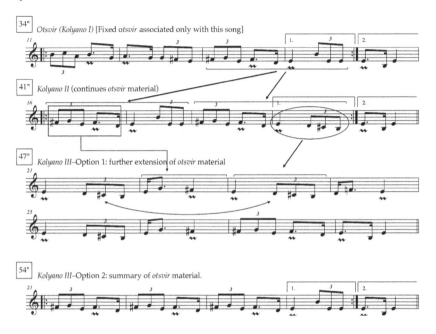

ment of narrow range. This shows that "you have nothing more to say about this material," Georgi remarked. It suggests that "you have exhausted or pumped dry the intervalic content." The *otsvir*'s characteristics become compressed into a few tones and a single idea, as a means of concluding its development. These three or four *kolena* work together as a set, Georgi noted, comprising the *horo*'s first large section.

Georgi provided us with two potential versions of a third *kolyano*. Option 1 (3/0:47″) develops motifs found in *Kolyano* II. Option 1, measure 21, repeats measure 19 of *Kolyano* II (the first ending). Measure 22 is a variation of measure 16. Thus, the first two measures of Option 1 emulate a move from the *Kolyano* II's first ending to its beginning. Measure 22 also looks back to the song, retaining the rhythm of its first measure. The [F♮] in measure 24 sets up another pair of chromatic variants, suggesting a fluctuation between the *otsvir*'s E Aeolian modality and the E Locrian flavor of the song's lower register. Measures 25–26 repeat measures 21–22, whereas measures 27–28 simply repeat the last two measures of *Kolyano* II, which also are the last two measures of the *otsvir*. Overall, this version of *Kolyano* III has a narrower range than that of *Kolyano* II, and its motivic content is less diverse: its first six measures (21–26) repeat a two-measure idea whose pitch content differs only in the [F♯] that appears in measure 24. The repetition and compression signify that the development of the *otsvir* is coming to a close, but modal and rhythmic links to the song help to bind this section of the *horo* together.

Georgi's second option for *Kolyano* III operates similarly, distilling a single, one-measure idea from the *otsvir*, that found in measure 13, as the section's essence (3/0:54″). Within the *otsvir*, this figure appears in the environment of a four-measure phrase. In *Kolyano* II, it becomes the initial measure of two two-bar phrases. Finally, in *Kolyano* III, Option 2, it stands on its own as a one-bar motif, whose repetition is rounded off by the cadential figures (the first and second endings) that also conclude the *otsvir*. Motivic links can thus easily be traced through the three lines, but in keeping with the character of Type III *hora*, the basis for those links derives from the *otsvir*, and not the song.

The preponderance of shorter note values (more eighth-note triplets), shorter motivic figures (one and two bars), and occasionally disjunct melodic movement (m. 14, 15, 20; Option 1: end of m. 21 to beginning of m. 22, m. 28; Option 2: m. 28, 29) found in these three *kolena* mark them as inherently instrumental in character. They represent the evolution of the *horo* into figures called *sitnezhi* (sing. *sitnezh*), a term referring to the idiomatically instrumental motivically based improvisations that are played after a dance song, usually in one or more new modes (cf. Levy 1985:188–189, 208). The word *"sitno,"* from which *sitnezh* derives, describes objects that are small or finely diced; a *sitnezh* is therefore characterized by a dense population of tiny things. In the *horo*, *sitnezhi* result from the subdivision of larger beat units into pitches of shorter rhythmic duration, creating a "pulsating, motoric effect" that may also possess a *Fortspinnung* quality (Rice 1994:315).[19] It is this increased note density, which showcases virtuosity and affords the illusion of a faster tempo, that can inspire dancers to elaborate their basic footwork with fancier, more energetic movements demanding smaller steps and emphasizing the shorter rhythmic units. Although instrumentalists today always structure *sitnezhi* in *chetvorki* and *kolena*, as Georgi does here, this was not always the case.

As the *sitnezhi* unfold, tradition mandates that an instrumentalist now move to new material in a contrasting mode, marking the beginning of the *horo's* second phase. Georgi characterized this as a developmental section, because the musician is free to explore a range of improvisatory and especially,

---

19. *Fortspinnung:* "The process by which melodic material is continuously derived from a brief figure. . . so as to produce a continuous melodic line rather than once characterized by balanced phrases of the type described as antecedent and consequent" (Randel 1986:322).

FIGURE 2.8. *The "B" section begins: Option 1. Transposing up a Fourth.*

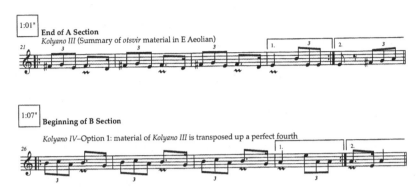

modulatory options. One typical technique is to create registral contrast by transposing the content of the previous *kolyano* up a fourth (here from E Aeolian to A Aeolian), prefacing the shift with a brief pause that draws the modulation to the listener's attention (figure 2.8; 3/1:10).

A second option involves modulating to a mode with a radically different color. If the previous *kolena* employ a minor-sounding mode—Georgi pointed to Aeolian, Dorian, and Phrygian, using the church mode names, as most common—the next *kolyano* might move to a major-sounding mode, like Ionian or Mixolydian. He cited shifting the tonal center up a fourth (from E Aeolian to A Mixolydian) as a highly effective and often used technique (figure 2.9; 3/1:13). Both of these modulatory practices underscore the importance of fourth, rather than fifth, relations in Bulgarian music.

Georgi characterized the effect of the latter modulation as "very sunny" and "full of light." Such timbral contrasts are key features of Bulgarian music, both in regard to *horo* structure and the intrinsic development of melodic lines. Variety is of utmost importance when thinking improvisationally. For instance, Stoyan insists that a long tone (what he calls an "open moment") never stand bare of embellishment. He employs both finger vibrato and a complex system of articulatory, decorative, and timbral ornaments as a means of decorating and linking every pitch, thus creating melodic density. The timbral ornaments are especially significant because they shade pitches microtonally, producing constantly shifting contrasts of what he calls "open" and "closed" sounds.[20]

20. In *kaval* performance practice, timbral ornaments are frequently produced using alternate fingerings that flatten or sharpen the pitch slightly, without changing the frequency to the extent that a new pitch is identified.

FIGURE 2.9. *The "B" section begins: Option 2. Modulating up a Fourth.*

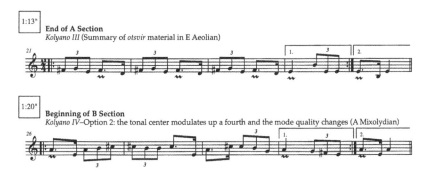

Stoyan describes tonalities, timbres, and registers in a synaesthetic fashion—as colors. They are his palette. It is also clear from his language that he perceives them spatially. Like Georgi's apprehension of *chetvorki,* they are places he grasps, moves to, and passes or spins through. "You start from one tonality," he explained,

> advance (*razvivash*) into another tonality, pass through.[21] These are the colors, I would call them. If you need the low register, you play *kaba*.[22] If you need the high register, you move [up]. . . . The whole objective is to seek out variety. . . . This is the fundamental task. . . . So I start to look for something else, something unexpected, something with another resonance, a different color—blue, green, red. Look, once you've played the theme, it becomes a question of improvisation—to constantly seek out and change the tonalities, not to stay in one place . . . and only play there. Always, you have to keep spinning.

A third technique employed to begin the *horo*'s "B" section is to move the tonal center down a major second, in this case from E Aeolian to D Ionian or D Mixolydian, following this material with a modulation to a *makam* that uti-

21. Stoyan's use of the verb "*razvivash*" is particularly appropriate because its meanings extend to three themes central to *horo* improvisation: development, movement, and spinning. It signifies to cultivate, develop, or work out; to evolve or advance; but also to untwine, unfurl, unwrap, unreel, unwind, and untwist.

22. The *kaval* can produce four registers: the main or "usual" register, as well as a high, low, and *kaba* register. The *kaba* differs from the low register in timbre rather than pitch. It is produced by slightly overblowing pitches in the lower octave. The air stream is positioned at the breaking point between the lower and "usual" register, so that both are sounded simultaneously, resulting in a vibrant, rich, resonant timbre awash in overtones.

lizes an augmented second, notably *Hicaz*. Such shifts are highly effective because, in Georgi's words:

> in this context a *makam* sounds very intense. . . . The use of the augmented second adds a tension to the whole structure. If you move into a *makam,* you need to stay there for a long time, to emphasize that this is the central, the culminative section of the work. This is the showiest part of the horo. It can continue forever—there are no rules. Here you can improvise; here is the place where you demonstrate your mastery.

"It's also mandatory to play with the registers of the instrument," Georgi continued, echoing Stoyan. When you shift the *makam* into a higher register, he noted, "this is the peak." Both Stoyan and Georgi observed that this moment is also frequently accompanied by a tempo acceleration, which further accentuates the climax. Figure 2.10 (3/1:25) presents the last, summary phrase of the *horo*'s "A" section, followed by a modulation to D Ionian, then to a *kolyano*

FIGURE 2.10. *The "B" section begins: Option 3. modulating down a Second and moving to a* Makam.

FIGURE 2.11. *Further modal mixture in Georgi's* Horo.

A Hicaz	A B♭ C♯ D
E Locrian	E F G A B♭
G Lydian	G A B C♯ D

pitched in the *gŭdulka's* lower register and the lower pentachord of *makam Hicaz* on C (C D♭ E F G), followed by further extemporization in the upper tetrachord of this mode.[23] Although never realized and possessing a different tonal center, the lower tetrachord of *makam Hicaz* is implied in the original modal content of the song, linking that melody with this distant portion of the *horo* (see figure 2.11).

At this point, instrumentalists face at least three options. First, they may elect to move on with the development. Second, they can segue to a new *horo*. When musicians play for weddings, where they must provide uninterrupted dance music for lengthy periods, they commonly string several *horos* together in a medley. They dwell on each section of a *horo,* improvising extensively in a particular tonality before moving on to a new song whose melody or *otsvir* is then spun into a new *horo* in turn. Third, they may end the piece. Whatever the case, before concluding, they may offer a reprise of the song. As Stoyan put it, "Once you finish the improvisational fantasia, you return to the song theme because it's easy—it's 'ready' [i.e., already composed] and hasn't been forgotten [i.e., it is readily recognizable]. Therefore, you improvise as much as you want, and then when everything has flowed out of your head, you return again to the very beginning." Musicians often re-approach the song by first reiterating the *otsvir,* which thus serves as a bridge between the *horo* and song, resulting in a ternary (ABA) form.

Type IV

A fourth *horo* type is woven exclusively from instrumental material, without any association with a song whatsoever. Here instrumental motives from the musician's personal vocabulary serve as grounds for improvisation. The devel-

23. Throughout the Middle East, *makam Hicaz* often employs a quarter tone on the sixth degree in the ascent, which is subsequently flattened in the descent. C *Hicaz* would thus comprise: C D♭ E F G A♭ B C B A♭ G F E D♭ C. Georgi employs A♮ as a tempered alternative.

FIGURE 2.12. Horo *structure*.

Section A

                   (Song)
    Kolyano I   Independent otsvir or melodic idea
    Kolyano II   Extension of otsvir
    Kolyano III
        Option A: Further extension of otsvir material
        Option B: Compression of previous material*

Section B
    Kolyano IV
        Option A: Previous material transposed up a 4th, usually prefaced by pause
        Option B: New material in major-sounding mode or makam, potentially
                  created by modulating up a 4th
        Option C: New material in major-sounding mode or makam, potentially
                  created by modulating down a 2nd
    Kolyano V   Modulation from "major" sound to "minor" sounding makam
    Kolyano VI   Registral play in makam of previous kolyano; tempo acceleration

Climax
    Kolyano VII   Modulation from makam of previous kolyano to new minor
                     mode or "minor-sounding" makam, sometimes with new tonal
                     center, but often in a tonality "parallel" or "relative" to that of
                     the previous kolyano

Section C (A')
    Kolyano VIII   Reprise of Otsvir
    Kolyano IX/X   (Further reprise of Section A material)
                     (Potential reprise of song melody)

*This may also comprise a fourth kolyano, when the third continues to develop the otsvir.

opmental principles and general format of the piece, however, are much the same, as summarized for all *horo*s in figure 2.12.

Application and Analysis: A Horo *by Stoyan Velichkov*

It remains now to apply these principles to a brief Type II *horo* improvised by Stoyan Velichkov on *kaval*. Its basis is an anonymous, twelve-measure dance song from strandzha called *Georgi le, lyubile* (Georgi, my love), which he first sang to better demonstrate the relationship between the song and the *horo* to come (figure 2.13; CD track 4).

FIGURE 2.13. Georgi le, lyubile.

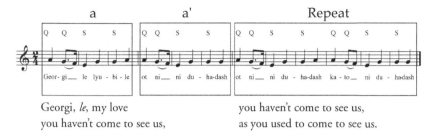

Georgi, *le*, my love
you haven't come to see us,

you haven't come to see us,
as you used to come to see us.

Text, Mode, Meter, and Form

At first glance the song appears quite simple. It is a love song whose lyrics express a dismayed young woman's suspicion that her sweetheart has lost interest in her. Like many Bulgarian songs, it is structured as a dialogue (of which only one verse is presented here). The phrasing of the text suggests that the melody comprises four three-bar phrases in duple meter, and that it would be danced as a *pravo horo* using a QQSS choreographic pattern. Phrase 2 varies phrase 1, differing only in its final pitch. Together the four phrases may be grouped in two six-bar periods, the second of which repeats the first. The melody's motivic composition comprises four melodic and two rhythmic motives (figure 2.14). Its range is very narrow, only a fourth, and its pitch content, diatonic.

But closer examination reveals that the song manifests considerable tonal and metric ambiguity, a feature of many Balkan and Slavic folk songs. Where is the tonic? Is it [E], [G], [A], or some other implied tone that does not appear in the melody itself? And what mode does the pitch content point to? There is no single or simple answer to these questions. The constant undulation between [G] and [A] might give the impression of a dual tonic.[24] It also affords the melody an intrinsic circularity. The end leads right back to the beginning, making for easy repetition in the course of dancing. However, when pitch content, text setting, and meter are taken into account, it is also possible to hear the melody as situated in any of three modes: A Aeolian, E Phrygian, or C Ionian.

The melody's meter may be perceived, for example, as a simple triple pattern (figure 2.15). Barring the melody in this manner emphasizes [A], which recurs on every other downbeat, as the tonic. This interpretation is supported by

24. This phenomenon is found in some other Slavic traditions, particularly Russian folk song.

FIGURE 2.14. *Motivic composition of* Georgi le, lyubile.

Rhythmic Motives: ♩ ♩.♪ and ♩ ♩

the syllabic setting of the text, which suggests groupings of three (i.e., *lyu-bi-le, du-ha-dash, ot ni ni*), as well as the gently rocking character of the [G]–[A] fluctuation.

A better solution might be to notate the song in compound duple meter, further emphasizing [A] as tonic by placing it on every downbeat (figure 2.16). This strategy additionally captures the line flow of the lyrics, setting one line of text to each measure.

A third option is to perceive the melody in terms of a larger beat unit—the half note—and the melody's first beat as an anacrusis (figure 2.17). This realization places the tonal center firmly on [E] through repeated metric accentuation that is further strengthened by the accentuation of the text, which when sung, emphasizes the syllables set here to the first half of the downbeat of each measure.[25]

Finally, consider the following three harmonizations, each of which offers a legitimate tertian setting for the melody, here presented in duple meter, in contemporary folk ensemble practice (figure 2.18).

The first two harmonizations situate the melody in A Aeolian and E Phrygian, respectively. The third, however, plays with the melody's two interlocking thirds ([E–G] and [F–A]), treating [E] and [G] as the third and fifth degrees of a C major chord. Harmonizing the first measure in F major sets up a IV–I progression that positions [C] as tonic, although it never appears in the melody. This harmonization maintains the Bulgarian preference for plagal relationships while also resulting in a Western European sound.[26]

25. One also could bar the melody similarly in 6/4 and treat the first two beats as an anacrusis, in which case the text syllables in question would fall on the downbeat of each measure.

26. Composer Ivan Kirev employed this harmonization in his arrangement of the tune for the Kutev Ensemble folk orchestra. A recording of this arrangement may be heard on the CD-ROM accompanying Buchanan 2006 ("*Ludi-mladi*"; track 4).

FIGURE 2.15. Georgi le, lyubile *in triple meter.*

Geor- gi___le   lyu - bi - le   ot   ni___ni   du - ha-dash   ot   ni___ni   du-ha-dash   ka - to___ni   du - ha-dash

The Otsvir and Section A

Because melodies such as *Georgi le, lyubile* exist in oral tradition and were not harmonized much before the late 1800s, it is difficult to know how their modality and meter were actually heard. In fact, their very ambiguity may well have opened up a larger number of improvisational options. Stoyan's instrumental rendition of the song and subsequent *otsvir* offer some clue as to his own perceptions (figure 2.19). He uses the tune, performed in two, three-bar duple-meter phrases without anacrusis, to build a *pravo horo* in compound duple time whose fundamental modality is E Phrygian.

Stoyan highlights the lyrical character of the song by strategically interpolating dotted rhythms throughout his instrumental rendition, which result in repeated and passing tones of a sixteenth-note's duration that ornament and smoothly connect the song's original pitches, and by employing *portamenti* in measures 2, 3, and 5. Such *portamenti* are a common *kaval* ornament, easily facilitated by the instrument's keyless construction. They also point to a key feature of Stoyan's aesthetic: to play song tunes effectively, he asserts that instrumentalists must sing the words in their head. He thus does everything possible—through *portamenti* and other techniques—to emulate the singing voice with his *kaval*, a practice that imparts a remarkably cantabile quality to his playing.

The tune's dotted rhythms hint at the compound-duple framework of the *horo* to come. This bears some explanation. Pairing a simple duple-meter song with a compound-duple instrumental *pravo horo* is a stereotypical scenario that juxtaposes the lyricism of the voice with the more virtuosic capabilities of the instrument. Although we have transcribed most of Stoyan's piece in 6/8, as this is how it is performed, the standard practice among Bulgarian musicians is to notate a *pravo horo* in 2/4 (a custom that we followed in transcribing Georgi's

FIGURE 2.16. Georgi le, lyubile *in compound duple meter.*

Geor- gi___le   lyu - bi - le   ot   ni___ni   du - ha-dash   ot   ni___ni   du-ha-dash   ka - to___ni   du - ha - dash

83

FIGURE 2.17. Georgi le, lyubile *in 3/2.*

Geor- gi___ le lyu - bi - le ot ni___ ni du - ha-dash ot ni___ ni du - ha-dash ka - to___ ni du - ha-dash

illustrations above).[27] However, in performance the dotted eighth and six-teenth note figures notated in 2/4 are frequently stretched or relaxed. They are typically—but not always—played as triplets comprising a quarter and eighth note, producing a compound-duple orientation.[28] This practice is not unlike the "swinging" of eighth notes in jazz. In both traditions, notation serves primarily as a guide; it does not definitively capture every convention of performance practice, which remains largely in oral tradition.

In Stoyan's *horo,* the forthcoming move to 6/8 becomes more obvious in the *otsvir,* in which a greater number of triplets are utilized. Triple beat divisions will soon come to dominate the entire piece; their prevalence in the *otsvir* effects a metric shift from 2/4 to 6/8, underscoring this *kolyano's* transitional function to the rest of the *horo.*

Stoyan's *otsvir* is neither fixed nor melodically independent of the song's content. It is closely related in terms of phrasing, modality, intervalic relationships, rhythmic figures, and melodic motives, as would be characteristic of a Type II *horo.* For example, the *otsvir* reveals that Stoyan hears *Georgi le, lyubile* in E Phrygian. He begins this *kolyano* with a rhythmic variation of measure 2, which also positions [E] on the downbeat. (See figure 2.20 for this and other motivic relationships in the *horo's* first section.) Continued metric accentuation and the cadence in measure 12, where the melody moves from scale degree 5 to 1, further establish [E] as tonic.

Kolyano II develops the *otsvir's* material but becomes increasingly more instrumental in character. Although the *otsvir* preserves the three-bar phrasing of the song, this *kolyano* marks a shift to *chetvorki,* whose most overt connections to the *otsvir's* substance are found in rhythm figuration and gesture, rather than melody. Thus, measures 13 and 15 of *Kolyano* II are rhythmically related to measure 9 of the *otsvir;* measure 15 is additionally related by gesture. Measure 14 is related, in rhythm and gesture, to measure 12. Measures 16 and 17, the first

27. This practice probably relates to the dance steps, which occur on the larger, duple beat. Thus, the dance choreography may provide the conceptual model for the notational framework of the *pravo horo* genre from an indigenous perspective.

28. This effect can be heard in Georgi Andreev's playing. Listen, for example, to the fixed *otsvir* and subsequent material.

FIGURE 2.18. *Three potential harmonizations of* Georgi le, lyubile.

and second endings, represent stereotypical *pravo horo* cadences that extend the conjunct pitch movement of the previous measure.

[E] remains the tonal center throughout the phrase, but the addition of a [G♯] takes the piece to a new, parallel mode, *makam Hicaz* on E (E F G♯ A B C D E), whose lower pentachord encompasses most of the *kolyano's* pitch content. Stoyan emphasizes this change by positioning the [G♯] on the downbeat of all but the *kolyano's* second measure. Beginning the phrase a major third above the previous *kolyano's* cadence also boosts the range of the *horo*

FIGURE 2.19. *Stoyan Velichkov's* Horo *on* Georgi le, lyubile.

FIGURE 2.20. *Motivic relationships in* Horo *on* Georgi le, lyubile.

upward, adding [B] and [C] to the range and contributing to an increase in intensity.

The third *kolyano* reduces the content of the *horo*'s first section to the scalewise melodic figure initially presented in the last half of *Kolyano* II (mm. 15 and 17). The reiteration of this figure, with its successive eighth notes, increases the *horo*'s note density, creating a vigorously rhythmic, driven effect that is uniquely instrumental in style. In other words, Stoyan is now improvising completely in *sitnezhi*, a transformation that began in the previous *kolyano*.

Section B: The Development

In keeping with the general structural format explored above, Stoyan now introduces new material in a major mode, modulating to A Ionian by shifting the tonal center up a fourth. However, rather than starting out the first four-bar phrase with the new tonic pitch, which becomes the norm for the *kolyano*'s subsequent *chetvorki*, he begins on [G♯], by reiterating the initial triplet of *Kolyano* III's two phrases. Repeating this figure establishes a firm motivic link between the *horo*'s first and second sections and highlights [G♯] as a pivotal tone with multiple modal functions. It was the added [G♯] that effected the shift from E Phrygian to E *Hicaz* in *Kolyano* II. Here it becomes the leading tone of the new Ionian mode, resolving to the tonic on the downbeat of measure 25 (the cadential measure of the *kolyano*'s first *chetvorka*).

True to form, *Kolyano* V moves to a "minor-sounding" *makam*, in this case *Hicaz* on A (A B♭ C♯ D E F G A). However, the *kolyano* does not advance to the new mode directly. Stoyan again employs a transition that also bears resemblance to Turkish improvisational practice. Throughout the Turkish and Arab Middle East, it is not uncommon to begin an instrumental improvisation in *makam Hicaz* on the scale-degree 4, and to dwell on this pitch before descending through the *makam*'s lower, signature tetrachord to the tonic. Stoyan begins this *kolyano* similarly. He reiterates [D] many times, embellishing it with rhythmically emphatic mordents and a timbral ornament, denoted by the symbol ‚ in figure 2.19. [D] is played by closing the thumbhole and top three fingerholes on the *kaval* with the left hand; the right hand produces the ornament by closing all of the remaining fingerholes, in rhythm, on the eighth note indicated, and then opening them on the following beat (denoted by o). The technique shades [D] microtonally, without producing a distinctive new tone. Turnlike, excursional dips through [C♯] and [B♮] further decorate the pitch while sustaining the Ionian flavor of the previous *kolyano*. Finally, in measures 44–45, the line lands solidly in *makam Hicaz*.

Stoyan's implementation of the timbral ornament and its accompanying rhythmic figure, which serve as the basis of the entire line, derives from the cadential measure (m. 37) of the previous *kolyano*, where the same technique is employed in an identical rhythmic environment on [A]. Utilizing the cadential rhythm of *Kolyano* IV to build *Kolyano* V is a summarizing move signaling that the *horo* is drawing to a climax.

Indeed, *Kolyano* VI remains squarely in *makam Hicaz* and demonstrates play in the upper register of that mode. The line begins like the previous *kolyano*, on scale-degree 4, but moves upward to the fifth degree, expanding the range, before descending to the tonic. In the last four measures of the piece, Stoyan provides the full scale of the *makam,* as if to say that this is the point to which the entire *horo* was leading. The attainment of the tonic in the upper register is the work's peak; it also leads immediately to its conclusion.

Significantly, a steady approach to the upper tonic and sounding the full scale of a *makam* are strategies also frequently utilized in Turkish and other Middle Eastern modal improvisations. Given the location of Stoyan's birthplace, which lies near the Turkish border, they may represent the influence of or a connection with these traditions. His repertory teems with similar patterns implemented in the climactic sections of other *horo*s, in a variety of meters, including the complex asymmetrical meters for which Bulgarian music is well known. (See figure 2.21 for representative excerpts.) These patterns represent a formulaic manner of spinning out an improvisation. They are indicators of the oral nature of the tradition, and the fluidity with which instrumentalists navigate through contrasting metric environments. They also speak to the tactility of the improvisational process. Certain patterns become ingrained; they "feel" right in terms of the hand's physiognomy (cf. Levy 1985:207). They represent the juncture of motor memory, stylistic knowledge, and the variational capacity of personal creativity.

The modal relationships evident throughout the *horo* are summarized in figure 2.22. To review, their progression develops in tandem with a steady move from lower to higher pitch levels, an increase in note density, and in some performances, a slight acceleration in tempo. Each of these processes contributes to an escalation in emotional intensity and as such, they comprise the *horo's* narrative.

FIGURE 2.21. *Improvisational similarities in Stoyan Velichkov's* Horo *repertory.*

88

FIGURE 2.22. *Modal relationships in Stoyan's* Horo *on* Georgi le, lyubile.

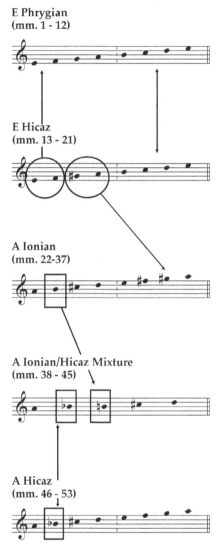

E Phrygian
(mm. 1 - 12)

E Hicaz
(mm. 13 - 21)

A Ionian
(mm. 22-37)

A Ionian/Hicaz Mixture
(mm. 38 - 45)

A Hicaz
(mm. 46 - 53)

The original tune relies on the lower Phrygian tetrachord to establish the tonal center of E. Although the tonic is somewhat ambiguous in measures 1–6, the cadence in measure 12 confirms the prevailing mode is E Phrygian.

The upper tetrachord remains constant while the lower tetrachord changes only one note. The characteristic augmented second of *Hicaz's* lower tetrachord not only provides modal variety, it also serves to connect the E Phrygian mode of the song and *otsvir* to the next *Kolyano's* A Ionian mode.

Since E *Hicaz* includes [G♯], the movement to A Ionian becomes simple and fluid. The common [G♯] becomes the leading tone to the new toanl center [A].

Measures 38–45 elements of Ionian and *Hicaz* by alternating scale degree 2. Each phrase begins with the Ionian supertonic [B] and ends with *Hicaz* supertonic [B♭].

The improvisation concludes with a complete A *Hicaz* scale utilizing only the lowered supertonic and both tetrachords.

Conclusion

Stoyan Velichkov's brief *horo* does not engage all improvisational options enumerated in figure 2.12, or that might be evident in a longer piece. He does not accelerate the tempo in the climactic *kolyano,* for example, or offer a reprise of the *otsvir* and song. Yet his *horo* does illustrate a consistent relationship to the general structural format that he and Georgi Andreev discussed. "Every *horo* is like an experiment," Stoyan told us, that elaborates upon an underlying "scheme." He improvised the *horo* on *Georgi le, lyubile* to teach us, in musical terms, how the principles germane to the scheme should be realized. Although he did not describe them in the analytical language employed by Georgi, and despite the many differences in their backgrounds, it is clear that both musicians had the same precepts in mind. Georgi observed that the art of *horo* improvisation pivots upon a contradiction: the best *hora*, those that are most characteristic, sound anonymous—as if they have been handed down through time immemorial rather than produced by a living person. "Their very anonymity demonstrates the mastery of their creator," he remarked. Yet in practice, such *hora* result from an individual's ability to wed creativity with learned techniques. Musicians such as Stoyan and Georgi depend on a personal, internalized stylistic vocabulary, gained and shaped through years of localized experience, in which motivic, modal, metric, rhythmic, registral, and timbral variation and contrast are key formative processes. From this repository, new melodies are woven through metered time and modal space, sonic places to and through which instrumentalists travel on the crest of the musical lines they create. This is how a good *horo* is spun.

References

Brody, Lauren. 1998. "An Abbreviated History." Liner notes to *Song of the Crooked Dance: Early Bulgarian Traditional Music, 1927–42.* Yazoo Records, Yazoo 7016.

Buchanan, Donna A. 2000. "Bulgaria II: Traditional Music." In *The New Grove Dictionary of Music and Musicians,* second ed., ed. Stanley Sadie. London: Macmillan Publishers, Ltd., 4:570–583.

———. 2006. *Performing Democracy: Bulgarian Music and Musicians in Transition.* Chicago: University of Chicago Press.

Forsyth, Martha. 1990. *"Two Girls Started to Sing . . .": Bulgarian Village Singing.* Rounder Records, Rounder CD 1055.

———.1996. *Listen, Daughter, and Remember Well . . . : The Songs and Life of Linka Gekova Gergova from the Village of Bistritsa, Sofia.* Sofia: St. Kliment Ohridski University Press.

Kachulev, Ivan. 1967. "Narodni muzikalni instrumenti" [Folk musical instruments]. In the *Entsiklopediya na Bŭlgarskata Muzikalna Kultura* [Encyclopedia of Bulgarian Musical Culture], ed. Venelin Krŭstev et al. Sofia: BAN, 44–48.

Katzarova-Kukudova, Raina and Kiril Djenev. 1976. *Bulgarian Folk Dances.* Cambridge, Mass.: Slavica Publishers, Inc.

Levy, Mark. 1985. "The Bagpipe in the Rhodope Mountains of Bulgaria." Ph.D. dissertation, University of California at Los Angeles.

Lloyd, A. L. 1994[1966]. *Folk Music of Bulgaria.* Topic Records, Ltd. TSCD905.

Macdermott, Mercia.1998. *Bulgarian Folk Customs.* London: Jessica Kingsley Publishers.

Raim, Ethel, and Martin Koenig. 1988 [1970, 1971]. *A Harvest, a Shepherd, a Bride: Village Music of Bulgaria; In the Shadow of the Mountain: Bulgarian Folk Music.* Elektra/ Asylum/ Nonesuch Records 9 79195–2.

Randel, Don Michael. 1986. *The New Harvard Dictionary of Music.* Cambridge, Mass.: The Belknap Press of Harvard University Press.

Rice, Timothy. 1994. *"May It Fill Your Soul": Experiencing Bulgarian Music.* Chicago: University of Chicago Press.

———. 2000. "Bulgaria." In *The Garland Encyclopedia of World Music, Volume 8: Europe,* ed. Timothy Rice, James Porter, and Chris Goertzen. New York: Garland Publishing, Inc., 890–910.

———. 2004. *Music in Bulgaria: Experiencing Music, Expressing Culture.* Oxford: Oxford University Press.

Todorov, Todor. 1974. "Problemi na melodicheskoto ravitie v instrumentalnata narodna muzika." In his *Sŭvremenni Problemi v Izuchavaneto na Bŭlgarskoto Muzikalno Narodno Tvorchestvo.* Sofia: BAN, 154–207.

CHAPTER 3

Flamenco in Focus

An Analysis of a Performance of Soleares

PETER MANUEL

[handwritten marginalia: what music do they understand in technical terms?]

Ever since the mid-nineteenth century when flamenco emerged as a public entertainment genre, it has meant different things to different people. Depending on audience and context, it has been party music for slumming Andalusian aristocrats, an exotic spectacle for tourists and outsiders, a private fiesta entertainment for gypsies, and, last but not least, an art form cultivated and cherished by serious music-lovers. Today, as before, many people enjoy—at some level—the "passion" and expressivity of flamenco without understanding it in technical terms, or even knowing how to tap their feet properly to it. Although there may be no point in belittling this rather uninformed sort of enjoyment, there is also no doubt that one's appreciation of flamenco can acquire an added dimension of depth and richness through understanding of some of its basic formal aspects. Furthermore, with its formal complexity, its idiosyncratic combination of European and Middle Eastern–derived features, and its distinctive harmonic, rhythmic, and stylistic conventions, flamenco offers particular interest to a transnational study of such musical parameters. This chapter provides some general background data on flamenco style and structure, and looks in detail at a single song-form called soleares, and a representative performance of it.

Although flamenco draws from traditions many centuries old, it was not until the first half of the nineteenth century that it can be said to have emerged as a distinctive form of Andalusian music.[1] Andalusian music culture was itself

---

1. Among the many books exploring early flamenco history are Lefranc (2000), Alvarez Caballero (1981), and Schreiner (1985).

Gypsy guitarist Diego del Gastor. Photo by Steve Kahn.

an eclectic entity, syncretizing the legacy of the Arabs, Berbers, Jews, Christians, and pagans who cohabitated for several centuries. While most Jews and Moors were expelled by the early 1600s, their musical influence persisted, and the ethnic mix of port towns like Seville and Cádiz was enriched by the presence of African slaves and influences from new forms of creole Latin American music.

93

Perhaps most important, the sixteenth century saw the arrival of substantial numbers of gypsies (whose communities may have come to accommodate many clandestine Moors and Jews). Although now constituting only around three percent of Spain's population, gypsies have long played a disproportionately important role as professional musicians. Socioeconomic underdevelopment, relative isolation from mainstream European culture, and the richness of the musical heritage itself together perpetuated the vitality of Andalusian folk music down to the present day.

In the districts of Seville and Cádiz, from the late 1700s references can be found to forms of music, which would subsequently come to be categorized, albeit ambiguously, as "flamenco."[2] Over the next century, this idiom evolved primarily as a stylized and elaborated adaptation of elements of Andalusian folk music. By the 1850s, most of the cantes, or song-types, of modern flamenco were not only coalescing but being performed publicly in clubs called *cafés cantantes*. Although many of its leading performers have been nongypsies, flamenco's core of artists and audiences remained the gypsy-centered subculture, which historically comprised not only ethnic *gitanos* (Romany gypsies whose ancestry and traditional language derived primarily from India) but also other lumpen-proletarian bohemians. In the course of the nineteenth century, as flamenco became a professional entertainment idiom performed in cafés and for the private parties of rich playboys (*señoritos*), it absorbed elements from other sources, including Latin American (and Afro-Latin) music, regional genres from other parts of Spain, and possibly even Italian opera.

As with other music styles, the effects of commercialization and professionalization have been mixed, often obliging artists to pander to the tastes of ignorant audiences (whether local or non-Andalusian), while at the same time stimulating higher technical standards and expansion of repertoire, increasing the sheer amount of performance, and attracting the attentions of nongypsy musicians. Since the early twentieth century, flamenco's trajectory has been irregular; it suffered considerably during the culturally stultifying and economically disastrous Franco era (1936–1975), but has enjoyed prodigious vitality in recent decades. Today, as in previous generations, polemics rage between purists and innovators, and traditionalists rant against the effects of commercialization

2. The origin of the term "flamenco" (whose original meaning is "Flemish") remains obscure. By the early nineteenth century it had come to mean "gypsy," possibly through identification of flamboyant, bohemian gitanos with the six thousand Flemish riff-raff that were brought to southern Spain after 1767 to alleviate the region's depopulation following the expulsion of the Moors. In the mid-1800s, it became common to refer to dancing or singing "a lo flamenco," that is, "a la gypsy" or "in gypsy style"; the term then came to be applied to the music and dance per se (see, e.g., Lefranc 2000:203)

(especially the pop-oriented forms of "nuevo flamenco"), but there is no doubt that the genre is flourishing, both in traditional and new forms.

Despite this vitality, it is worth mentioning that flamenco is by no means the most popular music in Spain. Most Spaniards, and even many Andalusians, have no interest in it at all, although the pop flamenco of recent decades has acquired a new sort of trendy mass appeal, and all Spaniards are well aware of flamenco's international renown. On the whole, flamenco's popularity is perhaps more akin to that of jazz or blues in the United States, with its primary audience consisting of a mixture of hard-core music lovers, and gypsies and interested Andalusians who grow up thoroughly immersed in the art.

The Musical Elements of Flamenco

Flamenco can be regarded as comprising *cante* (singing), *toque* (instrumental accompaniment, primarily on guitar), and *baile*, or dance. The latter tends to be the focus in specific contexts, whether a private gypsy fiesta, or a formal show put on for tourists in a *tablao* (the modern successor to the café cantante). For its part, solo flamenco guitar has evolved into a sophisticated idiom in the last half-century; it also has become particularly popular as an international art form, especially because, unlike vocal music, guitar-playing poses no language barriers. Nevertheless, in other senses, flamenco cante, or singing, with guitar accompaniment, remains the quintessential and most basic structural format of the genre, and that which will accordingly be the focus of this essay.

The flamenco repertoire consists of around a dozen basic song-types, themselves generally called cantes (or, more recently, *palos*), and a dozen or two subsidiary or obscure variants of these. The cantes are distinguished variously in terms of poetic form, characteristic vocal melodies, in some cases a metrical scheme called *compás*, and a distinctive guitar tonality and conventional accompaniment patterns. The cantes can be classified in several ways. Some of them can be seen as stylized forms of genres of Andalusian folk music, in particular the numerous regional varieties of the *fandango* family (including *malagueñas, granaínas, taranto/tarantas,* and the *fandango de Huelva*). Others, such as *soleares* and *siguiriyas,* are more strictly associated with gypsy music culture in that they lack counterparts in Andalusian folk music and appear to have been cultivated primarily by gitanos, to some extent in a semiprivate fashion. These cantes, because of their solemn character, are sometimes referred to as *cante jondo* or "deep song," as opposed to cantes such as *tangos* and *bulerías*, which are fast and festive, and may have evolved in more public, professional contexts. Some, such as *granaínas, malagueñas,* and *fandango libre,* are rendered in free rhythm, whereas most others are metered, that is, in compás. Among the latter, *tangos* and *tientos* are in duple meter, and most of the others, including soleares, are in some form of what could be regarded as triple meter. Most of these basic forms, including their conventional guitar accompaniment patterns, were standardized by the early twentieth century. The innovation that abounds today consists primarily of various sorts of elaboration and expansion within these inherited cantes rather than invention of new ones.

Musical Elements: Tonality

Much flamenco, including the soleares focused on in this article, is based not on common-practice Western tonality, but on what musicologists call Andalusian or Phrygian tonality. In this system, the chordal vocabulary derives not from the Western major or minor scales, but primarily from the Phrygian or "E" mode (or transposed variants thereof); however, in contrast to the Gregorian Phrygian mode, the tonic E chord is major rather than minor. This tonality is best regarded as a sort of modal harmony, in the sense that it has clearly evolved as a harmonization based on scale degrees of a modal system rather than a tonal one per se. The modes in question are the Arab *maqâms* (or vernacular versions thereof) which pervade most forms of art and vernacular music in the Arab and Turkish world, and also appear to have dominated Moorish music. Of particular importance are the modes Bayati and Hijaz, which have been for several centuries among the popular maqâms in Arab urban music. Their scales are roughly as follows, taking E as tonic, with the F+ in Bayati (like the C+ in Hijaz) denoting a neutral, half-sharp second degree, intoned between F and F♯:

Bayâti: E F+ G A B C D (E)

Hijâz: E F G♯ A B C+ D (E D C B A G♯ F E)

In both of these modes, the fourth degree (here, A) functions as a secondary tonic and a temporary resting point.

   In Andalusian Phrygian harmony, the chordal vocabulary derives primarily from the pitch resources of these modal resources. Thus, taking E as tonic and "rounding off" Bayati's neutral second degree (F+) to a lowered second (F) affords minor triads on the fourth and seventh degrees (Am, Dm) and major ones on the second, third, and sixth degrees (F, G, and C). The standard use of a major tonic triad (here, E major) rather than a minor one suggests affinities with the Hijaz mode insofar as it occasions the use of the raised third in some contexts, affording the characteristic ("Oriental"-sounding) augmented second interval between second and third scalar degrees (F and G♯). (A strikingly similar form of modal harmony is common in other musics where Arab-Turkish modes have syncretized with Western chords, such as Turkish, Greek and Balkan urban music, and klezmer.[3]) In E Phrygian, the role of the "dominant"—that is, the chord which demands resolution to the tonic—is thus played by a major chord on the lowered second degree—here, F major. The Western dominant chord—a B7—is basically nonexistent in this system (except for often being introduced briefly in the typical final cadential flourish, which shifts to standard Western tonality in the direct major key).

Andalusian Phrygian tonality is epitomized in the common chord progression Am–G–F–E (the "Andalusian cadence"), in which the E functions as the tonic, rather than the dominant of A. The progression should thus be understood as iv–III–bII–I, in the key of E Phrygian, rather than I–VII–VI–V in the key of A minor. This cadence can be regarded as providing the basic structure of most flamenco harmony in Phrygian/Andalusian tonality. Its importance can in that sense be compared to that of the IV–V–I progression in Western common-practice harmony, or the ii–V-I progression in mainstream jazz. Depending on context, the progression may occur in a quick and straightforward manner, or in the form of a deliberate semicadence on iv, followed by a leisurely and circuitous descent to I. (Vocal and guitar melodies in flamenco also tend to descend rather than ascend.) Movement by fourths is also common; thus, a movement to Am (iv) might be followed by the progression G7–C–F–E (III7–VI–IIb–I)—which could also be seen as a variant of the Andalusian cadence, adding a C (VI) chord between the G (III) and F (IIb) chords. In some contexts, including the soleares examined in this chapter, there may be a temporary cadence on the submediant VI (here, C). This may be regarded as the most characteristic contrasting tonal area, analogous to the relative major of a minor key. In some cantes, such as malagueñas and other forms of the fandango family, Phrygian tonality (e.g., on E) coexists or alternates with simple, common-practice I–IV–V harmonies on this relative major (VI, or in this case, C). Other cantes, such as alegrías and tanguillos, use simple common-practice harmony rather than Andalusian/Phrygian harmony.

Chord voicings in flamenco often include nontriadic tones, which are generally open strings on the guitar (using the standard tuning of EADGBE, or, with the capo as in our transcribed example, GCFBbDG). Thus, for example, in compás 10 and many other instances in figure 3.2, the Ab (IIb) chord is enriched with a high G, played on the open string, as is the D7 chord in the final bars. The F in the very beginning passage in the song, also played on the open string, is similarly idiomatic, adding an ambiguous hint of F minor to what is probably better regarded as an Ab major chord.

3. See Manuel (1989).

Musical Elements II: Performance Structure

A typical flamenco recital, with voice and guitar accompaniment, comprises a series of pieces (not exactly "songs"), in different cantes, each lasting around five minutes. (In a private gypsy fiesta, the festive, collective music-making might consist of endless bulerías or tangos with different amateur singers contributing verses.) Each song consists of a set of verses (called *copla, tercio,* or *letras*), usually from three to five lines each, which are punctuated by guitar interludes called *falsetas*. The guitarist also provides a short introduction which sets the tonality and, if relevant, the *compás* and tempo of the cante.

As the piece consists of an additive series of verses and *falsetas,* there is no long-term thematic development per se, nor any of the techniques of symmetry, recapitulation, and closure that characterize genres like sonata form or the thirty-two-bar AABA popular song. Hence the term "song," insofar as it implies some sort of coherent, rationalized formal structure, is somewhat misleading. (The only form of closure per se in soleares and bulerías consists of a short final verse—sometimes called *cambio* or change, or *macho*—which, as mentioned, uses standard tonic-dominant harmony and quickly accelerates to a close.) Structure and closure are present, but only on the local level of the individual copla, which—as we will see in the case of soleares—generally introduces an emotional tension and intensity, which is then melodically relaxed or resolved. This sort of mini-drama is repeated, with variations, with each copla. Also as discussed later, an even more short-term form of structure is provided by the internal dynamics of the compás, with its internal pattern of tension and release.

In accordance with this fundamentally additive (rather than long-term developmental) musical structure, each short copla section consists of an epigrammatic, condensed statement that is thematically independent from the other coplas in the song. Accordingly, although the lyrics in a given song do not illustrate the overall continuity of a poem per se, many individual flamenco coplas in themselves are minor masterpieces of concise expression, ideally suited to their musical rendering. Although verses often deal with the same topic—especially unrequited love—they often differ in mood and subject matter. Insofar as formal structures seeking development, climax, and closure are distinctively modern bourgeois creations, flamenco, in its essentially additive, sequential structure, is thus typical of many premodern forms, especially those relying on strophic forms using stock melodies.

In soleares, as in some other types of cante, a copla usually consists of three or four lines of verse. Each line is theoretically octosyllabic, but lengths often vary, and vocalists may change words somewhat in singing. The final and third-to-last verses generally rhyme (or are assonant); thus, in a four-line copla, the scheme would be *abcb,* and in three lines it would be *aba.* However, the assonance can be quite approximate, and in general, rhyme in soleares is not very important, especially given the loose, melismatic style of rendering.

Flamenco lyrics themselves derive from varied sources. Most are transmitted more or less orally, that is, through families, performances, or, nowadays, recordings. Many, however, are written by literary, nonmusician poets. A singer is free to combine verses from different sources, and on different topics, within a single song. Continuity of subject matter is only expected in pop-oriented songs, from the *cuplés* popular from the early twentieth century to the varieties of modern "nuevo flamenco" that seek and sometimes achieve true mass popularity. (The titles of most flamenco songs that are listed on CD covers merely consist of the first line of verse, and have no particular relation to the subsequent coplas.)

Flamenco Guitar

Although flamenco guitar has come in some contexts—especially international ones—to outshine flamenco singing, the primary role of the guitar in mainstream flamenco has always been to accompany the vocalist. Given the fact that even until the mid-1900s, guitars and guitarists were somewhat scarce, in informal domestic contexts flamenco cantes were often performed without guitar accompaniment, as purely modal monophonic songs. However, it is also clear that by the late 1700s, if not earlier, the guitar was widely used in Andalusia to accompany various kinds of folk song, including gypsy singing. By the time flamenco emerged as a public art form, guitar had become the standard accompanying instrument for professional contexts, and conventional playing techniques were already established. Traditionally, these consisted primarily of *rasgueado* (strumming) and melodies plucked especially with the thumb (*alzapúa,* from *alzar:* to raise, and *púa:* plectrum), both supplemented by rhythmic fingernail-strokes (*golpes*) on the face of the instrument. In the early decades of the twentieth century, Ramón Montoya (1880–1949) and other guitarists—to some extent inspired by classical guitarists—enriched flamenco guitar technique with new or greater use of arpeggio, four-fingered tremolo, and fast *picado* passages (single-note runs). The idiom of flamenco guitar solos was further cultivated in this period. Also established by this time was a repertoire of conventional guitar patterns and keys associated with particular cantes (e.g., B Phrygian with granaínas, and F# Phrygian with tarantas). Subsequent innovators—especially the brilliant Paco de Lucía (b. 1947)—have further extended guitar technique and harmonic vocabulary, while remaining faithful to the established repertoire of cantes rather than inventing new ones. Although traditional guitarists seldom strayed far from first position (i.e., playing only near the capo), more modern players have come to utilize the entire fretboard, and have explored other idiomatic guitar sonorities by playing in such keys as Eb and Ab Phrygian. In general—speaking of technique per se rather than structure and content—it might be said that classical guitar technique is somewhat richer and more varied than that of flamenco, but few classical guitarists can render the furious rasgueado patterns and machine-gun picado runs that flamenco players cultivate.

In accompanying a singer, the basic requirement of the flamenco guitarist is to provide the correct compás (in the case of metered cantes) and to support and enhance the singing. The guitar introduction to a song serves, on a basic level, to set the pitch and tonality for the singer and establish the mood of the cante. The falsetas in between the verses serve to punctuate them and allow the singer to catch his or her breath. The falsetas are invariably precomposed, and in general, flamenco guitar playing contains little or none of the sort of free improvisation encountered, for instance, in jazz. However, the choice of falsetas, and the ongoing extemporized flourishes and variations lend the guitar playing an essential flavor of looseness and spontaneity.

Traditionally, the guitar introduction and falsetas are relatively brief. In recent years, guitarists increasingly indulge in long, elaborate falsetas and introductions which, although pleasing guitar-lovers, might provoke an annoyed singer to rebuke the instrumentalist with a "¡Corta ya!" ("Cut it, already!"). (However, in most contexts, guitarists and vocalists who perform together are accustomed to working with each other.) The guitarist's primary task is to make the singer sound good, rather than to show off. This goal involves sensitively complementing the vocalist in various ways, by tailoring dynamics, intensity, and even tempo to particular passages, knowing when to be assertive and when to lay back, and generally intensifying the singing.

Soleares

Soleares enjoys a certain preeminence among flamenco *cantes*. It is sometimes referred to as the "mother of cantes," and it does appear to have been a primary evolutionary source for certain cantes (especially alegrías and bulerías). However, it is not as old as some cantes, such as siguiriyas, and its development has no particular relation to that of cantes like fandangos (which derive from Andalusian folk music) and tangos and guajiras, which derive in part from Latin America. In general, its "maternal" status would appear to rest on its inclusion

in almost every formal flamenco performance, on the way it seems to epito-
mize the structural features of the distinctively gypsy-associated cantes (including alegrías and bulerías), and on its essentially obligatory role in the repertoire
of any aspiring flamenco singer, regardless of regional or stylistic background.

Soleares (or soleá) appears to have evolved from diverse sources, predominant among which were Andalusian styles of singing *romance* (pronounced
"ro-MAHN-say"). Spanish *romances* are long narrative ballads, with octosyllabic verse lines, sung in strophic style, often with simple stock melodies. *Romances* would be traditionally sung in informal rather than concert-style contexts. However, Andalusian gypsies had long cultivated their own forms of
singing *romances,* often using text fragments rather than long epic passages,
and singing them in lively, rhythmic fashion with dance, at weddings, other
festivities, and even street shows. Cervantes describes one such public performance of a gypsy *romance* in his 1608 story, "La Gitanilla." By the 1850s, as performed in private fiestas and public cafés cantantes in the towns in the Seville
and Cádiz area, some of these styles had acquired distinctive forms and rhythms
and had come to be designated as "soleares." In the subsequent decades they
came to enjoy wide popularity, especially via the cafés cantantes, leading to the
publication of booklets of lyrics, and at the end of the century, a number of
gramophone and cylinder recordings revealing a cante basically cognate with
that of today.

The most distinctive and basic structural feature of soleá is its compás,
which in flamenco implies a structure that is somewhat more complex than a
simple meter. Flamenco pedagogues (whether dancers, guitarists, or some singers)
generally describe the soleares compás as comprising twelve beats, with accents
on 3, 6, 8, and 10, as shown here:

1 2 3 4 5 6 7 8 9 10 11 12
    >   >   >   >

Essentially the same compás, and the same moderate tempo (MM100–160) are
used in alegrías, which, however, is in major rather than Phrygian tonality; the
bulerías compás is also similar, but its *aire* (tempo, spirit) is fast and festive,
unlike soleares, which is prevailingly serious, although not necessarily so un-
mitigatedly tragic as siguiriyas. In the compás of soleares and alegrías—and
even more so in bulerías—the first beat does not have the same sort of structural emphasis and importance that it might in a Western meter, or, for that
matter, in an Indian *tâla;* rather, the most important beats are three and ten.

As we shall see later, guitar patterns themselves tend to reinforce the internal accents of the soleares compás, in which tension is typically introduced
at beat three and resolves at ten, with beats eleven and twelve being inactive.

Thus, the harmonic rhythm in solea (and bulerías) typically tends to consist of a loose ostinato moving to bII on beat 3 and cadencing on the tonic at beat 10, roughly as shown here:

```
beats:    1 2 3   4 5 6 7 8 9   10 11 12
chords: (I I) bII - - - (I I bII) I  - -
```

Furthermore, the guitarist, aside from playing on the strings, often executes a fingernail tap (*golpe*) on the wooden face of the instrument on the accented beats 3, 6, 8, and 10. Someone providing *palmas,* or hand-clapping accompaniment, also would usually render a variant of this structure, which is represented well in English as follows (clapping "seven" as two eighth-notes): one two THREE four five SIX SEV-EN EIGHT NINE TEN (eleven twelve).[4]

There are various ways of conceiving or analyzing this structure. To begin with, it constitutes a twelve-beat scheme with internal accents. More specifically, it could be regarded as a syncopated variant of the familiar horizontal hemiola or sesquialtera, literally, "six that alters," that is, from 6/8 to 3/4, in the sense of being 3 + 3 + 2 + 2 + 2. The distinctive syncopation lies in the accentuation of the final, rather than initial beat of each grouping. The 6/8–3/4 hemiola is, of course, a cliché of various Spanish and Latin American musics; in the form of yuletide *villancicos,* the Latin-American-derived *zarabanda* (sarabande), and other genres, it was well established in Spain from the sixteenth century. The 3 + 3 + 2 + 2 + 2 pattern emerges in a somewhat different manner when soleares (or alegrías) markedly accelerates, as often happens in dance, in which case its compás becomes like that of the lively bulerías. At that tempo, beat one effectively disappears, and beat twelve emerges as a sort of syncopated anacrusis to three. The 3–3–2–2–2 syncopation is quite clear at this tempo, but beginning from beat 12, not one:

```
12 1 2 3 4 5 6 7 8 9 10 11 (12)
>       >     >   >   >
(3  +   3  +  2 + 2 + 2)
```

In many ways, it is better to regard this compás merely as a cycle, with internal tensions and resolutions, rather than a meter in which the first beat has a special preeminence as a starting or finishing point. Further, such a compás, with its internal patterns of tension and resolution, is more complex than a meter per se, and is akin to a *rhythmic* ostinato. One also might point out, as suggested earlier, that this sort of pattern, along with the dynamics of the in-

4. If one finds verbal mnemonics useful, instead of "I like to live in Ame-ri-ca," the accentuation could be rendered (in moderate tempo) as "I want TO live on A CHICK-EN FARM in SPAIN (pause-pause)" (rendering "chicken," like "seven," as two eighth-notes).

dividual copla, provides a form of expressive local structure and dynamism that, in flamenco, is more important than any sort of extended formal structure.

Given its rhythmic ambiguities, soleares could be notated in various ways, for example, in 12/4, in alternating bars of 6/8 and 3/4, or—as is most common—in 3/4. In this chapter, it is notated (somewhat idiosyncratically) in 12/4, with a dotted bar line every three beats to suggest the 3/4 subdivision.

A typical formal rendering of soleares might comprise four or five coplas punctuated by guitar falsetas. The basic melodies to which the coplas are sung are not improvised, but are chosen from a finite set of stock tunes familiar to the singer. Flamencologists have described around fifty of these soleá tunes, some of which are quite distinct, but most of which are fairly similar, constituting slight variants of each other.[5] Thus, in the piece analyzed later, the different coplas represent five different soleá tunes, with distinct names and pedigrees; however, with the exception of the last, they are quite similar to each other. The tune variants are generally named after the towns or neighborhoods where they evolved (e.g., Triana—formerly the gypsy barrio of Seville—or Alcalá), or the individuals who fashioned or popularized them. These designated names of melodies might not be known to all vocalists but, rather, only to musicians or flamencologists who take an interest in such matters. Most of the melodies and guitar accompaniment patterns, including those in the song discussed here, tend to follow a few relatively standard patterns.

Before examining the recorded song in detail, it may be useful to look at a very schematic rendering of the most typical opening pattern, which also forms the basis of that in the recording. An explanation of the notation of key signature is also needed here. Flamenco cantes like soleares are most typically notated in the key of E Phrygian, as that accords with the "white-key" piano mode and with the fingerings conceived of by guitarists; hence, this chapter has up to this point used that convention. The actual concert pitch of a song, however, is usually different, as guitarists generally use a capo (*cejilla*) to match the comfortable range of the singer. Thus, for example, in the recording discussed in this essay, the guitarist has put the capo at the third fret, such that the actual tonic is G Phrygian rather than E Phrygian. Because this chapter is intended as an analytical study rather than a guitar accompaniment manual, the extended transcription later (figure 3.2) indicates the actual ("concert") pitches, in the key of G Phrygian (with three flats—not to be confused with E♭ major). However, to ease the transition and to assist guitarists, the schematic guide to basic

5. For thorough classifications and descriptions of soleares singing styles, see Lefranc (2000: ch. 6), Soler Guevara and Soler Díaz (1992), and—based on the latter—Norman Kliman's fine Web site: http://perso.wanadoo.es/siguiriya/soleares.htm, which contains sound examples of all the styles.

FIGURE 3.1. *Schematic model of opening soleares verse.*

soleá style shown as figure 3.1 also provides the guitar-oriented E Phrygian chords in parentheses. (Flamenco guitarists refer to the E-major chord fingering as *por arriba,* or "above"; however, soleares is often played in the fingering of A Phrygian, using as tonic the A major chord—called *por medio* or "in the middle"—with the "Andalusian" cadence thus comprising Dm–C–B♭–A.)

The pattern shown as figure 3.1 basically consists of two melodic lines (A and B), each rendered twice, and each with a standard guitar chordal accompaniment; since each melody line accommodates two lines of verse, each melody line can be divided into two sections, notated A(1–2) and B(1–2). As will be shown more clearly in the discussion of the recorded example, the melodic lines are typically rendered: A1–A2–(guitar break)–A1–A2–B1–B2–B1–B2. The pattern thus lasts nine compases. The vocal lines typically begin on or (in A2 and B2) slightly before the first beat of the compás, which generally is preceded by a guitar cadence on beat 10. However, the vocal melody, rather than overtly stressing the compás, is loosely free-rhythmic in style, offering no particular emphasis on strong beats of the compás. Melodies A and B are quite similar, each consisting of a rise from the tonic (G) to the fourth or fifth scale degree, and returning to the tonic. This contour—a quick initial ascent, followed by a somewhat more extended descent to the tonic—is typical of most soleares verse-line melodies.[6] In melody A, the guitar oscillates between chords on the tonic and flat second degree (A♭); more specifically, in keeping with the compás of soleá, it tends to move to A♭ on beat 3, and cadence back on G at beat 10. Melody B, by contrast, after moving on beat 3 to A♭ (bII), has a dramatic internal III7–VI (B♭7–E♭) cadence on the submediant (which functions as a "relative tonic"), on beat 10. Guitarists use the all-purpose term *cambio* (change) to describe this distinctive chordal cadence. In soleares, the cambio constitutes the climactic point in a copla, coming at the end of the penultimate line in the three- or four-line verse.

The first three beats of the next and final compás feature a clear rhythmic iv–III–II (Cm–B♭–A♭) progression, drifting to the tonic on beat 7, and resolving more definitively there on beat 10. The first rendition of the second melodic line (B), with its distinctive chord progression, and coinciding with verses 3–4, constitutes the dramatic climax of the copla, after which the melody subsides to rest on the tonic note. Note that the verse lines do not correspond exactly to the melodic lines; the typical format can be shown as follows:

Melodic lines: A1—A2—(guitar break)—A1—A2—B1—B2—B1—B2
Verse lines: 1   2   2   2   3   4   3   4

A second type of common soleares pattern or style (which, like the entities mentioned above, is also called cambio), is typically sung after the first one. The main difference is that during the first melody line, the guitar, instead of oscillating between tonic and flat second-degree chords, starts with a tonic seventh chord (or IV7 of iv) and on beat 10 of the compás resolves temporarily to the minor iv chord (figure 3.2, C minor). The vocal melody during this section heightens the tension by stressing the seventh scalar degree over the G7 chord (here, F).[7] The subsequent compás generally resembles the melody B

6. As Lefranc (2000:47–49) points out, it is also typical of and perhaps at least indirectly influenced by Arabic melodic contours such as that of the *adhan* or call to prayer, and by the aforementioned gypsy forms of singing *romances*.

7. Often, perhaps because they are singing at the top of their ranges, vocalists sing a major sixth-degree rather than a seventh, giving the impression that they are unable to quite reach the higher degree. (In other contexts, some vocalists, especially from Jérez, sometimes sing a bit sharp, as if through an excess of emotion.)

FIGURE 3.2. *Transcription of "A quién le contaré yo."*

FIGURE 3.2. *Continued*

FIGURE 3.2. *Continued*

pattern of figure 3.1 in returning to the tonic by means of a iv–III–II (Cm–B♭–A♭) progression, and thence to I. Because the third copla in the recorded example (from compás 27, henceforth "c. 27") exhibits this second type of pattern quite clearly, a schematic model is not shown here. The remaining coplas generally adhere to one of these two patterns, with the exception of the concluding verse (the *cambio/macho*), which modulates to major-key tonality.

The common tradition of singing soleares and other cantes a palo seco, that is, without guitar accompaniment, raises the question of to what extent, or in what way, the guitar's role is structural and essential. For modern listeners who are accustomed to hearing flamenco with guitar, the instrument's chordal harmonies may certainly affect melodic consonances and dissonances, determining, for example, whether a given pitch is perceived as restful or demands resolution. However, for those immersed in traditional flamenco and well familiar with the palo seco sound, it is more likely that a cante like soleá is essentially modal, such that the guitar chords are basically decorative rather than essential. When a soleá is sung without guitar, such listeners and the performer need not necessarily imagine the chordal accompaniment in their heads. Thus, when the guitar oscillates between tonic and flat second chords, it can be seen as basically reiterating a modal tonic; the movement to the minor iv chord essentially reinforces the clear melodic movement to the fourth degree. And, finally, the climactic "cambio" moment in the penultimate verse line is best seen as being *intensified*, rather than determined by, the salient III7–VI guitar semi-cadence. However, the way in which listeners hear and internalize chordal harmonies in flamenco may be far from simple and evident.

"A Quién le Contaré Yo," Sung by Juan Talega

Let us now turn to the recording included in the CD (track 5), which derives from a well-known and influential 1962 five-LP anthology. This set of recordings was the first to document, in a systematic and extensive form, the extant corpus of flamenco cantes, and is regarded as having played a substantial role in the general revival of flamenco in the following decade. This soleá, aside from being a fine performance, nicely illustrates the features discussed so far in this chapter.[8] It is also cited as a model by a number of flamencologists (e.g., Lefranc [2000:179, 183], and Kliman [n.d.]), partly because the vocalist, Juan Talega (or Talegas), was the creator or popularizer of some of the influential soleares styles performed here. Talega himself (1891–1971) was an influential performer of his era. His father and uncle were well-known singers from the gypsy community of Alcalá de Guadaira, a town east of Seville. The musical styles of these families, although closely related to those of Seville's gypsy quarter, Triana, were more directly linked by personal and musical ties to the influential flamenco singers in Marchena, some thirty miles further east. The styles of soleares that these singers created and codified—including three of the copla renderings here—are hence referred to by experts as soleás of Alcalá and Marchena. Although Talega performed mostly in domestic contexts, he traveled and sang extensively in Andalusia, and served as a mentor of sorts to Antonio Mairena (1909–1983), one of the most influential singers of the next generation.[9] He is accompanied in this recording by guitarist Eduardo él de la Malena (Eduardo de Malena, 1925–198?).

This solea comprises five coplas. As is standard, these constitute concise, thematically independent verses, which do not exhibit or require any particu-

8. From *The History of Cante Flamenco* (Everest 3366/5), disc 2, side B, track 1; also on *Archivo del cante flamenco* (Vergara 13.002 SJ), side 2, track 3, and on *Cantes de Utrera y Alcalá* (Ariola 85.425 N), side 1, track 2. This same piece is also transcribed and briefly discussed by Carol Whitney (1976).

9. LeFranc (2000:176–177, translated by this author) presents further data on Talega and the Alcalá/Marchena tradition:

The soleas of Alcala have great originality. Their complete and definitive character, and the classicism and austere respect for the past they manifest, constitute a

lar sense of continuity or development, whether literary or musical. Hence, as may be noted, the first is tragic and fatalistic, and the third seems to express the singer's indifference to his former beloved, and the final verse is an affirmation of his love.

(A note regarding the guitar notation: As mentioned, the transcription reflects the performer's use of a capo on the third fret. The singer often drowns out the guitarist, and where the guitar is too soft to transcribe rests are shown in the guitar staff. Also not shown are frequent golpes (fingernail-taps on the face of the instrument, generally on beats 3, 6, 8, and 10) as well as many of the routine chordal oscillations between A♭ and G.)

The recording commences with ten introductory compáses. In the first two, Malena plays standard opening soleá patterns, outlining the progression A♭–E♭–A♭–G (II–VI–II–I, or fa–do–fa–mi), cadencing in conventional fashion on the tonic G on beat ten. The II and VI harmonies are colored with nonharmonic tones: B♭, F, and G in the first case and F in the second. In compases 3–8, Talega sings the *temple* ("tem-play"), which consists of introductory, warming-up phrases, sung to the syllables "ayayay . . . ," and generally ascending to the fifth degree and back to the tonic. Note that Talega sings in Phrygian mode, with B♭ as its third degree, whereas Malena plays a G major tonic chord, with B natural. Following the *temple*, Malena plays two compases of very conventional *falseta* material (c. 9–10), the first of which constitutes a proper guitaristic rendition of the model *falseta* shown schematically in example 1.

The first *copla*, of four lines, is a characteristic flamenco lament, in which the singer hyperbolically relates his anguish, leaving its causes to the listener's imagination. The second and fourth lines rhyme, but the general tendency in

set of traits not seen anywhere else in these repertoires. It is said that in Alcalá they didn't so much innovate as deepen; being faithful to the tradition, they gave it depth and transmitted it, without being much interested in other repertoires, even those nearby.

The originality of this repertoire is realized through its essentially domestic character. It derives from a total of three persons: Agustín Fernández Franco, called Talega, born in the 1860s; his brother Joaquín él de La Paula (1875–1933) [Joaquín Fernández Franco]; and Juan Fernández Vargas, known as Talega (1891–1971), who was Agustín's son and the nephew of Joaquín (La Paula being Paula Franco Aguilera). We are in the presence of a repertoire whose narrow chronological limits, its development strictly in a family base, and its stability and classicism, imply with near certainty its origins in the earlier existence of a local set of cantes, undoubtedly from nearby Triana. Many gitano families after 1848 lived in caves beneath the old castle of Alcalá. For those who, at the beginning of the twentieth century, fled from the punitive nocturnal expeditions [against gypsies] of Triana, Alcalá was the most accessible refuge [translated by the author].

romances and many soleás toward an octosyllabic count of each line is clearly not adhered to here.

> A quién le contaré yo
> la fatiga [las fatiguitas] que estoy pasando
> se la[s] voy a contar a la tierra
> cuando me estén enterrando

> To whom will I tell my sufferings? I'll tell the earth when they are
>   burying me.

This verse is rendered here with a melody attributed to Talega's uncle, Joaquín él de La Paula (1875–1933). It has become a standard and popular melody, often used for the opening copla. It roughly follows the model presented schematically as figure 3.1, and allows us to examine more closely this style of rendering. The chart shows how the four-line verse is adapted to the melodic lines. The melodies can be regarded as comprising two pairs of lines listed as A(1), A(2), B(1), and B(2). Each pair is sung twice; verse line 2 of the copla is sung thrice, and the final pair of verse lines, 3–4, is sung twice, although it also could only be sung once. However, slight variations occur in the repetitions of both text lines and melodies. Each melody line lasts roughly one twelve-beat compás. The entire pattern could be represented as A(1)1, A(2)2, A(1)2, A(2)2, B(1)3, B(2)4, B(1)3, B(2)4, or more simply as A1–2, A2–2, B3–4 (in which B can repeat).[10]

verse line		melody	compás
1	A quién le contaré yo	A(1)	11
2	la' fatiguita' que estoy pasando	A(2)	12
	(one compás guitar break)		13
2	fatiga' que estoy pasando	A(1)	14
2	la' fatiguillita' que estoy pasando	A(2)	14–15
3	se la voy a contar [a] la tierra	B(1)	16–17
4	cuando me estén enterrando	B(2)	17–18
3	se lo (sic) voy a contar a la tierra	B(1)	19
4	cuando me estén enterrando	B(2)	20

Although loosely conforming to the model of Figure 3.1, the rendering of this copla also illustrates the sort of variation that can occur. The most notable

---

10. The latter representation is used, for example, by Lefranc (2000:146).

departure occurs from the start of the line "Se la voy a contar . . ." in compás 16. Normally, as in Figure 3.1, after finishing the third rendition of the second verse line, the singer would promptly begin singing at the start of the next compás. Here, however, Talega pauses, and starts halfway through the compás. This obliges Malena, who adheres like a rock to the compás, to adjust some of the standard chord accents to fit Talega's melody. In particular, he performs the climactic III7–VI "cambio" on beats 3–4, instead of the usual 7–8 and 9–10. Talega's evident readiness to truncate the compás illustrates the sort of flexibility that is tolerated in certain situations in flamenco. (In bulerías in fast tempo, the tendency to conceive of phrases in six rather than twelve beats makes such irregularities more common.) Talega starts the final rendition of the last text line in more standard fashion, at the beginning of the compás, such that it more closely conforms to the model shown in Figure 3.1. Because of his leisurely entrance in compás 16, the copla takes up ten rather than the more typical nine compases.

Aside from such adjustments, Malena's chordal accompaniment largely follows the pattern of the schematic model above, oscillating between I and IIb (G and Ab) during the first melody lines (c. 11–16), climaxing at the III7–VI (Bb7–Eb) cadence in the third melody line (c. 17, repeated at c. 19), and returning to the tonic via the "Andalusian cadence" of iv–III–II–I (Cm–Bb–Ab–G) at the fourth melody line (c. 20). As indicated by the chord names above the staff, the guitar progressions tend to stress the third and tenth beats of the compás. The guitar falseta following the copla, lasting one compás (c. 22), is highly conventional in its arpeggiated C–Bb–Ab–G descent cadencing on beat 10 of the compás.

Note that Talega sings with standard Andalusian Spanish pronunciation, which (like most Caribbean Spanish) often drops "s" before a consonant, and "d" between vowels. A distinctive flamenco singing mannerism is the addition of a concluding "o" on extended renderings of final syllables ending in "a." Hence, in c. 24, "el sentido te esvarias" is sung as "el senti'o te 'varia'o," and in c. 35, "escritura" becomes "escriturao." Another mannerism, heard in the second copla, is the occasional omission of entire words, which the listener is evidently expected to fill in.

The second copla (c. 23–25) is of three verse lines, with a loose rhyme between the first and third lines, and an even looser adherence to the standard octosyllabic line. This verse's melody is identified with Juan Talega himself (in the broader category of soleás of Marchena and Alcalá). It adheres basically to the second type of common soleá pattern described above, in that the first compás establishes a G7 (V7 of iv) chord, and cadences dramatically on Cm (iv), before proceeding to a Bb7–Eb cadence, and thence to the G Phrygian tonic. There is no repetition of text lines, such that the entire copla is rendered in only three compases. This pattern would not be sung at the beginning of a soleá.

> [Dices] que no me querías
> y cuando [d]'elante tu me tienes
> el sinti'o te [d]'esvaría'[s]

> [You say] you don't love me
> but when you've got me in front of you
> you get all flustered.

After one compás (c. 26) of standard guitar, Malena plays a short falseta (c. 27), outlining a typical descent from iv to I.

Talega then proceeds to sing the third copla (c. 28–35), in which the poet asserts his indifference to the fact that his former lover no longer loves him, since he never had any reason to expect constancy from her in the first place.

> Dices que tú a mí no me quieres
> pena yo no tengo ninguna
> porque yo con tu querer
> no tenía hecha escritura

> You tell me you don't love me
> but I don't feel any pain
> because in regards to your love
> I never had any written document

Talega sings this verse in a style associated with Triana rather than Alcalá and Marchena; oral tradition attributes it to a nineteenth-century female singer named La Andonda (Kliman [n.d.]; Lefranc [2000:145–146]). Its melody does not differ dramatically from the previous ones. In terms of the relation between poetic and melodic lines, it resembles the model shown as figure 3.1 in its threefold repetition of the second line of the verse. However, unlike in figure 3.1, the final two verses are not repeated, such that the entire copla rendering takes eight rather than nine or ten compases.

Meanwhile, in its movement from a tonic seventh chord to the minor chord on the fourth degree (Cm), this third copla more closely resembles the second copla of this recording. Here, the first melodic line (which is here repeated) starts on F, the seventh degree of the tonic chord (cueing the guitarist to play G7), half-cadences around the fourth degree, and then descends to the tonic. (The degree to which Talega sings in a fixed, rather than improvised manner, can be appreciated from his essentially identical rendering of this verse in a 1959 recording, audible on Kliman [n.d.].)

Following this verse Malena plays a three-compás guitar falseta (c. 36–38). This is a fine example of a traditional falseta; it follows the well-worn pattern schematized in figure 3.1, and involves no flashy display of technique, but builds in its second compás (c. 37) to a driving and exciting climax. The final compás is harmonically stable postcadential filler, that ameliorates the expressive tension of the previous passage.

The fourth copla (c. 39–43), as sung, is somewhat ambiguous in meaning. It appears that the verse is normally sung with two additional words, rendered here in brackets, which clarify it.[11]

> [Cuando] a ti nadie te quiera
> [ven,] que yo a ti te querré
> que aquello que me hiciste
> yo te lo recompensaré
>
> When no one loves you, come, I'll love you
> and repay you for what you've done for me

This melody is also attributed to Talega. He sings the verse straight through, with no textual repetitions, and with each line of text corresponding to a single melody line and compás. Aside from the lack of repetitions and the quick progression to Cm in the first line, it loosely conforms to the model of figure 3.1. Note the clearly audible iv–III–II–I (Cm–B♭–A♭–G) "Andalusian" progression in c. 40.

At c. 44, almost immediately after finishing the fourth copla, Talega again sings the second copla ("Que no me que querías . . ."). In doing so, he illustrates a number of points. First, his repetition shows how a flamenco piece is not a closely, precisely structured formal composition, like a pop song or a classical composition. Rather, it is a typical product of an oral tradition in being a loose, informal entity, in which fragments may be freely inserted, verses repeated or altered, and overall length and structure treated with flexibility. Furthermore, his second rendition of this copla offers a revealing comparison with the first. The melodic contour is largely the same. However, as with his rendering of the third verse of the first copla, Talega here begins the copla not at the start of the compás, but halfway through it. Again, Malena, rather than breaking the compás to fit this irregularity, adheres firmly to it, while being obliged to

---

11. The bracketed words are included in the rendering of the verse in the booklet accompanying the Westminster recording; this booklet, unlike some flamenco liner notes, is clearly compiled by an authority, who has perhaps edited such verses to conform to their more customary forms.

alter the standard chordal pattern (e.g., of the first rendering). The essentially free-rhythmic singing style enables this adaptation. Talega's irregularities might suggest that he conceives of the soleá compás not as a fixed pattern of twelve beats, but one that can at some level alternately be thought of as phrases of six, with a certain tendency toward twelve. This sort of conception further illustrates the fundamentally oral nature of the flamenco tradition.

Immediately after finishing this copla, Talega sings the short concluding verse (c. 47–49), which changes (and is hence called "cambio") to major tonality, and follows a conventional pattern, accelerating slightly. Talega's use of the major scale cues the guitarist to switch from Phrygian tonality to an alternation between G major and D7 chords. Because this passage functions primarily as a short cadence, Talega does not feel obliged to sing more than a fragment of verse, followed by the standard flamenco nonlexical syllables "tran tran tran."

> Ay, que te quiero
> y tú no lo sabes
> te tran tran tran

> Ay, I love you and you don't know it

The booklet accompanying the record adds a final verse, which is presumably sung in other renderings:

> tienes tu casa cerra' con llave

> You've got your house locked up with a key.

Note that the final guitar cadence falls not on beat 1 but beat 10 of the compás.

Afterword: Is There an Indigenous Flamenco "Theory"?

In a study such as this, the question may naturally arise as to the extent to which we have been employing analytical terminology and concepts that cohere with those used by flamenco musicians themselves. In other words, do flamenco musicians "have theory," in the narrow sense of the word "theory" as implying an explicitly articulated set of terms and concepts describing abstract entities like mode, harmony, and meter? Before attempting to answer this question, it should be clarified that the extent to which such an "emic" theory is lacking should not be taken as a deficiency. Whether or not a flamenco artist is able to verbalize such concepts has little or no bearing on that musician's ability to perform a variety of different cantes, each with their distinctive formal complexities and characteristics. "Theory," in this sense, is something that is primarily of use to outsiders studying the art (such as readers of this chapter), or helpful in particular sorts of communication between performers.

In general, it may be said that for at least a century there has been something of a continuum in terms of level of theoretical articulation among flamenco performers. At one end of this spectrum would lie the many performers—especially gypsies—who would be essentially innocent of formal theoretical knowledge, having learned their art as a domestic inherited tradition. Singers are particularly likely to fall in this category, as well as almost all musicians before the twentieth century. (For that matter, even today quite a few gypsies, including younger generations, have avoided school and remained illiterate.) We may picture, for example, a gypsy vocalist who has solid command of all the major cantes, and who perhaps is able to identify and sing many specific substyles by name, but who is unaware that siguiryas could be counted in twelve beats.

At the other extreme, we may take an educated, Spanish, middle-class, amateur flamenco guitarist, who also may have studied a bit of classical music; aside from avidly copying recordings of performers like that just described, he makes abundant use of pedagogical books and Web sites that describe and discuss cantes in abstract analytical terms, and that provide transcriptions, in staff notation, of guitar falsetas (some of them, of course, created by gypsies with no knowledge of theory). Such educated amateur performers are not an entirely recent phenomenon; in 1902 one Rafael Marin published a guitar manual for such players, complete with theoretical descriptions of basic cantes and pedagogical exercises to develop technique.

In modern times, most flamenco musicians might fall somewhere between these extremes. On the whole, it can be generalized that theory, in the narrow sense defined here, is not extensively developed in flamenco. (In this sense flamenco contrasts markedly with a genre like jazz.) Singers, despite their command of cante, are especially unlikely to be able to verbalize theory, such as harmonic and rhythmic concepts, in comparison to guitarists. In general, there might be little need for such verbalizations, except perhaps to instruct accompanying guitarists.[12]

What is important is that the singer be able to tell the guitarist where to put the capo, in order to accord with the singer's range; otherwise they may flounder about trying to match pitches, and the vocalist can end up singing

---

12. Thus, for example, if a vocalist performing bulerías switches from Phrygian to major tonality, singing a major scale with a prominent sixth degree, the guitarist is expected to follow along; if for some reason he fails to do so, the singer might be unable to tell him anything more specific than "¡Cámbialo, por Dios!" (Change it!).

disastrously out of his or her range. Thus, for example, Juan Talega might have known nothing of note-names and keys per se, but presumably learned from experience to be able to tell the guitarist before making this recording, something like "Ponla por er tre' y toca por soleá por arriba"—that is, "Pon la cejilla en el traste numero tres . . ." meaning that Malena should put the capo on the third fret and play soleares, in E Phrygian fingering (as opposed to por medio using A major as the tonic chord; the former would afford G Phrygian, and the latter C Phrygian).

Most guitarists nowadays—and certainly teachers of flamenco dance—would be able to tell someone, such as a student, that soleares can be counted in twelve beats. However, the conventions of counting certain other compás patterns accord with structural patterns rather than numerical beats per se.[13] Chordal vocabulary, insofar as it exists, derives from guitar fingerings and basic solfège. Alphabetical note or chord names are little used. Thus, from a por arriba Phrygian tonality using E major as tonic, the progression Am–G–F–E would be described as la–sol–fa–mi. A knowledgeable guitarist might be able to describe a G minor chord (as fingered on the guitar) as *sol menor.* Other guitarists, if trying to convey the concept, would have to demonstrate it on the instrument, and might refer to it as a *postura* (posture, fingering) rather than an *acorde* (chord). The F♯ Phrygian tonality of tarantas, with its distinctive tonic chord (from low to high: F♯–C♯–F♯–G–B–E) would be described as *tono de tarantas* rather than, for example, "F♯7 with a flat nine, thirteen, and no third degree." B Phrygian might be referred to as *tono de granaínas,* and C major as *tono de caracoles.* The term *por arriba,* denoting an E major chord, would also imply E Phrygian tonality, or, in certain cases, E major.[14]

The analysis in this chapter has not attempted to discover any particular deep structure or to make any novel interpretations, but rather to show what are essentially the familiar and conventional aspects of soleares. Few flamenco musicians read staff notation, and few would employ the alphabetical chord names used here, but these tools have been used in this article in order to illuminate rather than interpret flamenco conventions.

Academics might disagree as to the extent of theoretical knowledge of, say, the hypothetical aforementioned singer who does not consciously know that the soleá *compás* has twelve beats. Some might argue that his ability to perform, and to distinguish a correct soleá from a faulty one, indicates the existence of a passive, "implicit theory" in his mind. Others (such as myself) might

13. Thus, siguiriyas, of twelve beats in the pattern 2+2+3+3+2, is counted something like "one-and-two-and-three–ee-ee-four-ee-ee-five-ee." Fandango de Huelva, in six beats, is usually counted "one-two-three-four-five (pause)."

14. I am grateful to John Moore and Estela Zatania for some of this information.

argue that the notion of such an "implicit theory" is oxymoronic and that it extends the scope of the word "theory" to the extent that it is meaningless. Rather, according to this perspective, "theory," in order to be a meaningful concept, should be defined precisely as the conscious and explicit use of abstract concepts such as meter and mode to describe music. In this view, the singer in question would not have a theoretical understanding of his art per se, but rather a clear *intuitive* and operational understanding of it. Ideally, of course, theoretical descriptions of such music, whether fashioned by "insiders" or others, accurately reflect and describe the operational concepts of performers without forcing them into alien modes of analysis.

References

Alvarez Caballero, Angel. 1981. *Historia del cante flamenco.* Madrid: Alianza Editorial.

Kliman, Norman. Web site: http://perso.wanadoo.es/siguiriya/soleares.htm.

Lefranc, Pierre.2000. *El cante jondo: del territorio a los repertorios: tonás, siguiriyas, soleares.* Sevilla: Universidad de Sevilla.

Manuel, Peter. 1989. "Modal Harmony in Andalusian, Eastern European, and Turkish Syncretic Musics." *Yearbook for Traditional Musics* vol. 21:70–94.

Marín, Rafael. 1995 [1902]. *Método de guitarra: Aires andaluces (flamenco).* Córdoba: Ediciones de la Posada [Madrid: Don Dionisio Alvarez].

Schreiner, Claus, editor. 1985. *Flamenco: Gypsy Dance and Music from Andalusia.* Translated by Mollie C. Peters. Portland: Oregon: Amadeus Press.

Soler Guevara, Luís, and Ramón Soler Díaz. 1992. *Antonio Mairena en el mundo de la siguiriya y la soleá.* Málaga: Fundación Antonio Mairena and Junta de Andalucía.

Whitney, Carol. 1976. "Structure and Variation in Flamenco Song and its Guitar Accompaniment." *Guitar Review* 41:10–18.

CHAPTER 4

An Afro-Cuban Batá Piece for Obatalá, King of the White Cloth

Robin Moore and Elizabeth Sayre

A fro-Cuban *batá* drumming—music that salutes and calls to earth the Yoruba *orishas,* or deified forces of nature[1]—is one of the most complex percussion traditions in the Western hemisphere. Nevertheless, its musical aspect is understudied and poorly understood except by those who have had extensive training in batá performance. The analysis presented here will introduce the reader to the workings of the music by focusing on transitions, interactions, and variations in the recorded selection "Obbatalá" (Grupo Oba Ilú, *Santería, Songs for the Orishas,* Soul Jazz Records, 1998). The track is noteworthy for the range of *toques* (rhythmic patterns) it covers within just a few minutes[2] as well as for the outstanding performance of the lead singer, Marta Galarraga, and drummers Mario Jáuregui Francis (*iyá* or mother drum), Pedro Pablo

---

We would like to thank Michael Spiro, Michael Marcuzzi, and Thomas Altmann for their thoughtful comments on drafts of this essay.

1. The *orishas* are complex spiritual forces—deified West African historical figures who have multiple associations with natural phenomena, characteristics of human personality, and philosophical or life principles.

2. The recording's quality outweighs two significant drawbacks. First, the chorus is out of tune, although this quality lends a certain ceremonial authenticity to the example. In ritual settings, communal participation is more important than perfect intonation. The second difficulty is that the small head of the iyá (lead drum) is difficult to distinguish at times among the other sounds on the recording.

Bataleros Julio Edera Alán (Iyá), "Wichy," Cecilio Torres Sandrino (Itótele), and Carlos Herrera (Okónkolo), summer 2001, Playa, Havana. Photo by Robin Moore.

Martínez Campos (*itótele* or middle drum), and Máximo Duquesnes Martínez (*okónkolo* or small drum).[3]

Initially, we provide some basic cultural and historical information and a listening guide to the recording. Later we comment on the formal qualities of batá drumming, the dynamic interactions between singers and drummers, and movement toward greater rhythmic intensity and improvisational freedom in the final segments of the piece. All rhythmic sections are analyzed, but three of the six receive closer consideration as a means of understanding the overall musical progression. We suggest that the structure of "Obbatalá" unfolds in

3. Marta Galarraga is the daughter of Lázaro Galarraga, one of the finest living Cuban singer-bataleros, now resident in Southern California. Ms. Galarraga currently lives in France and tours internationally. Mario Jáuregui was trained by Pablo Roche (one of Fernando Ortiz' informants from the 1930s; one of the most famous and respected twentieth-century batá players), and was an original member of the Conjunto Folklórico Nacional de Cuba. "Pedrito" Martínez has been a resident of northern New Jersey since the late 1990s, and has had an important impact on Afro-Cuban music in the New York City area in recent years. In Cuba he was a member of Yoruba Andabo and other renowned folkloric groups. Máximo Duquesnes Martínez is known as one of Havana's best *cajal güiro* and rumba players (Spiro 2003, p.c.).

response to musical tensions generated through varying and combining the standard toques. Such variations include the utilization of differing calls and responses, constrained improvisations, and textural contrasts obtained through the juxtaposition and ordering of toques and songs.

The cultural roots of batá drums lie in West Africa, in what are now Nigeria and the Republic of Benin. Enslaved Yoruba[4] people brought memories of their religions to colonial Cuba in the eighteenth and nineteenth centuries and reconstituted them there. Batá drumming accompanies religious events associated with *la Regla de Ocha,* also known as *Santería.*[5] Traditional events that call for batá drumming include: the initiation of a new priest, the honoring of one's godparents' orishas,[6] the anniversary of an initiation, the celebration of an orisha's annual day,[7] a celebration mandated by orisha through divination, the honoring of a *santero/santera* (initiate, priest) who has passed away, and the consecration of a new set of sacred drums. Ceremonies typically involve the rendering of an extended series of distinct toques, played first alone and then accompanied by song and dance. This form of worship is intended to induce possession in initiates of the religion. "Bringing orisha down" into the bodies of *santeros* is intended to help to heal and unify the religious community; when orisha become present in a ceremony, they may offer advice, remedies, warnings, recommendations for restoring balance, spiritual cleanings, or blessings, among other communications, to initiates. Drumming, song, and dance are crucial for facilitating possession.

Drummers master considerable knowledge and experience in order to play competently in such a context. They must understand the composition of more than fifty distinct rhythms as a unit and as played on each of the three drums individually. They must learn to recognize hundreds of devotional chants, to

4. "Yoruba" is a term that that dates from the late nineteenth century. It refers to sets of related ethnic groups from areas that are now in southwestern Nigeria and the southeastern part of the Republic of Benin.

5. *La Regla de Ocha* is an Afro-Cuban religious practice primarily based on West African beliefs. Santería, often synonymous with *la Regla de Ocha,* derives from the association of *orisha* with particular Catholic saints. This process of cultural fusion took place over time in colonial Cuba. Most Yoruba *orishas* have a corresponding Catholic saint. *Ocha* practitioners participate in worship that incorporates drumming, dance, and song. "Ocha" is a contraction of the Nigerian term *orisa* or saint-deity.

6. *Santería* initiates form ritual kinship bonds with elders—"godparents" who guide them in practicing the tradition.

7. Each orisha has a particular calendric day of worship that often derives from the patron saint day of its corresponding Catholic saint. The day associated with Obatalá, for instance, is September 24, the feast of Our Lady of Mercy.

associate them with particular deities, and with particular forms of accompaniment. They must memorize complex sequences in which sacred repertoire is to be performed. Finally, they must be sensitive to constant musical cues offered throughout the ceremony from the lead singer and other drummers and to respond appropriately with metrical shifts, improvisations, or elaborations of the basic pulse. Good batá playing involves making seamless, smooth transitions between rhythms, which in turn facilitate transformations of consciousness in those gathered at the event. In effect, musical transformations accompany and support spiritual transformations. At key sections in ceremonies there are shifts in tempo, energy, intensity, and excitement. These are typically cued by the lead singer and responded to instantaneously by the drummers. Our analysis considers how such shifts occur and build upon one another, focusing both on microlevel variations within sections and on progression through the sections.

Three drummers play the set of three double-headed batás. Each drum, shaped something like an asymmetrical hourglass, has a larger head called the *enú* (mouth), and a smaller head called the *chachá* (butt); one head is struck with each hand, with the drum laying across the player's lap. The *enú* heads produce open tones and closed or muffed tones, whereas the *chachás* play slaps or smacks that have a higher, less clearly pitched sound.[8] The largest drum is called the *iyá ilú*, meaning "mother drum," or simply *iyá*. It leads the ensemble, performs the most extended improvisations, and sounds "*llamadas*," or calls between drums. The iyá usually has bells strung around each head (*chaguoro* around the enú head and *chaguorí* around the smaller chachá head) that sound continuously as it plays.[9] The middle drum, the *itótele*,[10] also performs considerable improvisation and elaborations of basic rhythms. The smallest drum

---

8. Cuban-style batá playing has two main regional styles, based in Havana and Matanzas. In this essay we describe Havana-style technique. In Matanzas, drummers play the chachá with their strong hand (in Havana the chachá is played with the weak hand), and the chachás of the okónkolo and iyá have an additional finger/rim-shot technique that is not usually heard in Havana (Spiro, p.c.). Occasionally the chachá of the itótele will be played with a leather strap (also seen in Nigerian batá performance).

9. We have heard various suggestions about the symbolic meanings of the *chaguoro* through various personal contacts. The *chaguoro's* bells are said to be pleasing to female deities Yemayá (the ocean, the spirit of maternity) and Ochún (the river, the spirit of beauty, joy, and sensuality). They are said to frighten away nonorisha spirits, who are not welcome in orisha ceremonies. Finally, the bells' constant ringing is consistent with an African musical aesthetic of continuous sound that produces great timbral complexity.

10. Ortiz (1954–55 4:210) speculates that the term may derive from the Yoruba *totó* meaning "completely" and "tele" meaning "one who follows."

is called the *okónkolo*.[11] It most frequently provides a basic rhythm that may serve as a pulse reference for the other drummers, though in a few toques it can depart from its usually static, short patterns and improvise extensively.

Sacred batá drums are constructed and consecrated through an elaborate process in which the orisha *añá* is placed inside the drums. Male performers undergo an initiation in order to perform at sacred events.[12] When they are ordained as ritual drummers, they become known as *omóañá*, "children of *añá*," or when they receive consecrated drum sets, they become known as *olubatá*.[13] Batá drumming was an entirely oral tradition until recently; for that reason the repertoire and its interpretation vary from performer to performer and from one group of drummers associated with a particular consecrated set of drums to another. Players usually learn the music in an informal apprenticeship process. Younger, aspiring artists begin on the okónkolo, then move on to the larger drums as they gain experience.

In the mid-1930s, *aberikula* or nonconsecrated drums were first created and used. These drums now appear in ceremonial contexts under certain conditions,[14] and are used in combination with Cuban symphonic compositions, dance repertoire, Latin jazz, and North American popular music. Additionally, they accompany staged performances of sacred music and dance as interpreted by Afro-Cuban folklore ensembles, some of which have become highly professionalized, organized and promoted by the Cuban government after the Revolution. The existence of aberikula drums has contributed a great deal to general knowledge about batá drumming, the notation of the repertoire, and its study among the non-initiated. This growing accessibility makes a study such as ours possible.

11. This term seems to come from *kónkoto,* meaning children's god or toy ("dios o jugete de los niños"; Ortiz 1954–55 4:212). It may refer to the fact that the okónkolo is smallest of the sacred batás, the baby or child of the ensemble. Marcuzzi (2004, p.c.) suggests that the name more likely reflects ways that supporting drum parts are vocalized in teaching/playing contexts.

12. The Cuban batá tradition does not permit women and homosexual men to play consecrated drums. Within the last twenty years, women in Cuba and abroad have begun to play batá drums in secular and some limited sacred settings.

13. There are many more *omoañá* than *olubatá,* who have significant ritual responsibilities associated with drum ownership.

14. In places where *añá* drums are scarce (outside Cuba, for example), *aberikula* drums play ceremonies more regularly. Or, in cases in which santeros cannot afford the expense of hiring *añá* drums for a ceremony, *aberikula* drums provide a less expensive alternative. *Aberikula* drums also demand less in the way of ritual protocol and maintenance than *añá* drums (Altmann, p.c.).

As mentioned, our essay analyzes a *tratado,* or drum and song sequence, which pays tribute to Obatalá,[15] the "King of the White Cloth," who stands for peace, wisdom, and purity in the pantheon of the orishas. We examine three distinct toques to illustrate the means by which the drummers build intensity into their performance.[16] We leave aside many important aspects of the batá tradition such as the relationships between drumming and dancing, or the analysis of melodic/textual variation used by lead singers to call and interact with the orishas. We focus instead on how the drum ensemble reacts to changes cued by the lead singer and how the drums respond to each other with variations on basic patterns, predetermined calls and responses, and improvisations.

Listening to Afro-Cuban Batá Drumming

One of the most important aspects of entering the sonic world of the Cuban batá is to understand how to listen to the drumheads of the ensemble as a unit. In existing literature one sees references to the complexity of hearing six skins sounding at once, but it is rarely mentioned that batá players do not hear each of the heads as having equal weight or an identical role in the music. Without mandating a single way of hearing batá drumming (the possibility of hearing the music in multiple ways is part of its power), we recommend that listeners focus on the relative importance of the different heads. Understanding how to listen is rather like understanding how two-dimensional lines and shapes on a canvas can represent three-dimensional space, or how to move back and forth between different perspectives in an Escher drawing.

In order to get the most out of the recording, we recommend listening with headphones and directing your attention in particular ways. Like many recent studio releases, Oba Ilú's disc is mixed with the okónkolo panned to the left, and itótele to the right—a distribution that replicates the experience of facing a batá battery seated in the traditional configuration (where the itótele player would be seated to iyá player's left and the okónkolo player to his right). The iyá is mixed to the center, with the enú slightly to the right, and the

---

15. Many variations exist in the spelling of Santería terminology. We choose to use the most typical spelling, Obatalá, although it differs from the spelling used in the title of our selection.

16. As scholars and musicians, we have had limited access to the spiritual aspects of batá performance. One of us trained in the musical aspects of the batá tradition with John Amira (New York), Orlando Fiol (New York, Philadelphia), Amelia Pedroso (Havana), Lázaro Pedroso (Havana), Michael Spiro (San Francisco), among others, and between us we have attended and even performed in minor ceremonial occasions.

chachá slightly to the left. If the listener focuses on the left channel, he/she will be able to distinguish the okónkolo, which plays the same ostinato from the beginning of the track through 4:38. The itótele's chachá is audible in the right ear (particularly from 2:04 through 3:17, as the itótele's enú does not play much in that section; in this passage it can be heard as a steady, dry sound on the "backbeat.")[17] Once that sound is distinguished in the texture, it will be easier to hear it in other parts of the selection. The itótele's enú is also audible in the right ear, but as a quieter, more melodic sound. The iyá's enú is easily distinguishable as the lowest pitch in the recording. The iyá's chachá is more elusive, most clearly audible when it plays at points in the texture when no other drumhead is sounding (for example, in the extended conversation between iyá and itótele from 1:22 to 1:42). We recommend that readers witness live batá drumming, or see it on video, to experience further the sounds of the six drumheads working in coordination.

As you learn to distinguish the different drum sounds, it may be helpful to focus on two distinct "planes" of listening within the composite texture.[18] The first is a "rhythmic bed"[19] or aggregate ostinato created from the sounds of the two heads of the okónkolo and the chachá of the itótele. The second plane is comprised of the composite of tones, open and muted, played by the enús of the iyá and the itótele that together create recognizable melodies.[20] It is in this second plane that the batás are understood to "speak"—creating phrases in imitation of Yoruba tonal languages, to be understood by the orishas and by priests. Below we transcribe parts of the recording in planes, while transcribing others separated into the parts played by each musician separately. Hearing the planes of sound is a step toward understanding batá drumming as drummers hear it, yet it is important not to think of the music only as "foreground" (melody) and "background" (rhythmic bed), but rather as multiple layers and coincidences of sound to be appreciated as an ever-shifting whole.

17. Itótele's chachá plays on the "and-of-two" and "and-of-five" of every 6/8 bar. If the music is felt in four with a triplet subdivision (that is, with pulses on "one," the "and-of-two," "four," and the "and-of-five" of every bar of six), these hits on itótele's chachá fall on the "backbeat," the "two" and "four" of every set of four beats. See the transcriptions of this section later in the article.

18. Kenneth Schweitzer (2003) was the first to write about this way of listening to the batás.

19. This is Orlando Fiol's term; our thanks to him.

20. As noted by Schweitzer, this distinction between "rhythmic bed" and "melody" is complicated by the fact that the rhythmic bed has a melodic aspect to it as well, often a descending melodic profile.

The chachá of the iyá helps define the rhythmic bed of the piece, but it also acts independently in various roles. For instance, it frequently plays at the same time as the enú of the itótele to reinforce the latter's melodic contributions. It may accent melody (enú) notes of its own patterns for emphasis or impact; and it invariably plays with extra authority in order to signal other players to begin playing or to change the toque. It also may play characteristic independent figures that add to the intensity and density of the texture. For this reason, we have assigned the chachá head of the iyá a unique graphic representation in the transcriptions (see transcriptions).

One must learn to recognize the relationship of toques to the *clave*, a two-measure rhythmic phrase that underlies almost all of the music, which has slightly differing forms depending on the underlying feel of the rhythm, duple or triple (figures 4.1 and 4.2).[21] Knowing where the clave is in the music is important as it determines the appropriate moment for drum and song entrances, rhythmic changes, and appropriate dance steps. This is true even if the clave rhythm is not audible.[22] Clave rhythms consist of two parts, a more syncopated half and a straighter half. Performers often develop an intuitive sense of clave over time so that they not only feel its presence in the music but also can predict its orientation in a song never heard before. If song melodies, rhythms, and sometimes dance steps are not all performed in the correct orientation relative to the clave, the music feels wrong to an experienced performer. In our basic transcriptions of songs and toques below we include the clave on occasion since it functions as a crucial, if unheard, reference point for lead singer and drummers.[23]

The 6/8 clave is also sometimes performed in a similar but distinct rhythm, as follows. Note that it is essentially the same as the figure 4.2 with the addition of two notes (figure 4.3).

The important relationship of batá drumming to the art of singing for the orishas cannot be emphasized strongly enough. The *akpwon* or lead vocalist may on occasion sing for the orishas with no drum accompaniment, with a *güiro* ensemble (conga drums and *chekerés*), or with other musical ensembles depending

21. Some batá toques are clearly in a duple feel, others clearly in a triple feel. Others have a mix of feels across the drum parts (i.e., itótele plays duple feel, whereas okónkolo plays triple feel). In yet other toques, the correct feel of the rhythm lies somewhere "in between" or may even shift phrase by phrase; these subtleties are virtually impossible to notate.

22. On occasion, the clave will be played on a maraca-like instrument called *atcheré* to accompany batá and singing, or it may be clapped by singers, but often its presence is only implicit. It is not played in Oba Ilú's recording.

23. Schweitzer's discussion of the clave in *ñongo* is the most extended in the literature to date.

FIGURE 4.1. *Clave in 4/4.*

on the occasion or regional origin of the musicians.[24] Singing with the batás, however, requires specialized knowledge of when and how to signal transitions to new rhythms that the drummers can follow. It is more complicated than singing alone or with the other percussion whose repertoire is less extensive.

Orisha songs are responsorial: the akpwon first sings alone, then others in the room answer with an appropriate *coro* (chorus). Songs may be lengthy, covering many claves, or short. The repertoire consists primarily of *rezos,* rhythmically free pieces that include long, partially improvised melodies and texts, or *cantos,* shorter songs with a strictly defined rhythm. The latter are much more common. All songs heard in "Obbatalá" are cantos. Song sequences are called *tratados* (literally, "treatments") and progress from slower to faster in tempo, and often from less dense to more dense in texture. Certain songs are grouped together within tratados, either because they are textually related or because they are sung to the same rhythmic accompaniment. Each song within a given sequence may be repeated any number of times until the *akpwon* decides to move on.

In a ceremonial setting, the akpwon monitors spiritual activity and directs his/her vocal energy accordingly through choices related to song sequence, tempo, and melodic and textual variation.[25] Such decisions aim to intensify participants' enthusiasm and attract the orishas into their dancing bodies. In turn, the drummers must be constantly attentive to the lead singer since certain songs necessitate immediate rhythmic changes. They constantly choose between ways of accompanying songs: through choice of toque, tempo, feel, or the amount of musical ornamentation played at any given moment. The iyá player leads the drum ensemble in these changes and follows the singer, enhancing his/her performance. "Obbatalá" as performed by Grupo Oba Ilú provides examples of both obligatory musical changes dictated by songs as well as others that reflect drummers' choices about what and how to play.

A great deal could be written about orisha song texts. Their translation is extremely difficult, as Afro-Cuban communities have lost African language fluency over time. Even master singers express doubt about the meaning of some

24. In Matanzas the *iyesá* drum ensemble accompanies singing for the orisha. In other contexts, violins and other instruments are used in worship. See Delgado (2001) for additional information on topics related to iyesá traditions.

25. Although there are no gender proscriptions in ritual singing in this musical tradition, male singers are more common.

FIGURE 4.2. *Clave in 6/8.*

songs and disagree about precise interpretations, although they still understand many phrases and words.[26] Complicating the issue further is the fact that
religious texts often speak in metaphors or through oblique references to stories about the orishas; their literal meanings do not necessarily help listeners
understand their true significance. Singers generally agree that song texts may
praise the orishas, tell their stories, or even insult them in order to provoke
their presence in a ceremony.

The Music of "Obbatalá"

Religious events involving batás often take place in the living room or base-
ment of a private home, or in the hall of a community center, rented especially
for the occasion. Preparations for the *tambor* or "drumming" involve the creation of an altar to a particular deity or deities and the cooking of ritual foods.
Animal sacrifices also may be made for the orishas, or for the drums themselves
in order to feed the religious force they are believed to contain. Animals offered
up in this manner are usually cooked and eaten by participants after the ceremony has ended. Musical activity begins with unaccompanied drumming in
front of the altar before most of the guests arrive. This part of the ceremony is
known as the *Oru del Igbodu* or *Oru Seco*. It involves playing a series of twenty-
three toques or "salutes" in a prescribed order to the orishas.

After the Oru Seco is completed and guests arrive, the second section of
the ritual begins. This is known as the *Oru Cantado,* a series of songs accompanied by drumming and dance that also salute the orisha in a prescribed
order. As each one is praised, initiates of that orisha are required to come forward to dance and salute the drums and prostrate themselves before the instruments in recognition of their spiritual power. Although the akpwon has
some freedom to choose which songs to sing in the Oru Cantado, only a few
pieces are entoned to any given orisha. In both the *Oru del Igbodu* and the *Oru
Cantado,* the energy level of the ceremony remains relatively contained.

26. The language has changed, or has been lost, in Cuba to the point where it is no
longer easily recognized by West Africans. The Australian scholar Amanda Vincent says
that Nigerian Yorubas may be able to interpret Cuban song texts when they are sung, because the melody provides clues to the tonal character of the words (p.c., January 2004).

FIGURE 4.3. *Clave in 6/8, variant.*

The climax of the event is known as the *Güemilere*. It consists of a freer series of songs with drum accompaniment in which participants dance and sing with greater intensity, inviting spirit possession. The Güemilere may last for hours, as long as is necessary in order to induce possession. During this period, the akpwon chooses songs with greater freedom, and may sing dozens of songs to the same orisha (often as long as twenty to thirty minutes per orisha), repeating them and varying them in a variety of ways. The ordering and execution of the song sequence is critical in the Güemilere, as the entrance of a new song can markedly increase energy or release the tension built up by many repetitions of a previous piece.

Participants "mounted" by their orisha are dressed in special clothing associated with that deity, and proceed to interact with the community in trance as the incarnation of a divine being. They may offer advice to community members, call for particular sacrifices to be made, or request music of various kinds. This period of interaction with possessed initiates may also last for extended periods of time. Ceremonies end with a *cierre* or closing section consisting of yet more prescribed instrumental salutes and songs followed by ritual actions that bring worship to a close. Any individuals still in trance are coaxed out of this ecstatic state and brought back to the physical world.

In Oba Ilú's recorded selection (CD track 6), Marta Galarraga sings seven different songs to Obatalá. This deity is the father of the orishas, associated with peace, serenity, wisdom, purity, mountaintops, and the color white. In visual representations, in dance steps, and in stories, Obatalá is often depicted as a slow-moving old man with a cane, although he appears in different incarnations in different songs and stories. In one story he is a warrior on horseback, for instance; in another, the deity is female.

The sequence of songs in this selection is traditional and is used in ceremonial contexts to "bring Obatalá down."[27] However, the relatively short length of our tratado and the fact that it repeats each devotional chant only a few times does not correspond to what would be heard in a ceremony. Its relatively rapid rhythmic shifts and increases in both tempo and rhythmic density within each subsection are more characteristic of performances in the Oru Cantado section than in the freer Güemilere section. However, our song sequence usu-

27. Michael Spiro (2003, p.c.).

ally does not appear in the Oru Cantado.[28] Clearly, performers have tailored the length and dynamics of the selection for the studio setting.

The first and second, third and fourth, and fifth and sixth songs are pairs that function as "verse" and "montuno" in relation to each other. Montuno is a word with many meanings, but by referring to a verse-montuno relationship here, we suggest that the first song of the pair is virtually never heard without the second. The montuno completes the previous song, and in most cases represents a shortened version of the same musical idea. Song #7, in its brevity (the chorus repeats itself within a much shorter time span compared to songs before it), might be considered a montuno or coda to the entire tratado. Lyrics for all of the song texts are included below, followed by a melodic transcription (figures 4.4 and 4.5). See figure 4.6 for the exact time in the recording when each of the songs begins, and for the toques that accompany them.[29]

As you listen to "Obbatalá," first try to get a general feel for its characteristics. Notice the relative pitches and timbres of the drums and voices, the subtle sounds of the bells strung on the iyá, and the increase in tempo over the course of the track. Hear the difference between the right and left channels to begin to separate the sounds of each drum and to locate the beat of the music. The beat regulates the music in the same way throughout the selection although the tempo increases. In order to feel this, it may be useful to tap out the song melodies against the clave and/or the implicit beat as transcribed here.

Use figure 4.6 to identify the sections of the tratado. These consist of song changes cued by the akpwon and related changes in rhythm signaled primarily by the iyá. In most cases, the akpwon's decision to change a song will provoke a response of some sort from the drum battery. This may be a shift to an entirely different toque or merely the addition of new calls or improvisational nuances.

We will now briefly analyze the six toques that the batás pass through during the course of the tratado.[30]

---

28. Spiro (2003).

29. As mentioned, definitive translation of these texts is problematic, a scholarly project in and of itself. Through conversations with Spiro and Marcuzzi, and using Lázaro Pedroso's work as a reference, we know that, in a general sense, the songs implore Obatalá to be present in ceremonies through possession of an initiate. The texts (particularly the akpwon lines at the end of the recording) mention several "roads" of Obatalá: Odu Aremu (which may also be a reference to Oduduá, another orisha sometimes described as a road of Obatalá), Ayaguna, Osagriñan, and Oba Moro.

30. We denote the chachás of the itótele and okónkolo with the same type of note head but at different pitch levels since both these drumheads are part of the "rhythmic bed," as opposed to the chachá of the iyá, discussed previously (see figure 4.7).

FIGURE 4.4. *"Obbatalá" song texts.*

#1	Lead & chorus:	*Odudu aremu* (2x)	5 claves
		Odu aremu odudu ifarawa	
		Odudu aremu, Odu aremu odudu ifarawa	
	("Montuno" response to #1)		
	Lead:	*Odudu aremu*	1 clave
	Chorus:	*Odu aremu odudu ifarawa*	1 clave
#3	Lead & chorus:	*Odu aremu o wimbio*	6 claves
		Odu aremu o belona (Obatalá)	
		Ala-agogo emi sele o	
		Aremu kwelaye	
#4	("Montuno" to #3)		
	Lead:	*(Baba, Iworo, Obatalá) Odudu kwelaye*	1 clave
	Chorus:	*Baba mi chokoto aremu kwelaye*	1 clave
#5	Lead & chorus:	*(L)Eriwode, (l)eriwode*	1 clave
#6	(Answer to #5)		
	Lead:	*Obatalá (Ayaguna) belona*	1 clave
	Chorus:	*Baba elona eriwode*	1 clave
#7	("Montuno" to entire tratado)		
	Chorus:	*Ayembele to*	"3 side"
	Lead:	*To to, y to to*	"2 side"
		(Lewa wo, Lewa wona	
		Lewa wo, Lewa wo'che	
		Ayaguna lejibo, Osagriñan lejibo, Oba Moro lejibo)	

Yakotá (0:00–2:04)

Yakotá (figures 4.8 and 4.9) is a frequently occurring generic song toque that usually appears at the beginning of tratados since its characteristic tempo and energy are relatively low.[31] Yakotá is not dedicated to a single orisha. The toque has a lilting, calm quality; songs accompanied by this rhythm tend to be longer, with more sustained melodic lines. When the lead singer calls Song #1 beginning with the phrase "Odudu aremu," the iyá player must respond with yakotá; any other choice at this point would be uncharacteristic. Interestingly, yakotá is unusual in that it does not "have clave," as some batá players say. By this they mean that in none of the three drum parts does yakotá imply the alternating measure-by-measure asymmetry of the clave. Yakotá's rhythmic bed

31. "Song toques" do not appear as part of the Oru Seco; on the other hand, some toques in the Oru Seco do accompany songs in the Oru Cantado, Güemilere, and the Cierre. Some Cuban teachers distinguish between *toques genéricos,* that accompany songs for many orisha, and *toques específicos,* those that are orisha-specific.

FIGURE 4.5. *"Obbatalá" songs.*

FIGURE 4.5. *Continued*

134

FIGURE 4.6. *Sectional flow of "Obbatalá."*

Time Code	Song	Drum Rhythm
0:00	Akpwon calls Song #1 (3 repetitions)	
0:03		Iyá player calls *yakotá*
1:47	Akpwon calls Song #2 (2 repetitions)	(no rhythmic change)
2:00	Akpwon calls Song #3 (2 repetitions)	
2:04		Iyá calls next toque, *hueso*
3:15	Akpwon calls Song #4 (3 repetitions)	
3:17		Iyá initiates *tambor*
3:33	Akpwon calls Song #5 (2 repetitions)	Iyá discontinues *tambor* and shifts into ride pattern
3:44	Akpwon calls Song #6 (3 repetitions)	
3:47		Iyá calls *ñongo*
3:59	Akpwon returns to Song #5 (2 repetitions)	
4:08	Akpwon returns to Song #6 (5 repetitions)	
4:33	Akpwon calls Song #7 (23 repetitions)	
4:37		Itótele calls *ichachalekefun*
5:23	(End of track)	

is distinguished by the positioning of the itótele's chachá (top line of staff). The chachá slaps on the "and-of-2" and "and-of-5" in each bar create a polymetric (duple) tension against the ternary feel of the okónkolo.

"Hueso" *(2:04–3:17; Figures 4.10 and 4.11)*

The term *hueso* is not accepted by all Cuban master players, but many use the word to refer to this rhythm. In Spanish, hueso means "bone." In the basic version of hueso there are no itótele enú tones, making it sound melodically empty or skeletal; presumably, the name refers to this quality. In effect, there is no composite melody in hueso since the only element in the basic melodic plane is the iyá's enú. Hueso is used at the beginning of toques to various orishas, and also to accompany particular songs, often at moments when an intensification of musical energy is required, as is the case in this recording. Hueso, unlike yakotá and other generic and orisha-specific toques, is a rhythm in which the itótele can "speak" relatively freely, most often with closed or muff

Figure 4.7. *Tone key to batá transcriptions.*

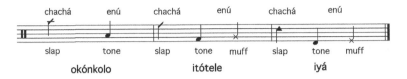

Figure 4.8. *Yakotá, basic rhythm.*

Figure 4.9. *Yakotá, composite sketch.*

Figure 4.10. *Hueso, basic rhythm.*

Figure 4.11. *Hueso, composite sketch.*

tones, and is not required to answer with a particular phrase when the iyá makes a call. This freedom is facilitated by the melodic emptiness in the basic itótele line.[32]

Drummers are not required to respond with hueso when the singer calls Song #2, "Odu aremu o wimbio." A typical accompaniment to this song would be the "ride pattern" heard between 3:33 and 3:47 in Oba Ilú's recording.[33] The choice of hueso was more than likely dictated by the iyá player's perception that musical energy (in terms of density of texture and tempo) needed to be propelled forward at that moment.[34] Hueso's syncopated itótele slap on the chachá, in combination with its relatively active iyá pattern, (and the resultant more differentiated rhythmic bed), has a tendency to push the time more than the ride pattern with its clearly ternary feel. The placement of hueso here demonstrates how the iyá player can make choices, within limits, based on his sense of what is needed to make the music work.

Tambor for "Baba mi chokoto aremu kwelaye"
(3:17–3:33; Figures 4.12 and 4.13)

This rhythmic sequence accompanies only a single song in the repertoire, "Baba mi chokoto aremu kwelaye" (Song #3 in our tratado), and does not appear at any other time. It is one of many examples from the batá repertoire in which the melody created between the enús of the iyá and itótele closely mimics a particular song text—specifically that of the choral response beginning with the phrase "Baba mi chokoto" (see transcription). In this type of song-specific toque,[35] the iyá's and itótele's enús create tightly interlocked composite melodies. Also, the iyá's chachá reinforces the itótele's part of the melody by playing at the same time as itótele's enú. When the akpwon calls for the song "Baba mi chokoto aremu

---

32. The relative freedom experienced by the itótele during this rhythm is most apparent during vocal accompaniment. At 2:20 and 2:58 in the recording, the itótele riffs in response to iyá calls (that themselves correspond to the choral entrances in this section).

33. In the recent *Abbilona* recordings of Obatalá praise songs (García 1990), for instance, the more typical ride pattern is heard (listen to the disc entitled *Obatalá,* track 4 at 5:13).

34. The only way to know why Jáuregui made this choice at this point would be to ask him (not currently feasible), but both Orlando Fiol and Michael Spiro agreed with our sense that considerations of tempo and energy probably dictated his choice.

35. "Tambor" is a term used by Orlando Fiol for any toque that imitates a song text; *invento* is another common Spanish term for these types of toques, which are thought to be relatively recent additions to the batá repertoire (Altmann, Fiol, Spiro, p.c.).

FIGURE 4.12. *Tambor, basic rhythm and chant.*

drum melodies imitate chorus

kwelaye," the iyá player responds immediately with a call for this toque. Listeners will note that as the itótele enters with its new pattern, its chachá shifts so that the rhythmic bed has a ternary feel. When done expertly, as it is here, listeners experience a smooth shift in energy from the previous polymetric beds to tambor's evenly subdivided, motoric drive.

"Ride Pattern" (3:33–3:47; Figures 4.14 and 4.15)

There is no known name for the toque played here when the akpwon calls the song "Eriwode, eriwode." This rhythm is a melodically spare framework with a ternary rhythmic bed. As in hueso, the toque contains no composite melody to speak of. We refer to it as ride pattern[36] since it appears before and between imitative song toques like "Baba mi chokoto aremu kwelaye." Drummers usually play it at the beginning or in the middle of tratados.Its appearance at this point in the recording represents another moment in which the iyá player makes a choice about the performance. Typically, "Eriwode, eriwode" would be accompanied by ñongo, yet the iyá player delays calling ñongo until the following "montuno" song ("Obatalá belona . . .") begins at 3:47. The delay builds tension and enhances the sense of arrival created by the next song, particularly because of the reentry of the itótele's enú. If the iyá player had chosen to call ñongo immediately, or to play an extended introduction/call (another typical choice), some of the sense of anticipation would have been lost.

36. John Amira and Orlando Fiol use this term.

FIGURE 4.13. *Tambor, composite sketch.*

rhythmic bed

O-du - du kwe - la-ye   BA-BA MI   CHO - KOTO/ARE-MU   KWE-LA - YE
composite melody

Ñongo (3:47–4:37; Figures 4.16 and 4.17)

Ñongo is a frequently occurring song toque played for virtually every orisha. In the Oru Cantado, drummers may play ñongo at the beginning or near the end of tratado sequences, but only briefly. In the final Güemilere, however, they play it often and develop it extensively with many conversations and variations on the itótele and iyá. Ñongo is simple in structural terms, yet can be hard to execute. This is because it must stay on the "forward edge" of the beat to maintain energy, but cannot be played too fast or the song texts that it accompanies will become unpronounceable. Ñongo is distinctive in batá repertoire because the calls and answers heard between the iyá and itótele are quite individualistic compared to other rhythms, requiring flexibility and virtuosity.[37] It is transitional and exciting, often creating a bridge between the opening of a tratado and its up-tempo conclusion.

Ichachalekefun (4:37–5:23; Figures 4.18, 4.19, 4.20)

Ichachalekefun (also referred to below as "chacha," without an accent on the final "a") is one of the most frequently played song toques in the repertoire; it appears at the end of tratados in both the Oru Cantado and Güemilere sections of the ceremony. A crowd pleaser, it is among the most rhythmically dense toques; commercial music that makes use of the batás often features it. Ichachalekefun typically follows ñongo. Chacha is one of only a few toques in which the okónkolo departs from the basic pulse and improvises along with

---

37. Schweitzer (2003) is the first work ever published on this important rhythm. He notes in analyzing a recording of ñongo by the younger Cuban group Abbilona that in contemporary practice the itótele and iyá players practically become equal partners in creating improvised conversations.

FIGURE 4.14. *Ride pattern, basic rhythm.*

FIGURE 4.15. *Ride pattern, composite sketch.*

FIGURE 4.16. *Ñongo, basic rhythm.*

FIGURE 4.17. *Ñongo, composite sketch.*

FIGURE 4.18. *Ichachalekefun, basic rhythm.*

the larger drums. Most commonly, the iyá marks beat one of the measure in chacha, though in certain moments and conversational exchanges downbeats are deemphasized, creating an ungrounded, floating effect in which the musicians feel the pulse together without actually playing it. The collective virtuosity of an ensemble shines in moments like these. Ichachalekefun is also notable because its basic "swing" is somewhere in between duple and triple meter. The itótele's pattern determines how the meter feels. This drum is also important because its chachá strokes are not evenly spaced, creating an asymmetry that drives the momentum forward.[38] Scholars typically transcribe the itótele line in 4/4, as in figure 4.18, yet its feel is often somewhere between duple and triple.[39] We have notated both the basic okónkolo pattern and a common variant from which *okónkoleros* initiate their improvisations. Once the okónkolo changes to its new pattern, the rhythmic bed becomes more subdivided and syncopated, adding to the intensity.

Drum Talk in "Obbatala"

Let us proceed now to the variations, conversations, and improvisations played by the drummers in response to the singer and to each other. As noted, our analysis in this section will concentrate primarily on drum talk in Yakotá, Tam-

38. In practically every batá toque, the itótele's chachá is evenly spaced across the clave. In ichachalekefun, by contrast, the chachá slaps fall on beats "3" and "and-of-4" of each bar of four.

39. In Matanzas, drummers playing *chacha* begin in triple meter and then shift later towards a duple feel as the energy and tempo build. In Havana, the meter stays more or less "in between," depending on the ensemble's taste.

FIGURE 4.19. *Standard okónkolo variation.*

bor, and Ichachalekefun. Figure 4.21 tracks overall musical events by time code in each of the three sections analyzed in detail, with song entrances indicated in boldface.

Variations in Yakotá: Re-combination and Effective Placement of Motives

In Oba Ilú's recording the drums stay in yakotá longer than in any other rhythm, due in part to the length of Song #1: five claves. The iyá's calls are relatively infrequent in this section and it plays few variations on its basic rhythm; this marks the ensemble's style as relatively "conservative" or "old school."[40] The relatively long time spent in yakotá results in a more effective contrast when the drums move into faster tempos, denser textures, and frequent conversational exchanges. At 0:26, the iyá delays its second enú note, but this is the only moment that it decorates its melody independently of conversations with the itótele (figure 4.22).

During yakotá, the iyá player calls the itótele to answer seven times, using four different rhythmic variations. Call #1 and itótele's response to it, heard at 0:15, 0:34, and 1:50, are basic, standard variations heard in yakotá (figure 4.23).

Calls #2 and #3 are the same length as Call #1 and use material both from iyá's basic pattern and from Call #1. In each case, the itótele gives the same simple response shown above, adding one open tone on the "and" of beat 6 before its open-tone downbeat on beat 1. Call #2 (heard at 0:45 and 1:08) takes iyá's basic melody and repeats it at twice its normal frequency. This is what Schweitzer calls "contraction"; compare the normal iyá open tones in figure 4.8 to those marked in the first and second measures.

Call #2 thus represents less of a rhythmic departure from the basic toque than other iyá variations during yakotá. Call #3 (heard at 0:52) takes the motive at the end of Call #1—a flam into three eighth note open tones—and repeats it. This cutting up and recombining of short phrases to produce variations is typical of Afro-Cuban traditional drum music (figures 4.24 and 4.25).[41]

40. Compare the yakotá heard on Abbilona's CD "Ochún," track 2; calls appear much more frequently.

41. François Zayas, p.c. The art of creating *quinto* phrases in Afro-Cuban rumba (secular, folkloric vocal and drum music) involves recombination of phrases and pieces of phrases in much the same way.

FIGURE 4.20. *Ichachalekefun, composite sketch.*

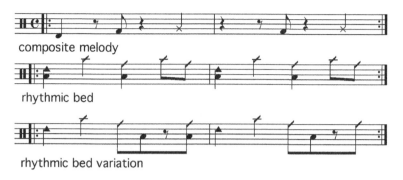

composite melody

rhythmic bed

rhythmic bed variation

Call #4 (beginning at 1:22, concluded by 1:42; figures 4.26 and 4.27) is a much longer exchange, quite different from the first three calls. Schweitzer refers to this as a "continuing conversation" (exchanges that go on for more than one clave in which the drums break out of their basic patterns), as opposed to a "simple call" (an exchange completed within one clave in which the drums stay on their respective sides of the clave).[42] The iyá alters its basic pattern and repeats the new rhythm over and over, provoking the itótele to repeat its simple response numerous times. The iyá's altered pattern, with the chachá playing on the "and-of-1" and on beat 4 in each bar, changes the rhythmic bed for a time to a more asymmetrical and syncopated feel than the basic bed of yakotá, which in turn intensifies the musical energy under the third cycle of Song #1.

The iyá concludes the exchange by taking the last motive of Call #1 (four open tones) and playing it three times. The itótele responds by ornamenting its two subsequent open tones more substantially than in its simple response. Itótele's conclusion goes on two bars (bars 10 and 11) past the point where the iyá stops its alteration. This appears be a decision by the itótele player to balance the iyá's long conversation with a slightly longer-than-normal conclusion.[43]

The placement of drum variations accompanying song and dance can strongly affect the buildup of musical energy at crucial moments. For example, the entrance of the chorus in any song is a significant point of arrival and can be enhanced by the drummers. The iyá may call for a conversation right before the

42. The "continuing conversations" that Schweitzer examines in ñongo are more varied than this relatively simple continuous repetition of the same figure heard from 1:22 to 1:34. Note that in ñongo, unlike yakotá, drum variations correspond closely in a rhythmic sense to cycles of the clave.

43. Schweitzer also suggests that this sense of proportion sometimes determines the length of itótele responses.

FIGURE 4.21. *Musical events in "Obbatalá."*

Time Code	Event Description
0:00	**The akpwon calls Song #1 "Odudu Aremu..."** (it repeats 3 times, lead-chorus)
0:03	**The iyá player calls yakotá.** It continues for 34 clave repetitions through the song change at 1:47
0:15	The iyá calls the itótele for the first time (Yakotá, call #1)
0:18	The itótele responds simply (see transcription below)
0:20	First chorus entrance
0:22-0:24	The akpwon says, *"Hekua Obatalá, Hekua Ye Unle!"*
0:26	Iyá delays the second note of its melody (a variation, not a call)
0:34	Iyá calls again at 0:15 (#1) in the same place relative to the song melody
0:36	Itótele gives the same response as it did at 0:18
0:38	Second entrance of the akpwon
0:44	A male voice in the chorus says *"Hekua Ye Unle!"*
0:45	Iyá calls by playing its melody three times in sequence (call #2)
0:47	Itótele gives the same response as at 0:18
0:52	Iyá omits its enú strokes, then doubles the second half of its call from 0:15; the call falls in same place relative to the song melody (call #3)
0:54	Itótele gives same response as at 0:18
0:56	Second entrance of chorus
1:08	Iyá repeats its call from 0:45 (call #2), at 1:10. The same itótele response is given, but the conversation falls earlier in the melody than in previous instances
1:13	Third akpwon entrance
1:22-1:42	Iyá begins a repetitive melodic figure that begins with an open tone on the "muff side" of the itótele melody (call #4). In response, itótele repeats its simple response over and over. The sequence repeats seven times before the iyá calls to resolve at 1:34. Iyá's resolution is essentially its first simple call repeated three times, while the itótele continues its simple response. Itótele's resolution, starting at 1:37, covers three cycles of yakotá and is more complex and extended than the previous response. This longer interaction bridges the chorus' third entrance at 1:30. By 1:42 the drums are back to their standard patterns.
1:47	**The akpwon calls Song #2, the montuno to *"Odudu Aremu"*** (repeated twice, lead-chorus); drums continue in yakotá (five more claves)
1:50	First chorus entrance; iyá calls as at 0:15 (call #1)
1:52	Itótele responds as at 0:18
1:53	Second akpwon entrance
1:57	Chorus entrance
2:00	**Akpwon calls Song #3 *"Ye...Odu aremu o wimbio..."***
2:04	**Iyá calls hueso** (it continues for 24 claves); increase in tempo and intensity
3:15	**Akpwon calls Song #4 *"Baba mi chokoto aremu kwelaye"*** (repeated 3 times, lead-chorus)

FIGURE 4.21. *Continued*

Time Code	Event Description
3:17	**Iyá calls tambor *"Baba mi chokoto aremu kwelaye"*** (continues for 5 claves)
3:18	First chorus entrance
3:21	Second akpwon entrance
3:24	Second chorus entrance
3:27	Third akpwon entrance
3:30	Third chorus entrance
3:33	**Akpwon calls Song #5 *"Eriwode, eriwode"*** (repeated twice, lead-chorus); iyá shifts to ride pattern (continues for 5 claves) - itótele plays no enú until ñongo
3:44	**Akpwon calls Song #6 *"Obatalá belona..."*** (repeated 3 times, lead-chorus)
3:47	**Iyá calls ñongo** (continues for 21.5 claves); first chorus entrance
3:59	**Akpwon returns to Song #5** (repeated twice, lead-chorus)
4:08	**Akpwon returns to Song #6** (repeated five times, lead-chorus)
4:33	**Akpwon calls Song #7 *"Ayembele to"*** (repeated 23 times, lead-chorus, into fade)
4:37	**Itótele calls ichachalekefun on the akpwon's third repetition of the song** (continues for 22 claves, into fade)
4:38-4:44	"Straight" ichachalekefun for 3 claves
4:45	Iyá opens conversations with two short calls to conversation (1 clave each); at top of first conversation, okónkolo goes to alternate pattern and continues in it
4:48-4:56	Iyá calls long conversation (2 claves in length) followed by two more short conversations
4:56-5:00	Unembellished ichachalekefun for 3 claves (extra iyá melody notes in the first 2 claves; extra itótele melody note in the second clave)
5:01-5:06	Iyá omits the enú for 3 claves; itótele adds extra melody notes in the first clave
5:07-5:11	Iyá brings the enú back in with two short conversations
5:11	Iyá plays straight, but itótele continues speaking for one clave
5:12-5:16	Iyá calls two more short conversations
5:17	"Straight" ichachalekefun for 1 clave into fade
5:23	TRACK ENDS

chorus' entrance in order to highlight it. Alternately, if a new song dictates a change to another toque, the iyá player may time his call so that the new toque is fully established only when the chorus answers the akpwon for the first time. Figure 4.28 shows how Mario Jáuregui places his calls in yakotá relative to the songs.

In five of the seven short calls and responses listed here, drum variations set up the chorus' or the akpwon's entrance so that the drums finish their conversation and return to their basic patterns one measure before a new cycle of

FIGURE 4.22. *Iyá variation.*

FIGURE 4.23. *Call #1 and itótele simple response.*

FIGURE 4.24. *Iyá Call #2 and itótele simple response.*

FIGURE 4.25. *Iyá Call #3 and itótele simple response.*

FIGURE 4.26. *Yakotá's basic rhythmic bed and the rhythmic bed variation created by Call #4's continuing conversation.*

FIGURE 4.27. *Iyá and itótele from 1:22. through 1:42. Call #4 and extended response.*

the song begins. Their apparently random placement thus turns out upon closer analysis to be chosen with precision. The only exceptions are the iyá variation at 0:26 and Call #2 at 0:45. The variation at 0:26 comes in the middle of the melody; it serves to fill in a space in the vocal line and lead into the third phrase of the song. Call #2 on the iyá, by contrast, directly mimics and supports the vocal rhythm sung by the akpwon. The placement of both these exceptional phrases thus relates to vocal performance as well. As an example of how calls coordinate with vocal performance, consider figure 4.29 (0:45–0:56). It includes Call #2 beginning in measure 3 and Call #3 beginning in measure 7. Call #2 mimics the rhythm of the akpwon's line, whereas Call #3 does the same, as well as setting up the chorus' entrance a measure before it begins.

Call #4, the extended conversation beginning at 1:22, initially creates drive under the akpwon's third repetition of the melody. As it continues under the following chorus, however, anticipation builds about what will come next. This turns out to be a shorter montuno-like version of Song #1—what we call Song #2—at 1:47, and then a transition into an entirely new song and rhythm at 2:00. The placement of Call #4 thus relates closely to vocal performance as well, contributing to the climax of Song #1. Call #4 ends during the fourth clave of the choral response, allowing the drums to play their basic pattern for the next vocal entrance. It introduces a great deal of new rhythmic material, suggesting that if the same variations are repeated many times, they begin to

FIGURE 4.28. *Song-rhythm relationships in Yakotá.*

Rhythmic Figure	Placement against song	Function
Call #1 at 0:15	Called leading into the 5th clave of the song	Sets up 1st chorus entrance
Variation at 0:26	Leading into 3rd clave of song	Fills space in chorus melody; sets up 3rd clave repetition
Call #1 at 0:34	Called leading into the 5th clave	Sets up 2nd akpwon entrance
Call #2 at 0:45	Called at the 3rd clave	Reinforces vocal rhythm of akpwon
Call #3 at 0:52	Called leading into the 5th clave	Sets up 2nd chorus entrance
Call #2 at 1:08	Called at end of 4th clave	Sets up 3rd akpwon entrance
Call #4 at 1:22	Called at the end of the 3rd clave while the akpwon is singing, this conversation bridges the 3rd chorus entrance and concludes at the beginning of the 4th clave	Sets up the next akpwon entrance which is the change to Song #2 (consisting of the last two segments of song #1)
Call #1 at 1:50	Called at the 1st chorus of Song #2 (one clave in length)	Sets up 2nd akpwon entrance, Song #2

lose their effect and must be balanced with freer ones. Jáuregui, like all outstanding iyá players, has mastered the art of enriching the basic toque to highlight certain points in the melody, and of giving the groove a kinetic push forward when needed.

Tambor:"Baba mi chokoto aremu kwelaye": The Batá Drums Speak

We do not analyze hueso's variations and conversations here, but proceed instead to the third toque, what we call tambor. We chose this rhythm for analysis because it is distinct from others in the sequence, and because it emphasizes the close relationships between drumming, speech, and song in the batá repertoire. As soon as Marta Galarraga calls Song #4, the drummers are required to respond with the rhythm that specifically accompanies this song and no other. No one knows ahead of time when or even if she plans to sing it; the iyá player nevertheless responds at a moment's notice and makes the following call to the itótele at the end of the akpwon's first line (3:17; figure 4.30).

As in the previous rhythmic change, this feel is different from what comes before and after. As soon as the itótele answers the iya's call to enter, it changes the placement of its chachá to beats 2 and 5 of every bar instead of the "and-

FIGURE 4.29. *Voice, iyá, and itótele, 0:45–0:56.*

of-2" and "and-of-5." The rhythmic bed thus shifts to an unambiguously ternary feel (figure 4.31). Secondly, the itótele's enú begins to play again, but in this toque it has little freedom to improvise (though if the song were repeated more times, as in a ceremonial context, it is possible that the itótele would ornament its basic pattern). The iyá is also limited in the variations it can play; both drums are constrained because they are imitating speech/song. Note that the batás play this toque for a short time relative to previous sections of the tratado. From this point on the rhythmic shifts become more frequent.

Ichachalekefun: Collective Virtuosity

We now skip over a relatively short section in which the ensemble plays its ride pattern rhythm (3:33–3:47), and a longer, complex section based in ñongo with

FIGURE 4.30. *Drum transition from hueso to tambor.*

FIGURE 4.31. *Tambor: Iyá and itótele, 3:19–3:32.*

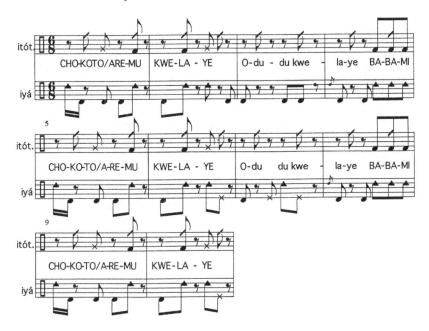

many variations (3:47–4:37)[44] to focus on the final rhythm, ichachalekefun. The entrance of ichachalekefun is the most dramatic change of the tratado; the feel shifts strongly toward duple subdivision at this point. It is very important to note, however, that chacha's characteristic swing derives from the ternary subdivisions that are still felt by the players and expressed in some of the parts—it is precisely this ambiguity in the rhythm that makes batá drumming difficult to notate and virtually impossible to learn without a teacher to emulate. In this particular recording, for example, the okónkolo part and the coro's melody are clearly duple once the rhythm is fully established (at about 4:38), but the itótele and the lead singer still use many ternary-feeling subdivisions in their renderings.

Several other characteristic features of this rhythm stand out from other sections. First, at 4:37 the itótele and not the iyá makes the call to change the toque. Iyá entrance calls for this toque do exist, but the itótele's *llamada* makes for the smoothest transition without disrupting ñongo or obscuring any part of its basic melody. Also, the itótele call's ambiguous meter serves as an effective bridge between the triple pulse of ñongo and the more duple character of

44. Schweitzer (2003) includes extended analysis of ñongo, including characteristic solos, variations, and insightful comments on the dynamics of performance in that toque.

FIGURE 4.32. *Itótele's call to ichachalekefun in three feels.*

ichachalekefun. The call at 4:37 can be interpreted in several ways; three possibilities are transcribed in figure 4.32. The first two represent ways that the call on Oba Ilú's recording could be notated.

The apostrophes in the first two calls in figure 4.32 are meant to indicate a very subtle sense of phrasing or pause between the three groups of notes. Some itótele players may play with a more distinct feeling of rest between the three groups, as in the third possibility.

As in other toques, song entrances and pauses in song melodies can be important points for variation or conversation in ichachalekefun. However, in this recording there is only a single song performed over the rhythm, consisting of rapid call-response alternations. It does not leave many long spaces between akpwon and chorus, and thus does not allow time for the drums to set up a transition from one to another. As a result, conversations and variations are relatively independent of the vocals, although the drums still must support the overall increase in tempo and intensity.

Ichachalekefun is one of only two toques in the repertoire in which the okónkolo improvises extensively (the other is *iyesá*). In our selection, the okónkolo's variations appear independently of deliberate signals from the other drums, yet the player nevertheless seems to alter his pattern in response to changes in their rhythms. The okónkolo begins the toque playing an altered basic pattern (figure 4.34, bar 4). When the iyá calls the first conversation at 4:45, he moves to it even before the call is complete (bar 8).[45] The okónkolo's

45. According to Michael Spiro (p.c.), older Havana *okonkoleros* only move to the improvising part after the iyá and itótele play a long conversation (2–3 claves). Younger okónkolo players, by contrast, often alter their pattern after a short conversation, or may not even wait for conversations to begin their riffs. Overall, younger players improvise

new pattern is more syncopated than the original; in combination with the uneven spacing of the itótele's chachá, it helps create one of the densest textures heard in the batá repertoire. In improvisations from 4:45 through the end of the track, the okónkolo returns to one phrase repeatedly (it first appears in bar 8 of the transcription)—a slap on "2" and an open tone on the "and-of-3." In bars 26–31 of the transcription in figure 4.34 (5:01 through 5:06), the okónkolo elaborates two-bar (clave-length) phrases that represent variations on this motive. In the first bar of each, the enú is silent or less active, in the second bar it plays more. These okónkolo phrases occur during a passage of maximum tension in the other drum parts, when the iyá omits its enú stroke on the downbeat in order to create the strongest possible impact when it subsequently reenters. The absence of the iyá's enú in this section guarantees that the okónkolo pattern is heard clearly, along with the composite chachá strokes of all three drums. Coinciding with the return of the iyá's enú to the texture, the okónkolo plays its basic rhythm from bar 32 through 37 (5:07 through 5:12). Starting in bar 38 through the end of the track, it shifts again, playing a contracted version of its alternate basic pattern.

In ichachalekefun the drums play sequences of short calls (with the iyá improvising mainly on the three-side and the itótele playing on the two-side), or combinations of long calls and short calls, to create interactions that last several claves. These interludes alternate with periods of unornamented performance. Older players (such as Mario Jáuregui and others of his generation) tend to play only characteristic short and long calls, with some variations, whereas some contemporary groups have worked out long sequences of their own material. Older performers sometimes frown on such experimentation.

Calls and responses in ichachalekefun typically overlap each other less than in other rhythms, consisting more of distinct alternating phrases of half a clave length. In Oba Ilú's recording, the iyá and itótele variations do not overlap at all with the exception of the second clave of the long call (4:48–4:52, bars 12 through the downbeat of bar 16). This is a characteristic, formulaic exchange in ichachalekefun, although its exact interpretation may vary from ensemble to ensemble. In the first clave of the call—bars 12 and 13 (4:48–4:49)—the iyá plays the practically the same phrase that it does in bars 14 and 15. However, the itótele's response differs from the first clave to the second. The itótele recog-

---

more than older players. Several of our teachers have said that they do not consider it appropriate to play too many *floreos* (ornaments) on *fundamento* drums. John Amira (p.c.), for instance, states that too many floreos interfere with the "speech" of the drums, that their composite melodies get lost in too many improvisations.

nizes the call in bar 12 and responds on the two-side of the clave with a variation (bar 13, 4:49). The next phrase (bars 14–15) is a tightly interlocked polymetric exchange in which the iyá plays where the itótele rests. Both drums play
on both sides of the clave here, although they never obscure each other's
melodic strokes (the iyá plays more melody on the three-side and itótele plays
more on the 2-side).[46] The short iyá call (4:52) that follows in bar 16, and the
corresponding itótele answer in bar 17 (4:53), along with the short call and answer in bars 18 and 19, represents a typical resolution of this long call.

Sometimes the drums move on from ichachalekefun to yet another toque
that represents an even higher peak of intensity, but tratados frequently end
here, as this one does. Because it is the rhythmic climax, chacha may not follow the pattern found in other toques such as ñongo of including consistently
longer and more frequent conversations. Drummers still improvise to maintain
or increase the intensity of the accompaniment whenever they deem it necessary. Nonetheless, the basic iyá and itótele patterns may be played many times
without variation and still create a high energy level, especially if the ensemble
plays with *sabor,* that almost indefinable collective swing that can make the
toque percolate.[47] Figure 4.33 describes conversational activity in ichachalekefun, clave by clave.

This version of ichachalekefun is typical, in its frequent use of short calls,
and less frequent use of the long call, which would represent a longer, more turbulent departure from the basic feel of the rhythm. Figure 4.34 is a complete
transcription of ichachalekefun (4:37–5:22).

Oba Ilú's recording fades to a close at 5:22. It is usually only in folkloric
and secular musical arrangements that batás end in a clean, coordinated fashion. In religious settings, tratados often end abruptly with a signal from the
singer or the iyá player. The music usually stops during a ceremony in order
for specific ritual events to take place, such as following the instructions of the
orishas who come down.

46. See bars 14 and 15 (4:50–4:52), the second clave of the long call. The iyá plays on
the first and the fifth triplet beats of the first bar, and on the third triplet beat of the second bar, or once every four beats. Itótele's pattern (both chachá and enú) fills in all the
beats in between the iyá's notes (2,3,4 . . . 6,1,2 . . . 4,5,6).

47. Students of batá drumming often describe a disorienting, but pleasurable, feeling of not knowing which head is producing which sound when they experience the
greater-than-the-sum-of-its-parts, tight interlock between the drums in ichachalekefun
and other very rhythmically dense, up tempo toques (*Osain, Tui tui,* and *Meta Meta* are
other examples).

FIGURE 4.33. *Variations and calls in Ichachalekefun by Clave.*

Clave #

1 (4:38, bar 2)	Regular ichachalekefun; okónkolo in altered pattern
2	Regular
3	Regular
4 (4:44, bar 8)	Short Call 1; okónkolo goes to alternate pattern with variations
5 (4:46, bar 10)	Short Call 2
6 (4:48, bar 12)	Long Call, 1st clave
7	Long Call, 2nd clave
8 (4:52, bar 16)	Long Call resolution (= Short call 2a)
9 (4:54, bars 17-18)	Short Call 3
10	Regular (with slight variation on the iyá)
11	Regular (with slight variation on the iyá)
12	Regular
13 (5:01, bar 26)	Iyá enú is silent; itótele plays variation at end of the clave; okónkolo shifts to two-bar riffs
14	Iyá enú still silent
15	Iyá enú still silent
16 (5:07, bars 31-32)	Iyá enú returns with Short Call 4; okónkolo plays straight again
17 (5:08, bars 33-34)	Short Call 3a
18	Regular
19 (5:12, bars 37-38)	Short Call 2a; okónkolo goes to contraction of first pattern
20 (5:14, bar 40)	Short Call 1a
21	Regular
22	Regular into fade...

Conclusion

In five brief minutes, Oba Ilú's recording "Obbatalá" provides an introduction to the intricacies of Afro-Cuban religious music; it has required many words and diagrams to begin to explain them. The aesthetics of this piece are similar to those of many other African-influenced traditions throughout the Americas, sacred and secular. Most integrate multiple artistic media (music, dance, costumes, visual art), allow for considerable improvisation, and require a high degree of sensitivity to group dynamics. Given their aesthetic complexity, musicians who play batá music commonly consider pieces such as the tratado to Obatalá as part of a "classical" tradition. Yet because of the close ties between these drums and Santería, a religion that has long been persecuted, the music has been frequently stigmatized by outsiders. It is also the case that batás are associated with poorer, socially marginal communities, that its practitioners

FIGURE 4.34. *Ichachalekefun: iyá and itótele, 4:37 to end.*

have guarded their knowledge from others, and that they typically have no training in Western music and thus cannot not discuss their drumming in academic terms even if they wished to.

As little as twenty years ago, bataleros might have considered analyses such as ours as violations of religious sanctity. Because of the legacy of persecution associated with the Santería, concern for the privacy rights of the Afro-Cuban community in this sense have been expressed many times through the years (e.g., Friedman 1982; Villamil in Vélez 2000) and continue to be an important issue.

FIGURE 4.34. *Continued*

The fact that our analysis was conducted by a woman and a religious outsider may be controversial to some individuals even now. Nevertheless, we believe the essay is appropriate for at least three reasons. First, we base our observations largely on informal conversations with experts and on percussion lessons unassociated with sacred events. Second, the analysis does not reveal sensitive ritual secrets. Third, general interest in Santería has grown considerably since the 1980s and with it the willingness of performers to share their expertise.

Our analysis foregrounds the general structures and rhythms of batá tratados as well as the fundamentally emergent and interactive nature of effective

FIGURE 4.34. *Continued*

performance. Musicians make constant split-second decisions about when and how to alter their rhythms and melodies in accordance with the dynamics of a given event. This is evident in the switch to the tambor rhythm discussed previously, in the use of rhythmic variations to enhance song melodies, in decisions about when to call sectional rhythmic shifts, and in other ways. Both the iyá and itótele constantly evaluate the energy level and rhythmic density of the performance, filling in and creating additional rhythmic material as needed. The best okónkolo players are also constantly aware of changes in the music, as the "feel" of their playing can have a profound effect on musical dynamics.

In the same way, the akpwon has considerable flexibility to improvise, and to regulate the energy or intensity of the event at any given time.

In the tratado to Obatalá and in most religious contexts, the akpwon and drummers work together in building musical intensity. They begin slowly and in a relatively prescribed fashion, but by the end of the piece, they increase tempo and make improvisation a more central component of performance. Tratados in the batá repertoire have clear openings, middle sections, and up tempo final sections. Each song called by the akpwon opens a subcycle whose length is determined by the musicians according to the demands of the musical-spiritual situation at any given moment. Repetition serves to increase tension and energy, like the gradual heating of an engine as it turns over and over, with changes from section to section feeling like shifts from lower to higher gears.[48] Thus, the musical forms of tratados are similar to other African and African-descended musics that are cyclical, open-ended, and context-determined (in contrast to fixed or non-improvised forms in traditions elsewhere). The open-ended progression from "cool" more structured beginnings to "hot" open-ended final sections is also the basis for popular music form in many parts of the Americas, especially those where African-derived cultural expressions have flourished.

Although the purpose of this chapter was to discuss musical style and structure, we stress again that the separation of music from context is especially problematic in the case of batá repertoire. Batá drumming has as its primary purpose praise of and communication with divine beings. Its significance for practitioners cannot be appreciated without recognition of this fact. Even more important, the parameters of music-making in traditional contexts are inseparable from factors such as the need to induce possession. Batá performance never involves the interpretation of rigidly precomposed music; it emerges in dialogue with particular communities and ritual needs, as well as through the efforts of individual performers, each with their own respective styles. The creation of written scores for the purpose of analysis has heuristic value, but we should never lose sight of the influence of the countless contextual variables and religious parameters that help determine the substance of a performance.

We hope this chapter will make batá music more comprehensible to a wider audience and that this in turn will lead to increased appreciation of and respect for all African-derived traditions. Considerable additional reading, or experience working with religious elders, would be necessary in order to understand the religious philosophies that have given rise to the batás. Still, an appreciation for the music as such constitutes an important initial step in cross-

---

48. Thanks to Michael Spiro for this metaphoric language (p.c.).

cultural understanding. We hope that the listener will learn to hear this music not only as intricate and virtuosic but also as a beautiful form of expression with its own internal logic and aesthetic parameters.

References

Altmann, Thomas. 1998. *Cantos lucumí a los orichas (a Santería songbook)*. Hamburg: Oché.

Amira, John, and Steven Cornelius. 1992. *The Music of Santería: Traditional Rhythms of the Batá Drums*. Crown Point, Ind.: White Cliffs Media.

Brown, David H. 2003. *Santería Enthroned: Art, Ritual, and Innovation in an Afro-Cuban Religion*. Chicago: University of Chicago Press.

Charry, Eric. 1996. "A Guide to the Jembe." *Percussive Notes* 34(2):66–72.

Coburg, Adrian. 2002a. *Oru seco. Batá scores*. 5th ed., rev. Bern, Switzerland: Adrian Coburg.

———. 2002b. *Toques especiales. Batá scores*. 4th ed., rev. Bern, Switzerland: Adrian Coburg.

Cornelius, Steve. 1990. "Drumming for the Orichas: The Reconstruction of Tradition in New York City." P. Manuel, ed., *Essays on Cuban Music: North American and Cuban Perspectives*. New York: University Press of America, 139–155.

Delgado, Kevin. 1997. *Negotiating the demands of culture: Batá drumming in San Diego*. Master's thesis, UCLA.

———. 2001. *Iyesá: Afro-Cuban music and culture in contemporary Cuba*. Ph.D. dissertation, UCLA.

García, Nanette, and Maurice Minichino. 2001. *The Sacred Music of Cuba: Batá Drumming Matanzas Style*. Melantone Productions. Book and recording; practical performance guide.

Hagedorn, Katherine. 2001. *Divine Utterances. The Performance of Afro-Cuban Santería*. Washington, D.C.: Smithsonian Institution Press.

Mason, John. 1985. *Four New World Rituals*. New York: Yoruba Theological Association.

———. 1992. *Orin Orisa: Songs for Selected Heads*. New York: Yoruba Theological Association.

Mason, Michael. 2002. *Living Santería: Rituals and Experiences in an Afro-Cuban religion*. Washington D.C.: Smithsonian Institution Press.

Ortiz, Fernando. 1950. *La africanía de la música folklórica de Cuba*. Havana: Ministerio de Educación.

———. 1951. *Los bailes y el teatro de los negros en el folklore de Cuba*. Havana: Ministerio de Educación.

———.1954–5. *Los instrumentos de la música afrocubana*, 5 vols. Havana: Ministerio de Educación.

Pedroso, Lázaro (Ogún Tolá). 1995. *Obbedi, cantos a los orishas: Traducción e historia*. Havana: Artex.

Roberts, John Storm. 1972. *Black Music of Two Worlds*. New York: Original Music.

Sayre, Elizabeth. 2000. "Cuban Batá Drumming and Women Musicians: An Open Question." *CBMR Digest* 13:12–15.

Schweitzer, Kenneth. 2003. *Afro-Cuban batá drum aesthetics: developing individual and group technique, sound, and identity.* D.M.A. dissertation, University of Maryland, College Park, MD.

Summers, Bill. 2002. *Studies in Batá, Sacred Drum of the Yoruba, Havana and Matanzas.* Book and CD. New Orleans: Bilsum Music BMI.

Vélez, María Teresa. 2000. *Drumming for the Gods: The Life and Times of Felipe García Villamil, Santero, Palero and Abakuá.* Philadelphia: Temple University Press.

PART II

Isoperiodicity

From Strict to Discursive, with Variations

CHAPTER 5

Aka Polyphony

Music, Theory, Back and Forth

SUSANNE FÜRNISS

R esearch in ethnomusicology has shown that behind polyphonic performance in oral traditions there are patterns and sets of rules which are the
reference for any music making. The purpose of this chapter is to demonstrate
how a high degree of complexity in vocal polyphony may result from the simultaneous or successive variation of a substratum of puzzling simplicity. Although the rules in such performance are mainly implicit, they are based on an
autochthonous conception that reflects the complexity and links to the music's
social and symbolic signification.

These principles will be demonstrated through the polyphonic system of the
Aka from Central Africa with the help of five different versions of one song—
dìkòbò dámù dá sòmbé—that belongs to the divination repertoire *bòndó*. After
an introduction to Aka culture and a presentation of the problematics of analyzing oral polyphonies, I shall present the bases of the Aka's theoretical conception of polyphony with two series of rerecording, a process of analytical re-

This text is a largely augmented adaption of a previous article published in French:
"Rigueur et liberté: la polyphonie vocale des Pygmées Aka (Centrafrique)," in *Polyphonies
de tradition orale. Histoire et traditions vivantes,* C. Meyer (ed.), Paris, Créaphis, Coll.
Rencontres à Royaumont, 1993, 101–131. The basic material used here, both recordings
and fieldwork data, has been collected by Simha Arom between 1971 and 1983. His findings concerning the rules that underly Aka polyphony are illustrated in detail and linked
to later research on this music, including my own. I thank Simha Arom warmly for the
permission to use his material.

cording. The results will then be applied to solo and duo performances of the same piece, which will give additional insight into how the material is realized, modeled and transformed in collective "real-life" situations. The discussion will also touch on topics intimately related to this analytical work, such as the functionality of Aka music-making, fieldwork, linguistics, and apprenticeship.

Introduction to the Aka

The Aka live in the rain forest on both sides of the border between the Central African Republic and the Popular Republic of Congo. They belong to a group of populations widely called "Pygmies"[1] and to which belong the Mbuti— including the subgroups Efe, Asua, and Kango—from the Democratic Republic of Congo, the Twa from Rwanda, the Baka, Bakola/Bagyieli and Bedzan from Cameroon and the Babongo from Gabon. They all share the use of counterpoint as a musical technique to which one can add, for some of them, the yodel technique.

Originally hunter-gatherers (Bahuchet 1985), the Aka are now more and more sedentary and live partly from their own agriculture, in the immediate proximity of other populations of villagers of different ethnic groups (Thomas et al. 1981–2004; Kisliuk 1998:65). Their musical tradition testifies to their ancestral nomadic lives, as it is deeply structured by hunting (Olivier and Fürniss 1999:119–123): the majority of the musical repertoires are related—in a direct or indirect way—to this activity. One finds not only collective ritual repertoires preceeding or following a hunt but also others originally reserved for either men or women during the periods of the year when the men were out in the forest for weeks following game, while the women stayed at home. Figure 5.1 shows a representation of all musical repertoires of the Aka from Mongoumba in the very Eastern part of the Aka area.[2] In the inner circle of this schematic representation, you find the tools of music-making (voice, hand clapping, instruments), in the intermediate one the name of each repertoire, and in the outer one the circumstance or function of its execution.

---

1. As to the "invention" of the concept of "Pygmy," see Serge Bahuchet (1993). This term is derived from the Greek word *pugmaios,* "tall as an elbow." It refers to several different ethnic groups living along the equator on the African continent and speaking languages from different linguistic families. The criteria for grouping these people together are not very clear, but all of them share more or less a bundle of features such as small height, relatively clear skin, being originally hunter-gatherers and singing in polyphony.

2. This kind of circular representation, inspired by Arom (1994), is now used by several scholars working in Africa (Fernando-Marandola, Le Bomin, Olivier, Vallejo, and myself).

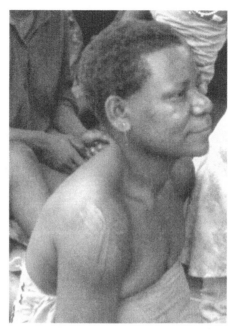

Moako, Central African Republic, Mongoumba, December 1990. Nineteen years after her first recording (CD track 10), she is still a major collaborator with ethnomusicologists. Photo by author.

Dialectal and musical variability is quite strong in this culture. Many songs and dances circulate with the people that move a lot throughout the area (Bahuchet 1995:61; Kisliuk 1998:99). As these movements reflect partially the dynamics of family links between lineages, the musical and choreographical repertoire is never identical from one place to the other, although the main repertoires and rhythms are the same.

A consequence of their nomadic past is that the Aka use only a few musical instruments, none of which is played without simultaneous singing. Most of the melodic instruments—such as one- and two-stringed musical bows, a harp-zither, a harp, and a pair of one-tone flutes[3]—accompany intimate songs. These can be sung by one singer alone, but the structure of the songs is nevertheless based on a multipart conception of call-and-response between a soloist and a polyphonic choir (Fürniss and Bahuchet 1995). Some readers might miss the mentioning of a harp or a lamellaphone, both widespread in this part of Central Africa. They may be heard in an Aka camp, but as these instruments

---

3. A four-hole notched flute seems not to be in use anymore. Music of these instruments is published on CD (Fürniss 1998).

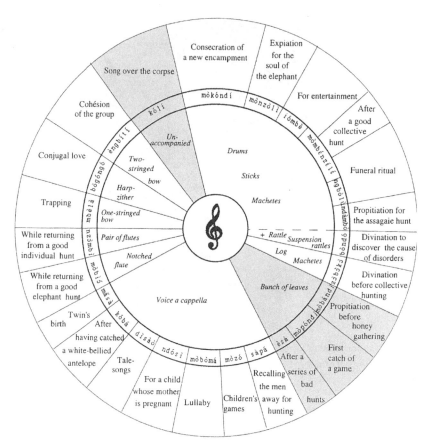

FIGURE 5.1. *The musical universe of the Aka. All Aka music is sung, with or without in-strumental accompaniment. The unshaded areas signify the use of handclapping; shaded areas denote its absence.*

have been borrowed recently from other populations, they have neither their own song repertoire, nor another social function than individual entertainment. This is why they are not included in figure 5.1.

Music-making is closely linked to spirituality: "The Aka present an extreme example where religion is nearly exclusively expressed through music and dance, without officiant, without prayer and without offerings, that is without any perceptible religious gesture . . ."[4] (Bahuchet 1995:59). Singing and dancing *is* the offering to the forest spirits and to the spirits of the ancestors that are supposed to take care of their children. But their attitude depends on human behavior toward them and within the living community. The verb *kàmuz-* denotes a musical aspect of the concept of happiness: "to be happy,"

4. Translations from Bahuchet's French are my own throughout.

"to agree," "to give the response in a song" (Bahuchet 1995:64–65). This explains why the majority of musical repertoires call on polyphonic singing and are—in one way or another—related to spirituality.

The religious component of music and dance is not always visible. Nevertheless, through the social dynamics that operate in a performance, even what appears as a mere "Saturday night" event is an important issue for the camp as a whole, as is demonstrated throughout Kisliuk (1998). In this sense, all Aka singing can be considered "a reflection of the community as well as a communion of religious essence" (Bahuchet 1995:64–65). In spite of the progressive loss of hunting rituals, the dances that belonged to them are often maintained and perpetuated in a context of entertainment when men and women meet to dance together.

The main rhythmic basis for singing and dancing is provided by two drums,[5] a pair of wooden percussion sticks and a pair of metal concussion blades to which can be added a rattle or a pair of suspension rattles attached to the legs of the main solo dancer. In practice, you might find that the percussion sticks are missing or that the rattle is added only in certain circumstances. Other repertoires are sung *a cappella* with a simple meter-defining accompaniment provided either by handclapping or by the flagellation of the body. The main function of flagellation is to purify the body of evil forces (Bahuchet 1995:62). In three ritual dances that call on purification of humans, this symbolic action is integrated in the musical activity: the legs are regularly struck with bunches of leaves which produce a thumping, but clearly audible sound that provides the meter for the singing of the dancers.

Each dance can be identified by its own polyrhythmic formula, which is a combination of different rhythms repeated together in a cyclic, or periodic structure. The generic name of a dance refers to this formula as well as to the specific choreography and the song repertoire that goes with it. The polyrhythmic formulæ for all Aka music are isolated and analyzed *in extenso* by Simha Arom (1991:486ff). His study further illustrates the principles that underly the process of rhythmic variation within a framework of strict periodicity.

The structure of Aka music is based on repeating cycles of either eight, twelve, or sixteen beats. Because for each song all cycles have strictly the same length, we call them isoperiodic. For most repertoires, each beat is split into three minimal values, or subdivisions, such that an 8 beat cycle has twenty-four possible "positions" at which a tone may be sung or a percussion instrument struck.[6] The regular recurrence of similar musical material at identical posi-

5. One repertoire calls for a struck wooden bar and a pair of metal concussion blades.
6. This is a ternary metricity. Some repertoires call on a binary metricity so that the beats are split into two or four minimal values.

tions of each cycle demonstrates the general rigour of the periodic framework (Arom 1991:408). This leads the author to talk of this music as *ostinatos* with variations.

Group singing is based on several different vocal parts that unfold simultaneously in polyphony. Two polyphonic techniques can be observed: counterpoint, in which voices are rhythmically and melodically independent, and homorhythmic singing in parallel intervals (Arom and Pahaut 1993; Fürniss 1999). We will concentrate here on the contrapuntal repertoire as it is this musical trait that distinguishes Aka music from their neighbors' music.

There are no professional musicians, every interested person can join in singing or learn to play an instrument.[7] Musical knowledge—as with knowledge in any other domain—is acquired by observation and imitation from birth on, as children are never kept apart from any musical activities of elders. They learn by trial and error with hardly any verbalized instruction. As for the practice of music-making, all members of the community have an equivalent status, that is, nobody earns his/her living from music making and nobody is excluded from a performance, although certain singers are more competent or virtuoso than others. The *kònzà-lémbò*, "master of the song," is the person who has acquired the most important musical knowledge (Bahuchet 1995:61). He/she masters not only the entire song repertoire but also the polyphonic parts of each song and sees to a complete and correct performance. A parallel function exists for the dance: the *kònzà-èbókà*, "master of the dance," or *ginda* (Kisliuk 1998:58) may gain a widespread reputation so that people come from far away to be initiated in the dance and its secrets.

Melodic and rhythmic variation is one of the main concerns of good Aka musicians and there is virtually no limit to the number of contrapuntal lines that can be interwoven. Thus, with the increasing number of participants, the polyphonic texture gets richer and leads to a more and more complex musical expression.

Research Method

Considering the great number of participants and voice-crossings, making a transcription and musical analysis from a conventional recording is extremely difficult, if not impossible. CD track 7 is a *tutti* version of the divination song,

---

7. Nevertheless, only men play instruments, except for the two-stringed bow, which is reserved for women.

dìkòbò dámù dá sòmbé, with the rhythmic accompaniment of two drums, struck metal blades and a rattle. An attentive listening gives the impression that under a dense sound magma there are nearly as many parts as there are singers. In fact, separating out the individual parts presents a formidable challenge.[8] Figure 5.2 presents another version of the same song with only six singers, three women and three men.[9] The different parts of the notation were obtained through a research technique I am about to explain, and they illustrate the aural phenomenon just experienced: some melodies are alike and meet for a while, but they do not stay identical for very long.

I shall not discuss the issues of transcribing Aka music with Western notation here. The latter is well-enough adapted to the notation of rhythms—under the condition that one abandons the concept of measures (Arom 1991:183). But as to the notation of melodies, it may certainly sometimes seem imprecise, as the Aka's realization of a degree of the scale may vary within a margin of a half-tone. Although melodic and harmonic fourths, fifths, and sevenths are quite clearly definable, intervals between neighboring degrees are less so. The melodic contour being an essential issue for the conduct of the constituent parts of the counterpoint, a graphic representation as proposed in Arom and Fürniss (1992) may be closer to the vernacular conception than transcription in staff notation. But the latter is more suited to introducing readers that are used to staff notation to an African repertoire.[10]

Given the complexity of a polyphonic performance and the absence of verbalized apprenticeship, this study could not be possible if I used only conventional recordings. The only practical way to transcribe each part is to isolate it from the others. Simha Arom (1976) developed the technique of rerecording as an analytical device for the study of orally transmitted polyphonies, and it has been applied to the material presented here: the different constituent parts are not recorded simultaneously but successively, each of the singers hearing in headphones the part or parts of the previous singer(s).[11] For the singers, the

8. The heuristics and the difficulties of the discovery of the Aka's four part conception are very well illustratred in Arom (1994).

9. Archive Arom BM83.4.

10. Other musical transcriptions of Aka polyphonies are published in Arom 1973b, Fürniss and Bahuchet 1995, Fürniss and Olivier 1997, Kisliuk 1998, and Fürniss 1999. A system of graphic visualization has been used in the CD-ROM Arom et al. 1998.

11. The evolution of computer technology at the beginning of the twenty-first century allows now direct multitrack-recordings even in difficult field conditions (Fernando-Marandola 2002).

FIGURE 5.2. Dìkòbò dámù dá sòmbé. *Superposition of six isolated parts of a re-recording series. Only the first singer uses words.*

Figure 5.2. *Continued*

FIGURE 5.2. *Continued*

FIGURE 5.2. *Continued*

introduction of this process takes some getting used to, as in real-life perfor-mance the melody can vary from one cycle to the next. But in order to under-stand the essential structure of the music and to get access to the reference pat-tern for any variation, one needs to work first with versions that are nearly unvaried. A second step is to add variations and to determine, through analysis, the rules from which they are made. Each participant is asked to sing without variations to obtain a minimal version of each part of the song, which enables transcribing, evaluating and comparing the variations later. The superposition of the isolated parts results in a synthetic version of the complete polyphony (see figure 5.2, which illustrates nine twelve-beat cycles). The rerecording tech-nique is validated when the different individual recordings are overdubbed and played back to the bearers of the tradition, and then recognized as an accept-able version of the given song.[12]

But before going into the analysis itself, I would like to pay tribute to our musicians. Although I was not yet an ethnomusicologist when this material was recorded, I worked myself with the same singers between 1989 and 1994. Ndolé, Mokenzo, Botambi, Moako and Dikondi are members of a family that lives near Mongoumba in the southeast Central African Republic. All of them are excellent singers with a solid knowledge of their musical heritage. Working with my research colleagues and me, they became experts at making analytical recordings, adept at producing minimal versions of any song. Their patience during the quite tiring rerecording sessions was remarkable. The discussions initiated by this type of work were very enriching for all of us. One day, Ndolé did not agree when I wanted the children to keep away in order not to disturb the recordings: "No, Susanne, I want them to share what we are discussing here. They would never hear it in this way again."

The Aka's Conception of Polyphonic Singing: Cognitive Premises

Constituent Parts of the Polyphony

According to Arom (1994), Aka counterpoint is based on four constituent parts (though, as mentioned, the number of *actual* melodies sounded may be greater), each of which is named and has distinctive features. For every song, each of the four parts has its own essential melodic pattern. It consists of a minimal and nonvaried version of the part, determined by the presence of certain scale

---

12. The validity of this *a posteriori* synchronization can be experienced in the section "Analyser" of the CD-ROM *Pygmées Aka. Peuple et Musique* (Arom et al. 1998).

tones that are systematically located in specific positions of the cycle. This pattern is a reference for the several variations, in terms of which it is realized.[13] The four parts are:

- The *mòtángòlè*, literally "the one who counts," which is generally sung by a man. It is the principal voice that contains the essential words of the song and allows the other singers to identify the piece without ambiguity.
- The *ngúé wà lémbò*, literally "the mother of the song," is a male part as well. It is generally situated lower and has longer rhythmic values than the *mòtángòlè*. It is the equivalent of a bass part.
- The *òsêsê*, literally "below" (which means inferior in hierarchy to the *mòtángòlè*), is a female middle voice characterized by fairly little melodic and rhythmic movement. These three parts are sung with the "chest voice" or laryngeal mechanism 1.[14]
- The *dìyèí*, literally "yodel," is sung above all the other parts by women. It is determined by the yodel technique, a constant alternation between laryngeal mechanisms 1 and 2, which is commonly called "falsetto," or "head voice." It consists of melodies of mainly wide intervals and uses specific vowels correlated to the two yodel registers: low yodel register—mechanism 1—open vowels as [e, a, o];[15] high yodel register—mechanism 2—closed vowels as [i, y, u] (Fürniss 1991).

The three latter parts do not use words, but are sung with meaningless syllables. This relates to musical and linguistic issues, as the Aka language, like the majority of African languages, is a tone language in which the pitch of the syllables has a relevant lexical or grammatical significance (Cloarec-Heiss and Thomas 1978). It has two tones—high and low—that change the sense of the words; for example, *mbókà* means "village" and *mbòká* means "plantation." In printed text, the tones are indicated above the vowels that support them: *ò* is a low tone, *ó* a high one.

The consequence of this linguistic constraint on singing is that the melodies have to follow roughly the tonal scheme of the language if the words are to be understood by a listener. Generally, in traditional African multipart singing,

---

13. The conception of the vocal polyphony is synthesized in the entry *lémbò*, "song," of the *Encyclopédie des Pygmées Aka* (Thomas et al. 2003: vol. 2(5):146–148).

14. In order to clarify an abundant and often unclear terminology concerning voice production, the term of "laryngeal mechanism" is proposed by Henrich, Roubeau and Castellengo (2003).

15. In order to avoid phonetic transcription, I underline the open vowels: *e* is pronounced like in "bed," *o* like in "four."

all parts pronounce the same words.[16] This means that the melodies of the parts progress with the same curve and therefore produce parallelism (Jones 1959:217). But in the specific case of contrapuntal polyphony, where the melodies move in different directions—such as the example we are considering—words are not articulated by all parts simultaneously because their sense would be lost. This is why only the *mòtángòlè* uses words, whereas the other parts do not (Arom and Pahaut 1993).

Knowing the names and features of the four constituent parts of the polyphony, one may be tempted to consider that it is easy to get access to the formal structure of *any* polyphonic song. But in reality Aka hardly ever refer to the parts and their patterns explicitly. Indeed, they are immanent concepts that are never taught to the musicians as such. Many singers don't know them and learn about the parts only when there are too many errors in the performance (Arom 1994:148). This is a particularly delicate issue in ritual performances, as the spiritual efficiency of music making is compromised when the polyphony is not well sung. Then, the "master of the song" interferes and indicates the parts that are poorly executed. He reminds the singers of the importance of a complete polyphonic texture, which pleases the spirits and inclines them to help the community achieve a successful and harmonous life. Many elder informants confirmed that this was the way they discovered the existence of the polyphonic parts; some of the younger ones learned them while working with Simha Arom or myself.

Varying the Melody

In order to give life to the basic parts, the Aka use three realization types of the patterns. Again, their specific features are as immanent as the features of the parts, and the terms are rarely used (Arom et al. 1998; Thomas et al. 2003:2 (5):146–148):

- *Kpókpó*, literally "straight on," is the equivalent of the English word "pattern," as a song realized "*kpókpó*" is the mere reproduction of the unvaried pattern. It can be heard at the beginning of a performance, when a singer is not particularly inspired or very experienced. When developing the variations during a normal performance, a singer may also use the pattern as one of the possible variants.
- *Kété bányé*, literally "take a shortcut" or "take a small path alongside of the large way," is the variation of the melody around the pattern. For each

16. Exceptions and an interesting discussion of this phenomenon can be found in Agawu (1988).

song, each constituent part has its stock of variants that the singer uses following his/her musical capacities and inspiration.

- *kùká ngó dìkùké*, literally "simply cut it," is a process of rhythmic variation that transforms the cycle into a succession of several short segments (see later, *dìyèì*). This is combined with several melodic variation techniques and therefore demands a high mastery of the voice and a knowledge of all variation possibilities for a given song.

Dìyèí (yodeling) is not only one of the constituent parts but also a yodeled variation technique that can be applied to any of the parts as we shall see later. The way of projecting the voice is part of Aka musical aesthetics: "one should not taper off the phrases but project them out brightly, letting the notes ring through the trees while listening for the echo" (Kisliuk 1998:26).

Patterns and Variation Techniques

Let's come back to the song *dìkòbò dámù dá sòmbé* and examine the patterns and variants of each part individually. In the present rerecording series,[17] some parts have been recorded more than once in order to identify their minimal pattern. The series contains nine "takes": we have one *mòtángòlè*, two *ngúé wà lémbò*, one *òsêsê*, and five *dìyèì*. As the parts were recorded one after the other during the same session, the same singer may sing the same part twice or s/he may sing different parts successively. I shall not focus especially on the succession of the variants in this first part of the analysis, but concentrate on the essential patterns and the techniques singers use to vary them.

Aka melodies can be described as being based on an anhemitonic pentatonic system—a five-tone scale in which neighboring degrees are separated by intervals that can vary between about a major second and a minor third. Musicians, however, are more concerned with correct relationships between parts than they are with a rigid idea of interval sizes, and these may vary even within a single performance.

Aka music does not operate with absolute pitch. Every singer who begins a song situates it in a comfortable tessitura for his/her own voice. The other singers will follow him/her by choosing the parts and variants that correspond the best to their voices. In order to facilitate direct comparison between the versions, I transcribe for convenience in relative pitch using the degrees [D], [E], [G], [A] and [C]. Everything is notated in metrical transcription that reflects

17. Archive Arom BM83.4.

the underlying structure of the cycle: twelve beats with a ternary subdivision.[18] The notation is layed out in a paradigmatic representation that for current purposes can be defined as a vertical alignment of all possible variants of a part. Beat 1 is determined by the beginning of words as sung by the the *mòtángòlè*, although the *ngúé wà lémbò, òsêsê*, and *dìyèí* do not begin at the same position in the cycle.

Mòtángòlè

Figure 5.3 is an inventory of all variants sung by Mokenzo, the singer of the *mòtángòlè*. He sang without any accompaniment except for his own hand-clapping, which gave him the metrical framework (left channel of CD track 8). The letters on the left identify the variants. They are arranged on the paper from top to bottom following the increasing dissimilarity from the minimal version *a*. The order of variants in this particular realization is indicated by the numbers on the right of the notation and results in the following sequence: *a-a-a-a-c-e-b-e-a-d-g-b-g-f-g*. Boxed notes indicate the first appearance of a variant.

The principal characteristic of this main part is the enunciation of the words of the song: *dìkòbò dámù dá sòmbé*, literally "The hair of my pubes is dense."[19] When words are sung, Aka music is strictly syllabic, which means that one syllable of the words is allotted to one note of the melody like in beats 1–6 of variant *a*. The tonal scheme of the words determines the melodic oscillation between the two degrees [G] and [A]. The periodicity, however, is independent of any linguistic consideration. As a multiple of the four-beat formula of the rhythmic accompaniment that underlies all songs of the *bòndó*-repertoire, it could have ended after the words with beat 8, but in this particular song the cycle is extended to twelve beats. This is why the *mòtángòlè's* phrase ends with nonsignificant syllables that allow a melodic extension to include [E] in addition to the two initial tones.

One can see both melodic and rhythmic variations. These mainly take place on beats 1–2, 6–8, and 10. The variant *g* is strikingly different and is sung without words, which liberates the singer from both the rhythm and tonal scheme of the words on beats 1–3.

The types of rhythmic variation seen here are *binary splitting* (var. *c*, b. 10), *division of long durations* (var. *c*, b. 6–7) and *smoothing* of small oscillations (var. *g*, b. 1+3; var. *c*, b. 8). All variants, however, respect some essential rhyth-

---

18. For the distinction between rhythmic and metric transcription, see Arom (1991:228).

19. The Aka ideal of a harmonous life is having many children and plentiful meat to eat. Sexuality is therefore a recurrent theme in song texts.

FIGURE 5.3. *Variants of* mòtángòlè *sung by Mokenzo.*

mical events that can therefore be considered as relevant identificatory features of this vocal part:

- the commetrical progressions on b. 2–3, 5–6, 9–10, 11: the melody is on the beat;
- the contrametrical progressions on b. 8/2[20] and 4/2: the melody is off the beat;
- a hemiola on b. 3–4;
- the silence on b. 12.

Furthermore, the *mòtángòlè* is rhythmically defined by a constant ambiguity between ternary and binary subdivision of the beat, as beats 1 and 10 are divided in two, whereas beats 3, 4, and 8 follow the ternary subdivision of the percussion support.

20. The number after the slash indicates the subdivision within the beat.

The melodic variations can be made according to a principle of *equivalence between* or *commutation of fifths*. According to the structure of the scale, some degrees in a variant can be substituted by another one a fifth below or a fourth above—here [D] instead of [A] on beat 7 and 10. There is also commutation of *neighboring degrees*—[G] instead of [A] on beat 1, 2, and 8; [E] instead of [G] on beat 1. These are the operational principles in the song we study here. Much work has still to be done in order to establish true general rules of interval combinations in Aka polyphony.

The realization of [G] instead of [A] on beat 1 calls for further explanation. The tonal scheme of the words—*dìkòbò dámù dá sòmbé*, three low-tone syllables followed by a high tone—might suggest a melodic pattern such as that found in variants *d* and *e*. So, if [G] is the musical representative of the low speech tone, it is [A] that, in this position, is in fact the neigboring variant above [G]. This kind of variation may bear on the comprehension of words since it modifies their tonal scheme. But as all words of this song—as of all other songs of the contrapuntal repertoires—are contained in a single sentence which is repeated over and over—and with very few variations within a performance or from one performance to another—the comprehensibility is finally a minor concern and cedes importance to musical variation.

Because all versions of the cycle are considered equivalent, one can summarize the variants of *mòtángòlè* with the paradigm shown in figure 5.4.

Ngúé wà lémbò

The following inventory of *ngúé wà lémbò*'s variants (figure 5.5) includes those of two versions of this part sung by Ndolé in two different octaves (low octave: variants *b-k*, high octave: variants *a, k-o*). The variants are here put together following the similarity of their musical material. The notation starts with the beginning of the melody of the *ngúé wà lémbò*, but as this coincides with beat 6 of the *mòtángòlè* part, beat 1 appears in the middle of the staff.

CD track 8 is the combination of the lower *ngúé wà lémbò* (right channel) and *mòtángòlè* (left channel). The succession of the variants is *b-b-c-f-g-e-i-e-j-d-h-i-i-h-k*.

CD track 9 is the combination of the higher *ngúé wà lémbò* (left channel) and *dìyèi* (right channel) in another sequence of the variants: *a-m-l-m-o-k-n-m-m-m-m-l-m-l*.

In the melody, the [A] of beats 2 and 6 can be replaced a fifth higher by [E]. Neighboring degrees are used to *embroider* around the sustained [D] of beats 8–9 and to fill out the descending fourth [D]–[A] on beats 9–10. In fact, there is only a very reduced stock of melodic variations, which are summarized in

FIGURE 5.4. *Paradigm of variations in the* mòtángòlè.

figure 5.6. Thus, the melody can be presented as a *succession of variable sections,* the combination of which gives way to a patchwork of realizations.

The most interesting developments in this part have to do with phrasing and its relationship to periodicity. The minimal version, variant *a* of figure 5.5, is characterized by very few occupied positions within the cycle which leaves a large section musically blank. One of the main principles of variation in this part appears to be the *filling out of silences.* As a consequence, there are *variations in segmentation* resulting from the emergence of different ways to group the same pitches when they return in subsequent cycles. As more and more tones substitute for the rests that were present initially, the resulting phrases have new relationships with the cyclic framework.

For instance, the minimal pattern of variation *a* contains a single melodic segment lasting from beat 7 to beat 12; the introduction of the [D] on beats 3–4 and its anacrusis on beat 2 (var. *b-j*) adds a second one. The filling out of beat 1 (var. *k-o*) causes an important switch in the perception of the part: the two segments are linked to become again a single one that covers the whole cycle. This link is reinforced by the syncopation on beat 12, which has a rhythmic impact on beat 1.

The way the silences are positioned influences the perception of the period's beginning and ending points: either it can be considered as identical to the *mòtángòlè*'s or *overlapped* with it, which makes the overall structure of the song much more complex. In variation *a-k,* the period can be considered identical to the *mòtángòlè*'s, because the two segments fit in the frame between beat

FIGURE 5.5. *Variants of* ngúé wà lémbò *sung by Ndolé.*

I and beat 12. But in variation *k-o*, the period of the *ngúé wà lémbò* is clearly desynchronized with the *mòtángòlè*'s, because it starts six beats later, going from beat 6 to beat 5. This is an eloquent example of a variation technique that gives the Aka singers the possibility to efficiently modify the melodic and rhythmic combinations of a limited collection of material. Other examples of this variation technique will be found in the *dìyèì* part (figures 5.8.a and 5.8.b).

Apart from variation *c + f,* the variants presented here are not subject to *syntactic constraints,* they can be sung in any random order. Variation *c,* how-

FIGURE 5.6. *Paradigm of variations in the* ngúé wà lémbò.

ever, mandates a determined sequence: as beats 5–6 are tied together, it can only be followed by variation *f.* More examples of this kind of phenomenon also will be found in the *dìyèí* part.

Òsêsê

Like the *ngúé wà lémbò,* the women's part *òsêsê* (figure 5.7) does not begin on the same beat as the *mòtángòlè.* Except for one, all variations tie beat 12–1 and most of them have a silence on beat 4. Although there is not much variation, the *òsêsê* confirms the variation techniques of commutation of fourths—[G]–[D] on beat 7–8—and of filling out a descending fourth with an intermediate degree—beat 2 and 6/3.

The order of variants sung by Botambi during this re-recording session is *a-c-c-b-b-b-c-d-d-e-b-b-c.*

Dìyèí

Other variation techniques can be discovered by the analysis of five different realizations of the yodelled part *dìyèí* (CD track 9), of which Dikondi's version (right channel), sung together with the higher *ngúé wà lémbò* (left channel), is the most interesting one. She sings with many variations in the following order: *k-k-l-k-k-k-n-o-l-l-l-l-m-l.* She starts on beat 11 as indicated by a star.

FIGURE 5.7. *Variants of* òsêsê *sung by Botambi.*

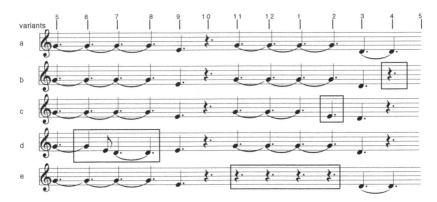

The inventory shows twenty variants that I have grouped following a rhythmic trait that underlines the structural overlapping of *dìyèí*'s cycle with *mòtángòlè*'s. The variants of figure 5.8.a contain a change of pitch at the first beat of *mòtángòlè*'s cycle, whereas the variants of figure 5.8.b reinforce the overlapping by a tie between beat 12–1.

Apart from some rhythmic and melodic variations that have already been introduced, this large stock of variants illustrates another particularity of Aka music: the *equivalence of octaves* in melodic composition. This can be seen on beat 1 + 2 of variation *h-j:* the high [A] is transposed to the lower octave, whereas the melodic surrounding stays identical and the metric position of the degree is maintained. The same phenomenon appears in variation *r-t* on beat 3 + 4 and in variations *n* and *o* on beat 7 + 8. Its use gets more complex and creates very interesting variations when it is combined with the commutation of the fifth or the fourth (var. *f-j*, b. 7–8).

The period is filled out with mainly two melodic segments. The syntactic liberty in lining up the great majority of these variants (var. *a-q*) can be illustrated with the sequences realized in other versions of this part, as sung in our rerecording series (unfortunately we don't have the space to put them all on the CD):

- *dìyèí* sung by Mokenzo to the *mòtángòlè: a-a-a-a-d-d-a-d-c-a-a-d-e-b-a;*
- *dìyèí* sung by Mokenzo to the *òsêsê: a-a-a-a-a-e-a-e-a-e;*
- *dìyèí* sung by Mokenzo again to the *òsêsê: f-g-g-g-h-g-i-g-j-h.*

But still, some variants are subject to syntactic constraints. Variations *r-t* are compatible as such only with each other because they introduce a unique segment going from beat 3 to beat 9–10. This causes a shift of the initial segmentation of this part. Although each of these variants can follow any other, the

FIGURE 5.8.a. *Variants of* dìyèí *sung by Dikondi and Mokenzo.*

switch back to the other ones is only possible in the middle of *dìyèí*'s cycle, that is, on beat 11. In this context, variation *q* appears as a transitional variant that facilitates the switch-back, as we can see in the sequence of the second *dìyèí* sung by Dikondi to the higher *ngúé wà lémbò: p-p-p-k-k-p-k-k-t-r-s-q-l.*

The principles of variation showed here all belong to the variation technique *kété bányé.* The metaphor of the "small path alongside of the large way" is easy to recognize as the main segments of the melody can clearly be identified. This is not always easy when the *dìyèí* is sung in the variation technique

FIGURE 5.8.b.

kùká ngó dìkùké. Let us consider a take from a different rerecording series[21] in which completely new variants are introduced (CD track 10).

As the name of this technique indicates—"simply cut it"—the melody is split into smaller slices of up to four segments by the introduction of very short breaks. The melodic variation makes a large use of both commutation of intervals and equivalence of octaves, creating a succession of mainly large intervals that gives a special importance to the minor seventh. Whereas the ear may have difficulties recognizing the pattern, a trained eye can nevertheless follow it through the whole paradigm.

21. Archive Arom BM74.31.6.

FIGURE 5.9. *Dìyèí realized by Dikondi in the variation technique* kùká ngó dìkùké.

Yodelling and Melodic Variations

The equivalence of octaves as a principle of melodic variation has a direct bearing on the application of the yodel technique. Although the alternation between laryngeal mechanism 1 and 2 (chest and head voices) is generally correlated with melodic movement in large intervals such as fourths, fifths, and minor seconds, the yodel is also used in melodic progressions with a reduced ambitus. Thus, in figure 5.8, one can find yodeled major seconds (var. *f-j,*

b. 8–9 and var. *n*, b. 9–10) and even the change of mechanism on the same degree (var. *o*, b. 9–10 and var. *t*, b. 1–2. All degrees sung in mechanism 2 are indicated by a "°" in the transcriptions.) What is important for the singer is that the regular alternation of the yodel registers is maintained: there is a change from head to chest voice (or vice versa) with each new note.

Nevertheless, this principle seems not to be respected in variations *d-e*, *l-m*, *o*, and *q* with the succession of two sounds in the same laryngeal mechanism. A closer look enables us to identify a rule underlying the treatment of small intervals in Aka yodelling (Fürniss 1991:183–185): the second sound of an ascending interval belongs always to the high yodel register (mechanism 2) and the second sound of a descending interval belongs to the low yodel register (mechanism 1):

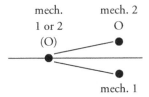

Thus, the execution—yodelled or not—of two adjacent degrees depends on the vocal register of the first degree, which is itself determined by its position within the melodic pattern and the type of variation chosen by the singer.

The Polyphonic Pattern and the Substratum of the Song

The superposition of the four parts (figure 5.10) illustrates the structural overlapping that operates in *dìkòbò dámù dá sòmbé*.

The *mòtángòlè* begins on beat 1, *dìyèí* and *òsêsê* on beat 5, and *ngúé wà lémbò* on beat 6 (or even 7 if one does not take in account the possible anacrusis on b. 6). All pieces of the contrapuntal repertoires are based on this type of structural overlapping, but the specific relationship between the parts varies from one piece to another.[22]

---

22. For two other songs of the same divination repertoire *bòndó*—which means that they have the same rhythmic accompaniment—the overlapping is as follows:

- *kòkòyàndóngó*: *mòtángòlè* and *dìyèí* begin on b.1, *ngúé wà lémbò* and *òsêsê* on b.5;
- *mábé*: *mòtángòlè* begins on b.1, *ngúé wà lémbò* on b.3, *dìyèí* on b.8 and *òsêsê* on b.12.

Three different types of overlapping are visualized in the section "Recomposer" of the CD-ROM *Pygmées Aka. Peuple et Musique* (Arom et al. 1998).

FIGURE 5.10. *Structural overlapping of the four constituent parts.*

189

The musicians do not necessarily think of any particular position as being the "beginning" of the cycle. There are many points where you can start: in the recording of the *òsêsê*, for example, the singer began on beat 3 of variation *d*. But, in general, one of them is more appropriate than the others and appears statistically as the most common place to start. This is the point I have called "beginning."

The inscription of the most frequent minimal version of each part in the framework of *mòtángòlè*'s cycle (figure 5.11) shows that the cycle is filled out in such a way that there is never a common silence, no interruption in sound. It is a structural reinforcement of the cyclic character of the music: not only are the parts perpetually repeated and their beginning—indicated by a star—more statistical than conceptual, but their imbrication makes the music spin around without an overall beginning or ending. This is corroborated by the way a song and dance performance begins: one singer starts alone and the others join in after a while; endings are loose, with the voices fraying out successively. And those who begin, don't necessarily start with the *mòtángòlè*, as the reader can hear on CD track 7: the singer who begins the performance does not start with the *mòtángòlè*'s incipit, but with a variant of the yodelled part *dìyèí*. It seems that there are variations from one region to another, but Kisliuk (1998:112) describes this phenomenon very well: "At the beginning of a round, in the early stages of a dance, it is usually men and boys who establish support parts. . . . Usually, once some support parts have been voiced, people follow by taking up the theme. Sometimes, though, when the eboka [dance] is going strong, people begin a song with the theme itself."

As to the vertical structure of the four-part construction, the polyphonic pattern shows that at several points, some parts meet others on the same pitch:

- On beat 1+2, *mòtángòlè* and *dìyèí* meet on [A];
- On beat 3, *dìyèí*, *òsêsê* and *ngúé wà lémbò* meet on [D], which the latter maintain on beat 4;
- On beat 5, *dìyèí*, *mòtángòlè* and *òsêsê* meet on [G], etc.

Scanning for other vertical phenomena, we see three kinds of dyads: fifths, fourths, and major seconds.[23] It is remarkable that [C] does not appear here. Indeed, in the individual parts, it is only used as a passing note between [D] and [A] and thus is excluded from the patterns. Therefore, in the polyphonic pattern of *dìkòbò dámù dá sòmbé*, we can find all other possible combinations of neighboring degrees or of intervals that skip one degree, except

23. This is what lead Arom to speak of a "polyphony of consonances" and made him compare this music to medieval *Ars Nova* composition processes (1978).

FIGURE 5.11. Dìkòbò dámù dá sòmbé. *Polyphonic pattern.*

for those including [C]. This is why there are hardly any dyads of thirds. Only the minor third [E]/[G] may appear on beat 12 or in two positions where three tones meet at the same time (b. 1 + 6).

If the rules of variation allow for the inversion of these consonances—introducing the minor seventh and, exceptionally, the major sixth—their position within the cycle is nevertheless predetermined and invariable. Thus, the succession of a given combination of tones in given positions of the cycle gives the *substratum* that bears the identity of a particular polyphonic song. The substratum for *dìkòbò dámù dá sòmbé* is shown in figure 5.12.

I have to underline that here we are at a point that lies beyond the Aka's conception as expressed through naming or describing verbalization. The substratum is a complete abstraction of any musical realization and a pure product of musical analysis. Nonetheless, its cultural relevance—that is, its validity for Aka culture—can easily be recognized through any realization of *dìkòbò dámù dá sòmbé,* because all variants presented above can be generated from this very simple harmonic and metric scheme.

Musical Practice: Juggling with the Substratum

Free Movement in a Polyphonic Context

Facing the disconcerting simplicity of the substratum, one may ask: how come Aka polyphony sounds—or is—so complex? In spite of the modular character of their combinations, the variation techniques within a constituent part

FIGURE 5.12. Dìkòbò dámù dá sòmbé. *Substratum.*

are quite limited. Paradoxically, the simplicity of the substrata is what makes the complexity so possible to achieve: points at which two or more parts meet on the same tone are pivots that allow individual singers to switch from one part to another. And this is what brings music to life and what is interesting for the Aka. In their musical practice, distribution of the constituent parts is neither determined in advance nor invariable during performance. Singers are at liberty to change parts in the middle of a song, not only to another part theoretically assigned to the singer's gender but also to any of the four parts (Arom 1994:145); men may yodel and women may sing the *ngúé wà lémbò.*[24] In an excellent and dense performance—where the best singers are in the groove— the voices rebound from one part to the others like billiard-balls.

The ideal is that all parts be always present, but this is not always so. If during a ceremony, ritual efficiency is compromised, this is a point where the "master of the song" intervenes to remind the singers of the importance of a complete polyphonic performance. If I expose here an ideal, it is far from being consciously fixed in the mind of the singers. They just do it. And sometimes, it doesn't matter if the polyphony is complete, as soon as the groove is there. But even then, for the analyst, the interchangeability of the parts is what makes them so difficult to grasp and disentangle, and what necessitated the rerecording technique.

To this analytical difficulty we must add that a singer not only spontaneously chooses the part he wants to sing but also its variants. "Thanks to his inculcation—that is, his own cultural apprenticeship—each member of the community knows perfectly, at any point of the period of each song, and in relation to such a point, which variations he can execute" (Arom 1978). Thus, the melodic course of each singer depends on his capacity to use the pivot tones to move freely among the parts and to create original combinations of both parts and their variants. Some of these creations may be so successful that they become popular and are sung over and over by the whole camp before fashion changes for the benefit of another melodic combination (Kisliuk

24. Another description of flexibility and interchange of the parts can be found in Kisliuk (1998:112).

1998:99); some of them may become part of an individual's "signature song style" (ibid.:102).

The musicality of a singer seeks an echo in others' capacity to respond,[25] as "nobody knows in advance what any other singer except himself will sing in the following second" (Arom and Dehoux 1978:70).

Pathways Through the Material

Singing Alone

All Aka singing is collective, at least in concept. Even lullabies and love songs have a musical structure based on the complementarity of at least two parts. We nevertheless find solo realizations of contrapuntal pieces that—after an evening dance session—are repeated during daytime as an accompaniment to activities and marching (Kisliuk 1998:98–99). Indeed, even ritual songs can be performed out of context—lacking some ritually indispensible elements— and the presence of at least four singers is not necessary in order to sing a polyphonic song. Look at figure 5.13, *dìkòbò dámù dá sòmbé* sung by a young girl, for her own entertainment.[26] Only twelve years old, Moako is already a very good musician; the readers of this book may find it difficult to recognize the song.

This version illustrates the lining up of different constituent parts and their variants very clearly. All segments are derived from one of the four constituent patterns as indicated under the staff (M-*mòtángòlè*, N-*ngúé wà lémbò*, O-*òsêsê*, D-*dìyèí*). The transcription takes in account the multiple realizations of some of the pitches. When [F] or [B] appear, they can be considered variants of [E] and [C], respectively, and are included to show how flexible the performer's conception of singing "in tune" can be. They are nevertheless part of the anhemitonic pentatonic system, as the melodic minor seconds [E]–[F] or [B]–[C] never appear as such.[27] The determination of a segment's origin in a particular constituent part is sometimes difficult, as the structural overlapping allows for the same melodic movement to be interpreted as belonging to either of two different parts. These points are indicated.

25. You may experience reactivity in the interchange of parts. Take any four-part polyphony (Renaissance . . .) and four singers, switch freely from one part to the other, and try to have all of them present through the entire performance.

26. Can be heard on *Aka Pygmy Music*, UNESCO, Musics and Musicians of the World, Auvidis D8054, tr. 3.

27. For more on the Aka scale system, see Fürniss (1993b), and Arom and Fürniss (1993).

FIGURE 5.13. Dìkòbò dámù dá sòmbé. *Solo sung by Moako.*

The singer uses mainly segments from the women's parts òsêsê and dìyèi, plus others from the mòtángòlè part. In the first part of most of the cycles, derivations from mòtángòlè and òsêsê are predominant, whereas the middles and the ends of the cycles are dominated by segments derived from dìyèi; some of them could be interpreted as belonging to ngúé wà lémbò, as its rhythmic structure merges with dìyèi's. Figures 5.14 to 5.16 depict the derivations of the main variants. One finds the same variation principles as those described above, but one also finds segment combinations that did not appear in the rerecording version. These derivations are used both in figure 5.13 and figure 5.17. Their occurence is indicated to the right of the notation.

FIGURE 5.14. *Segments derived from* mòtángòlè.

We can consider the solo realization of a contrapuntal piece as if it were one voice within a polyphonic performance, since—as with each singer's line in a polyphony—choices stem from a concern for diversity that has its origin in a vertical, contrapuntal conception.

Singing in Duo

The solo version of *dìkòbò dámù dá sòmbé* shows only one of many possible ways to create a pathway through the musical material. Listen to a duet version (CD track 11), where Moako is joined by her friend Dikondi. This perform-

FIGURE 5.15. *Segments derived from òsêsê.*

ance contains roughly the same material as in the solo version, but it is integrated into a pair of distinct melodic lines in which the segments are distributed between the two singers very differently (figure 5.17). There is much less *dìyèí*, a bit more *ngúé wà lémbò*, but mainly derivations of *mòtángòlè* and *òsêsê*.

The responsiveness of each singer to what the other sings determines the trajectory of each one's melody. Indeed, as soon as two singers join in a song, they try to be *complementary*. This can be a very simple procedure. Periods 2–4 and 9–11 illustrate the *exchange of parts:* the girl who sang *mòtángòlè* switches to *òsêsê* while her companion switches the other way round, from *òsêsê* to *mòtángòlè*. Moreover, the transcription shows that there are very few points where the two voices meet or are in a real unisson. During some of them (cycles 4

FIGURE 5.16. *Segments derived from* dìyèí.

and 11) an ingenious procedure can be observed, the *simultaneous variation* that deploys the material in a mirror thanks to the equivalence of octaves:

This simultaneous variation of identical material testifies to the extremely rapid reaction of the singers and their ability to immediately and economically trans-

Figure 5.17. Dìkòbò dámù dá sòmbé. *Duet sung by Moako and Dikondi.*

form the musical material. Moako, the solo singer, used the same kind of mirror principle in successive periods (figure 13, per. 1, 2, and 4).

Some segments of these two realizations are very difficult to assign to one of the conceptual parts. The mirror variants just mentioned (var. 1, 3–5, and 9 of the *dìyèí*s derivates, figure 5.16) are good examples. I mentioned earlier that yodelling can be used as a variation process in other parts than *dìyèí*. The prox-

FIGURE 5.17. *Continued*

imity between variation 1 of figure 5.16 (*dìyèí's* derivates) and variations 5 + 6 of figure 5.14 (*mòtángòlè's* derivates) illustrates this. They are quasi identical but nevertheless linked organically to both parts. We are here at the limit of systematic analysis as in practice, the girls we heard in CD track 11 varied the basic material in such a way that the parts are interwoven and it is hard to determine the segment's origin. When the singers push the combination of variation techniques to its limits, the parts seem to merge until they dissolve in an individual's creation, which transcends them.

Conclusion and Perspectives

Aka polyphony does not substantially differ from any other Central African polyphony, although others are generally instrumental. They share the main variation techniques—as commutation of intervals and free combination of variants (Dehoux 1986; Arom 1991)—and a substratum that underlies different parts (Le Bomin 2004:21) and may generate simultaneous instrumental and vocal realizations.

One particularity of Aka—as of most other Pygmies'—polyphony is that, in an African context, vocal *counterpoint* is quite rare. The other vocal polyphonies are usually built on a responsorial alternation between a soloist and a choir, the latter singing two parts in mainly parallel movement. Kubik (1968:28) described the skipping process that combines a scale degree with the one two steps away, and that leads to the main harmonic areas described by Jones (1959:220). This principle is valid all over the continent and also characterizes most of the Aka's noncontrapuntal repertoires (such as *mòbándì, dìsàò* and *kóbá,* see figure 5.1). Independent melodic lines in homophony, that is, in homorhythmic progression, are sung by South Africa's township choirs (Coplan 1985), but real counterpoint—independence of melodies and rhythms—is significant only in two other African regions: in the East, where Ethiopia and Tanzania are good representatitves,[28] and in the South, mainly in Botswana and Namibia.[29]

These different vocal counterpoints do not work in the same way everywhere. One important outcome of musical analysis as practiced in this article is that—combined with observation and interviews—it gives solid access to the singers' *conception* of their own music. Bringing to light the musical principles that underly a performance gives insight into the cognitive—mainly nonverbalized—processes that guide a singer intuitively. Applied to different musics, analysis allows a comparative study of similar musical styles in order to determine their proximity or distance. As an example, in Olivier and Fürniss (1999), Aka counterpoint has been considered alongside the contrapuntal polyphony of the Jul'hoansi of Namibia to consider the possibility of a relationship between Pygmy and Bushmen music. This comparative study of mu-

28. Ethiopia: Dorze (Jenkins 1968; Lortat-Jacob 1994), Ghimira, Maji (Jenkins 1968), and so on; Tanzania: Wagogo (Vallejo 2004).

29. Botswana: Bushmen (England 1967); Namibia (Olivier 1998).

sical characteristics has shown that, although many musical and extramusical features converge and though the acoustic results are very close, the conception that the Jul'hoansi have of their music is radically opposite to the Aka's. In fact, Jul'hoansi music does not proceed from a basic multipart pattern, but it is generated from a single melody that is simultaneously materialized in different tessituras (Olivier 1998).

The theoretical musicological concerns developed here are, as we said earlier, not shared by the Aka. Still, the interaction and complementarity of four named—and thus explicitly conceptual—parts in any Aka music reflects an important philosophical perspective. Life is only possible within the community; no project can be achieved alone. But among the Aka, having a "generally egalitarian lifestyle" (Kisliuk 1998:131), nobody makes decisions for the group as a whole, and there is leeway for negotiating individual behavior within the limits of social acceptability.[30] Transposed to music, this constrained liberty finds its parallel in the contrapuntal conception of the most important ritual musics (Arom 1978). There is a necessary complementarity between the parts as is the case in society: "as in daily life, everybody is responsible for his acts in relation to the survival of his entire community, [and] in musical practice, every musician realizes his part in relation to what the others sing around him" (Bahuchet 1995:61–62). The variation techniques offer important means to individual expression and creativity. Virtuosity may exploit the entire margin of liberty offered by the pattern until the underlying theoretical framework of constituent parts may be hidden or transcended.

Performers do not think about structural features and thus access to structural elements is difficult to obtain by observation. And here is where systematic analysis as practiced here elucidates the relationships that exist among musical grammar, autochthonous terminology, symbolic conceptions, and implementation in performance. There is no doubt anymore that analysis is more than an objective in itself. We have known since long ago that Aka singing is complex and perpetually varying. But only after describing the parts and the way they are modeled do we have *concrete criteria* to recognize and appreciate individual expression and interaction in performance. Experience this when listening again to CD track 7.

We know that as much as the grammar of a language is not literature, musical rules are not performance. In this sense, the demonstration of the basic concepts of Aka music theory does not tell us how music is experienced. But it allows us to understand the formal musical elements that are interwoven

---

30. This is an important issue in Kisliuk: "Elanga [the elder of a camp] was quietly ignored, as is often the case when BaAka issue authoritive statements to each other" (1998: 78); for the question of egalitarian lifestyle, see also pp. 131–133.

with social, religious, economical, and aesthetic factors for any culturally relevant performance. As in language, musical rules are neither necessarily explicit nor formally taught, but the fact that people don't speak about them doesn't mean that they don't exist. Thus, a systematic approach to traditional music is not antagonist to a dynamic approach. The study of structure is complementary to the study of interaction and I am rather tempted to say that it should precede it: under the condition that it is conducted in very close relation to ethnography, musical analysis provides relevant criteria concerning the musical material that is brought into operation during a performance and becomes an excellent starting point for the study of aesthetic and social realms.

References

Agawu, Kofi V. 1988. "Tone and tune: The evidence for Northern Ewe music." *Africa* 58(2): 127–146.

Arom, Simha. 1973a. *Aka Pygmy Music.* UNESCO, Coll. "Musical Sources," Philips 6586–016 (reedition as CD 1994. Coll. "Musics and Musicians of the World," Auvidis D8054).

———. 1973b. "Une méthode pour la transcription de polyphonies et polyrythmies de tradition orale." *Revue de Musicologie* 59(2):165–190.

———. 1976. "The Use of Play-Back Techniques in the Study of Oral Polyphonies." *Ethnomusicology* 20(3):483–519.

———. 1978. *Anthologie de la Musique des Pygmées Aka.* OCORA/Radio France 558 526–28 (reeditions as CD 1980, 1985, 1987 and 2003, C559012/13).

———. 1991, *African Polyphony and Polyrhythm. Musical Structure and Methodology.* Cambridge: Cambridge University Press.

———. 1994. "Intelligence in traditional music." In *What is Intelligence?* Jean Khalfa, ed. Cambridge: Cambridge University Press, 137–160.

Arom, Simha, Serge Bahuchet, Alain Epelboin, Susanne Fürniss, Henri Guillaume, and Jacqueline M. C. Thomas. 1998. *Pygmées Aka—peuple et musique.* CD-ROM. Paris: CNRS, Montparnasse Multimédia, ORSTOM.

Arom, Simha, and Vincent Dehoux. 1978. "Puisque personne ne sait à l'avance ce que tout autre que lui-même va chanter dans la seconde qui suit . . ." *Musique en jeu* 32:67–71.

Arom, Simha, and Susanne Fürniss. 1992. "The Pentatonic System of the Aka Pygmies of the Central African Republic." In *European Studies in Ethnomusicology: Historical Developments and Recent Trends.* M. P. Baumann, A. Simon, and U. Wegner, eds. Wilhelmshaven: Florian Noetzel Edition, 159–173.

Arom, Simha, and Serge Pahaut. 1993. "Une voix plurielle," entretien sur les polyphonies orales. *Cahiers de musiques traditionnelles* 6. "Polyphonies," 184–196.

Bahuchet, Serge. 1985. *Les Pygmées Aka et la forêt centrafricaine.* Paris-Louvain: Peeters.

———. 1993. "L'invention des Pygmées." *Cahiers d'Etudes africaines* 33(1):153–181.

———. 1995. "De la musique considérée comme une philosophie (chez les Pygmées Aka de Centrafrique)." In *Ndroje balendro, Musiques. terrains et disciplines. Textes offerts à Simha Arom.* V. Dehoux et. al., eds. Paris-Louvain: Peeters, 57–65.

Cloarec-Heiss, France, and Jacqueline M. C. Thomas. 1978. *L'aka, langue bantoue des Pygmées de Mongoumba (Centrafrique): Introduction à l'étude linguistique. Phonologie*. Paris: Selaf.

Coplan, David B. 1985. *In Township Tonight! South Africa's Black City Music and Theatre*. London: Longman Group Ltd.

Dehoux, Vincent. 1986. *Chants à penser gbaya (Centrafrique)*. Paris: Selaf.

England, Nicholas. 1967. "Bushman Counterpoint." *Journal of the International Folk Music Council* 19:58–66.

Fernando-Marandola, Nathalie. 2002. "New Perspectives on Interactive Field Experiments." *Yearbook for Traditional Music* 34:163–186.

Fürniss, Susanne. 1991. *Die Jodeltechnik der Aka-Pygmäen in Zentralafrika. Eine akustisch-phonetische Untersuchung*. Berlin: Dietrich Reimer-Verlag.

———. 1993a. "Rigueur et liberté: La polyphonie vocale des Pygmées Aka (Centrafrique)." In *Polyphonies de tradition orale. Histoire et traditions vivantes*. C. Meyer, ed. Paris: Créaphis, 101–131.

———. 1993b. "The pentatonic musical system of the Aka Pygmies of Central Africa." *ESCOM-Newsletter* 4. European Society for the Cognitive Sciences of Music, 26–32.

———. 1998. *Central Africa. Aka Pygmies. Hunting, Love and Mockery Songs*. CD, Ocora/Radio France C 560139.

———. 1999. "La conception de la musique vocale chez les Aka: Terminologie et combinatoires de paramètres." *Journal des Africanistes* 69:147–162 (with CD).

Fürniss, Susanne, and Serge Bahuchet. 1995. "Existe-t-il des instruments de musique pygmées?" In *Ndroje balendro. Musiques, terrains et disciplines. Textes offerts à Simha Arom*. V. Dehoux et. al., eds. Paris-Louvain: Peeters, 87–109.

Fürniss, Susanne, and Emmanuelle Olivier. 1997. "Systématique musicale pygmée et bochiman: deux conceptions africaines du contrepoint." *Musurgia: Analyse et Pratique Musicales* 4(3):9–30.

Henrich, Nathalie, Bernard Roubeau, and Michèle Castellengo. 2003. "On the use of electroglottography for the characterisation of the laryngeal mechanisms." *Proceedings of the Stockholm Music Acoustics Conference, August 6–9, 2003 (SMAC 03)*, Stockholm, Sweden.

Jenkins, Jean. 1968 [reedition]. *Ethiopia. Vocal and instrumental Music*. Two CDs, OCORA C580055/56.

Jones, Arthur Morris. 1959. *Studies in African Music*. London: Oxford University Press.

Kisliuk, Michelle. 1998. *Seize the Dance! BaAka Musical Life and the Ethnography of Performance*. New York: Oxford University Press (with two CDs).

Kubik, Gerhard. 1968. *Mehrstimmigkeit und Tonsysteme in Zentral- und Ostafrika. Bemerkungen zu den eigenen, im Phonogrammarchiv der Österreichischen Akademie der Wissenschaften archivierten Expeditionsaufnahmen*. Vienna: Österreichische Akademie der Wissenschaften.

Lortat-Jacob, Bernard. 1994. *Ethiopia. Dorze Polyphonie*. CD, CNRS-Musée de l'Homme, CNR-274646.

Le Bomin, Sylvie. 2004. "Ameya: Méthode et perspectives comparatives en ethnomusicologie." In *Langues et cultures: Terrains d'Afrique, Hommage à France Cloarec-Heiss*. P. Boyeldieu and P. Nougayrol, eds. Paris-Louvain: Peeters, 12–24.

Olivier, Emmanuelle. 1998. "The Art of Metamorphosis or the Jul'oan Conception of Plurivocality." *Proceedings of the Khoisan Identities & Cultural Heritage Conference—Cape Town 12–16 July 1997.* Cape Town: University of Western Cape and InfoSOURCE Publishers, 261–268.

Olivier, Emmanuelle, and Susanne Fürniss. 1999. "Pygmy and Bushman Music: A New Comparative Study." In *Central African Hunter-Gatherers in a Multidisciplinary Perspective: Challenging Elusiveness.* K. Biesbrouck, S. Elders, and G. Rossel, eds., Leiden: CNWS, 117–132.

Thomas, Jacqueline M. C., Serge Bahuchet, Alain Epelboin (since 1993), and Susanne Fürniss (since 2003), eds. 1981–2004. *Encyclopédie des Pygmées Aka.* Paris-Louvain: Peeters [10 of 17 volumes released].

Vallejo, Polo. 2004. *Mbudi Mbudi Na Mhanga. The Musical Universe of the Wagogo Children from Tanzania.* Madrid: Polo Vallejo.

CHAPTER 6

Oleg Tumulilingan

Layers of Time and Melody in Balinese Music

MICHAEL TENZER

Time and Culture in Music

This chapter introduces the music of the Balinese *gamelan* and explores the layers of structure of a well-known composition in its modern repertoire. I pursue this as an end in itself, but the composition's structural features and temporality help me draw attention to the broader challenge of how to experience and imagine time in particular musical contexts, both through Balinese music and in comparison with other musics. Let me begin with a view of the latter aims.

One of the reasons music is so important to people relates to its depiction and seeming resolution of the paradoxes of the human dimensions of time. Once we have taken a moment to reflect, little else is as compelling. Of course time is many things. We perceive it in our world, but must invent ways to describe and understand it. Whatever its actual nature from a physicist's point of view, or from a mystic's, for most people time is conceived through conventionalized images and metaphors. Time is felt at the least to be both a progression (because we age and die) and a regeneration (because of the Newtonian mechanics of orbits and seasons). Anthropologists might explain this duality in terms of individuating, bodily experience versus communal, life-cycle experience. Some philosophers might speak of it as becoming (motion) and being (stasis). Oriented as we are in the contemporary world toward the visual, we often think of these two perspectives as opposed, rather like lines and circles are opposed in a two-dimensional plane—no matter what we know of Einstein's curved time, and no matter what higher nonspatial resolution we suspect exists in religious or cosmic realms. Or one may think of oneself as stationary while time moves "through" us, as opposed to actively moving together along with time. It is hard to imagine how *not* to experience a tension between these contrasting qualities, because they shape experience at the most basic level. But are these extremes as opposed as the geometry of lines and circles suggests? Music has other ideas.

In music patterns of repetition proceed together with those of development and change. Such is also the case with many other experiences we have of the world, including visual and verbal ones. But music holds a special place because, like time, sound is ephemeral and cannot be held. Music's enactment of time can only be roughly approximated by visual, verbal, or mathematical means. Its ineluctability causes us to consider music to bear essential truths that we crave knowledge of. In music we can grow and be reborn simultaneously.

There are many ways in which line and circle—or, if one likes, progression and stasis—can be simulated and merged in music. Some music is almost irreducibly elemental and static, built up from the simplest of short, repeating, circlelike patterns. Yet it moves progressively, too, and is invariably inflected, at the very least (with the arguable exception of certain repetitive electronically made musics), with perceptible fluctuations in intensity and delivery that superimpose a sensation of time moving directionally. At the other extreme, some music aims to eschew repetition by constantly changing and striving to move forward though time. It will nevertheless, despite intentions, exhibit recurrences and contextual relationships between sounds or melodies. Even if one could imagine a music in which pattern and repetition were truly absent, our obsessive, order-seeking psyches would try to find ways to impose them or else, in all likelihood, reject the music as incoherent. Music can do no more than represent or suggest certain temporal qualities but the perception of them—the experience of them—is up to us, and depends upon our habits and perspectives.

The piece of music from Bali under consideration contains layered, culturally distinctive constructions of progressive and repetitive time structures. The encounter with Balinese music is itself worthwhile in terms of taking the lid off of it per se, and getting to know some of its ingenious features. This possibility alone justifies the study, but as a knowledgeable outsider to the music I have gone further in some regards. I hope that my analysis can provoke an unsuspected cross-cultural experience that even Balinese listeners are quite unlikely to be conscious of. That my perspective is not in itself especially Balinese I can say with some confidence, having spent countless hours in discussion with Balinese about music and related ideas. But it is both fitting and inevitable for a world in which musics are internationally available, and our imaginations lead us to create new, and hopefully beneficial, meanings and uses for

Oleg Tumulilingan *by Anak Agung Gdé Sobrat. Courtesy Neka Gallery, Ubud, Bali.*

them. One can realistically hope that Balinese might thank us for our thoughts on their music, as we might thank them for thoughts on ours.

In terms of any general discussion about time, some additional implications (at least for those likely to read this book) will be cultural. The distinctions between so-called "linear" and "cyclic" have become for many—both in music and other cultural domains, and consciously or not—associated with certain perspectives in a regrettably black-and-white way. Their symbolism is enormous and tenacious. The linear, always-changing kind of time is associated with historical progress and a Western, bourgeois, capitalist (call it what you will) view. On the positive side, this kind of time symbolizes the modern and liberated cutting edge of humankind's inventiveness; on the negative it signals hegemony, domination, elitism, and rootlessness. By contrast, repetitive musics are associated with "traditional" cultures—or their modern heirs, popular musics. On the positive side, this is thought of as communal and participatory; offering needed antidote and resistance to the decadence of the modern and hyperindividual; seen negatively it is crude and naïve, or else an overcommercialized, mechanistic commodity corrupted by the same capitalism it holds out against.

These symbols are old-fashioned and simplistic beyond the point of cliché. Nowadays they may grate on the sensibility of any of the millions who love and identify unproblematically with groove-based popular or traditional musics, the formally elaborate narratives of modern Western music, the patient trajectories of North Indian classical music, or others among the vast possibilities that exist. Why, then, do the symbols persist, embedded in cultural norms that pit the West against the rest? Merely asserting, as has been done, that they are false and outdated has not yet put them to bed. We are better off trying to dislodge them with concrete counterexamples such as the one I will discuss. Balinese music is a good place to do this kind of work because it has often been invoked (for the wrong reasons, in my view) as an exemplar of nonlinear time, an icon of an exotic culture that is irreconcilable with the cosmopolitan West. In a nutshell, the tired assumption is that Balinese music is static and Western music isn't.[1] I am not here to argue that this is or isn't the case as much as I am to persuade that the distinction between static and progressive musical time is itself false. Musical time, consistent with experience of lived time, is not either/ or. It is both/and.

Balinese Gamelan

Fabled Bali isle, a small province of Indonesia with a culture blending Southeast Asian and Hindu elements, has a deep and continuing history of musical abundance. Chant, song, and ensemble musics flourish there, often combined with poetry, dance and theater. Music remains as indispensable in the twenty-first century for Bali's many religious rituals as it was also for royal ceremonies of former times, and it continues in many informal, "folk" contexts. This is not to suggest that Bali itself is stable; it is engaged in constant debate and struggle over how to variously alter, adapt, discard, and reinvent its traditions to cope with modern Southeast Asian and global realities. Curiously, however, in the face of all this, its dense, dynamic instrumental music has proliferated with a vengeance. One part of its success has to do with the fact that for about a century it has been heard not only in ongoing, well-anchored ritual roles, but with growing frequency at secular events. In conjunction with recordings made and distributed worldwide, this has created considerable international demand. Like its home, Balinese music became famous. Ensembles have toured

---

1. This idea of "static time" in Bali generally (and gamelan particularly) flourished throughout the mid-twentieth century, reaching an apogee with Geertz (esp. 1973). It was stressed in ethnomusicology beginning with Colin McPhee's writings of the 1930s, up to Becker and Becker's seminal article about Javanese music (1982; see reference to this also in the Vetter/Sutton chapter in this volume), and Bassett 1995. The impact of such thinking is waning though slow to dissipate, as it is linked to perceptions about the irreducibility of cultural differences (Agawu 2003).

abroad since 1931, and since the 1950s thousands of foreigners have been drawn to learn the dance and music either by going there to study or by using exported instruments. I am one of them, captivated by playing, researching and composing it since 1977.

The nonvocal music is played on one of many different kinds of sets of mainly percussive instruments (with some bamboo flutes and one bowed instrument, the *rebab)* called *gamelan,* a word related to one for "hammer," which refers to the variously shaped mallets used. *Gamelan* in Bali can be owned by temples, schools, government offices, tourist resorts, individuals and especially by village districts called *banjar,* which store them in a public hall where people meet to practice together. More than eighty players and as few as two may be required, and the many varieties of instruments can be of wood, bamboo, leather (for drum skins), and, most characteristically, forged bronze shaped as keys or gongs of all sizes.

Historically, *gamelan* genres have specific uses and repertoires; for example, there is one genre called *gamelan gender wayang,* which has only four instruments of ten bronze keys each and a cohesive family of music compositions used for shadow puppet plays (an important theater form) and a few other kinds of rituals and theater. Every *gamelan* genre has a certain instrumentation, musical style, and particular way of adapting Balinese scales and tuning systems that makes it audibly and visually unique. The compositions, too, are distinctive and composed-out, though as intellectual property they are fluid, varying from village to village and subject to changes and modifications made by thoughtful players or ensemble leaders. As carefully composed and detailed as they are by the time a group commits itself to learning one, however, compositions are always taught orally and memorized strictly. This lengthy and satisfying transmission process catalyzes group social cohesion. And *gamelan* organizations also vary dramatically, both in terms of the sound of the instruments they play on and the character, skill, spirit, and history of the generations of musicians in each group.

The quintessential and most popular Balinese *gamelan* since Indonesia's 1945 independence is an ensemble requiring some twenty-five to thirty musicians. It includes about fifteen impressive bronze-keyed metallophones in several ranges spanning over four octaves, many sizes of gongs, from large and profound to tiny and pealing, two conical, double-headed drums, and bamboo flutes. It is known as *gamelan gong kebyar,* or *kebyar* for short. *Kebyar* is also the associated style: virtuoso, capricious, dazzling, complex—both in performance and musical concept. Listening to kebyar on CD as a newcomer can be overwhelming if one wants to know how the music is organized. One contends first with the sheer fact of a hail of reverberating, mallet-beaten bronze producing storms of crashing overtones. The music pulsates and throbs and is often thunderous and breathless, but sometimes suddenly hushed, and just as startlingly, loud and breakneck again. It is in a tonality all its own and saturated with stops, starts, turns and jumps between multiple melodies, textures, and tempi.

Yet cosmopolitan ears—alive to the way that foreign sound worlds beckon like secret epiphanies—sense order regulating the fury. But how to know it? There is no substitute for the "real thing" of immersion study. But with the help of CD track 12 and the transcriptions provided, I will guide you quickly through the basics and into some subtleties.

We are concerned with a *gending,* or musical composition, called *Oleg Tumulilingan,* created in 1951. It remains popular in Bali to this day, where everyone saves their breath and just says *Oleg. Oleg* is modern and secular: it was commissioned from musician Pan Sukra and dancer Ketut Maria for the occasion of the first major international tour of Balinese music and dance, in which the troupe from Peliatan village spent six months of 1952 in England and the United States, finishing with a much-hyped run in Las Vegas (the same group had also played at the Paris International Exposition in 1931).[2] But there is a well-known story about how the Peliatan musicians refined and elaborated what they took to be Sukra and Maria's "rough draft" after learning it and peremptorily dismissing the unwitting pair back to their home village. The anecdote is instructive both for demonstrating how malleable Balinese compositions are in performers' hands and equally because it indicates that the *Oleg* under discussion later, performed by musicians at the STSI music academy in 1991, is only one of many possible versions. With a popular piece like *Oleg,* variants would all use mostly the same music; the differences would come in the ordering of things, the tempi and dynamic changes overlaid, and the outlay of various kinds of melodic and rhythmic detail. Our analysis is thus only of this version, not of any elusive "*Oleg*" itself. Other versions would to a certain extent provoke their own analyses.

Oleg is associated with its choreography, which is every bit as fixed as its music (though similarly variable in detail from village to village). The movements, postures, and choreographic patterns of Balinese dance comprise a complex mirror of the music. Although a proper exploration of these essentials cannot be made to fit into the primarily musical concerns of the present chapter, the dimensions of richness they impart should be invoked and borne in mind. *Oleg*'s begins with an elaborate, abstract solo depicting a seductive female bumblebee flitting among flowers. With fingers outstretched and eyes sharply

2. *Oleg*'s creation is described in Coast (1953).

focused, the dancer's body is angled into the S-shaped basic posture of Balinese female dance, with feet slightly apart, fingers and toes bent up, and arms half-extended and raised to shoulder height (see page 207). Movement, by turns for arms and facial expressions only, or by small footsteps or knee bends, or in running sweeps around the stage, is organized into segments that correlate closely with musical phrasing and form. Costumed with a shimmering gold headdress and elegantly patterned sarong, the dancer's torso is wrapped in long strips of bright purple (or red, or green) and gold layers. A pair of thin scarves hanging from either side of a waistband are often lifted with the fingers and outstretched to where they hang just below the arms to simulate wings. Two-thirds of the way through, a dancer portraying a male bee joins her for a flirtation.

My observations on *Oleg*'s music are limited to the tightly constructed five minutes and twenty-two seconds of music (in this recording) accompanying the first half of the solo part of the dance. Although never performed separately, the music there is self-contained and could stand alone. It is not used later in the piece, and when it ends, after a very clear and slowed-down cadence, there is a full pause before the remainder commences. *Oleg* in full lasts for about fourteen minutes.[3]

Basics of Balinese Gamelan via Oleg

Skipping over *Oleg*'s dramatic, fragmented introductory passages for the moment, let us take our entrance into the music during the ensuing slow section. Our concern is with melody and formal structure; the drumming, although clear and engaging on the recording and important for many reasons, is not of itself vital to the present analysis and will merit only tangential mention in what follows. One also hears the bamboo flutes prominently here. Although much prized for their sweetness, these essentially duplicate, via decorative paraphrase, the melodies played on the bronze instruments. Hence, we will focus on the latter to explain the music, as would the Balinese. Bear in mind the following practical terms, all of which have fairly precise Balinese equivalents: *beat,* understood as one of a series of equal time units of fundamental importance; *cycle,* a series of (in this case) sixteen beats "filled" with melody, drumming, and so on; *punctuation,* the stressing/marking of certain beats in each

---

3. For analysis of other parts of Oleg, see Tenzer (2000, passim) and Ornstein (1971, passim). For more on the dance, see Bandem and DeBoer (1995).

cycle with an identifying pattern of strokes played on gongs of different sizes and sounds; and *strata,* the numerous layers of melody, punctuation and drumming that fill out cycles, each with a mainly consistent rate of subdivision.[4]

Oleg is composed within the scale/tuning environment characteristic of *gamelan gong kebyar.* This is a five-tone subset of a seven-tone aggregate found regionally and well-known by the Javanese word *pélog.*[5] Different *gamelan* reflect the system in their own ways, and historically there has been no standard. What makes the *kebyar* five-tone scale recognizable is its pitch level (the first of the five tones will lie somewhere between Western [B] and [D♯]), and the general pattern of intervals within each octave: small-small-large-small-large. The "smalls" can vary from less than a half step to more than a whole step, and the "larges" between a wide minor third and a narrow perfect fourth. Approximating one possible version, my transcriptions use the Western sequence [C♯–D–E–G♯–A–(C♯)]. Connections among adjacent pitches in this list are stepwise moves in *kebyar* even though it may not look that way on the Western staff (as between [E] and [G#] or [A] and [C#]). Admittedly the use of Western notation creates these sorts of problems, but the familiarity of the system itself is compensation. Throughout the transcriptions, too, there is nothing on the [F] or [B] places on the staff; analogs of these tones are not present at all. This explanation, however, can not really account for the special sound-world of the ensemble. The gamelan shimmers and pulsates intensely, as a result of the complex overtone clouds created by the action of wood striking bronze, and also the purposeful mistuning of pairs of instruments to create rapid acoustical beating.

Consider first the slow, settled passage lasting a single cycle from 1:00 to 1:32, at the entrance of the bamboo flutes (the sixteen beats last for a generous two seconds each at this pace). Five strata of the bronze instruments playing in this passage are transcribed in figure 6.1. One sees and hears how they are rhythmically stratified, like an inverted trapezoid set over a base of gongs at stratum 5. Each stratum is strictly set at a given rhythmic density (at least in this passage, which is a more or less default arrangement subject to much variation later).

---

4. Throughout I avoid Balinese terms for names of instruments and musical techniques when possible, fearing that an abundance of these would muddy the waters for my intended audience of mainly newcomers to Balinese music. Similarly, I avoid any discussion of general aspects of the music not directly related to the present analysis. Of course such information is readily available. Writings in English on Balinese music include McPhee (1966); Tenzer (1998, 2000); Harnish (1999); Basset (1995, 2004 [in French]); Gold (2001, 2004); Vitale (1990, 2003); and McGraw (2005).

5. The sixth and seventh tones of the scale are simply not present on the tuned bronze *kebyar* instruments, though flutes, rebab and occasionally-used singers can make them available. Other types of Balinese gamelan do avail themselves of all seven tones.

FIGURE 6.1. Oleg: *Melodic Strata and Gongs in cycle 8 (1:00–1:32. see appendix for fuller transcription).*

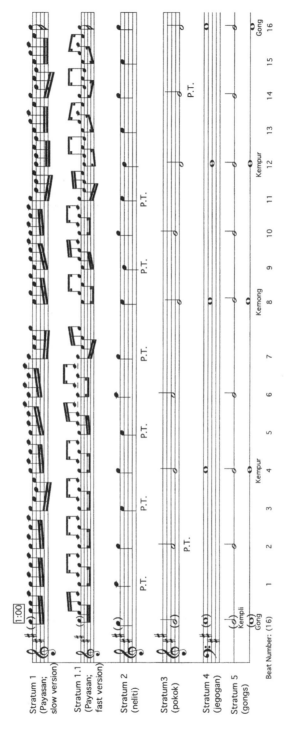

Although the music looks a bit rhythmically monotone on paper, we hear the musicians articulating the individual notes in varied ways, whereas the flutes and the drums add extra rhythmic and melodic nuance. Melodically, each stratum from 1 to 4 has its fixed sequence of tones. Scan the score vertically for the beats at which each stratum aligns with the ones above or below it. These nodal points are always related at the unison or octave or else by locally passing or neighboring tones (labeled P.T.). In this way one also hears, and can see, that the whole complex is unified through pitch-class identity and function as reflections of a single melodic concept.

The concept applies to each stratum in a different way. Stratum 1, played by the *payasan* (figuration) instruments is the densest and most prominent. I represent it here with a single sixteenth-note line despite the fact that there are actually twelve musicians working it out in different ways on three different kinds of instruments.[6] Only two of the twelve musicians play what I have written; two others play it an octave higher. Eight more play complementary parts in various possible configurations and registers that, in the end, all meld into a seamless, articulate band of sound (see appendix for a detailed and complete rendering of this passage including flutes, drums, and all melodic configurations).

Stratum 1.1 shows the same material as it would be played at a fast tempo (this is for illustration only, because even elsewhere in *Oleg*, because of alterations in phrasing, it is never actually rendered in precisely this way). Here two musicians would play the stems-down tones and two more play the stems-up part, interlocking closely to create a line just like that in stratum 1 but impossible for individuals to play at such a speed. Four others would double this quartet an octave higher, and the remaining four players in the stratum 1 group would play complex complementary parts as before. Balinese music is renowned for such interlocking (called *kotekan*), and it has been documented copiously.[7]

Stratum 2, what is termed *neliti* ("that which is correct or precise"), proceeds once per beat. Although there is a metallophone called *ugal* that *can* play the *neliti* if its player wishes, at slow tempi he or she is much more likely to ornament it. When the twelve players of stratum 1 drop out momentarily, as they often do, ornaments in stratum 2 stands out (1:50, 2:41 etc.). But in the passage shown in figure 6.1, not only is the *ugal* close to inaudible, the *neliti* is itself something of an imaginary guide, analogous to the sequence of chord changes present in a jazz tune, which are certainly *there* even though they may be liter-

6. They are *pemadé*, a set of four metallophones with a two-octave range; *kantilan*, another set of four identical to the first but one octave above it; and *reyong*, a row of twelve tuned gongs two octave plus two tones) played by four musicians each commanding two or three of them, and sharing one or two others with the player(s) beside them.

7. Bandem (1993), Vitale (1990), Tenzer (2000), Tilley (2003).

ally present only in an abstract way. And as with jazz changes, following this quasi-imaginary progression is important.

Strata 2, 3, and 4 are usually each played on one of three specially desig-nated pairs of instruments , each pair in its own register. A pair called *penyacah,* not heard on this recording, play the *neliti* verbatim. Balinese call stratum 3 *pokok,* or core (or root, or trunk) tones, because of its central place in the tex-ture. In stratum 4, the deep *jegogan* support the *pokok,* playing at half its rate.

Stratum 5 displays the punctuating gongs so indispensable to the structure and feeling of Balinese *gamelan.* The upper part shows the *kempli,* a small mounted gong making a "tk" sound. Here it plays every two beats, reinforcing the *pokok.* At faster tempi, to help the interlocking parts stay oriented, it would play at *neliti* rate. Below we see the hanging instruments *gong, kempur,* and *klentong* (abbreviated G, P, and t), aligned in density with stratum 4. The deep *gong* marks cycle endings/beginnings, the midsize *kempur* marks the first and third quarters, and the high "tong" sound of the *klentong,* harder to hear on the recording, the midpoint.

Oleg's sixteen-beat cycle, as a generative space for melody and a regenerating seed for form, is defined and identified by this pattern of gong, kempur, and klentong. The music should be counted and felt in such a way that the gong arrival at beat 16 receives the strongest accent. Because this is also the point at which the cycle begins, the notation commences with a labeled beat 16. But all the tones above it are in parentheses, as if to suggest the end of a previous cycle.

Oleg does not "own" this punctuation pattern; in fact, it is used in so many compositions and is so taken-for-granted that Balinese have no agreed-on name for it.[8] In the part of *Oleg* we have taken up this formation is always present, hold-ing fast while everything changes around it, like signposts in a shifting landscape.

Oleg's Architecture I: Tempo and Dynamics

Architecturally speaking, what makes *Oleg Oleg* is the combination of the hanging gongs' unchanging, repeating punctuation cycle and the directed pro-gressions of melody (and drumming) that fill this framework. In all the gong cycle occurs twenty-seven times, but the way it fills clock-time is elastic. Con-sider this first from the perspective of tempo and dynamics. In figure 6.1 the sixteen-beat distance from gong to gong was thirty-one seconds (equivalent to about MM = 32) but elsewhere—at 0:29, 3:53, and 4:42, and others—it com-

---

8. Some call it *tabuh dua; tabuh* means cycle-type and *dua* means two, which refers to the two *kempur* strokes before each gong stroke (Wayan Beratha and Wayan Sinti, per-sonal communication, 1998). The pattern is also called *bapang.* (Tenzer 2000:257).

presses to 5 seconds (MM = 192), a 600 percent difference in speed! (In other words, when the music is fastest, six notes fill the time that one note filled when it was slowest.) Still elsewhere, it accelerates or slows as if it had been suddenly stretched or relaxed, while ranging between loud and soft often and with comparable unpredictability. Depicted on a graph, the tempo displays a clear but imperfect sinusoidal shape. The shifts between slow and fast are dramatic and intriguing: they both mask the regularity of the sixteen-beat gong cycle and exploit that same regularity as a way of keeping the music unified, even (Balinese would say) simple, despite the fluctuations. Because of the gong's recurrences, throughout we grasp that the twenty-seven cycles are identical in some way, despite changes in tempo and dynamics.

Figure 6.2 graphs the twenty-seven cycles, measuring the speed of the beat against the "arbitrary" elapsing of minutes and seconds. If we could somehow set aside our reliance on the framework of clock-time for comparison we might feel as though time itself was speeding and slowing. The twenty-seven gong strokes are numbered and circled, with their clock-times indicated. The continuous black line passing through the gongs represents the musical continuity, curving up or down at accelerations or ritardandos. Balinese are emphatic that gong comes at the *ends* of cycles, even though cycles are also considered circular by them (which is their own version of the pleasant contradictions between regenerative and progressive time as, of course, circumferences have no beginnings or endings). Nonetheless, later, for essential reasons relating to the construction of the melodies, when discussing the music within a given cycle, I refer to the portion of the black line approaching the *left* of the numbered, circled gong strokes in this figure.

The thick band across the middle of the graph depicts orchestral texture and dynamics. The wider the band, the louder the sound. Narrow vertical lines within the band represent textures where part of the ensemble is not playing, and thicker ones are used when all play together. Here it can be seen that generally speaking, soft dynamics are associated with slower passages and loud dynamics with faster ones.[9] The music leading to gong 7 and continuing to

---

9. It must be understood that structurally insignificant changes from soft to loud or vice versa often occur within a cycle; what I have tried to characterize in the graph and in this paragraph is the structural dynamic character of cycles as wholes. For example, I speak of cycle 16 as being at peak dynamic though its final four beats are *subito piano*. There are many other such very surface, "expressive" changes, although I concede that in the present analysis, in order not to digress too much, I have not furnished sufficient criteria for distinguishing between these and structural ones. A more thorough (although still inchoate) approach to the interrelation of surface and structural aspects of dynamics and tempo is suggested in Tenzer (2000: 343–52).

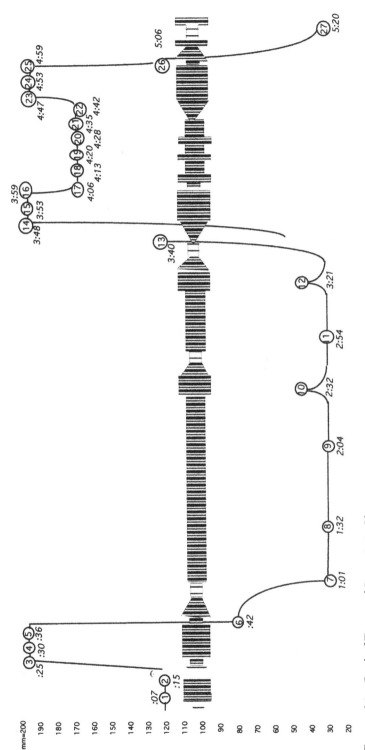

FIGURE 6.2. *Graph of Tempo and Dynamics in* Oleg.

gong 13 (just after 0:48 to 3:40) is soft except for the supple fluctuations leading to and away from gongs 10 and 12. The very fastest passages, spanning cycles 4 to 6 (0:25–0:42), 15 to 17 (3:48–4:06) and 24 to 26 (4:47–5:06), are all at high dynamic; all cadence with a sudden dropoff in volume and speed. The slightly less-fast music between gongs 18 and 23 is exceptional because of its sequence of abrupt dynamic changes, making it something of a climax in the evolution of tempo and dynamics through the composition.

Tempo and dynamics cooperate to articulate several possible perspectives on musical form. The pattern of their organization can be represented by letters as ABCBDBE. The intro A (the fast cycles 1–3) and the outro E (cycle 27, slow) flank the whole as though a set of musical parentheses. They in turn enclose the three symmetrically placed tempo "peaks" represented by B, each three cycles long. Bridging the three Bs are the two six-cycle center sections, the slow C and fast D. But these elegant proportions are thrown gently askew by the one-cycle transitions bracketing C, the first of which slows the tempo while the second speeds it up (cycles 7 and 14). This is an enrichment heightened also by the fact that C is so dramatically slower than the rest of the music. Indeed, the tempo differences between A, B and D feel more like gradations than genuine contrasts. Together, they comprise a large region of fast music, all of which is heard in clear juxtaposition to the central slow section C. To close the music E gradually returns to C's tempo as if to remind us that the latter is a stable, grounded state. For another view, one also could say that because C and D last for an extended number of cycles they claim the lion's share of our focus, and because of their contrasting tempi balance each other suitably. They are the central, most substantial passages. Seen this way, B's function is merely to link the other sections together.

The foregoing discussion is condensed into figure 6.3. In the next section's melodic analysis, we will layer on many additional observations about form.

Oleg's Architecture II: Melody and Figuration

Which of the various strata in figure 6.1 can be said to be the *actual* melody of *Oleg?* We have a semantics issue here, in that the closest vernacular equivalent of the word—*lagu*—is more flexible than the English one. In Bali "melody" can be any of the whole complex of strata. It is as if together they form a many-edged prism: there is a beam of light going in (the full ensemble) and separate spectral components coming out (the strata). In effect, whichever stratum one has under consideration can be called the melody because it is understood that the others are joined to it, cooperative with it.

FIGURE 6.3. *Tempo and dynamics in* Oleg, *shown in relation to the 27 gong cycles.*

Cycles (1-27)	Number of Cycles	Tempo	Dynamic	Formal Pattern
1–3	3	(Intro)	Varied	A
4–6	3	Peak	Loud	B
7, 8–13, 14	1,6,1	(Trans.) Slow (Trans.)	Soft	C
15–17	3	Peak	Loud	B
18–23	6	Fast	Soft/Loud	D
24–26	3	Peak	Loud	B
27	1	(Outro)	Varied	E

We are to be concerned with the two strata that appeared in figure 6.1 as strata 1 and 3. The former I have described as the figuration (or *payasan*). For the latter (the *pokok*) I shall use the term core melody, because its function is foundational. Figure 6.4 is a transcription of the figuration of the entire twenty-seven cycles of the performance. Each is numbered; the cycle shown in figure 6.1 now turns out to be the eighth of these. The various tempo designations used in figures 6.2 and 6.3 (slow, fast and peak) appear in the conventional place at the upper left of each line of music. The word "solo" (cycles 1, 3, 7, etc.) indicates a passage when the twelve *payasan* instruments drop out temporarily, leaving the *ugal* exposed above the slower metallophones—including the core melody, which is always playing—and usually the drums as well. As in figure 6.1, stems-up tones indicate tones that interlock at fast or peak tempi; at slow tempi, the stems-up parts move in parallel or at the unison.

Analysis of the transcription, including the core melody underpinning each of the twenty-seven lines of figuration shown, proceeds in four stages. The first three develop typologies of the various permutations used in the music for a specific aspect of the melodic/figurational structure. In a final stage the typologies are combined, overlaid, and integrated with the tempo analysis above to create a composite picture of these factors.

Permutations of the Core Melody and Their Affiliated Figurations

With the exceptions of the introductory cycles 1, 3 and 4, the remaining 24 cycles in *Oleg* all have the same core melody, however varied their figuration and other characteristics may be. The core melody also has some (very basic) transformations of its own: it appears in its original form, labeled "A," as well as in transposition down by two scale steps, "B," and in two forms that enable

FIGURE 6.4. *Full transcription of figuration stratum.*

FIGURE 6.4. *Continued*

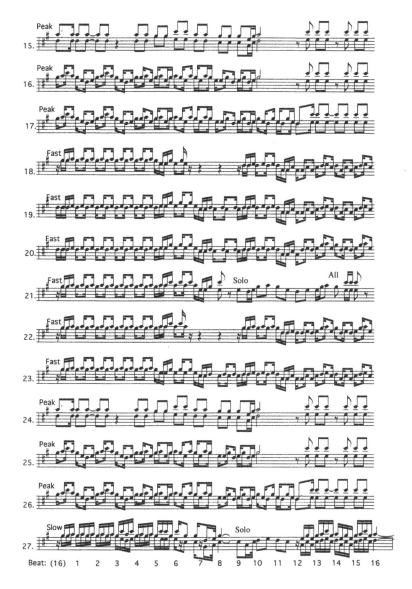

transition between A and B or vice versa: "A–B" and "B–A." (Cycles 1, 3, and 4 all use a sole, mildly contrasting core melody. Although not analyzed here, I mention it to stress the music's economy of means.)

Figure 6.5 displays cycles 2 and 5 through 27 (24 cycles), taken verbatim from figure 6.4 and rearranged in vertical alignment with their affiliated transfor-

FIGURE 6.5. *Transformations of the core melody aligned with the styles and phrasings of their figurations.*

mations ("styles and phrasings") of the core melody. Those that go with A are grouped in the upper left of the figure, those with B on the lower left, with A–B on the upper right, and with B–A on the lower right. The forms of the core melody itself are clustered at the center for comparison, and the sixteen beats of the cycle are numbered across the page between these central staves.

The core melodies are notated without stems and with alternating closed and open noteheads. The latter represent moments of greater metric impor-

FIGURE 6.5. *Continued*

tance; in other words, beats 4, 8, 12, and 16 are stronger than 2, 6, 10, and 14. This hierarchy is reinforced by the gong punctuations (Gong, Kempur [P] and Klentong [t]) on the stronger beats and also by the tones in stratum 4 (as seen in figure 6.1). Although these distinctions and reinforcements are present, the core melody itself, as a sounding stratum, is heard on each even-numbered beat with utter regularity.

One can verify the transposition relationship between A and B by keeping the *pélog* scale in mind. Since the five tones are represented by [C#, D, E G#, A], two steps below core melody A's gong tone [G#] is B's [D], and so on. As shown with the dotted lines, ovals and brackets, A–B and B–A are easily derived from their parent versions. In the former case the melody begins just as A does until beat 6, but from beats 6–16 the tones of B are spliced on. B–A begins just as B does up to beat 14, where the last two tones of A are substituted. What happens in these transitions is that the gong tone changes from [G#] to [D] and vice versa.

What does it mean to say that the music in the various staves above or below the core melodies are in fact figurations of them? Scanning along a vertical axis from the core melody to its affiliated staves one finds consistent Balinese-style heterophony. Specifically, this means that the scale tones on each of the strong beats, and on most of the weaker beats, too, are always the same. Thus, for example, in core melody A's figurations, [G#] is always present on beats 4 and 16, [E] on beat 8 and [D] on beat 12.[10] The figuration is actually a kind of filling-in at a greater rhythmic density, done in one of many possible styles drawn from a palette of possible figuration types.

Last, observe the variety of figurations, noting that the transformations of the core melody each have a different number of affiliated figurations. There are nine associated with A, only two with B, five with A–B, and three with B–A. Some of these clearly contrast with each other, while others are closely related and may only be different in one or two small features. Such differences are easily perceptible, however, and are not to be disregarded. I label the contrasting types *styles* and discuss small differences between two instances of a given style in terms of *phrasing*.

---

10. An exception can be seen at version I (staves 2 and 3) of the figurations lined up above core melody A. On beat 8, the core melody lands on E while the figuration is on D. This brief clash is resolved at beat 10. The alignment splits again at beat 12 and resolves again at 14. In effect, the figuration reverses the progression of the core melody at beats 8 and 12: it is D–E in the former case; E–D in the latter. These displacements do not alter the identity relationship.

Styles of Figuration

Because of their often quick rate of change and textural prominence, for most Balinese listeners figuration styles are expressive, influencing musical mood and meaning. Beyond this, for musicians and composers the palette of figuration styles comprises a collection of specific compositional techniques available to create desired musical impressions. Some styles are newly invented, while others originate, and are often uniquely associated with, certain older pre-twentieth-century gamelan genres. Thus, the use of a certain figuration style may constitute a clear reference to an older music, and the reference in turn evokes the particular ritual or social associations of that music. Or it may be something innovative and self-consciously new.

The vocabulary of styles appearing in *Oleg* happens to be small and conservative, consisting essentially of four historically derived types known respectively as *norot, nyog cag, ubit telu,* and *malpal* (there are no English equivalents). The references invoked draw, moreover, on a common and standard repertory of more-or-less "classical" composition techniques. By the same token the four styles contrast with one another clearly, and in so doing shape a series of clear structural profiles. As combined or contrasted within or among cycles, their expressive qualities are extremely familiar and unlikely to be lost on any (even minimally) competent Balinese listener.

IIa. Most prominent of the four is *norot,* which was already introduced (but not named) as stratum 1 (and 1.1) of figure 6.1. Norot is associated with the repertoire of the grand *gamelan gong gdé* of the former royal courts, whose many ritual compositions, developed over centuries, are heard regularly in temple ceremonies. It is spiritual and serious music, but as used for *Oleg*'s graceful bumblebee character it reflects also an association with untrammeled nature, and a sense that the bumblebee, although playful and sensuous, has a sacred dimension.

Referring back to figure 6.4, norot appears in slow tempo for cycles 7–13, and, divided into interlocking parts, in fast tempo at cycles 18–23 and 27. Cycle 14 comprises an acceleration that begins slowly with the players dividing up into interlocking parts on the fourth beat. In cycles 7 and 11, the norot gives way to an *ugal* solo midway through. In other cycles, other kinds of phrasing changes occur as well. In cycles 8–10, 12, 14, 19, 20, and 23, the style's very elemental design is most apparent. It consists of regular alternation, in sixteenth notes, between the current core melody tone and its upper neighbor. When the core melody moves, the norot moves three sixteenths in anticipation, articulating the change with a double-note figure.

For the ensuing remarks, bear in mind that a reference to beat 1, for example, includes the tone that falls on the beat as well as the three sixteenth

notes *preceding* it, in order to remain faithful to Balinese end-accented perceptions. Norot's pattern of regular alternation can be seen at beats 2, 3, 5, 7, 9,
and 11; the double-note figure at beats 6, 8, 10, and 12. The double-note figure
also appears in beat 1, but as a kind of embellishment rather than as an anticipation. The purely decorative diversion at beat 4 is something added to give
the overall line a distinctive shape so that it is not a purely generic realization
of norot patterns. Ditto for the four-beat cadential figure at beats 13–16, which
borrows from another kind of figuration style, *nyog cag*.

IIb. Nyog cag is associated with the innovations of gamelan gong kebyar in
its early years, the 1920s and 1930s, though it is used widely in all kinds of
music today. It is an interlocking style in which one part plays on the even and
the other on the odd subdivisions of the beat; each part taking a disjunct shape
that allows their composite to be conjunct through a kind of leap-frogging
action. Nyog cag is athletic and traverses a much wider range than norot. Because it covers more pitches in less time, it has a stronger musical momentum.
Its particular kind of interlocking makes it suitable for playing at very fast
tempi, though it can also be slowed down enough so that a single player can
play all of the notes, as in the four-beat cadential figure just mentioned.

In *Oleg* nyog cag is less pervasive than norot, and is used in balanced combination with other styles. Cycle 6, for example, begins with norot and ends
with a different kind of figure (discussed later under phrasing), but features
nyog cag centrally at beats 5–12; cycle 5 is identical save for a change in the
phrasing at beats 11–12. Nyog cag also appears dramatically at the beginnings
of cycles 16–17 and their repeat at 25–26, where it is soon supplanted by the
third kind of style, *ubit telu*.

IIc. Ubit telu patterns interlock using a total of three scale tones every two
beats (ubit is a term for interlocking parts; telu means three). They are heard
in cycles 16 and 25 from beats 5–11 and cycles 17 and 26 from 5–13. Instead of
nyog cag's exact alternation, in ubit telu the two interlocking parts coincide
whenever the middle of the three tones in use appears. Their association with
sacred repertoire recalls norot's, but because they generally appear at fast tempi
they have a more virtuoso, human character.

IId. Malpal, the last of the figuration styles, is heard at two key junctures:
cycle 15 and its repeat at 24 (recall from figure 6.2 that these cycles initiate the
passages in peak tempo that flank the fast passage at 18–23). The style is characterized by rhythmic unisons and repeated pitches played at fast tempi at a
mainly eighth note rate. As such it contrasts ringingly with the density of norot,
nyog cag, and ubit telu. Malpal is actually a dance term connoting large steps
used to circle or traverse the stage rapidly. The dancer does just this at these
points in *Oleg*, whereas elsewhere her feet remain comparatively more static,

or take smaller steps. The contrast provided by the judicious introduction of malpal underlines the shifts taking place at those moments.

Varieties of Phrasing

In a Balinese composer's imagination, the art of shaping a figuration for a core melody can be described in terms of two stages. First, a style or styles is selected according to the expressive quality desired. It is a matter of applying imagination plus various grammatical rules to work out a good fit between the selected style(s) and the core melody. Normatively, figuration fills the entire cycle in a rhythmically continuous succession, the way, for example, norot and nyog cag do in cycle 8 (or 23). But cycles where figuration does not, in the end, unfold in this way, can still be *conceived* thus, at least initially. In the second stage of composing, to add detail and contrast, or to synchronize with key dance movements, the composer removes some segments of the figuration and substitutes other motives, or sometimes just leaves a "hole." All of these phenomena can be classified under the Balinese music rubric of *angsel*, that is, an interruption in a normatively continuous texture introduced for contrast and accent.

There is a hole in cycle 5 at beats 11–12, for in the following cycle the same nyog cag figuration continues through those same two beats. Cycles 16–17 and 25–26 are similarly related. The norot in cycles 18 and 22 is interrupted by a pause at beats 8–9; were it filled in, the cycle at 22 would give us the normative version shown in figure 1, stratum 1.1. The fact, moreover, that a normative version of the material in cycle 22 never appears underscores the flexibility of the materials. *Oleg* is strictly cyclic at its root, but one cannot overvalue the compositional importance of shading and altering materials in each cycle in unexpected ways.

There are two types of angsel in which melodic material or rhythmic motives are substituted for normative figuration. In one of these types, the figuration instruments drop out at beat 8, and are followed by an ugal solo lasting to gong. This occurs in cycles 7, 11, 13, 21, and 27 (in 27, the figuration also moves to a kind of subcadence at beats 6–7, and reenters at beat 13). The other type, which has three subtypes, comes at the concluding beats of the cycle. Figuration is replaced by a rifflike rhythm on the repeated pitch [E], complemented by the higher [C♯]. The first of the subtypes, lasting four beats, is found in cycles 5, 15, 16, 24, and 25; the second, also four beats, is in cycles 6, 17, and 26. The third subtype, combined with the ugal solo in cycle 21, occupies on the last two beats.

I have now accounted for all of the twenty-seven cycles in figure 6.4, except for numbers 1 through 4. 1, 3 and 4 were excluded because they are based on a different core melody. But cycle 2, based on core melody A, is unique. It uses none of the figuration nor phrasing strategies so far described, and its materials do not reappear elsewhere. They are, in fact, unique not just to cycle 2 but to *Oleg* itself, having the fanfare-like quality of a signature, inaugurating phrase. Nearly any Balinese could identify *Oleg* given just a segment of it.

The Composite Analysis: Core Melody, Style, Tempo, and Phrasing

Drawing on figures 6.2–6.5, figure 6.6 summarizes the progressions of the four parameters described above, aligning each in columns of a table whose rows correspond to the twenty-seven cycles. The rightmost column compiles the designations from the others into a single code. Bold horizontal lines within columns reveal macrorhythms comprising groups of cycles. Evidently, even though the parameters are well delineated within individual cycle boundaries, the cycles themselves cluster into diverse formations. These veiled, asynchronously layered shifts reside at a level of structure located between the individual cycle and the entire composition, a level that I have elsewhere called metacyclic (Tenzer 2000:276, 452).

A bird's-eye view make it plain that metacycles in different columns are often unaligned. The core melody's metacycles throw this asynchronicity into sharpest relief vis-à-vis the whole. Cycles 7–15 and 16–24 turn out to be iterations of a nine-cycle macropattern (numbered at the right margin of the column). Cycle 7 shares a boundary with the style and tempo columns, but it is out-of-synch with these when cycle 16 begins and aligned with the phrasing column instead. The nine-cycle group is thus reinforced by other structural parameters at each occurrence, yet differently. (For years I taught and performed *Oleg* and was provoked by an intuitive sense that a process of this sort was in motion, but it was masked by the progression of the other parameters and inaccessible until I worked out this analysis in detail.)

In the next two columns, the four different figuration style combinations are seen to align closely with tempo changes. Styles in cycles 2 (labeled X) and 5–6 (norot and nyog cag, labeled I) do not recur later. It is the consistent use of style combination II (norot with the four-beat nyog cag cadential pattern) that sets up the metacycles for this column. II appears in cycles 7–14, changing to III (malpal) and IV (nyog cag and ubit telu) when peak tempo is attained at cycles 15–17. The return to II at cycle 18 occasions the beginning of a second metacycle, which similarly shifts to III and IV at cycles 24–26. The two metacycles last 11 and 9 cycles, respectively; they are unequal but one may also say that at this level of structure they are balanced. This can be felt especially if one perceives the *fact* of II's extreme prolongation as the important thing,

FIGURE 6.6. *The composite analysis.*

Cycle #	Core Melody		Style	Tempo	Phrasing	Complete code
1.	(-)		(-)	Fast	(-)	(-)
2.	A		X	Fast	x	A/X/F/x
3.	(-)		(-)	Fast	(-)	(-)
4.	(-)		(-)	Peak	(-)	(-)
5.	A	(1)	I (*norot & nyog cag*)	Peak	a (angsel subtype 1)	A/I/P/a
6.	A	(2)	I	Peak	b (angsel subtype 2)	A/I/P/b
7.	A	(1)	II (*norot & nyog cag cad.*)	(Rit.) Slow	c (hole & ugal solo)	A/II/S/c
8.	A	(2)	II	Slow	d (normative 16th)	A/II/S/d
9.	A-B (= trans. A to B)	(3)	II	Slow	d	AB/II/S/d
10.	B	(4)	II	Slow	d	B/II/S/d
11.	B-A (= trans. B to A)	(5)	II	Slow	c	BA/II/S/c
12.	A	(6)	II	Slow	d	A/II/S/d
13.	A	(7)	II	Slow	c	A/II/S/c
14.	A-B	(8)	II	Slow (Accel.)	d	AB/II/Acc./d
15.	B-A	(9)	III (*malpal*)	Peak	e (malpal & angsel "a")	BA/III/P/e
16.	A	(1)	IV (*nyog cag & telu*)	Peak	a	A/IV/P/a
17.	A	(2)	IV	Peak	b	A/IV/P/b
18.	A-B	(3)	II	Fast	d' (d with hole)	AB/II/F/d'
19.	B	(4)	II	Fast	d	B/II/F/d
20.	B-A	(5)	II	Fast	d	BA/II/F/d
21.	A	(6)	II	Fast	c' (c & angsel subtype 3)	A/II/F/c'
22.	A	(7)	II	Fast	d'	A/II/F/d'
23.	A-B	(8)	II	Fast	d	AB/II/F/d
24.	B-A	(9)	III	Peak	e	BA/III/P/e
25.	A	(1)	IV	Peak	a	A/IV/P/a
26.	A	(2)	IV	Peak	b	A/IV/P/b
27.	A-B	(3)	II	Slow	h	AB/II/S/h

rather than the exact length of its prolongation. When II returns again in cycle 27, it is as if the process is to begin again, but is truncated by the ending.

Phrasing, the most nuanced and variable element in the music, is consequently hardest to group and analyze. Using lowercase letters, the numerous angsel types (motives and holes) have been identified in the table according to their description in the discussion earlier. Some differences among them are so slight, such as between cycles 18 (d') and 19(d), that the decision was taken to use the designation "prime" for the former rather than a new letter. The rationale for identifying metacycles between cycles 5–15 (eleven cycles inclusive) and 16–24 (nine cycles) rests upon the way each group begins with [a, b] and ends with [d,e], with various combinations of c and d in-between. When a metacycle begins again at 25, it also starts with [a,b] only to be cut short, as with other parameters, by the ending.

Because the core melody proceeds at a medium (i.e., half-note) pace, as opposed to the figuration's quick (sixteenth-note) one, we may perceive the former as a kind of structural movement somewhat akin to harmonic rhythm in Western tonal music. Like harmonic rhythm, the core melody has that powerful ability to cast an organizing shadow over our other perceptions. Heard against other parameters, the core melody's nine-gong metacycle strongly supports the central, concluding points of the entire analysis, which can now be stated unambiguously: *Oleg* may be rigidly based on a sixteen-beat cycle of gong punctuations, but is irregular at higher levels and, in terms of combinations of parameters, essentially devoid of repetition altogether. In the rightmost column of figure 6.6, we see that when all of the parameters are combined, there is only one instance of precise repetition, at 15–17 and 24–26. But this is an exception that proves the rule. However efficiently related to their companions they may be, every other cycle in the piece is uniquely constituted. *Oleg* displays a clear tension between temporal qualities: a solid periodicity at the cyclic level is heard in productive conflict with sets of staggered periodicities at metacyclic levels. The multiple layering of these factors yields a forceful linear drive at the level of the entire composition.

An Experience of Oleg, and the Uses It May Have

The materials of the preceding analysis were presented in the order in which I became aware of them, first as a player, then in contemplation: the regularity of the sixteen-beat cycle, then the tempo and dynamic plan, then the unity behind the core melody's transformations, and so on to the multidimensional composite of all the factors. Now I experience an unnameable temporal complexity as I listen, in which a repetitive, circular time intensifies, expands and contracts at multiple other levels through the building up of metacycles. I concede that the pair of nine-gong core melody metacycles (the grouping that is most asymmetrical and decoupled from other parameters, therefore most enriching of the overall complexity) are easier to comprehend than to follow. My own direct awareness of them varies according to how narrowly I focus my perceptions toward them, without ever disappearing entirely when my focus is broader. The point is that when "taking it all in," when I listen to *Oleg* as an organic, end-directed narrative, the experience is textured by the many sublevels, each independent and clearly articulated in its own right, that are always moving and standing still, returning and departing, ebbing and flowing at different rates, some regular, some not, some closed, some open.

Balinese music, for which *Oleg* stands here, offers a range of other temporal experiences, some more intensively cyclical, others more loosely discursive. *Oleg's* asymmetrical layering does not make it unique in Bali, for there are select other, comparable pieces, but along with those it is distinctive in its special recipe for temporality: that is, it is hypertypical, a special achievement of the culture. That Balinese recognize its particular value is evident from the permanent place it was accorded in the repertoire, in a century that produced much music already forgotten. At the level of the culture one might describe *Oleg* as definitive, having remarkable musical qualities (plus terpsichorean ones) that, because of the ingenious trio of stratified structure, rooted cyclicity and directed compositional process, only Balinese music is capable of achieving in such a way. Any such representative of a culture, moreover, rightly deserves the opportunity to be juxtaposed and compared with its counterparts in other cultures, and here is where concentrated listening to *Oleg* may have a broader application.

As suggested at the outset, all music, or more precisely, all music as we perceive it, suggests both motion and stasis in time. Within Indonesia there are other, regional musics analogous to *Oleg* (see the following chapter, on Javanese gamelan) and still others stressing either periodicity or linearity to much greater degrees.[11] Because there is nothing particularly Balinese or Indonesian about any of these qualities in the abstract, by letting temporality be our linchpin we can wander worldwide. Much jazz, to give a sole example from elsewhere, has its own kind of stratified structure (rhythm section, riffs, and soloist(s)), its own periodicities (cycles such as the blues chord progression), but with a com-

---

11. For a wealth of information and examples, see Yampolsky 1990–2000. The forest music of Mentawai (vol. 7, tracks 13–16) contain examples of minimally adorned cyclicity, whereas bamboo music from the Kenyah River of Kalimantan (vol. 17, tracks 5–6) are complex and asymmetrical.

positional process that tends to be much looser than in Bali, owing to the prominence of improvisation (insignificant in Bali). Ingrid Monson's graphic reduction of her analysis of *Sent For You Yesterday,* a blues by Count Basie and his band, although done for different reasons and different purposes, can be profitably compared to figure 6.6 above (1999, figure 1; shown here as figure 6.7). She also discovers a multilevel progression of periodicities, comprising layered blues choruses, melodies, riffs, call and response patterns, orchestration changes, and so on that is kin to *Oleg's* metacycles.

How far could we imagine extending this comparative potential? Might we use periodicity to compare Count Basie to a Burmese *hsaing-waing* ensemble or Shona *mbira?* If we found common elements there would be nothing to stop us; and there just might be some, if the example of the far-flung encounter between Bali and Basie has any persuasive power. It may be unsettling to think this way, though, because in the study of world musics it is axiomatic that music aids in isolating and according special value to a culture's identity. We may, perhaps aptly, feel at sea without this orientation. Even where musics blend and change across borders and through diaspora, the tendency has been to disentangle structures to relate them to cultures of origin, or to new and emerging cultures, again to assert, or at least problematize, identity. And there is no question that cultural and musical relatedness have historically gone hand in hand.

Would the integrity of cultural identities be threatened if we stressed features uniting disparate musics rather than dividing them? What both Monson and I have shown analytically is that periodic musics can yield complex linearity. Taken together, our examples reveal how this is achieved in related ways for extremely different case studies. We did so, moreover, without first dutifully doffing hats to Mozart symphonies or Schoenberg quartets, as if linearity is something for which Western art music gets to set the terms. (Conversely, the conventional downplaying of repetition in most writing about Western music impoverishes our view of it too, and equally segregates it from the rest of the world.) And rightly so, since in our lifetimes Western cultural prestige has shifted and shrunk to more realistic and fair proportions, a reality paradoxically at odds with the continued urge to articulate cultural identities that were originally formed in a defensive response to its dominance. Thinking musically, it is no surprise that integrated linear/periodic structures proliferate well beyond and outside Balinese gamelan, jazz, hsaing-waing or symphonies, yet why do we still have so few demonstrations of these phenomena? I suggest that a critical mass of such demonstrations would ultimately require us to view linearity and periodicity as elements of a larger unity rather than as oppositions, and that to accept this would be to truly bind Western art music to the

FIGURE 6.7. *Monson's analysis of "Sent for You Yesterday."*

	A				B			A				
	Intro	Chorus 1	Chorus 2	Chorus 3	Interlude	Chorus 4	Chorus 5	Interlude	Chorus 6	Chorus 7	Chorus 8	Coda
	8 bars	12 bars	12 bars	12 bars	4 bars	12 bars	12 bars	4 bars	12 bars	12 bars	12 bars	8 bars
	Piano 4 & Reeds 4	Ensemble	Piano Solo	Tenor Solo	Reeds	Vocal	Vocal	Trumpet	Trumpet solo	Ensemble shout	Ensemble shout	Reed 4 & Piano 4
		C&R brass and reed riff & solo alto sax	C&R piano solo & trombone with plungers muted	Over continuous brass riff		C&R voice & trumpet solo, piano improv. in background	C&R voice and reeds over continuous brass riff, piano off-beat hits		Continuous riff in reeds	C&R brass & reeds	C&R brass and drums over continuous wind riff	
(Unit of periodicity)		2+2	2+2	1		2+2	2+2 (voice + reeds) 2 brass 1 piano		1	1+1	1+1 (brass + drums) 1 (reed)	

(Monson 1999:35, reprinted with permission). "Sent for You Yesterday" (Count Basie-Eddie Durham-Jimmy Rushing) New York: 2/16/38 Smithsonian RD 030-2. Personnel: Buck Clayton, Ed Lewis, Harry "Sweets" Edison, tps; Dan Minor, Benny Morton, Eddie Durham, tbs; Earl Warren as; Jack Washington, as, bs; Herschel Evans, Lester Young, cl, ts; Count Basie, p; Freddie Green, gt; Walter Page, b; Jo Jones, d; Jimmy Rushing, vcl. (C&R = Call and Response)

233

Figure 6.Apf. Oleg: *detailed transcription of 1:01. to 1:32.*

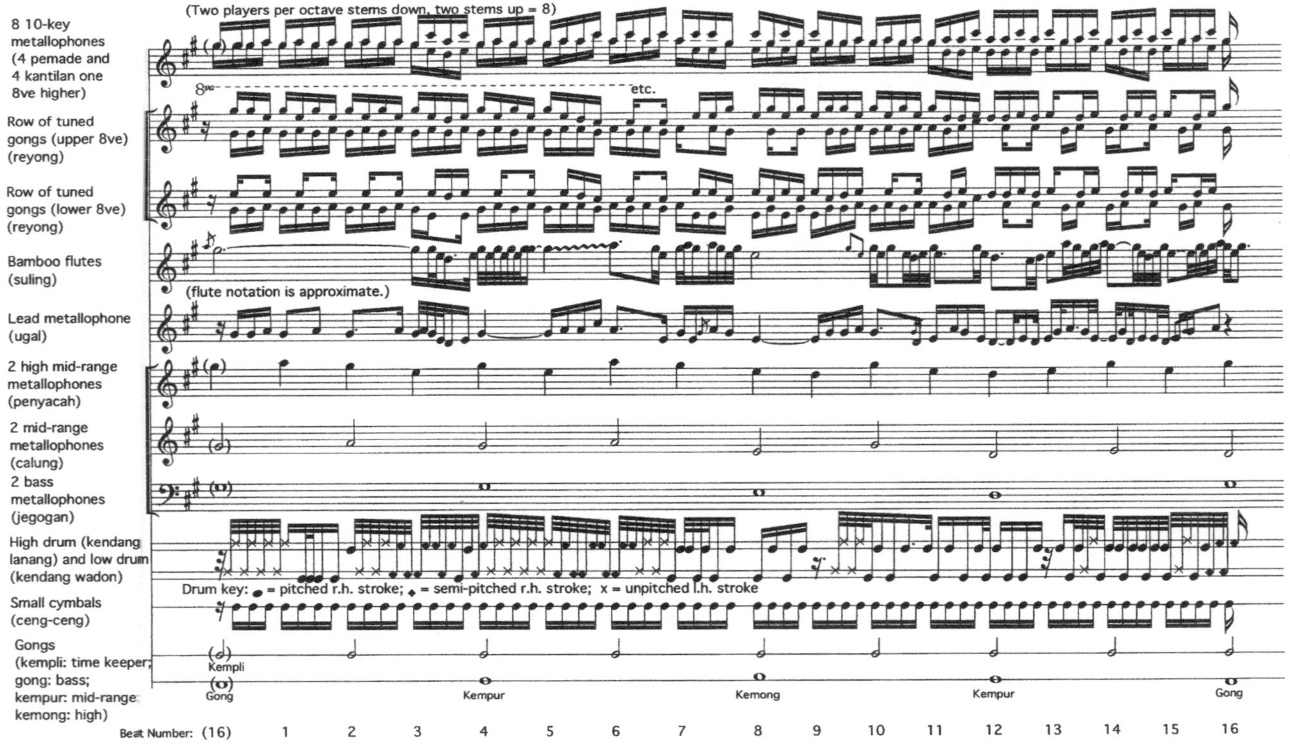

rest of the world's music, to finally be rid of any assumption that its temporality is uniquely set apart.

People all over are preoccupied in wildly varying degrees by the contradictory desires to both fortify and transcend their identities, which music helps equally to define and to destabilize. One thing is clear: musics themselves, steered by human actors, now connect more rapidly and frequently and across greater distances and circumstances than before, and "culture" is by no means the primary force of attraction in all cases. It could be mere accessibility, taste, the internet, individual imagination or creativity, or any of a million factors that confront us with opportunities and pathways for refreshment. I am far from the first to note that this laboratory is music's destiny for the foreseeable future, just as it is humanity's.

References

Agawu, Kofi. 2003. *Representing African Music: Postcolonial Notes, Queries, Positions*. New York: Routledge.

Bandem, Madé. 1993. "Ubit Ubitan: Sebuah Teknik Permainan Gamelan Bali." *Mudra: Jurnal Seni Budaya* Edisi Khusus. Denpasar: STSI, 59–91.

Bandem, Madé, and Frederik E. de Boer. 1995. *From Kaja to Kelod: Balinese Dance in Transition*. New York: Oxford University Press.

Basset, Catherine. 2004. vol. I: *Gong, Vingt Ans de Recherche;* vol. II: *Musiques de Bali à Java: L'Ordre et la Fête;* vol. III: *Gamelan, Architecture Sonore* (internet site: /www.cite-musique.fr/gamelan/); vol. IV: *Roue Sonore, Cosmogonie et Structures Essentielles de L'offrande;* vol. V: *Bibliographie et Table des Matières*. Thèse d'Ethnologie: Université Pars X-Nanterre, Laboratoire d'Ethnomusicologie UMR 8574.

————. 1995. *Musiques de Bali à Java: L'Ordre et la Fête*. Paris: Cité de la Musique/ Actes Sud.

Becker, Judith, and Alton Becker. 1981. "A Musical Icon: Power and Meaning in Javanese Gamelan Music." In W. Steiner, ed., *The Sign in Music and Literature*. Austin: University of Texas Press, 203–225.

Coast, John. 1953. *Dancing Out of Bali*. New York: Putnam.

Geertz, Clifford. 1973. *The Interpretation of Cultures*. New York: Basic Books.

Gold, Lisa. 2004. *Music in Bali: Experiencing Music, Expressing Culture*. New York: Oxford University Press.

————. 2001. "Bali." In *The New Grove Dictionary of Music and Musicians*. Ed. S. Sadie and J. Tyrrell. London: Macmillan. Vol. 12, 289–308.

Harnish 1998. "Bali." In *The Garland Encyclopedia of World Music,* vol. 4: *Southeast Asia*. Ed. Terry E. Miller and Sean Williams. New York: Garland, 729–761.

McGraw, Andrew Clay. 2005. *Musik Kontemporer: Experimental Music by Balinese Composers*. Ph.D. dissertation Wesleyan University.

McPhee, Colin. 1966. *Music in Bali: A Study in Form and Orchestration in Balinese Orchestral Music*. New Haven: Yale University Press.

Monson, Ingrid. 1999. "Riffs, Repetition, and Theories of Globalization." *Ethnomusicology* 43(1):31–65.

Ornstein, Ruby. 1971. *Gamelan Gong Kebyar: The Development of a Balinese Musical Tradition*. Ph.D. diss. University of California, Los Angeles.

Tenzer, Michael 2000. *Gamelan Gong Kebyar: The Art of Twentieth Century Balinese Music*. Chicago: University of Chicago Press.

———. 1998[1991]. *Balinese Music*. Periplus Editions: Berkeley and Singapore.

Tilley. Leslie. 2003. *The Technique of Reyong Norot Elaboration in Balinese Gamelan Music*. M.A. thesis, University of British Columbia.

Vitale, Wayne. 2002. "Balinese *Kebyar* Music Breaks the Five-Tone Barrier: New Composition for Seven-Tone *Gamelan*." *Perspectives of New Music* 40(1):5–69.

———. 1990. *"Kotekan:* The Technique of Interlocking Parts in Balinese Music." *Balungan* 4(2):2–15.

Yampolsky 1995. "Forces for Change in the Regional Performing Arts of Indonesia." *Bijdragen tot de Taal-, Land- en Volkenkunde* 151(4):700–725.

———. 1990–2000. Music of Indonesia, Vols. 1–20. Smithsonian Folkways SFW CDs. Set of 20 Compact Discs. Recorded, annotated and compiled by Philip Yampolsky. Numerous musicians. (Vol. 7: *Music from the Forests of Riau and Mentawai.* SFWCD 40423; and Vol. 17: *Kalimantan: Dayak Ritual and Festival Music.* SFWCD 40444.)

CHAPTER 7

Flexing the Frame in Javanese Gamelan Music

Playfulness in a Performance of Ladrang Pangkur

R. ANDERSON SUTTON AND ROGER R. VETTER

The composition of central Javanese gamelan music chosen for analysis in this chapter exemplifies many of the techniques evolved in Java for distorting and enriching symmetrical, periodic melody. It is perhaps no surprise—yet nonetheless a wonder to contemplate—that this venerated large ensemble music, largely founded upon such elegant and logical binary structures, allows for them to be stretched to the limits of perception in ways that challenge and satisfy listeners and performers alike. We shall examine the extent of at least some of these distortions in one particular performance, relating them back always to their regular substrate and the conventions that govern the tradition as a whole, and in so doing provide a reading of the music as flexible, multidimensional, and, in many aspects, anything but regular.

The Indonesian island of Java is home to an enormous variety of musical traditions, including a number of regional gamelan traditions. In this country of roughly five thousand inhabited islands and more than two hundred ethnolinguistic groups, each with its own particular approaches to music-making, the Javanese represent the largest single group, numbering more than seventy-five million. The music under consideration is associated with the court city of Surakarta (known more familiarly as "Solo") and the inland areas nearby; and if we visited regions within central and eastern Java remote from Solo we would likely find musicians playing at least some music in Solonese style, though other styles persist. If we travel to the western portion of the island, the province of West Java, we would encounter a substantially different set of traditions, not "Javanese," but "Sundanese."

The piece we explore, *Ladrang Pangkur* (CD track 13) is not attributable to any known composer, living or deceased. It is known to have existed in some (probably many) forms for several centuries at least, and many musicians have contributed to the actual shapes that it takes in performance. The performance here, dating from the 1970s, is by Condhong Raos, one of the top two or three gamelan groups of Java from the late 1960s through the 1980s, under the direction of master musician-composer-shadow puppeteer Ki Nartosabdho (1925–1985).[1] The performance is part of a medley from an audio cassette commercially released by a company no longer in existence and widely available throughout central and eastern Java during the late 1970s and 1980s.

Although not every Javanese is intimately familiar with gamelan music, all have heard it in public ceremonies, family rituals (especially weddings and circumcisions), and through the mass media (radio, television, and recordings). The extent to which casual listeners are aware of the structure of the music— the relationships between the many parts heard simultaneously and the shape given by the musicians to the piece as it unfolds—is difficult to say. Although many Javanese would claim little or no "theoretical" understanding of gamelan music, most would know, for example, that the sounding of one of the largest hanging gongs articulates the largest phrases of the piece, that the musicians respond primarily to the drummer's signals for changes in tempo and dynamics, and perhaps that the main melody (called *balungan,* lit. "skeleton," "outline") is generally played by some or all of the single-octave metallophones (*saron*). Many have had at least some instruction in gamelan music during primary or secondary school, and others may have more extensive experience. What we intend to convey in this chapter is something approaching what gamelan musicians themselves and knowledgeable gamelan music lovers would "hear" and "understand" in the particular rendering of a single piece of music. *Ladrang Pangkur* is one of the best known and most frequently played items in the entire repertory, which consists of several thousand pieces generally identified as "traditional" (i.e., known for at least several generations), and a rapidly growing body of new, mostly light pieces composed since about 1950 (after Indonesia gained its independence from the Netherlands).

As Tenzer points out (see chapter 6) with respect to Balinese gamelan music, Javanese gamelan music seems to play with our sense of time, stretching and compressing it through its unique approaches to rhythm and tempo. The performance we have chosen undergoes a number of shifts in tempo, both gradual and abrupt, leading the knowledgeable listener through eight succes-

---

1. For a short biography of Ki Nartosabdho, told mostly in his own words, see Sutton (2002:307–312).

Instruments of the Javanese gamelan at Pura Pakualaman, Yogyakarta, in 1974—(clockwise from top left) gendèr panerus *(foreground) and* gendèr barung; kendhang gendhing; gambang; kempul *(left) and* gong ageng *(right). Photos by Valerie Mau Vetter.*

sive statements of a main phrase, followed by one statement of a (partially) contrastive phrase. In a variety of interesting ways, the underlying sense of repetition is constantly disrupted and obscured by changes in tempo, changes in emphasis on different instrument types and voices, and omission and substitution of melodic material. Indeed, in comparison to the way many Javanese pieces are performed, this one is among those that frequently undergo some of the most radically playful alterations, in which the basic framework is, as we have indicated in the chapter title, "flexed" (but not broken). A number of textbook descriptions of Javanese gamelan music[2] stress the regularity and recursive-

2. Including a chapter by one of the current authors; see Sutton (2002).

ness of gamelan musical formal structure and performance practice, its binary symmetry and predictability. Indeed, the simpler renditions of the simpler pieces are remarkably regular, recursive (some would say monotonously repetitive), and predictable. Yet musicians of even modest accomplishment do not limit themselves to the simpler renditions of simpler pieces. Most would readily attest to the greater musical depth and aesthetic delight taken in playing and listening to pieces performed with changes in tempo and with melodic variation, pieces whose performance leads the listener through differing aural worlds, corresponding to different moods and different technical challenges.

Javanese "Compositions" for Gamelan Ensemble: Gendhing

Javanese refer to compositions for gamelan ensemble with the word *gendhing.* They may use the term *komposisi* (an Indonesianization of the *compositie,* the Dutch word for "composition"), but usually in reference either to the process of composing, or to a new work in which most or all of the parts have been determined by a composer. A printed collection of "compositions" would normally contain all the parts written out, perhaps with additional verbal explanation by the composer as to how parts should be realized. A *gendhing,* by contrast, takes its particular shape in performance. Multiple performances of the "same *gendhing*" can actually differ quite substantially from one another, but will share at least the same, or very similar main melody (*balungan*), and the same or very similar patterns of punctuation by the large gongs and other punctuating gong instruments.[3] Details of melodic variation, number of repetitions, tempo, and dynamics are all at least partially determined in performance, often in response to the unique demands of the dance or puppet drama they accompany, though limited by a shared knowledge of prior performance conventions (what we might call a shared knowledge of the "tradition" of rendering that particular *gendhing* and others of similar structure and mood).

Javanese *gendhing,* as realized in performance, produce a complex texture that some have characterized as "stratified polyphony" (Hood and Susilo 1967) others as "heterophony" (Sutton 1993, *inter alios*). One useful way to conceive of the texture—that is, the nature of simultaneous sound structures—is to think of the following layers:

1. a main melody, or melodic skeleton (*balungan*), is usually played by single-octave metallophones;

3. Three performances of the Javanese *gendhing Ketawang Puspawarna* are compared in Vetter (1981).

2. this main melody is punctuated in a (mostly) regular, repeated pattern known to musicologists as "colotomic" punctuation, played on various knobbed gong instruments, some hanging vertically, others mounted in wooden cases;

3. other melodic instruments, playing at faster densities (usually 2, 4, 8, 16, or 32 times faster than the beat of the main melody), provide melodic elaboration, in complex heterophonic relation to the main melody and to each other (and to the vocalists, if present);

4. (in many, but not all *gendhing*), voices and several non-percussion instruments perform less rhythmically rigid, sometimes florid melodic lines; these include fiddle (*rebab*), flute (*suling*), a florid vocal line performed by a solo female vocalist (*pesindhèn*), and a more rhythmically regular vocal line performed by male chorus (*gérong*), all in heterophonic relation to the main melody, to each other, and to the elaborating instrument parts;

5. one or two drums (out of three at the drummer's disposal) sound patterns which may simply be *gongan* (the melodic phrase between consecutive strokes of the largest gong)-length ostinatos (played on the largest drum or a combination of the largest and smallest drum) or more complex and lively patterns, usually originating from dance or dramatic accompaniment (played on the middle-sized drum).

These five layers are all interdependent and involve complex codes of interaction in performance, a topic thoroughly explored by ethnomusicologist Benjamin Brinner in his book on competence and interaction in Javanese gamelan music (1995).

Ladrang Pangkur

Rather than proceeding with further generalizations about *gendhing* we turn now to *Ladrang Pangkur,* or, to give its complete designation, *Ladrang Pangkur laras sléndro pathet sanga.* The full title of the *gendhing* conveys important information about formal structure (*ladrang*), the particular melody (*Pangkur*), tuning system/*laras* (*sléndro*) and mode/*pathet* (*sanga*).

The word "*ladrang*" tells us the pattern of punctuation used: the large hanging gong (*gong ageng*) plays every 32 beats, marking off the largest cyclic phrase unit, known as a *gongan;* the large horizontal kettle gong (*kenong*) plays every 8 beats, marking off the secondary phrase units, known as *kenongan;*[4] a

---

4. In Javanese and Indonesian, plural is not marked when implied from context; thus, we speak of a piece in *ladrang* form having four *kenongan* (not four "kenongans").

smaller hanging gong (*kempul*) plays at the midpoint in the second, third, and fourth *kenongan;* and the small, single horizontal kettle gong (*kethuk*) plays on the second and sixth beat of each *kenongan.* Thus, the *kenong, kempul,* and *kethuk* each mark different levels of subdivision of the 32-beat *gongan,* interlocking to form a regular, recursive pattern as follows (with t standing for *kethuk,* n for *kenong,* p for *kempul,* w for *wela,* a "rest" in the punctuation, and g for *gong,* sounding simultaneously with every fourth *kenong* stroke): t w t n t p t n t p t n t p t n/g. The *kenong* strokes mark the quarter points in the cycle (1/4 of the way through, 2/4 of the way through, etc.), the *kempul* (or *wela*) mark every other of the eighth points (1/8 of the way through, 3/8 of the way through, etc.) and the *kethuk* every other of the sixteenth points (1/16 of the way through, 3/16 of the way through, etc.). These audible guideposts make for a highly predictable sequence that, especially in more complicated pieces, can actually help musicians and dancers keep (or regain) their bearings, knowing "where they are" in the flow of the piece. As we will see in the analysis below, referring to these structure points is essential in understanding both the frame and the flexing thereof.

The word "*Pangkur*" identifies the main melody of this piece as distinct from the many hundreds of other such melodies with *ladrang* structure. In the narrower sense, this is the core title of this *gendhing.* By itself, the term *pangkur* refers to one of more than a dozen common sung poetical forms, differentiated from one another by verse structure (number of lines, number of syllables per line, and final vowel of each line) as well as melody. In fact, there are several different *pangkur* melodies, all with the same verse structure, each melody identified by additional words: *Pangkur Dhudha Kasmaran* ("Widower/Divorcé in Love" Pangkur), *Pangkur Ngrenasmara* ("Enjoyment/Pleasure of Love" Pangkur). Sometimes the *pangkur* that forms the basis of the *gendhing* we have chosen is referred to as *Pangkur Paripurna* (lit. "Whole/Complete" Pangkur) although there is nothing "incomplete" about the other *pangkur* melodies.

The words "*laras sléndro*" tell us in which of the two tuning systems (*laras*) the *gendhing* is played. *Sléndro* is a tuning system (in this case also a scale system) involving five tones per octave, separated by nearly equidistant intervals (each larger than a major second and smaller than a minor third). The other tuning system is *pélog,* comprising seven tones per octave, with uneven intervals, ranging from roughly a minor second to a minor third. Many whole pieces in *pélog,* or phrases within them, employ one of several possible pentatonic scales built of small (S) and large (L) intervals (e.g., S, L, S, S, L, etc.). In fact, *Ladrang Pangkur* can be played in two different *pélog* scales, with contours mostly similar, but intervallic structures markedly different from one another.

The final portion of the full title tells us the Javanese modal (*pathet*) category in which the *gendhing* is played. In *sléndro* there are three *pathet* in all (*nem, sanga,* and *manyura*), usually interpreted as differing in register (*nem* being the lowest, *manyura* the highest), but in actuality determined by a number of factors, including featured and avoided tones, contours, and their positions within the formal structure of the *gongan.* Although Javanese musicians and theoreticians discuss and argue more extensively about *pathet* than most other aspects of Javanese music, it is not essential for an appreciation of this performance. Had we time and space to analyze a large number of *gendhing,* questions of *pathet* designation would emerge naturally.[5] Suffice it to say at this point that musicians whose parts are partially created as they perform must have a sense of the *pathet* of the *gendhing* in order to make idiomatic choices.

A great deal has been written and published already about the instruments of the Javanese gamelan and the singers that often join with the gamelan music for performances of *gendhing* such as *Ladrang Pangkur;* in fact, nearly all gamelan performances in recent times involve singers and a large combination of instruments, both "soft-playing" and "loud-playing." Besides the punctuating gong instruments already mentioned, the "loud-playing" ensemble consists of three octaves of single-octave metallophones (*saron*), two kettle gong chimes (*bonang*), and a set of three drums (*kendhang*). The "soft-playing" ensemble incorporates the florid melodic playing of a two-stringed fiddle (*rebab*) and end-blown flute (*suling*), and the rhythmically regular and binary elaborating instruments: multioctave metallophones (*gendèr*), xylophone (*gambang*), zither (*celempung* or *siter*), and a soft-playing, single-octave metallophone (*slenthem*) that usually is also played for "loud-playing" style as well. Note that in current practice, the "loud-playing" instruments keep playing, albeit softly, for pieces or sections of pieces in "soft-playing" style. In most cases, when the soft-playing instruments are used, vocalists also join the ensemble, usually consisting of female soloists (*pesindhèn*) and a small male chorus (*gérong*).

Treatment (Garapan): Realizing Ladrang Pangkur *In Performance*

The performance we have chosen to analyze exhibits a number of features that are typical in most or all performances of this particular *gendhing,* or of all *ladrang,* or even of all *gendhing.* For example, nearly all *gendhing* begin with a melodic solo introduction (*buka*) joined first by the drum and then the other instruments at the first gong stroke. In many cases the *buka* identifies the *gendhing* to knowledgeable listeners; and in this largely oral tradition, musi-

5. For extensive discussion of *pathet,* see especially Kunst (1949/1973), Hood (1954), Becker (1980), Powers (1980), McDermott and Sumarsan (1975), and Perlman and Powers (2001).

cians may not be informed beforehand what *gendhing* they will be playing, or in what order, but will recognize the *buka* and play appropriately. The *buka* played for this performance is most closely associated with *Ladrang Pangkur,* but in fact can be used for several closely related pieces as well.

In the course of our analysis, we need to cover a number of topics. These include the following: tempo levels (*irama*), changes between levels (I, II, III, and IV), and resultant melodic expansion and contraction; various kinds of instrumental variation (simultaneous and sequential); contrastive drumming styles and signals; male and female vocal melodies, vocal solos, and vocal text; and the dynamics of interaction among musicians as the *gendhing* is performed. See the key to transcriptions for information.

In its most basic, reduced form, *Ladrang Pangkur* (here in *laras slendro pathet sanga*) consists of a 32-beat melody, often conceived and taught as a succession of eight measures (*gatra*) of four beats. (Slight variations of this melody exist, but this version is standard within the Solonese tradition.) For close to one hundred years, the notation system used most frequently to represent this and other *gendhing* basic melodies (*balungan*) is a cipher system. The main transcriptions we will analyze for the remainder of this chapter are given in standard Western notation, modified to accommodate, as best as possible, the musical features of gamelan music. But readers should know that Javanese almost never use Western notation to learn or study gamelan music. Instead they would write the basic 32-beat melody of this version of *Ladrang Pangkur* as follows, each line representing a *kenongan* of eight beats, that is, two *gatra*.[6] A slightly larger space is given between the two *gatra* than between the individual numerals within each *gatra,* not to indicate greater rhythmic duration but simply to make it easier to see each *gatra* as one unit, comparable to a measure or bar in Western music:

2 1 2 6   2 1 6 5

6 5 2 1   3 2 1 6

2 3 2 1   5 3 2 1

3 2 1 6   2 1 6 5

This notation has not only proven very practical (compact, easy to read, easy to type or enter on a computer), but also shows the binary symmetry that characterizes the *ladrang* form. Indeed, most Javanese musical forms are based on

6. This "basic" version is the one played at the faster tempo levels (*irama* I and II); a more elaborated main melody, in some sections containing two melody tones per structural beat is played at the slower tempo levels (*irama* III and IV).

a comparable symmetry, with the number of beats per *gongan* equaling some factor of 2 (i.e., 2, 4, 8, 16, 32, 64, 128, or 256 beats per *gongan*).

The Macro-Form

Now, let us take a close look at figure 7.1, what we are calling the "macro transcription," which shows the introduction (*buka*), and *saron* melody and colotomic punctuation as actually played for the entire performance.[7] We are using the Western five-line staff but in many ways, because of the nature of gamelan music, our transcription requires some substantial explanation. First, we chose in the macro transcription to place the strongest beat at the end, rather than the beginning, in order to conform with Javanese conceptions of beat, identifying the strongest beat—that is, the one corresponding with the gong stroke—as the last, not the first beat. Thus, in *ladrang* form, the main melody beat heard simultaneously with the gong stroke is beat 32, not beat 1, even though Westerners not familiar with gamelan music would almost certainly identify this strongly weighted beat as the "downbeat" (or "first beat").

We also chose to represent pitches that do not correspond exactly to the Western pitches implied by the notation. In the key to the transcriptions we provide fairly precise measurements of the actual pitches used, showing divergences from Western pitches in "cents" (one octave consisting of 1200 cents; i.e., 100 cents for each semitone of the Western tempered scale). Most important, however, is to realize that the intervals between what appear as major seconds are slightly larger than major seconds, and between what appear as minor thirds are slightly smaller than minor thirds, as this tuning system tends toward equidistant intervals (five per octave, as explained above). The "translation" we have used assigns the Javanese *sléndro* tones as follows: 1 = d; 2 = e; 3 = g; 5 = a; 6 = c. (Note: there is no tone 4 in *sléndro;* 3 and 5 are conjunct.[8])

---

7. The *saron* melody played here is nearly always what Javanese would identify as the main melody (*balungan*), the only exceptions being the quarter note (double time) variations played in the middle of sixth and seventh *gongan* (pitches [c e g a], leading to [c]) instead of what in this context would be half notes (pitches [c e g])—the standard *balungan,* as can be seen in comparable passages between *kenong* (n) and *kethuk* (t) at the same horizontal position in previous lines.

8. The omission of "4" in the ciphers for *sléndro* is very likely due to the Western origin of this notation system, in which the tone 5 (not 4) is a fifth above tone 1. In *sléndro* this interval is slightly larger than a tempered fifth, but close. Also in older Javanese nomenclature, though the first three tones are *barang* ("thing"), *gulu* ("neck"), and *dhadha* ("chest"), the next two have long been known as *lima* ("five") and *nem* ("six").

Key to transcriptions.

Ⓐ Pitch

actual pitch 230 260 235 265 210 cents

-10 +20 -20 +15 -20 -10

transposed pitch (used in transcriptions)

-10 +20 -20 +15 -20 -10

Ⓑ Drum Sounds

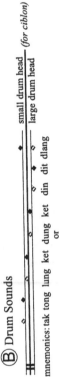

small drum head *(for ciblon)*
large drum head

mnemonics: tak tong lung ket dung ket din dit dlang
or
du

Ⓒ Form

$\left[\begin{array}{c} 32 \\ \rho, \circ, \bullet \end{array} \right]$ = 32 structural beats/*gongan*

= note value of a structural beat

Ⓓ Colotomic Events

g = *gong ageng*
s = *gong siyem*
n = *kenong*
p = *kempul*
t = *kethuk*

Ⓔ Tempo

($\downarrow$, $\downarrow$, $\circ$, $\bullet$ = 48) tempo of the structural beat
(in beats per minute)

Ⓕ Tempo Level (*irama*)

I = *irama tanggung*
II = *irama dadi*
III = *irama wilet*
IV = *irama rangkep*

Ⓖ Interruptions

// = a momentary cessation
to the flow of the performance
(*andhegan*)

pes. = solo *pesindhèn*
following a halt

Ⓗ Timings

2:02
$\lor$
timing (elapsed)
of an event

246

The *buka,* played by *rebab,* ends on pitch "a" (tone 5) at which point the full ensemble joins in, including the two most important colotomic punctuators: the large gong (*gong ageng*) and the *kenong.* The drummer enters part way through the *buka* to guide the tempo and confirm the formal structure. As shown, each of the subsequent lines of the transcription represents one *gongan* (full melodic phrase),[9] which may take as little as nineteen seconds (the first *gongan*) to as long as three minutes sixteen seconds (the last *gongan*). This fact by itself gives you some sense of the degree to which the basic framework of the *gongan* can be flexed with respect to duration alone. This dimension of flexibility is generally talked about in relation to the Javanese concept of *irama* level. Observe that:

- The first five lines after the *buka* (i.e., first five *gongan*) are played in *irama* I (also sometimes called *irama tanggung,* meaning "in between" or "not yet settled"). The actual duration can vary slightly; what makes all of these "*irama* I" is the ratio between the main melody (the part shown in its entirety in figure 7.1) and the subdividing parts. Figure 7.2, which shows many (but not all) of the instrumental parts played in the first *gongan,* reveals that both the *bonang barung* (medium sized gong chime) and the *saron peking* (smallest and highest pitched single-octave metallophone) subdivide the basic melody (played by *saron barung* and *saron demung*)[10] at a ratio of 2:1.
- In *irama* II, as shown in the first portion of figure 7.5 (and portions of figures 7.3 and 7.4; and sometimes called *irama dadi,* meaning "settled") the main melody, played on the *saron barung* (and others not notated here) has slowed to about half of what it was in *irama* I, now shown as half notes instead of quarter notes, and the *saron peking,* playing at more or less the same rate as in *irama* I, and therefore shown as eighth notes, is subdividing the *saron barung*'s half notes at a ratio of 4:1. In this performance, it is only the middle portions of the sixth and seventh *gongan* that are performed in *irama* II.
- *Irama* III (also called *irama wilet,* meaning "intricate"—referring to the nature of the elaborating parts), as one might expect, is realized with a ratio of 8:1, with one beat of main melody represented by a whole note; and

9. We decided not to add bar lines but simply offer a time signature that shows relative tempo and the number of beats per *gongan.*

10. Not shown is the *slenthem* part, which also plays the main melody, but an octave lower than *saron demung.*

FIGURE 7.1. *Macro transcription of the performance of* Ladrang Pangkur *by Condhong Raos, Ki Nartosabdho, director (source: "Aneka Pangkur," P.T. Wisanda cassette WD-508. n.d.).*

248

FIGURE 7.1. *Continued*

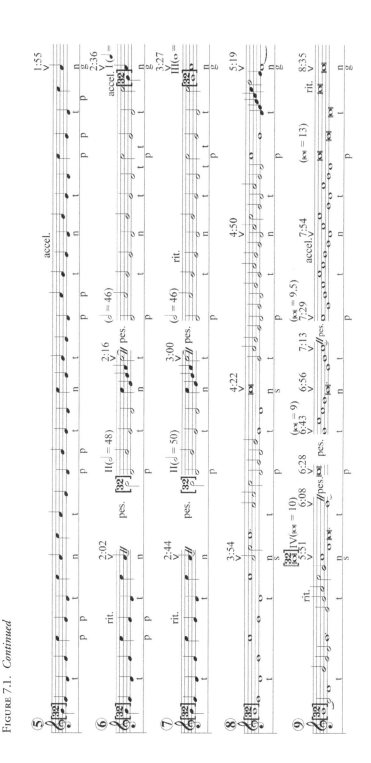

249

FIGURE 7.2. Gcngan *1 and 2, illustrating contrastive garapan (treatments) within irama* tanggung (*I*).

250

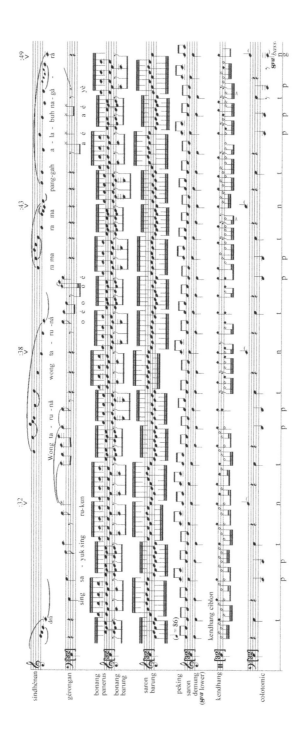

251

- *irama* IV (also called *irama rangkep,* meaning "double density") is realized at a ratio of 16:1, with one beat of main melody represented by a double whole note. Irama III and IV appear only during the last two cycles, as described later.

The eighth *gongan* is in *irama* III and, as can be seen in figure 7.1, is characterized by a combination of some whole notes, representing a slowed down version of the same melody we have heard in all the previous *gongan* ([e d e c e d c a]; or 2 1 2 6 2 1 6 5), followed by a passage with more varied rhythm (half notes, dotted whole notes, and even quarters at the end of the *gongan*) and a melodic contour that, while tracing the same basic path as in *irama* I up to near the end of the line, diverges somewhat.

The main melody (and hence all the other melodic parts) in the ninth and final *gongan* of this performance contrasts markedly with those in all the previous *gongan.* This ninth *gongan* is referred to as the *lik* (verb form *ngelik,* lit., "to get small"; that is, to go up to the high register). It is, strictly speaking, an optional section, one that is only played in response to a signal from the lead melodic instrument, the *rebab,* which goes "up" (Javanese say "gets small") to high [d] (tone 1) near the end of the previous *gongan,* between the final *kempul* and *kethuk* strokes (at 5:09). The other instruments and voices follow, the *pesindhèn* and *gérong* clearly singing in the high register and the *saron* instruments playing the ascending scalar passage of quarter notes approaching the end of the line (see last line of figure 7.6). Thus, one of the important ways in which the frame can be flexed is for this contrastive *gongan* to be played. Another is the slowing of the tempo in this *gongan* in approach to the first *kenong* stroke (at 5:51, melody on pitch [a], tone 5). At this point the *irama* level drops from *irama* III to *irama* IV and the elaborating parts double their density, even though the tempo of the main melody in *irama* IV has not dropped to half that of *irama* III. Because the subdividing parts must therefore play faster in *irama* IV than in any other *irama* level, this is often considered the most challenging for the musicians playing those parts. Also, because the *gongan* is stretched to such a remarkable length (more than three minutes) it can be more of a challenge not to get lost at this *irama* level than at the others.

Toward the end of the *ngelik gongan,* beginning with the last *gatra* of the third *kenongan* (c.7:45) and continuing through most of the fourth *kenongan,* the main melody, still in *irama* IV, is identical to that of the "normal" *Ladrang Pangkur* melody of *irama* III (eighth gongan). The acceleration of the tempo in approach to the final gong prepares for the end of this stretched-out *irama*-IV playing, but instead of going back to the regular *irama*-III *gongan,* the *rebab* plays a high [d] (tone 1, at 8:34) and the drumming changes just before the gong beat to lead without interruption into *Ayak-ayakan laras sléndro pathet sanga,* and from there to still other pieces, before finally ending (*suwuk*).[11]

Rather than let each line of figure 7.1 represent roughly the same amount of clock time, we chose to let each one present the *saron* melody for one *gongan.* This was to facilitate comparison between the various *gongan,* the first five of which consist of identical *saron* lines in *irama* I, the next two of which involve some interruptions and passages in *irama* II (shown here as half notes). In each line, the prevailing *irama* level is given in the time signature: 32 over a quarter note means 32 "*irama*-I" beats per *gongan;* 32 over a half note, as found right after the first gaps in sixth and seventh *gongan,* means 32 *irama*-II beats per *gongan.* Although the "value" of the beat may change (i.e., to use Western notation terminology, from a quarter to half-note, etc.), these changes in *irama* are never predetermined by a composer, however, but rather are signaled during performance by the drummer, who can decide to change tempo by playing a particular combination of drum strokes, which must in turn be heard and correctly interpreted by the musicians. Without the specific signals, the musicians would not change *irama* level, but simply keep repeating the *gongan* at the same tempo. Similarly, to end (*suwuk*) or proceed to another *gendhing,* the musicians also follow the tempo lead of the drummer, and a lead melodic instrument player (*rebab* or *bonang barung*).

An important aspect of the performance that leaps out at us from the macrotranscription (figure 7.1) is the appearance of gaps part way through the sixth, seventh, and ninth *gongan.* These represent short time intervals, leading up to which the instrumental music has been brought to a halt by the drummer's special pattern and during which the *pesindhèn* sings a short solo, only to be joined again by the instrumentalists just a bit further on in the *gongan.* Listen again to the sixth *gongan,* and look at figure 7.3. Analytically we can see that the *pesindhèn* fills a portion of the *gongan,* her short solo replacing a *gatra* (four beats) of the normal measured rhythm we have heard in the main melody, its elaborators, and the drumming through the first five *gongan* and in most of the subsequent ones as well. This coordinated halt in the middle of the *gongan* is known simply as *andhegan* (lit., a "stop") and is an intentional and playful interruption of the regular and predictable binary rhythm that has led up to it, and will return following it. Socially, an *andhegan* is a time for spe-

11. They could have ended their performance with a return to the regular *irama* III *gongan* of *Ladrang Pangkur,* or even gone back to *irama* I (*kébar*). But here the *rebab* and the drum signal *Ayak-ayakan,* not a surprising choice for those knowledgeable of the range of performance possibilities. (Because of time limitations, we have not included the subsequent pieces of this medley on the book CD.)

cial focus on the female singer, whose voice, and often whose dress and manner, are often found to be appealing, even erotic, by the many male audience
members.[12] Musicians and seasoned listeners (again, mostly male) often sigh
at the end of the *pesindhèn*'s solo, simultaneously marking the transition from
free, florid time back to measured instrumental rhythm and expressing a kind
of stylized, flirtatious appreciation for the *pesindhèn*'s melody. (A bit more will
be said in relation to figure 7.3.)

Before turning our attention to the particular details of this performance
that are shown in the subsequent transcribed figures, let's consider what else is
evident in this macrotranscription. For most of the first line, we see the standard colotomic punctuation pattern for *ladrang,* but toward the end of even
this line, in addition to the *kempul* (p) sounded on the fourth beat (pitch c)
after the *kenong* beat (its "normal" point in *ladrang* structure), we see two additional *kempul* strokes: one on the very next beat (pitch e) and another in between the following pitches (d and c). This livelier *kempul* part is not simply
an arbitrary choice made by the *kempul* player, but rather is a response to the
change in drumming style from the calmer *ladrang* ostinato, played on the
large and small drums (*kendhang gendhing* and *kendhang ketipung,* referred to
in combination as *kendhang loro,* lit. "two drums") up to the third *kenong*
stroke, to the much livelier dance-oriented drumming played on the middle-
sized (*ciblon*) drum from that point until the end of the piece. The *kethuk* part
also becomes somewhat more active just before gong in the sixth and seventh
gongan, sounding on the half beats immediately before and after the *kempul*
stroke. We will say more about this as we scrutinize figures 7.2 and 7.3 more
closely. Finally, although the large gong (*gong ageng*) only plays at its appointed
colotomic point, the final beat of each *gongan,* we hear the slightly smaller
gong (*gong siyem* (s)), play at certain other points in some *gongan,* for example,
a low [c] (6) at the end of the first and second *kenongan* of *irama* III (eighth
gongan, at 3:54 and 4:22) and at end of the first *kenongan* in the *ngelik gongan*
(the moment of "arrival" at *irama* IV; 5:51). These additions enrich the sound
with their deep, resonant tones, often stressing the main tone in the passage
immediately following, but do not articulate formal structure.

12. Although many individual Javanese *pesindhèn* rebuke flirtatious advances by male
audience members, their appearance at events that often last all night, such as shadow
puppet (*wayang kulit*) performances or all-night gamelan concerts (*klenèngan*), with instrumentalists who are all, or nearly all, male continues to suggest a degree of sexual avail-
ability greater than that of most Javanese women. And the historical antecedents of the
Javanese *pesindhèn* are the *talèdhèk* (or *ronggèng*), female singer-dancers who often served
the sexual desires of their male audience members (see further Sutton [1987], Walton [1996],
Tohari [2004]).

FIGURE 7.3. Gongan 6, *illustrating* trommel rem *treatment with* andhegan.

255

Enriching the Form: Tempo Changes, Interruptions, and Irama *Shifts*

Gongan 1 and 2

Figure 7.2 offers a detailed look at the first two *gongan,* both played in *irama* I, but contrasting in a number of aesthetically significant ways. Since it is the drumming style that is the primary determinant of the stylistic orientation employed in many of the other instrumental and vocal parts, let us look at that part first. Up to the third *kenong* stroke (at 0:21) the drummer plays a standard *ladrang* pattern on the large and small drums, at a fast steady tempo. But at this point he switches to the medium-sized (*ciblon*) drum and slows the tempo a bit (with no *irama* change), thereby signaling a shift to what is known as *kébar* treatment. The drumming in the following *gongan,* as can easily be seen in the transcription and heard on the CD (starting after 0:26), is much livelier and more varied than the highly repetitive drumming motif used over and over again in the standard *ladrang* drumming. This same style continues through the third, fourth, and fifth *gongan,* and into the sixth *gongan* until it is interrupted by an *andhegan. Kébar* drumming might sound lively and spontaneous, but it is actually a mostly fixed accompaniment for the *kiprah* (preening) movements of the flirtatious female dance known as *gambyong.* Even though no dancer is present, the drummer here, and in much of the remainder of the performance, plays *gambyong* dance patterns, following, as it were, an imagined choreography.

Let's consider now what this change to *kébar* style (or *kébar* "treatment") means for the other parts. Though some *saron* (the lower pitched *demung*) continue to play the main melody, the two *saron barung* play in a lively interlocking style (*imbal*), the composite of which is four times the rate of the main melody (here the *imbal* is shown as sixteenth notes against the quarter notes of the main melody). One *saron barung* plays on each beat of the main melody and half way in between ("on beat"), as the other *saron barung* plays in between those beats ("off beat"). The resultant melody is mostly conjunct, and follows the melodic contour of the main melody quite closely, pairing two notes at a time.

The two *bonang* (*barung* and *panerus*) for most of the first *gongan* have employed a technique known as *pipilan* (lit. "pick off one at a time"), in which each one varies the main melody two tones at a time by playing each pair in alternation, one at a time (the *panerus* at twice the rate of the *barung*). However, in response to the *ciblon* drum, the two *bonang* switch just after the gong stroke at 0:26 to an *imbal* technique, playing interlocking octaves with the *bonang barung* mostly anticipating every second tone of the main melody and the *bonang panerus* playing the tone one step (or, more often, one octave and one step) above that of the *bonang barung*. Despite the octave transposition, the ear tends to hear these two parts as creating mostly conjunct interlocking, like the *saron barung*, as the lower tone of the *bonang panerus* is always conjunct with either the higher, or (more rarely) the lower tone of the *bonang barung*. Together the two styles of interlocking (both generally referred to as *imbal*) create a very lively feeling Javanese would identify as *sigrak* ("lively"), *lincah* (Ind., "lively," "light-hearted"), even a little *urakan* ("unmannerly," "rude," "bawdy").

Adding to the lively feeling of this *kébar* passage are the vocalizations of the male chorus, here mostly vocables (syllables with no lexical meaning), such as "o é o" and "a é", the phrase *sing sayuk, sing rukun* (lit., "that which is congenial, that which is compatible/harmonious"). In addition to vocalizing, the male chorus members perform interlocking handclapping to add to the liveliness. The *pesindhèn* also enters, singing light-hearted, didactic verses in a form known as *wangsalan* The *pesindhèn* inserts short phrases (*abon-abon*) between the lines of the main *wangsalan* text to fill the *gongan*. Her melody floats over the steady beats of the instrumental parts, guided by the structural framework, but partially obscuring it or, as it were, softening its edges, by arriving at the important goal tones (usually those at the end of *gatra*, i.e., the *kenong* tones and the tones half way in between) late. This delayed arrival creates a layer of heterophony much appreciated by Javanese musicians and listeners, who will criticize a *pesindhèn* who arrives "too soon" at those goal tones.

The main melody in the *kébar* passages remains the same as beforehand, although it is only the *saron demung* (and *slenthem*, an octave lower, not shown) that continue to play the main melody, the *saron barung* having switched to *imbal* technique. The colotomic punctuation still articulates the *ladrang* form, but the *kempul* part becomes more active, playing on the fourth and fifth beats of each *kenongan* (instead of only the fourth beat of only the second, third, and fourth *kenongan* that characterizes the basic form and "standard" playing). And near the end of the fourth *kenongan* it also adds a syncopated stroke between the sixth and seventh beats, right before the gong beat. Thus, even among the instruments whose function is generally described as the articulation of formal structure, the *kempul* playing responds to and enhances the livelier mood with added strokes.

Gongan 5, 6, and 7

In the midst of what begins as the fifth *kébar gongan* (the sixth *gongan* in *irama* I), the drummer's signal brings the musicians to an abrupt halt just before the first *kenong* stroke (2:02). He has hinted at his intentions by accelerating the tempo towards the end of the previous *gongan*, and confirms it by the special pattern he plays for the second half of the first *kenongan*. The instrumentalists drop out and pause before playing the *kenong* beat, seemingly floating in measureless time. This kind of acceleration and fast first kenongan in *irama* I, leading to a sudden halt is sometimes referred to as *trommel rem*, which translates literally as "drum-brake(s)"—a pun on the word *trommel* (borrowed into Javanese from Dutch) as it is the *ciblon* "drum" which, as it were, slams on the brakes (*rem* in Javanese, also borrowed from Dutch) in this playful flexing of the *gendhing*.

After a moment of silence, the *pesindhèn* then enters alone and the drum soon resumes, inviting the other instrumentalists to join in again, but now at *irama* level II (main melody shown in half-notes). No sooner have they done so than the drummer signals yet another stop, and the main melody instruments respond with a double time (quarter-note) ascending passage (2:13–2:16), at variance with the standard main melody. The progression of measured musical time stops again, the *pesindhèn* sings, and again the drummer enters and brings the other instrumentalists back in, playing in *irama* II up to the end of the *gongan*.

Figures 7.3 and 7.4 show in more detail some of the parts played in this frame-flexing sixth *gongan*. Figure 7.3 shows the *pesindhèn's* part (the *sindhè-nan*), along with the main melody (here shown on *slenthem*) and the colotomic punctuation. Here we can see clearly how the vocal part floats rhythmically over the instrumental playing, in the same florid style whether in the moments of instrumental silence (the *andhegan*) or with the instrumentalists playing. The words are in a light, playful poetical form known as *rujak-rujakan* because each couplet begins with a description of one or another form of *rujak* (a spicy salad snack food, often sold by street vendors).

The play of *irama* level is a bit tricky here. Following the first halt and the first few syllables of the *pesindhèn's* short solo ("*rujak dlima*") the drum, colotomic (and some other) instruments join in, now suddenly in *irama* II. The main melody ([d g e d], now in half notes) is implied, but not actually played by any instrument. When the main melody instruments rejoin, they play the variant melody [c e g a c] as the drummer signals a second halt. After the second halt, again the *pesindhèn* sings a few syllables ("*sarwa cethä*") at which point all but the main melody instruments join back in, in *irama* II, the main melody instruments joining at the end of this third *kenongan* on ⌊d⌋ (tone 1) and continue in *irama* II up to the final beat of the *gongan*. At this point, if the tempo has neither been gradually slowed nor gradually accelerated, one might normally expect the musicians to continue by playing the next gongan in *irama* II. Figure 7.4 shows that the *irama* level suddenly shifts back to *irama* I at the gong stroke (2:36), for a second *trommel rem* (drum brake) passage. This is in response to a slight acceleration and particular configuration of

FIGURE 7.4. *End of gongan 6 and beginning of gongan 7, illustrating shift from irama dadi (II) to irama tanggung (I).*

259

drum strokes, which tell the musicians that at the gong stroke (2:36) the *irama* level will suddenly shift back to *irama* I. Here the *saron barung* (and other main melody instruments) jump back to the faster tempo characteristic of *irama* I. The *peking* reverts to its *irama* I style, merely sounding and echoing the main melody tones, and the *gambang* (along with other soft-playing elaborating instruments) drop out altogether.

In the subsequent (seventh) *gongan* the same treatment occurs again, but with the *pesindhèn* taking slightly more of the unmeasured time in between the "stop" (*andhegan*) and the reentrance of the instrumentalists. And instead of speeding suddenly back to *irama* I yet again, the drummer slows the tempo gradually, and the performance makes a seamless transition from *irama* II to *irama* III.

Moving Between Irama Levels

This kind of seamless shift is a hallmark of Javanese rhythmic treatment and is difficult to show accurately in staff notation. Different instruments shift their ratio of subdivision of the main melody beat (i.e., their *irama* level) not all at the same point, but where it is "comfortable" (*kepénak*) for the individual player and the idiom of his particular instrument. Look now at figure 7.5, which shows the transition from *irama* II to *irama* III at the end of the seventh *gongan*. The drummer directs this transition with a special sequence of drum strokes, beginning at the third *kenong* stroke (at the very beginning of figure 7.5, just before 3:10, and continuing to the gong beat at the end of the fourth *kenongan*, at 3:27). This leads directly into the first of a number of *ciblon* patterns (repeated sequences of strokes, ranging in length from two to six main melody beats) that fill out the *gongan* in *irama* III. This first one is called *lampah sekar* (lit., "flower walk/movement"), the first portion of which appears in the latter part of figure 7.5 (3:27 to 3:35). In longer performances of this and other comparable *ladrang* pieces, each *gongan* in *irama* III involves a different main *ciblon* drum pattern, corresponding, as in *kébar*, to one of the dance movements of the female dance *gambyong*. In this performance, we hear the second pattern (*pilesan*) in the final *gongan*. Integrated into the main pattern of each *gongan*, transitional drum patterns—mostly the same from one *gongan* to the next—articulate the formal structure, leading to *kenong* strokes, the final *kempul* stroke, and a new drum pattern just before the gong stroke.

The point by which one could say that the performance has fully reached *irama* III is the beat at which the gong plays (the [a] just slightly before 3:27). From this moment on, for this *gongan* and the first part of the next, the subdividing parts have all shifted to the level of subdivision appropriate for *irama* III. We show in the transcription a shift from 32 half-note beats per *gongan* to

FIGURE 7.5. *End of gongan 7 and beginning of gongan 8, illustrating shift from irama dadi (II) to irama wilet (III).*

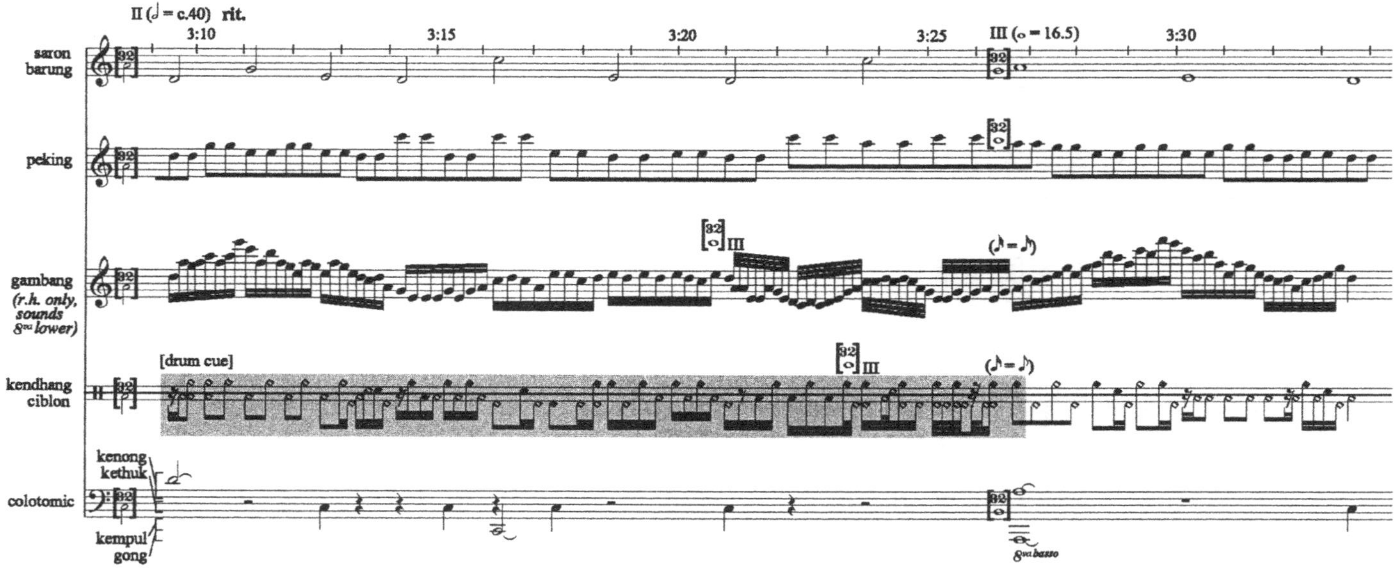

32 whole-note beats per *gongan,* as the tempo of the main melody structural beats by this point has slowed to about half of what it was in *irama* II (in the first part of figure 7.5) to accommodate the shifts in subdivision. But some instruments, including drum and *gambang,* have shifted a few beats beforehand. It is perhaps easiest to hear, and to see in the transcription, the moment where the rhythmically regular playing of the *gambang* has slowed to the point that the player feels comfortable to double his speed, moving from an *irama* II ratio (8:1 with the main melody) to *irama* III ratio (16:1 with the main melody). At the moment that this happens, the *gambang* playing literally jumps from a speed that is rather slow (for *gambang*) to one twice as fast, but which will undergo immediate, steady ritard until it has reached the "comfortable" range for *gambang.* We show the *gambang* part shifting (at 3:21) from sparser and sparser sixteenth notes to tightly crunched thirty-second notes. By the gong stroke, however, where we commence to show the main melody in whole notes, we adjust the *gambang* notation back to sixteenth notes, to show that the *gambang* speed is the same or similar to its speed in the steady portions of *irama* II immediately preceding.

Varying the Main Melody

Also note the shift in the *peking* part, which plays at a ratio of 4:1 with the main melody in *irama* II, to a ratio of 8:1 in *irama* III. The *peking* plays simple variations of the main melody. In *irama* I it almost always just sounds the main melody, but articulates each tone twice: once on the beat, and once "echoing" it a half a main-melody beat later.[13] In *irama* II, as you can see in the first half of the passage shown in figure 7.5 the *peking* part takes two successive tones of the main melody, reiterating one, then the other, then the first again, then the second again, ending this little figuration just one *peking* beat after the second main melody tone has been played. After the first tone (*kenong* beat, melody tone [d]) the main melody sounds [g] and [e], then [d] and high [c]. The *peking,* in the octave register above the *saron barung,* takes these tones, a pair at a time, playing [g g e e g g e e], and then [d d c c d d c c] (c's high). When the *peking* shifts to *irama* III, right at the gong beat (3:27), it becomes a little more independent from the main melody, still playing *peking* style [x x y y], but adding tones other than the main melody tones to create figures leading to

13. In the regional styles of Yogyakarta (south central Java), and Semarang (north coast of central Java) the *peking* "anticipates" by sounding the main melody tone a half beat before the main melody beat and then reiterating it on the beat (no echoing after the beat).

each tone of the now slow-moving main melody, beginning with [g g e e g g e e] to lead to main melody pitch [e], then [g g d d e e d d] to lead to main melody pitch [d].

This variation, though still quite limited, gives us a glimpse of the simplest kind of melodic *garapan* or variation treatment that characterizes many of the elaborating and vocally oriented (freer rhythm) parts. Although not "flexing" the frame in the sense of rhythmic alteration, the many layers of *garapan*—from the simple *peking* variations to the more elaborate meanderings of the *gambang* (shown here) and other instruments, including *gendèr*, the zithers, *rebab*, *suling*, and the vocal parts—flesh out the main melody, which, you will recall, the Javanese appropriately have designated by the Javanese word for skeleton (*balungan*). We can think of these melodic variations as yet another flexing of the basic melodic frame, in the dimensions both of pitch and of melodic density.

Before we focus in on the particulars of instrumental playing in this expanded *gongan*, mention should be made of the vocal texts here and throughout this performance. In the first *gongan*, *irama* I, we only hear the *pesindhèn* enter following the drummer's switch to the lively *ciblon* drum, and she sings different kinds of texts (*wangsalan*, *abon-abon*, and *rujak-rujakan*) that are typical of many *gendhing* performances, but bear no relationship to the particular sung poetic form from which this piece takes its name (*pangkur*). Finally, in the first *kenongan* of *irama* III (c.3:27 to 3:54), the *pesindhèn* sings the first line of a famous *pangkur* text, from the nineteenth century didactic treatise known as the *Serat Wedhatama*. Following the first *kenongan*, the *gérong* join in and sing the remainder of the verse in a rhythmically measured melody, with the *pesindhèn* singing the same text, but in a much more florid, rhythmically free style, heterophonically trailing the *gérong*. The text of the first verse, with English translation by the Javanese language scholar Stuart Robson is given below (Robson 1990:20–21):

Mingkar mingkur ing angkara	Turning away from selfish motives,
Akarana karenan mardi siwi	As one is pleased to give instruction to sons,
Sinawung resmining kidung	It is cast in the form of a delightful song,
Sinuba sinukarta	Finely finished and well turned,
Mrih kretarta pakartining ngèlmu luhung	In the hope that they may prosper in their practice of noble sciences
Kang tumrap nèng tanah Jawa	That pertain to the land of Java,

Agama ageming aji[14]   As the spiritual tradition adhered
to by its kings.

In *irama* I, and the portions of the sixth and seventh *gongan* in *irama* II, the basic melodic contour of the main melody and, consequently, the vocal parts, has been derived from the melodic contour of the usual *pangkur* melody associated with this piece (*pangkur paripurna*). But not until this *irama* III *gongan* are the text and the vocal melody both "fully" *pangkur,* and for this reason many Javanese musicians consider this more expanded (*irama* III) *gongan* to be the "real" *Ladrang Pangkur,* the *irama* I (and II) being like something of a condensed introduction, although sometimes played without ever slowing and expanding to *irama* III. In the *ngelik gongan,* which in contemporary practice nearly always proceeds to *irama* IV toward the end of the first *kenongan* and thereby eliminates the possibility of a *gérong* part (never present in *irama* IV), the vocal melody sung by the *pesindhèn* follows the contours of this variant main melody and thus can be said to be "not *pangkur*" (melodically) even though the text is *pangkur* (second verse), and the section is identified musically as "the *ngelik* section of *Ladrang Pangkur.*" Javanese listeners place great importance on the vocal parts, particularly the florid patterns of the *pesindhèn.*

Many of the *garapan* instruments cover a range of several octaves, and players conceive the *balungan* part in multioctave format, even though its manifestation on the *saron* is, as it were, folded in.[15] Thus, a pattern of main melody such as the final four beats of the *gongan* in *Ladrang Pangkur* ([e d c a]) is conceived of as a conjunct descent from [e] down to [a], though on the *saron* and *slenthem,* limited as they are to one octave (or just slightly more, ranging from [c] up to [d] in the higher octave), the part is played with a leap up from the [d] to the [c] above, followed by conjunct descent to the [a].

The thick texture of Javanese gamelan music makes it difficult to hear all of the *garapan* parts completely, as most of them involve dense and constant activity, often overlapping and coinciding with one another. Moving in diverse directions between predictable points of repose (described by some musicians as *nunggal-misah,* lit. "join and separate"), this kind of texture is a defining fea-

14. Final syllables with an open "a" vowel and penultimate syllables with "a" preceding these final syllables are pronounced "aw" and rendered in the transcriptions for this article as "å," but here we reproduce the text as it would normally be written in Roman alphabet (and as given in Robson [1990]).

15. In fact, all competent musicians recognize that acceptable *garapan* sometimes diverges from the *balungan,* even in its multioctave form. Some have theorized about an inherent, conceptual melodic line, referred to by Sumarsam and others as "inner melody." (See Sumarsam [1975], Sutton [1979], Sumarsam [1984], and Perlman [2004].)

ture of good Javanese ensemble playing. The melodic patterns performed by most of the *garapan* instruments and voices are known as *céngkok,* some of them identified by specific names, others simply by the final tone (and the *pathet*) of the passage in which they are used. Several book-length studies have been devoted primarily to the theory and practice of *garapan* and *céngkok;*[16] here we would like to draw your attention to a few examples in the *gambang* part. Javanese explain that the *garapan* parts "lead to" a particular tone, or that they "fill" a particular melodic context, usually a *gatra* (four beats of main melody).

As an example, we can talk about the *gambang céngkok* going to 6 (c) filling the gatra 3 2 1 6 ([g e d c]) in *sléndro pathet sanga* by scrutinizing the pattern filling the first *gatra* shown in figure 7.5 (the first *gatra* of the fourth *kenongan,* seventh *gongan*), and compare it to the *gambang* part played for the same passage, same *irama* level (II), of the previous *gongan* (the first *gatra* of the fourth *kenongan,* sixth *gongan*) as shown in figure 7.4. The transcriptions both begin with the third *kenong* tone [d] (tone 1, which is actually the last tone of the sixth *gatra* of the piece), followed by this *gatra* [g e d c] (3 2 1 6 in Javanese cipher notation). We can see in figure 7.5 that the *gambang* part (like the *peking* part) starts from the main melody tone at the *kenong* (tone d), but climbs more than an octave over the next eight sixteenth notes to sound a high [e] (tone 2) simultaneously with the next main melody tone [g] (tone 3). By the next main melody tone [e] (tone 2), it has descended an octave to join the main melody in unison, then proceeds down to a low [g] (tone 3) with the main melody tone [d] (tone 1) and finally up to join the main melody again at the end of the *gatra,* on [c] (tone 6). In the "same" passage in the previous *gongan* (figure 7.4), the *gambang* climbs to [a] (tone 5) against the first main melody tone [g] (tone 3), rather than all the way up to high [e] (tone 2). On the remaining three beats of this *gatra,* the *gambang* part actually articulates the same pitch degree as the main melody ([e], [d], and [c]; or 2, 1, and 6), but it soars up to high [a] before descending more almost two octaves to land at the end of the *gatra* on a low [c]. In keeping with the constraints of the modal system (*pathet*), the *gambang céngkok* emphasizes the prominent tones of *pathet sanga* (5, 1, and 2, here [a], [d], and [e]) and avoids giving emphasis to the weak or "enemy" tone (3, here [g]). The *gambang*'s [g] (tone 3) against the main melody's [d] (tone 1) in figure 7.5 actually does not emphasize this "enemy tone" as it is immediately followed by three successive [e]s (2's).

Thus this "same musical context"—that is, the "same *gatra*"—is realized differently in successive occurrences in the *gambang* part. Some musicians would

16. See especially Marc Perlman's *Unplayed Melodies* (Perlman [2004]); Brinner (1995), Sutton (1993).

say the *gambang* player chose a slightly different *céngkok*. Others would say that the two are similar enough to be called the same *céngkok*, since they start and end on the same tone and have other similarities in shape, but are, instead, different *wiletan* (i.e., different "meanderings," from the same Javanese word, *wilet*, used to refer to irama III, where playing can become intricate and winding around).[17] As is characteristic of the *gambang*, and most other *garapan* parts, the melodic motion is continuous. Thus, it does not rest (or sustain) even for one brief subdivision, but instead continues immediately into the next *céngkok*.

Other instrumental parts work in similar ways to the *gambang*, stringing variable *céngkok* together, one after the other, in a seamless progression through the *gendhing* as it unfolds. Vocal parts also consist of *céngkok*, in two contrasting styles: (group) *gérong* and (solo) *pesindhèn*. The male chorus (*gérong*) sing melodies that exhibit regular, proportional durations, almost always ending their phrases on the same tone as the main instrumental melody at the same rhythmic moment that the instrumental parts reach the same tone (albeit in different octave registers, depending on the tessitura of the instrument). The *gérong* part moves heterophonically with the main melody, tracing a similar contour overall, but often contrasting in motion between these moments of repose (*sèlèh*, in Javanese). The exact melodic shape and rhythmic particulars are variable, at least in some instances, but because it is sung by a small chorus of voices, and expected to sound as a single melodic line, the *gérong* part is usually worked out prior to the moment of performance, rather than being sung spontaneously (although exceptions to this occur). The *pesindhèn* part, though based on extant *céngkok*, is more variable, with individual preferences and spontaneous decisions determining the shape and sequence of *céngkok*. Figure 7.6 presents the vocal parts for the entire eighth *gongan*, in *irama* III, where the first verse of the *pangkur* poem is sung. We have identified the repose (*sèlèh*) tones of the main melody, encasing each in a shaded box, and similarly identified the ends of each vocal phrase in both the *gérong* and the *pesindhèn* parts.

---

17. *Wiletan* can be understood as the precise realization of a *céngkok* in all its details, variable in performance. But musicians do not agree universally on just how different two passages have to be to constitute a difference in *céngkok* rather than "merely" a difference in *wiletan*. One often hears musicians say something to the effect that so and so plays the same *céngkok* as someone else, only the *wiletan* are different, or that a single player enriches his performance by playing different *wiletan* of the same *céngkok* for passages that repeat in performance. Maximum variation is not the goal, but exact repetition in *gambang* and other *garapan* parts is considered overly rigid and the mark of a beginner (on variation in gamelan performance, see further Vetter [1981], Sutton [1993], Sutton [1998], Perlman [2004]).

There are six phrases in the *gérong* part, two in each of the last three *kenongan* of this *gongan*. (By convention, only the *pesindhèn* sings in the first *kenongan* of pieces such as this in *irama* III, the *gérong* joining in the second *kenongan*.)[18] The transcription shows the *gérong* phrases, two per system (as each system presents one *kenongan*), ending on the same pitch degrees as the main melody at those points: [d] and [c] in the second *kenongan*, [d] and [d] in the third, and [c] and [d] in the fourth.[19]

These are not the only moments at which the *gérong* part is in unison with the main melody (and, of course, with many of the other instrumental parts as well). The first *gérong* phrase (second system of the transcription) begins on pitch [c] while this same pitch is being sustained in the main melody. Near the middle of the second phrase, on the syllable "*bå*" (of "*sinubå*") both the *gérong* part and the main melody sustain pitch [e] before moving, each in its own idiom, to the phrase final [c]. Similarly, both the *gérong* and main melody sustain pitch [e] near the middle of the fourth phrase, on the syllable "*ning*" (of "*pakartining*"). The fifth phrase (first part of the fourth *kenongan*) shows an even closer relationship between these two parts, as the *gérong* melody moves through each successive pitch of the main melody [a c e d a e d c], albeit with auxiliary tones that make it an idiomatic *gérong céngkok*. The sixth and final phrase is a response to the *rebab*'s signal, beginning just after the previous *sèlèh* tone [c], directing the singers and players of multioctave instruments to proceed to the upper register, ending on pitch [d] with the gong stroke, in transition to the *ngelik gongan*.

In contrast to the *gérong* part, with its proportional and metric rhythms and its arrival at repose tones simultaneously with the main melody, the *pesindhèn* part seems to float freely over the measured rhythms of the other parts, in *parlando* style, always arriving at phrase-ending tones well past the moment when the main melody, the *gérong*, and most other instrumental parts have reached the end of their *céngkok*. We have inserted arrows in the transcription to link the final tone of each *pesindhèn céngkok* with the main melody tone that guides her singing. In most cases her *céngkok* is rather independent of the intermediary main melody tones, but in all cases except one, she sings a *céngkok* that ends on the same tone as the *sèlèh*. Because the *pesindhèn* phrase lags behind the others, as it were, we have had to draw arrows between systems to show, for ex-

18. This is very likely so because in most *ladrang* pieces, *irama* III, the *gérong* text is set in a poetical form consisting of six lines of eight syllables each (*kinanthi*), each line conveniently filling one half of one *kenongan*, ending with the last syllable coinciding with the gong stroke at the end of the fourth *kenongan*.

19. The final phrase ends on high [d], rather than the usual low [a] because the *rebab* has signaled a transition to the *ngelik gongan*.

FIGURE 7.6. Gongan 8 *in* irama wilet *(III), illustrating contrastive vocal styles (female and male) and their relationship to one another and to* sèlèh *(goal) tones.*

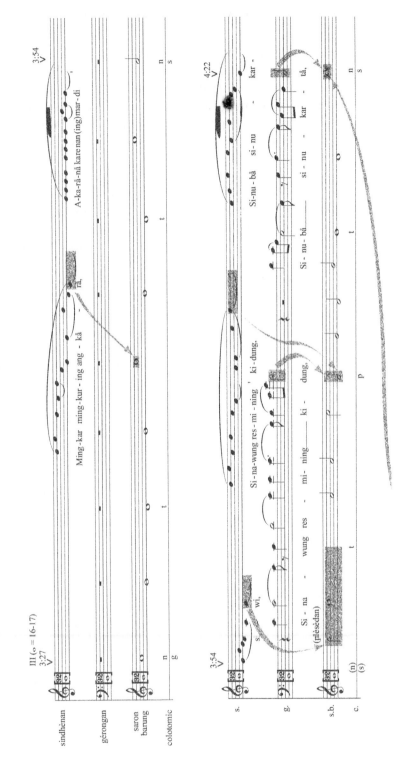

268

FIGURE 7.6. *Continued*

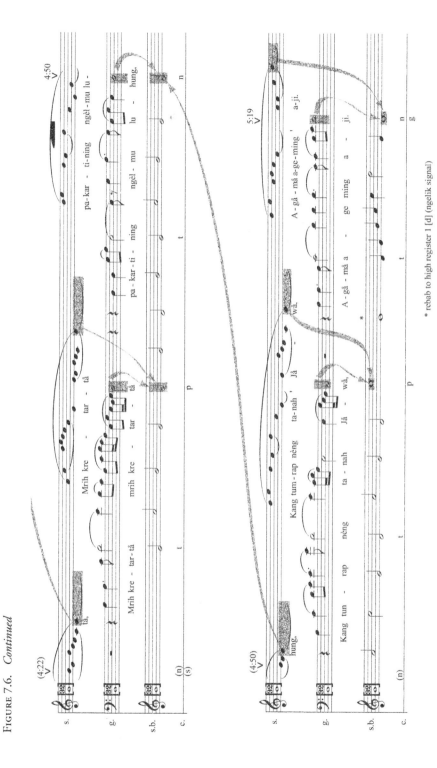

* rebab to high register 1 [d] (ngelik signal)

269

ample, that the pitch [c] she reaches in the first part of the third system, is actually determined by the final [c] in the main melody of the previous system. The exception occurs at the beginning of the second system, in which, instead of ending her phrase on the final pitch of the first *kenongan*, pitch [a], she makes a "slip" (*plèsèd*) to pitch [c], as it assumes special prominence in the main melody at this point, being both reiterated and sustained for the first quarter of the second *kenongan*.

We can get a sense of the variability of vocal *céngkok* by comparing the successive approaches to pitch [d] in the third system. In both the *gérong* and the *pesindhèn* parts the *céngkok* contours for the first phrase differ significantly from those for the second. The differences are partially a result of the contrasts between the main melody in each half, and also between the implied, underlying or "inner" melody for each half (see footnote 15). Of the two, the *gérong* is more constrained by these contrasts than the *pesindhèn*, whose *céngkok* choice is determined mainly by phrase final and by personal preference. In this gongan, for example, note that the very first *pesindhèn céngkok*, starting on pitch [d] and descending somewhat circuitously to pitch [c] in the lower octave, is nearly identical to the first phrase in the last *kenongan*, even though the main melody is different. Through their choice of *céngkok*, then, the singers, like the instrumentalists, contribute to flexing the melodic framework of this piece in terms of pitch and, in the case of the *pesindhèn's* later arrival at *sèlèh* tones, also in terms of rhythm. The ways in which these two vocal styles vary the main melody and contrast with each other constitute an important dimension in gamelan musical aesthetics.

Conclusion

In this chapter, we have taken a Javanese musical piece that might be analyzed solely in reference to its main instrumental melody, whose abstract structure presents a binary symmetry typical of nearly all Javanese pieces but whose particular sequence of tones belongs to this piece alone. Javanese writing for other Javanese do this routinely, but can assume of their readership a familiarity with the many processes that come to bear as the piece is realized by an ensemble of performers. Writing here for readers who mostly have little or no familiarity with such processes has made it imperative for us to foreground these performance processes, and we have done so in reference to a particular performance. This rendition of *Ladrang Pangkur* proceeds in just over eight minutes through four different tempo (*irama*) levels, each with characteristically different treatment by melodic instruments, singers, and drummer. In several places the instrumentalists stop altogether, with only the female singer continuing, later joined by the ensemble to finish out the phrase as if the loss of beat and momentum were only a passing memory. Transcriptions have illustrated aspects of interplay between melodic instruments, contrasts in drumming style, and laid out some of the various changes in tempo and treatment that make for an aesthetically rich and exciting performance, maintaining the integrity of the formal structure but roaming wild within it. Symmetry is never sacrificed; rather, it is radically offset by changes in tempo, melodic shape, and a whole range of factors that at times may seem intended to obscure or even obliterate the formal frame. What these techniques in fact do is intensify the power of the music by stretching the cognitive capacities of its performers and listeners, creating a magnificent, hardwon experiential realm unlike any other in Java or the world. The music's range and depth of expression, fully accessible only to practiced insiders, is the product of centuries of sustained generational collaboration and transmission among Javanese artists.

It is hardly surprising that scholarship on Javanese music, by Javanese and foreign scholars alike, has emphasized—even celebrated—formal balance and regularity, as this importantly models the music's simple, elegant basis. Many musics in the world can be described in terms of such conceptually clear, often fundamentally binary and periodic structures. But this level of understanding does not reflect the more human, artistic, and culturally specific properties of music, which are shaped over time (the time of history, musicians' development over lifetimes, and the time of individual performances) by a predilection to seek diversity and proliferation of possibilities within a system governed by simple constraints. This performance of *Ladrang Pangkur* illustrates a Javanese response to this imperative. And although some young Javanese musicians now engage in radical new forms of composition and playing techniques, the approach to performance we have encountered here—flexing what is at core a binary, symmetrical frame—continues to be the measure of good musicianship and a source of deep aesthetic delight.

References

Becker, Judith. 1980. *Traditional Music in Modern Java: Gamelan in a Changing Society.* Honolulu: University of Hawaii Press.

Brinner, Benjamin. 1995. *Knowing Music, Making Music: Javanese* Gamelan *and the Theory of Musical Competence and Interaction.* Chicago: University of Chicago Press.

Hood, Mantle. 1954. *The Nuclear Theme as a Determinant of Patet in Javanese Music.* Groningen: J. B. Wolters (repr. New York: Da Capo Press, 1977).

Hood, Mantle, and Hardja Susilo. 1967. *Music of the Venerable Dark Cloud.* Los Angeles: Institute of Ethnomusicology, UCLA.

Kunst, Jaap. 1949. *Music in Java: Its History, Its Theory, and Its Technique,* second ed. 2 vols. The Hague: Martinus Nijhoff. (Third enlarged ed., E. L. Heins, ed., 1973.)

McDermott, Vincent, and Sumarsam. 1975. "Central Javanese Music: The Patet of Laras Slendro and the Gender Barung." *Ethnomusicology* 19(2):233–44.

Perlman, Marc. 2004. *Unplayed Melodies: Javanese Gamelan and the Genesis of Music Theory.* Berkeley: University of California Press.

Perlman, Marc, and Harold Powers. 2001."Mode: South-east Asia: *pathet.*" In *The New Grove Dictionary of Music and Musicians,* second ed., edited by Stanley Sadie. Vol. 16. London: Macmillan Publishers Limited, 844–852.

Powers, Harold. 1980. "Mode as a Musicological Concept." In *The New Grove Dictionary of Music and Musicians,* edited by Stanley Sadie. Vol. 12. London: MacMillan Publishers Limited, 422–50.

Robson, Stuart. 1990. *The Wedhatama: An English Translation.* Leiden: Koninklijk Instituut voor Taal-, Land- en Volkenkunde (KITLV) Press.

Sumarsam. 1975. "Inner Melody in Javanese Gamelan Music." *Asian Music* 7(1):3–13.

———. 1984."Inner Melody in Javanese Gamelan Music." In Judith Becker and Alan Feinstein, eds., *Karawitan: Source Readings in Javanese Gamelan and Vocal Music.* Vol. 1. Center for South and Southeast Asian Studies, University of Michigan.

Sutton, R. Anderson. 1979."Concept and Treatment in Javanese Gamelan Music, with Reference to the Gambang." *Asian Music* 9(2):59–79.

———. 1987. "Identity and Individuality in an Ensemble Tradition: The Female Vocalist in Java." In Ellen Koskoff, ed., *Women and Music in Cross-Cultural Perspective.* New York and Westport, Conn.: Greenwood Press. (repr. Urbana and Chicago: University of Illinois Press, 1989), 111–130.

———. 1993. *Variation in Central Javanese Gamelan Music: Dynamics of a Steady State.* DeKalb, Ill.: Center for Southeast Asian Studies, Northern Illinois University.

———. 1998. "Do Javanese Musicians Really Improvise?" In Bruno Nettl, ed., *In the Course of Performance: Studies in the World of Improvisation.* Chicago: University of Chicago Press, 69–92.

———. 2002. "Asia/Indonesia." In Jeff T. Titon, ed., *Worlds of Music: An Introduction to the Music of the World's Peoples,* fourth ed. New York: Wadsworth Publishing/ Schirmer Books, 279–330.

Tohari, Ahmad. 2004. *A Dancer of Paruk Village.* Trans. Rene T. A. Lysloff. Jakarta: Lontar Press.

Vetter, Roger R. 1981. "Flexibility in the Performance Practice of Central Javanese Music." *Ethnomusicology* 25(2):199–214.

Walton, Susan Pratt. 1996. "Heavenly Nymphs and Earthly Delights: Javanese Female Singers, Their Music and Their Lives." Ph.D. dissertation, University of Michigan.

→► PART III ◄←

Linear Composition in
Periodic Contexts

CHAPTER 8

"Yang's Eight Pieces"

Composing a Musical Set-Piece in a

Chinese Local Opera Tradition

JONATHAN P. J. STOCK

This chapter looks at how a musician in an oral tradition creates a new musical utterance.[1] Its topic is the creation of a twenty-three-minute scene,
"Jin Yuan Seeks Her Son," in a drama entitled *The Prostitute's Tears,* a major
work in the Shanghai opera tradition (*huju*). Developing this scene as a musical set-piece in the early 1950s, star singer Yang Feifei (b. 1923) fused together
a set of traditional tunes to set wronged mother Jin Yuan's reflections on her
unfortunate adult life. An analysis of Yang's artistic and aesthetic choices in
constructing this set-piece illustrates how a skilled specialist musician composes
a large-scale musical form without recourse to music notation, and introduces
us to the music of this Chinese regional opera style.

Many aspects of opera repay close analysis, including: design and production; patterns of movement and gesture; reception history; social roles and political symbolism onstage; the life histories and experiences of opera's creators;
and the performance of musical and textual content. No one analysis is likely
to take in all these perspectives or to attempt to weigh equally those it does
embrace. For the analyst, the act of concentrating closely on selected aspects
of a performance, recording, or score necessarily requires the temporary exclu-
sion of others but the reader is always expected to then return to the original

---

1. I am most grateful to Yang Feifei for her permission to include an excerpt from one
of her recordings of the scene "Jin Yuan Seeks Her Son" in this chapter. Information on
Yang's life and career comes from an interview held with her in Shanghai on June 10, 1993,
and from the published text of an earlier interview; see Yang (1986).

object of study, mentally reassessing it in light of the new insights that concentrated study has generated. In this particular case, I concentrate on the music of the scene in question, presenting information from other media as supporting or contextual data. The aim is to understand how Yang Feifei reshaped traditional musical ingredients in her scene, which we can do by comparing the conventional forms of these elements (phrase patterns, scale, register, cadence notes, etc.) with the changes she introduced.

Shanghai Opera and Yang Feifei

Experts list more than three hundred distinct genres of musical drama in China, from exorcism theater to farce, historical romance, contemporary tragedy, shadow puppetry, and stylized acrobatics.[2] A few, like Beijing opera, are widely disseminated but most occur in one region only. Shanghai opera, *huju*, is a relatively recent genre, with a documented history of just over two centuries. Early performances occurred at religious and calendrical festivals in rural areas. Most of those involved were part-timers, young men from the same village who got together when the agricultural cycle allowed for fun, to make a little money, and in order to visit neighboring communities. Small-scale professional troupes gradually became numerous too, and historical sources record the names of one or two female performers among the many men active in the tradition, this at a time when women were legally prohibited from taking to the stage in China. The professionals roved the region seeking engagements at fairs, temple ceremonies, village festivities such as weddings, and the homes of the wealthy. Dramas elaborated themes that interested the ordinary people, including the struggles of young couples to avoid arranged marriages, and the elopement of neglected wives with their lovers, although we can assume that these latter stories were avoided at wedding performances. Legal measures attempted, largely unsuccessfully, to restrict the performance of these dramas—the authorities feared that traditional opera drew crowds to situations in which gambling occurred, and that the stories encouraged illicit love affairs. Moreover, records noted that the performances were often bawdy in content. Nevertheless, we should not overlook the potentially positive aspects of these dramas. Musician Wu Zhimin told me about rural performances he had attended as a child in the 1940s: "The stories were mostly about young people whose families tried to prevent them from marrying, or about hardships after marriage," he said.

2. There is a very substantial amount of publication on Chinese opera in European languages, Japanese, and, of course, Chinese. Key sources on *huju* are Shanghai tong (1936), Zhu and Xu (1988), Sun (1996), Wang, Chen, and Lan (1999), and Stock (2003).

Yang Feifei as Jin Yuan. Photo by author.

"It was close to everyone's experience of life, and sometimes people started to cry" (personal communication, September 21, 1997). This emotional outlet was likely very useful, allowing people to understand that others shared their own hardships. Street acquaintance and opera fan Shen Wei stressed the educational role of opera: "In the countryside the people didn't have any schooling," he explained, "but from watching opera they could see how to behave. Husbands could learn that beating their wives was bad, for example" (personal communication, September 6, 1997).

Song texts and dialog were rarely written down at this time. In fact, very few performers or listeners were literate. The singing seems to have been improvisatory, with words extemporized by the actors being set to local folk song tunes. Musical texture involved both monophonic (unaccompanied) song and heterophony. In the latter, a small instrumental ensemble accompanied the singer. Musicians who played the two-stringed fiddle *huqin* and the wood clappers *ban* led the ensemble. Chinese music is somewhat like Western music in that it predominantly uses seven-note scales. Actually, there are written records from Chinese antiquity of what we would today call a major scale, so we could even say that contemporary Western music is rather like Chinese in its reliance on seven-tone scales. Shanghai opera was no exception. Most of its traditional melodies use seven-tone sets, even if, as in much Chinese music, one of several anhemitonic (i.e., containing no semitones) pentatonic subsets within each octave are treated as primary melodic tones and the remaining two tones appear mostly as expressive decorations, if at all. (In recent decades, musicians have shifted from tunings extrapolated from well-tuned fifths to equal-tempered Western tuning, a small change that has slightly altered the sound of *huju* opera.)

This essentially rural tradition was reshaped in the late nineteenth and early twentieth centuries. When it opened to foreign trade in the mid-nineteenth century, Shanghai expanded rapidly to become China's principal industrial center and its most densely inhabited city. Many rural folk migrated to this city, among them opera performers. In Shanghai, they had to compete with the performers of many other traditions, and competition led them to assimilate various new stylistic traits and musical materials. Dramas gradually expanded to better entertain urban audiences, resulting in a wider range of stories and dramatic situations. Urban courtesans also took up Shanghai opera. The private performances of these women represent the first direct involvement of women in the urban strand of this tradition. Troupes slowly expanded, and in the 1910s women performers began to appear on public urban stages beside their male fellows. By the 1930s, female performers were numerous, at least in younger roles, and over the next twenty years female impersonation largely disappeared.

In common with many other Chinese opera styles at this time, the Shanghai tradition relied not on a specialist composer but on what we might call pre-existing melodic elements. These elements were fleshed out in performance by singer and accompanists alike, and were essentially of two categories:

- set tunes, often in strophic form, performed at appropriate moments in the drama, probably with a new song-text extemporized by the actor; and
- more flexible tune outlines, performed at different tempi, rhythmic densities, or meters, and in realizations appropriate to each of the several basic role-types found in Chinese opera. Several researchers call these "tune families," a term that reminds us that multiple versions of the tune coexist at once, not a single theme that is varied by the performer.

The exact balance of set tunes and tune families varies from one opera tradition to another in China: Beijing opera, for instance, relies predominantly on the latter, whereas the classic *kunju* style concentrates on the former. Shanghai opera uses each of these categories quite regularly, and the passage analyzed here encompasses examples from both. It also incorporates a hybrid form: we will see a set tune beginning to be subjected to the kind of systematic transformation process that underpins the tune families.

By the 1920s, Shanghai opera was highly popular in Shanghai as a whole, far outstripping other styles on the city's numerous radio stations. Successful performance groups were often large and musically innovative, and numerous star performers enjoyed a good income and citywide reputation, this much in contrast to the earlier low social standing of actors just a generation before- hand. Although many new dramas had been devised (or borrowed from other Chinese opera traditions, Western-style spoken plays, films, modern novels, and classical stories), the most celebrated were those that concentrated on fam- ily settings close to the lives of the ordinary people. Particularly prominent in the *huju* repertory of this period are dramas where the central role is that of tragic woman, brought to temporary life through the efforts of one or another of a succession of star actresses.

The period since 1940 saw several new trends become prominent in the *huju* tradition. Specialist composers, librettists, and directors were recruited, and troupes adopted many of the staging conventions of Western drama. These processes began well before the establishment of the People's Republic of China (October 1949)—the first nonperforming directors, for instance, were hired as early as the 1920s—but they accelerated under the new Communist govern- ment, which established a centrally planned network of cultural institutions (such as opera training schools, festivals, and competitions). Today, traditional- style melodies remain paramount, but a mixed ensemble of Chinese and West- ern instruments accompanies many performances. There may be some harmo- nization of tunes, and Westernized meters are used. The melodies are composed into notated scores memorized by the singers prior to performance, rather than assembled partly through improvisation during performance. Yet the tradition has not been completely transformed. Most *huju* dramas of the last sixty years have sustained the earlier concentration on subjects from family life, exploring in music and action how ordinary people come to emotional terms with un- expected changes in their lives.

One of the most significant actresses of *huju* in the twentieth century forms the subject of this chapter. This is Yang Feifei, a singer whose stage name is modeled on French name "Fifi" (pronounced Feifei in Mandarin but Fifi in Shanghai dialect), which was considered exotic in the Shanghai of her youth. When I asked Yang Feifei why she took up *huju* in the 1930s, she explained that she had a very poor family background. Society valued sons above daughters, and so poor families like hers concentrated their resources on bringing up boys and teaching them to read. Daughters (who would soon enough marry out of the family) were put out to work at any age if the financial situation demanded it, which is what happened to her. Instead of going to school, Yang was put into a Western-style spoken drama troupe as a child actress, switching as a teenager to an apprenticeship in Shanghai opera, which she much preferred. Her training was extensive and elaborate, and included acting as well as singing, and much participation in minor roles for actual performances—learning on the job was highly valued in this tradition. Yang Feifei described her lessons as follows:

> Teacher sat here. Someone with a *ban* sat there. If Ding Shi'e, my fellow apprentice, knew the opera she'd call out a phrase and I'd learn it. After she'd called out a section of ten or more lines, and once I'd learned it, we'd go on to the next section. After this, we'd go through them both one more time. A whole act might have ten or more sections. When all those had been learned we'd go through it one more time. The next time through, if I couldn't sing it, Teacher would hit the chair. But I was very clever. She never actually beat me. I worked very hard, because I liked this thing I was doing.

This rigorous instruction equipped Yang well for a long career as a professional actress. She confronted many hardships in her early life, both as a child worker and then a young female professional in Shanghai. Yang drew on this experience throughout her career, turning to her own emotions to invest the tragic roles she favored with great expressive intensity. She also created numerous new roles, honing her personal vocal qualities to sound quite distinct from the other actresses of her time. As her career proceeded, Yang worked out her own ways of singing:

> I found the old tunes too simple . . . I took what I had learned from many other kinds of drama, including Beijing opera and Shaoxing opera . . . and worked out their specialties. But it still had to sound like *huju*—otherwise it would just be singing and no one would want to listen . . .

> I can't write music down. I would sing it until it was very familiar and then get a musician to come and write it down for me. The musician might also help me work out the instrumental interludes, and I'd ask for his opinions on the vocal passages too. There weren't composers then, just musicians.

Because the repertory of *huju* was undergoing rapid change, even established dramas were typically performed in newly elaborated ways, Yang needed to constantly revise her style, create new roles, and generate new ways of performing existing tunes. Her success in these tasks allowed her to acquire and retain a considerable following among the fans of this opera form. She ended her career as the leader of one of Shanghai's most respected *huju* troupes, and even in retirement, Yang remains in high demand as a teacher.

Analysis: "Jin Yuan Seeks Her Son"

Yang Feifei's creation of the role of Jin Yuan embodies exactly the kind of musically moving but dramatically powerless female so often found in Shanghai opera. The drama *The Prostitute's Tears* appears to have originated as a traditional opera in 1939, its direct inspiration being a pair of influential 1930s Chinese films. *The Prostitute's Tears* shows us a young mother, Jin Yuan, who has a small child and a husband to support. Her husband was blinded and badly injured by Japanese military action, which has also driven the family from their home and jobs. Faced with starvation, Jin is forced to work in a brothel. Her husband dies of shock when he discovers the truth about his wife's income, and Jin Yuan is subsequently taken against her will to become the kept mistress of a rough gangster, Zhang Laohu. Zhang returns drunk one night and attempts to steal her savings, which support her son's education. After a struggle, he slips onto a kitchen cleaver and dies, with the unfortunate Jin Yuan placed in prison for manslaughter. Her only remaining hope is her son, taken away to distant Beiping (Beijing) by his school teacher. Ten years on, Jin Yuan, now ill herself, has served her time. Receiving news of her son's impending wedding, she journeys painfully on foot across China. There, before even she sees her son, she is recognized as a prostitute and reviled. She flees into a storm, eventually drowning herself into a river, anguished at having destroyed her son's chances of a good marriage.

The lead role in *The Prostitute's Tears,* Jin Yuan, is rarely in control of her own destiny, or even her own body. Yet music in opera can lend a powerful voice to those who otherwise lack one, and, in developing her version of this drama in the early 1950s, Yang Feifei devised a substantive scene in which Jin Yuan takes time out from the dramatic narrative to reflect in song on the various tragedies of her adult life (see photo). The scene, entitled "Jin Yuan Seeks Her Son", is positioned just before Jin's anticipated reunion with her son; it is performed solo, providing the audience an extended chance to become deeply moved by this woman's emotional plight.

In all, Yang's solo scene draws on ten of the melodic elements used in *huju*. These are listed in figure 8.1, and sections 4–6 are recorded on track 14 of this book's CD. The first three tune elements together form the scene's introductory passage, which is why the scene has become known also as "Yang's Eight Pieces" and not "Yang's Ten Pieces." As Yang Feifei noted, several *huju* singers before her had combined two or three elements to form a continuous musical whole. Nevertheless, it was far more usual for singers to create long passages by selecting a single tune and iterating it over and over. As some of these tunes comprise just two musical lines, the once commonplace solo passages of one or two hundred lines were musically very repetitive, even despite some ongoing improvisatory variation. This repetition, of course, freed *huju* singers to con-

FIGURE 8.1. *Melodic Elements in "Jin Yuan Seeks Her Son."*

Melodic element	Lines	Approximate Timing	Timing on CD
1. Fenghuang tou	1	0:00	—
Changqiang zhongban	2		
San song	3-4		
2. Zhongban	5-10	4:03	—
3. Kuaiban manchang	11-19	5:07	—
4. Man fan yinyang	20-27	7:53	0:00
5. Sanjiaoban	28-37	10:37	2:42
6. Daoqing diao	38-45	12:12	4:19
7. Migui diao	46-51	16:19	—
8. Manban	52-65	18:25	—

centrate on thinking up appropriate song texts, which was essential at a time when troupes were expected to give two performances per day, very often of newly worked out dramas. Indeed, some singers preferred the flexibility of this system even for well-established dramas, fearing that agreeing on a set text and a fixed number of repetitions with the instrumental ensemble opened them to new risks in live performance. From this perspective, Yang's new scene was unprecedented not for its length but in its careful planning and melodic richness.

As already mentioned, Yang's set-piece was much more than simply an unusually concentrated rush of tunes. There is also a refined sense of musical construction here. The traditional tune elements Yang drew on are carefully crafted, but the changes she made to them took this further by manipulating and elaborating melodic details, phrase structure, and form. Yang and several singers of her generation talk about "playing" with a tune over several weeks until they had shaped it the way they wanted and of "borrowing" bits of other tunes in the search for new expressive impact. But they rarely go beyond this, a common situation when the musicians concerned have not been schooled to explain their actions in detailed technical or theoretical terms. Even when direct questioning fails, the researcher can still investigate composition in such traditions by observing and perhaps participating in the creation of new pieces, or, as in this case, through musical transcription and analysis. We will focus on Yang's contributions in just part of the scene, the central sections (4–6), which are broadly representative of *huju* opera and demonstrate processes found across much Chinese music. After looking at each section separately, we consider their setting in terms of the whole musical scene, pondering for a moment Yang Feifei's attention to larger-scale issues.

Figure 8.2 is an outline transcription of Yang Feifei's vocal line during sections 4–6. This transcription uses contemporary Chinese conventions, although for this book it uses staff notation rather than the cipher notation more widely found in China today. Parts for the heterophonic accompanying instrumental ensemble are omitted, except during Yang's rests when a single line, an undecorated version of the music for lead *huqin* two-stringed fiddle, appears in parentheses. The song text is given below the vocal part in romanized pronunciations, with a summary translation at the end of the figure (and Chinese characters in the appendix at the end of this chapter). A little more attention has been paid to the details of Yang's ornamentation than would be the case with a transcription designed for use in China, where familiarity with Yang's vocal style and with *huju* more generally would guide those employing the transcription. Careful listening to the CD recording will reveal additional details of the performance, as well as providing a much richer impression of the accompanying ensemble's role. Other than the music, figure 8.2 is also marked with some analytical observations, such as labels to identify each phrase. These are explained in the notes at the foot of the figure and in analysis that follows, which looks at each section in turn to see how Yang took musical principles and materials from her tradition and applied them in the new scene. Including these annotations on figure 8.2 makes it possible to relate the analytical diagrams that follow back to the extract as a whole.

Man Fan Yinyang

The tune *man fan yinyang* is part of the Shanghai opera tradition's second most prominent tune family. Literally translated, the prefixes man and fan mean slow and converse (i.e., transposed).[3] *Yinyang* could be translated as female-male, and this tune was originally used for the alternation of female *(yin)* and male *(yang)* voices in question-and-answer dialog. In contemporary *huju*, *yinyang* is the name of a specific tune, one more fully called *yinyang xue*. The vocal material of *yinyang xue* has three main components:

- An opening *qiqiang* phrase (distinct male and female versions exist).
- A central stage of short, more-or-less syllabic *pingqiang* phrases (repeated as the song text required, or as the imagination of the singer permitted in improvised performances).

3. The word converse is accurately chosen by Chinese musicians. In *yinyang xue* the main accompanying fiddle's higher string is tuned to the fifth note of the scale and the lower string to the first; in *fan yinyang,* the lower string is taken as being tuned to the fifth degree and the higher string is set to the second degree. There is thus a change of string involved for the fiddle player. Singers and composers pitch these tunes somewhat differently in contemporary practice, but in many cases *yinyang xue* is sung with its fundamental note equivalent to a Western C while that of *fan yinyang* is an F.

FIGURE 8.2. *Transcription of sections 4–6. "Jin Yuan Seeks Her Son."*

- A final *luoqiang* phrase (shorter, and generally less distinct in its male and female forms).

Instrumental introductions, brief interludes, and codetta phrases fill out the tune. The whole structure can be repeated, as when one of the onstage characters has multiple questions. In duo performance the components are typically

FIGURE 8.2. *Continued*

Section 5. Sanjiaoban 1 = C vocal passages are in free meter; instrumental in two- or four-beat units

(l. 28:) Dong-seng see yeu ngo gen ko-li,

(l. 29:) Pa xia bao bei ling Zi-ziang. (l. 30:) Vu-se xiao bei ngo xing ze,

(l. 31:) Ling zao zen-yi si ou li-liang. (l. 32:) Ze neng ji - zuo zou ji - nü,

faster

(l. 33:) Lia dou zao cei hen mi-zang. (l. 34:) Vei u ge liu-mang Zang Lao-hu,

(l. 35:) Ta sang si qi ren tei xiong-wang. (l. 36:) Yi bi de ngo vu neng ying lei zo,

slower

(l. 37:) Ngo se sou jiang ta xing - ming sang.

Section 6. Daoqing diao 1 = F

(l. 38:) Sa zen ling

seu nei da, (l. 39:) Ku - li ngo

tei yu wang, (l. 40:) Yu cen hei di

FIGURE 8.2. *Continued*

Translation

Beleaguered Shanghai was steeped in hardship, The city was in chaos and prices rising. Poor folk borrowed money at high rates, Without choice—like sheep to the slaughter. Endless interest on top of interest, Madame Liu San forced me into a living hell. I prostituted myself secretly from my blinded husband, His life continued to ebb away. After Tongsheng died my situation became even worse, I brought up my treasured Lin Cixiang. Supporting my young one was my duty alone, I had no strength to search for work. I could only carry on as a prostitute, two times disaster had struck me. The vicious gangster Zhang Laohu, he used his connections to bully people so violently. He pushed me until I was no longer human, I accidentally killed him. It was hard to bear the crime of taking a life, Poor me—it was so unjust, unjustly thrown into a prison cell. Mr Chen took him [Cixiang] to Beiping, I still had hopes for my son's future. My traumatic experiences remained hidden, From then on mother and son exchanged no news—each distant and separated from the other.

Explanatory Notes

The transcription follows Chinese convention in compressing all melody parts to a single line. While the singer is active, only the voice part is shown; during vocal rests, the transcription shows an outline of the music played by the main accompanimental two-stringed fiddle. In fact, several melody instruments perform heterophonically throughout.

FIGURE 8.2. *Continued*

Transliteration of the lyrics is based on the Shanghai-dialect pronunciations heard on the recording. A Chinese text is given in the appendix of this chapter. Padding syllables are placed in square brackets: [a]. The lyrics are marked with line numbers following those in the scene as a whole.

No time signature is used for the central free-meter section (sanjiaoban).

Terms used in the analysis that follows are also given, including the local terms for sub-sections and my own alphabetical labels applied to each new musical phrase (a, b, etc.) as it appears. Inclusion of a number shows that the phrase is seen as related rather repeated (for example, f1 and f2) and instrumental passages (the most significant of which are identified as i and numbered throughout).

distributed as follows: the female-role singer opens by singing the first *qiqiang,* often a question. The male answers her with a few phrases of *pingqiang,* himself going on to supply the full answer in a final *luoqiang* phrase. Then, either the female singer asks another question or the male-role actor takes the lead, his question leading to responses in the *pingqiang* and *luoqiang* sections from the female-role performer. When sung solo, meanwhile, it is more common for the first *qiqiang* phrase to be extended by an instrumental codetta, which is followed immediately by a *luoqiang* phrase. A second *qiqiang* leads to two or more brief *pingqiang* phrases and the tune is then rounded off with a second *luoqiang.*[4]

Figure 8.3 summarizes this tune in tabular form, with the male and female versions of this tune placed side by side for ease of comparison. In duo performance, of course, the resulting song combines parts of each version. In preparing this, I have looked at all the examples of *yinyang xue* that I can find, so the resulting figure represents a typical version. The first row in each table just gives a label to each phrase so that they can be talked about conveniently. These labels are essentially alphabetical, except that "i" is used for the instrumental interludes. I will include most of my analytical observations about *yinyang xue* in the comments on the other rows but for now note that the female version has an extra "a" phrase at its very start, which I call "ao." This tells us that "a1" is the true first phrase to compare either with phrase "a" in the male version or with phrase "d" in the *luoqiang* section. (This detail makes fuller sense with sample song texts to hand, which, for linguistic reasons, I'm largely leaving out of this analysis; see further Stock 2003:144–47.)

The second row counts the beats given to each segment. This tune is normally sung at moderate or brisk speed in the Chinese equivalent of 2/4 time;

4. Examples of duo and solo versions of *yinyang xue* occur in Stock (2003:141–50).

FIGURE 8.3. *Tabular summary of Yinyang xue.*

Male Voice

1. Qiqiang (fairly fixed)

Phrase:	a	i1	b	i2
Beats:	4	2	6	14-16
Pitch structure:	5 → 2	(2 → 3)	3 → 1 → 2	(2 → 1 → 5)
Comments:	interlude	length as a & i1	long interlude balances a, i1 & b	

In duos, the first singer exchanges with the second here

2. Pingqiang (very flexible)

	c
	4
	3 → 1
	may repeat in varied form

3. Luoqiang (fairly fixed)

Phrase:	d	i1	e	i2
Beats:	4	2	6	variable
Pitch structure:	1 → 6 → 5	(2 → 3)	2 → 1 → 6	(2 → 1 → 5)
Comments:	synthesizes qiqiang structure & pingqiang style		long interlude, if tune repeats	

Female Voice

1. Qiqiang (fairly fixed)

	a0	i1	a1	i1	b	i2
	4	2	4	2	6	6
	6 → 5	(6 → i)	i → 6 → 5	(6 → i)	3̇ → 5 → 6	(6 → 5 → i)
	extra a & i1					sometimes 12 beats or more

2. Pingqiang (very flexible)

	c
	4
	i → 3 → 5
	may repeat in varied form

3. Luoqiang (fairly fixed)

	d	i3	e	i1/i2
	4	2	6	variable
	3 → 6 → 5	(2 → 3)	3 → 5 → 6	(6 → i)

Note

The third row in each table uses symbols from Chinese cipher notation: "1" represents the first note of the scale, etc.; sub- and superscripted dots show lower- and higher-octave pitches. The scale in question is the equivalent of a Western major scale. Yinyang xue is generally pitched so that "1" is equivalent to a Western C.

there would be one measure for each two beats in a staff notation transcription. We can see from this row that the male and female versions are quite similar in duration and distribution, although not entirely identical. Some observations include:

- The *qiqiang*'s 4 + 2 beats of phrases "a" and "11" are answered by phrase "b" at a matching 6 beats;
- A long interlude then either matches the length of "b" or approximately the length of the whole *qiqiang*.
- Central *pingqiang* phrases are much "squarer," fitting into a regular 4 beats each without interludes;
- The *luoqiang* returns to the opening 4 + 2 + 6 pattern.
- The *qiqiang* and *luoqiang* are quite fixed in form, but the *pingqiang* is much more flexible.

Row 3 puts forward a kind of characteristic melodic outline for the segment in question. It identifies the degree of the scale where the tune starts and then shows its final cadence note. Some segments of *yinyang xue* also have a fairly fixed middle point; if so, that is shown as well. Comments in row four add a little more detail. Reading these outlines comparatively tells us quite a lot about the versions of *yinyang xue*, for instance:

- Each version varies its final cadential target notes from *qiqiang* to *pingqiang* and to *luoqiang*. Setting aside the interludes, the male version can be summarized as 2 → 1 → (lower octave) 6 and the female 6 → 5 → 6.
- The male and female voices lie a fifth apart in their *qiqiang* and *pingqiang* cadences and an octave apart in the *luoqiang*—the female version is not simply the male version transposed.
- *Pingqiang* phrases are always varied, if multiple, in both male and female versions.
- The *luoqiang* phrases of each voice share the same duration, interlude, and cadence notes (an octave apart).
- The interludes often prepare the vocal start pitch for the next phrase to come.

Figure 8.3 and the discussion above tell us what Yang Feifei could draw from tradition when making a new version, *man fan yinyang*. A comparison of the older *yinyang xue* forms and this new version, as seen in measures 1–26 of figure 8.2, reveals that:

- *Man fan yinyang* adopts the sectional and phrase structure of the *male* version of *yinyang xue* (no doubled "a" phrase in the *qiqiang*) with the number of beats expected in each phrase doubled, with some adaptations.

- Yang's overall pitch emphasis is that of female *yinyang xue* performances (the outline of main cadence notes is 6 → 5 → 6—as seen at the end of the second, seventh and middle of the ninth staves, respectively). Yet, because she sings in the *fan* tuning (1 = F, rather than 1 = C), her actual pitch is a fifth lower, falling into the register usually occupied by male-role singers in *yinyang xue.*

- The *pingqiang* is now the longest section, not the slightest; it also shows a clear innovation—Yang alternates two *pingqiang* phrases, c1 (lines 21, 23, and 25) and c2 (lines 22, 24, and 26), each with a contrasting cadence and accompanimental interlude.

Further comment on each of these three results will briefly identify Yang's approach to composition in this section. First, we see that each beat in *yinyang xue* has become two beats in *man fan yinyang.* This is a standard principle of transformation applied in many of the tune families used by performers in numerous genres of traditional Chinese music, and normally in such music tempo is also halved when beat count doubles, so that the resulting music is around four times as expanded in duration as that of *yinyang xue.* This expanded tempo matches well the scene's mood of bitter personal reflection, but it poses technical challenges to the singer, who must sustain long phrases. Yang copes with this challenge in several ways. For instance, she inserts a considerable amount of surface-level melodic ornamentation to ensure that her new version has appropriate flow—she could hardly expect to move her listeners by simply singing the original melody at one-quarter speed. She also revises phrases that are too long for her breath, for example breaking the *qiqiang's* "b" phrase into two parts around a central interlude. (Including this new interlude, the phrase still lasts the expected 12 beats.) Since the overall tempo is now so slow, however, she concludes the *qiqiang* with a short interlude in place of the more usual longer one. Yang includes short interludes in her *pingqiang* section to allow for breathing, and she gives the *luoqiang* phrases slightly more flexible durations, which helps provide variety after the regular 8-beat phrases in the extensive *pingqiang.*

Second, although Yang chose the slightly simpler male-role version of the tune as her model in terms of phrase structure, she selected the female version for pitch emphasis. Male and female versions of tunes arose in Shanghai traditional opera at a time when men performed all the parts. Use of distinct pitch regions for the male and female voices lent some musical variety to the performances, particularly in dialog. These tunes lived on as parts of inherited tradition when actresses joined male performers on the stage, and skilled singers, male and female alike, began to cross the former boundaries for expressive impact. Yang's compositional process here was to experiment with each possible combination until she had the one that best brought out the emotional content of the song's words and exploited the musical qualities of her voice. Although she sings squarely within the usual male register in this *fan* tuning section, selection of male cadential targets would pitch the song contour too low for Yang to make the most of her trademark expressive lower tones at phrase ends.

Third, we can see that Yang Feifei has expanded the *pingqiang* segment much more considerably than the others. The *yinyang xue* model itself allows for this possibility, but I have not found any existing example as extensively expanded as this one—in fact, most performers of Yang's generation appear to have treated *yinyang xue* largely as a set tune. In making this development, Yang was applying to *yinyang xue* her awareness of musical procedures in other *huju* tune families, where many phrases of *pingqiang* are commonly sandwiched between one statement each of *qiqiang* and *luoqiang*. Moreover, and notably, she organizes her *pingqiang* phrases into pairs, reusing two forms of the *pingqiang* phrase, c_1 and c_2, in alternation. The *yinyang xue* model gave only a single *pingqiang* phrase repeated in variant form. In revising the *yinyang xue* model, Yang was again drawing on practice found elsewhere in *huju*, where phrases are regularly ordered into couplets. Given the expanded length of the *pingqiang*, which results from both its slow tempo and the number of lines of lyrics, it made clear musical sense for her to design melodic balance and variety into the new structure as well.

In sum, Yang revises the *yinyang xue* model into a slower, transposed version that suits the scene in question. To do so, she abstracted structural principles learned in connection with other *huju* melodic elements. We have already heard that singers acquired their trade in performance and by a regimen of drilling with other apprentices and, sometimes, a teacher. They were not taught to compose, or required to analyze music and abstract theoretical principles. Those who have looked back on how they came to form new versions of the traditional materials speak, as we saw, of "playing" with a tune until they had refashioned it the way they wanted. Analyzing Yang Feifei's reworking of phrase structure, balance, and melodic content on the journey from *yinyang xue* to *man fan yinyang* illustrates just how musically detailed such "playing" can be.

Sanjiaoban

In the *sanjiaoban* section we are now back in the *zheng* tuning, where C is the first note of the scale. The conventional expectations for *sanjiaoban* are that there will be an alternation of instrumental interludes, played in strict time, and free-time unaccompanied vocal phrases ordered in repeating pairs. (Listening to this passage on the CD reminds us that music described as free meter need not be random or formless; the durations of successive notes still contribute to a sense of phrasing. Or, to put it another way, free meter does not mean that the music is necessarily devoid of pulse, just that there may be different pulse speeds in successive phrases.)

Huju researchers point to three possible elements in the instrumental music. The first is a short interlude of just two beats (for example, measure 30 in figure 8.2). Sometimes, this is replaced by a longer interlude of nine beats, which might be used for musical variety, to generate greater dramatic tension, or to allow onstage movement. (This substitution most commonly occurs before the last line of a section, but none appear in Yang's scene transcribed here, perhaps because the singer wants to keep up tension throughout the section.) Both the two- and nine-beat interludes emphasize movement from the fifth to the sixth degree of the scale. The third kind of interlude lasts four beats and shifts melodic emphasis down to the scale's third degree. Normally, it is used to round off sections of *sanjiaoban* (as in measure 48; it also appears as measure 28, as an introduction to the section). As in *yinyang xue* a further *sanjiaoban* may then ensue. In Chinese *huju* notations, all these interludes are marked off from the vocal passages by barlines, a convention I have adopted in figure 8.2 also.

The vocal music, meanwhile, consists of pairs of phrases that are typically syllabic and, despite one or two zigzags, show an overall falling contour. Male-role singers generally fall to the sixth or first degrees of the scale, females to the first. Accounts of conventional practice describe each phrase as longer or shorter according to the number of syllables in its song text, so no time signature is used in Chinese notation for this music. A couplet of two melodic phrases is repeated freely by the singer over and over as he or she works through the lines of lyrics. Emphatic instrumental punctuations sustain a tense atmosphere until the partial winding down of the third kind of interlude. In all, this is known by *huju* musicians and audiences as a highly flexible song form, and one that is very suitable for moments where the lyrics contain important information that the audience must hear clearly or when the singer needs to pass quickly through a series of emotions, adapting each phrase to match the developing mood. Yang's text includes several changes of mood, and her lyrics deal with the central tragedies of her life, from the death of her husband to her accidental killing of another man. Typical in those senses, her use of *sanjiaoban* in this scene is nevertheless patterned in a more complex way than the conventional description just given leads us to expect. Figure 8.4 simplifies the melody of Yang's ten lines a little and omits the song text to allow her underlying pattern to emerge from the surface details.

FIGURE 8.4. *Outline of the* Sanjiaoban *Section.*

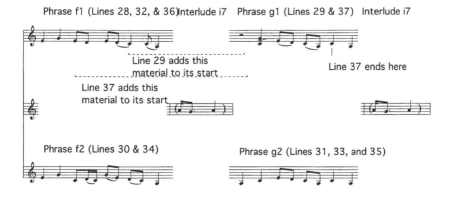

starting and closing interludes omitted

As figure 8.4 shows, Yang does not simply repeat two phrases of music over and over (with the requisite interludes). Instead, her plan for text lines 28–37 could be described as: f1, g1 (with some borrowing from the end of "f1" and a silent pause); f2, g2; f1, g2; f2, g2, f1, g1 (borrowing more from "f1" and again with a central silence). Yang Feifei's alternation of two versions of the first phrase lends some shape to the section. More significantly, her unusual inclusion of an expressive silence in the first "g1" phrase marks that gesture for the listeners' attention. Recurrence of such a silence in the final line encourages us to hear that line as satisfactorily summing up the whole section, an impression strengthened by the recapitulation prior to this pause of most of the "f1" phrase's music. This final phrase is furthermore the only one that ends on C (pitch 1), the cadential target note that we would expect from a female singer in *sanjiaoban*. Each of the earlier nine phrases ended on the sixth degree of the scale (A), which is also emphasized in every interlude. As such, the full impact of the final phrase, where Yang sings "I accidentally took his [silent pause] life away" is prepared on several levels.

In organizing her *sanjiaoban* passage in this way, Yang brings some overall shape to a notably flexible melodic element; essentially, she fits it into a profile that is especially suitable for the scene, which she can then reuse time and again in her fixed-form performances of this scene. Her compositional procedure has been to rationalize the phrase-by-phrase structure of *sanjiaoban* and pay particular attention to the overall form of the section. In doing so, Yang looks well beyond the traditional guiding principle of freely repeating the same melodic couplet over and over with varied punctuation provided by the various interludes. Existing academic writing on the music of Chinese opera traditions sometimes rather too readily accepts the conventional guidelines of these traditions as a full description of what musicians actually do in practice. In fact, analyzing the details of recorded performances can give us real insights into the kinds of musical ideas and values that underlie these traditions. As in this case, it sometimes turns out that musicians go well beyond the straightforward principles found in the words that accompany their traditions. (Stock [1999] presents an example from Beijing opera.)

Daoqing diao

Man fan yinyang is an example of melodic material that began as an imported set tune around the time of Yang's childhood and has by now completed the process of becoming one constituent of a larger tune family. *Sanjiaoban* also falls into the tune family category, although its very flexibility means that performers today do not really need to learn distinct versions of *sanjiaoban*—any one rendition can include fast, moderate, and slow phrases, for instance, and the phrases can be shaped to reflect the vocal style of any role. The third melodic component we analyze here, *daoqing diao* is an example of a set tune, although this, too, has both a female and a male version. The former is typically pitched in C or D and the latter a fifth lower (using the fan tuning). Its origin, at least according to its title, was in a song form employed by Daoists who sang while they begged for alms, and, indeed, early uses onstage in *huju* were confined to the personification of destitute characters.

Yang utilizes the male-role version of this tune in her scene. She told me that this suggestion came from a musician named Shao. Shao had heard her try out the female form of *daoqing diao* at this point in the scene and recommended that she try the lower-pitched one instead. This decision reminds us that composition in many traditions, including much contemporary popular music, regularly involves musical collaboration—effective creators in these circumstances are often those who can critically take on the ideas of their fellows. Nevertheless, Yang still reworked the tune to fit her own artistic conception. Figure 8.5 compares aspects of *daoqing diao* as sung by three male singers (Xiao Wenbin, Ding Hongsheng, and Xie Hongyuan) with Yang's version.[5] The figure shows that *daoqing diao* generally has what we might call a displaced two-part form. That is, each part normally comprises a quatrain of three musical

---

5. These examples are transcribed in Zhu and Xu (1988:401–403), and Shanghai shi (1984:102–103).

FIGURE 8.5. *Three male-voice performances of* Daoqing diao *compared to Yang's version.*

1. Xiao Wenbin

Phrase:	h	h1	j	k
Measures:	4	4	5	4
Pitch structure:	6 → 3	6 → 1	5 → 6	6 → 6
Comments:		as "h", cadence varied	end of text phrase	

Phrase:	h2	j	k1	k
Measures:	4	5	3	4
Pitch structure:	5 → 1	5 → 6	6 → 6	6 → 6
Comments:	as "h1", start varied	end of text phrase		

2. Ding Hongsheng

Phrase:	h	h1	j	k
Measures:	4	4	5	4
Pitch structure:	6 → 2	6 → 1	5 → 6̣	6 → 6

Phrase:	h2	j	k1	k
Measures:	4	5	3	4
Pitch structure:	5 → 1	5 → 6̣	6 → 6	6 → 6

3. Xie Hongyuan

Phrase:	i	h	h1	j	k
Measures:	4	5	4	5	3
Pitch structure:	6 → 5	6 → 3	6 → 1	6 → 6̣	2 → 6̣
Comments:	interlude based on "h"	extra measure at start			

Phrase:	j2	i
Measures:	5	2
Pitch structure:	5 → 6	3 → 6
Comments:		based on "k"

4. Yang Feifei

Phrase:	i7	h	h1	j	k
Measures:	2	4	4	5	4
Pitch structure:	3 → 5̣	3 → 3̣	3 → 6̣	5̣ → 6̣	6̣ → 6
Comments:	based on "h"				

Phrase:	h2	j	k1	k2
Measures:	4	5	4	4
Pitch structure:	5̣ → 6̣	5̣ → 6̣	6 → 6̣	2̣ → 6̣

phrases, one of which is heard twice: in the first half it is the opening phrase that is repeated; in the second, the final phrase. This three-phrase, four-segment format with immediate, modified repeat is unlike anything we have encountered so far in this scene, and it contains a distinctive asymmetry in its phrase lengths. This concerns the "j" phrase, which lasts five measures. In some performances, the singer follows "j" with a three-measure version of the phrase "k," so that the two together still add up to eight measures, but this is by no means universal. Although no two of the four performances are identical in primary pitch structure (let alone surface-level melodic treatment), the sixth degree of the scale functions as the point of departure for many phrases in all four performances and as the tune's primary cadential target note.

As explained earlier, Chinese dramatic music relies on set tunes, often in strophic form, and tune outlines that might be likened to sets of related melodies. Learning the different versions of tunes in these latter "families" provided singers with a set of materials that they were used to performing in multiple distinct forms. As such, we might surmise that Yang would create most readily when using melodic material and related principles from the tune families. Yang's employment of the conventional (male-role) phrase and pitch emphases in her *daoqing diao* section seems to bear this out. What figure 8.5 does not reveal is that Yang has expanded the song form from a flowing 2/4 (used in all the other three performances) to a slower 4/4 meter. This adaptation involved the same kinds of musical finishing as discussed above in connection with *man fan yinyang*, as shown in figure 8.6, which illustrates this input by directly comparing the first vocal phrase of her version with that of Xiao Wenbin.

We can see that Yang builds some new melodic work onto the surface of the male-role tune outline. Most distinctively, she begins her song higher than Xiao Wenbin, entering at the usual start-point of the female-role version of *daoqing diao*. This relatively high start, of course, gives Yang the musical space in which to fall and fall. With just one exception, each syllable in Yang's rendition of this phrase takes a falling contour, and even the level fourth syllable is decorated with a falling grace note. The phrase becomes, in Yang's version,

FIGURE 8.6. *Phrase "h" in Yang's and Xiao's versions of* Daoqing diao.

Syllables replaced by numerals (to mark position)

a seemingly inexorable descent that gradually encompasses an octave. In combination with her version's deliberately slow tempo and the special timbre of her voice, the result is a musical setting that well underlines the feeling of inevitable tragedy projected by the song lyrics. As this single phrase illustrates, even in the set tunes, and even in her performance of a melody suggested by another musician, Yang fashioned the small-scale details of her creation to contribute meaningfully to her overall dramatic aims.

Larger-Scale Issues: Putting It All Together

Now, we briefly sample aspects of Yang's larger-scale musical thinking. Yang has ordered the three tunes analyzed here to maximize contrasts between contiguous sections. This is summarized in figure 8.7:

At the heart of this design is the *sanjiaoban* section, with its palindrome of paired phrases: f1, g1; f2, g2; f1, g2; f2, g2; f1, g1. The text in this section has, perhaps significantly, a somewhat palindromic narrative shape. It contrasts the tragic death of Jin Yuan's husband Lin Tongsheng (line 28) and Jin's tragic killing of Zhang Laohu (line 37). With one death, Jin's lawful but weakened husband is wrongly taken from her; with the other, Jin wrongly slays the lawless but powerful man who has illegally seized her as mistress.

This same symmetrical principle can be detected at the general level throughout the rest of the scene. Although distinct in terms of their internal structures, the sections that directly adjoin the *sanjiaoban* share several characteristics with one another. For instance, both *man fan yinyang* and *daoqing diao* drive toward the sixth scale degree at their cadences, and, indeed, in Yang's version the openings of each section look rather similar (compare measures 1–4 and 51–54 in figure 8.2). Yang may even have decided to begin her male-role

FIGURE 8.7. *Sectional contrast at the heart of "Jin Yuan Seeks Her Son."*

Feature/Section	4: man fan yinyang	5: sanjiaoban	6: daoqing diao
tonality	fan (converse)	zheng (regular)	fan
	F	C	F
meter	fixed (4/4)	irregular	fixed (4/4)
tempo	slow	variable	slow
texture	heterophonic	demarcated vocal and instrumental lines	heterophonic
text-melody relationship	distributed, melismatic	condensed, syllabic	distributed, melismatic

modeled *daoqing diao* with this high opening because doing so, and so hinting back to the music of *man fan yinyang,* strengthened the continuity of the scene as a whole.

Looking now at sections 3 and 7, we see that *man fan yinyang* is preceded, and *daoqing diao* followed, by moderate-speed 1/4-meter tunes in the *zheng* tuning with a relatively unornamented vocal style (see figure 8.1). Each of these tunes (*kuaiban manchang* and *migui diao*) is somewhat like *sanjiaoban,* overlaying rhythmic instrumental music with a seemingly independent, slower-paced vocal line.

Taking one more step again toward the start and end of the scene, we find that *kuaiban manchang* and *migui diao* are themselves preceded and followed respectively by slow-tempo tunes in 4/4 with decorated yet densely packed song texts. Counting strictly, this gives us a symmetrical design that now stretches from section 2 to section 8 of the scene. In fact, section 2 continues the same rhythmic and musical style as section 1, relying on the very significant *huju* tune outline called *changqiang zhongban.* (In section 1, this was preceded and quickly interrupted by the insertion of decorative phrases, known as *fenghuang tou* and *san song,* respectively.) This is the only such continuation of a tune element from one section to another in the whole scene, and we might quite easily see the ten lines and 5 minutes of sections 1 and 2 together as well balanced by the fourteen lines and 4 minutes 40 seconds of section 8. Many *huju* dramas center on a woman who is tragically treated by the men around her, but few, if any others, build this theatrical dilemma right into the musical structure in such a concrete manner.

Conclusions

The most important aspects of Yang's compositional technique, revealed through the foregoing analysis, can be summarized as follows:

- She carefully and imaginatively selects existing musical material that best suits her artistic conception.
- She develops personal versions by abstracting principles from the traditional repertory, applying these in new ways to go beyond conventional models.
- She composes with an ear for structure within and also between sections.
- She is able to benefit from the input of other musicians, whether as sources of material or as sources of criticism.
- Yang applies these skills in combination to create a mirror-form scene that distills much of the musical and dramatic essence of *huju.*

As far as I am aware, listeners in the contexts of live or recorded perform-ances do not explicitly perceive this as a mirror-form movement ordered around Jin Yuan's reflections on the central misfortunes of her life, although they can do this when so requested in the context of study. I did not notice this feature myself until analyzing the scene in detail, and I have not yet had the chance to ask Yang herself about it. Nevertheless, musical analysis shows that a principle of structural symmetry is very much present, perhaps emerging from Yang's striving to hold together her rich succession of melodies with a genuine sense of musical balance. This purpose may have guided her during the long processes of trying out and honing prospective material, encouraging her to feel that cer-tain tunes, tune elements, and renditions of these materials particularly suited the various places in her scene. As this suggests, musical analysis generates ques-tions that can guide future fieldwork enquiry; it need not be an after-the-event procedure carried out, as an end in itself, away from the musicians.

Analysis also offers us an appreciation of how the scene works on a musi-cal level, which is more detailed than any we could derive through viewing a live performance. Analysis does more than offer rich details, however. It can (potentially) transform an understanding of music in question. An effective analysis should inform our imagination and listening, such that our experience of the music is deepened, and a new understanding (and new questions) can emerge. Acknowledging the transformative power of analysis, many ethno-musicologists have expressed concern that we not impute through analysis musical ends or experiences foreign to the musicians involved or their habit-ual listeners. The point is well taken, but, sometimes, we forget to emphasize as well the other side of the same coin—analysis is an outstanding means of thinking deeply about music. Analytical readings such as this one encourage us to listen more deeply to musics from around the world, studying them closely, and giving due acknowledgement to the artistry we uncover. In China, for instance, opera experts tend to speak of the aesthetic heights of the Chi-nese tradition as a whole as lying in the older and more prestigious styles, such as *kunju* and Beijing opera; the scene studied here suggests that contempora-neous musicians in much less widely renowned genres are also well able to pro-duce very carefully designed creative work. By providing us a means for the close exploration of music of all kinds, including that for which there is little explicit theory, analysis enables us to make a case for the recognition of musi-cal excellence wherever it occurs.

Appendix: Glossary of Chinese Characters

Terms use the pinyin system of romanization following Mandarin Chinese pronuncia-tion, except for song texts in the transcription, which reflect Shanghai dialect pronuncia-tions as heard on the recording. (The pinyin system is adapted to approximate those pronunciations also; speakers of the dialect in question will note some departures from Shanghai dialect as spoken, resulting from the transformations of vowels and consonants in sung performance.)

Many pinyin vowels and consonants are similar to those in standard English; those important for this chapter are illustrated here:

Pinyin	English	Example	Approximate Pronunciation
a	ar	Yang	yarng
c	ts	Ci	tsir
ei	eh	*Feifei*	fay-fay
i & *q*	ee	*qiang*	chee-arng [dipthong smoothed together]
x	hs	*xue*	hs-eh [second syllable unstressed]

A. SONG TEXT

慢反阴阳

孤岛上海多罪恶啦，市面混乱物价涨。
穷人借仔高利贷，身不啊由主似屠羊。
重重啊折息利滚利，刘三太逼我入火坑。
我瞒着啊丈夫私娼做，他病中一气命丧亡。

三角板

同生死后我更可怜，抛下宝贝林慈祥。
扶植小辈我尽责，另找职业是无力量。
只能继续做妓女，两度遭灾恨绵长。
万恶个流氓章老虎，他仗势欺人太凶横。
伊逼得我勿能人来做，我失手将他性命丧。

道情调

丧人命罪难当，可怜我太冤枉，冤沉海底坐牢房。
陈先生领他到北平，但愿我儿有希望。
将我隐痛要瞒脏，从此后母子两人，嗯嗯嗯嗯无音信遥隔他方。

B. PRINCIPAL NAMES AND TERMS

ban	板	wood block
Beijing opera	京 剧	*jingju*
daoqing diao	道情调	tune element, literally story-telling tune
Ding Hongsheng	丁洪声	actor, contemporaneous with Yang Feifei
Ding Shi'e	丁是娥	actress, 1923–1988
huju	沪 剧	Shanghai traditional opera
huqin	胡 琴	two-stringed fiddle
"Jin Yuan Seeks Her Son"	金媛寻子	*Jin Yuan xun zi*, solo scene in *The Prostitute's Tears*
kunju	昆 剧	classical opera originally from Kunshan, Jiangsu Province
luoqiang	落 腔	"falling phrase," term for the final component in many *huju* song forms
man fan yinyang	慢反阴阳	tune element, literally slow, converse *yinyang*
Prostitute's Tears, The	妓女泪	*Jinü lei*, drama
pingqiang	平 腔	"level phrase," term for the central component in many *huju* song forms
qiqiang	起 腔	"rising phrase", term for the first component in many *huju* song forms
sanjiaoban	三角板	tune element, literally triangular meter, which alternates fixed-meter instrumental and free-meter vocal phrases
Xiao Wenbin	筱文滨	actor, 1904–1986.
Xie Hongyuan	解洪元	actor, b. 1915
Yang Feifei	杨飞飞	actress, b. 1923; primary creator of the music studied here
zheng	正	"regular," opposite of *fan* tuning

References

Shanghai shi qunzhong yishuguan, ed. 1984. *Huju changqiang ji yunyong*. Shanghai: Shanghai shangwu yinshua chang.

Shanghai tong she, ed. 1936. "Shenqu yanjiu," in *Shanghai yanjiu ziliao*. Shanghai: Zhonghua shuju, 564–578.

Stock, Jonathan P. J. 1999. "A Reassessment of the Relationship between Text, Speech Tone, Melody, and Aria Structure in Beijing Opera." *Journal of Musicological Research* 18:183–206.

———. 2003. *Huju: Traditional Opera in Modern Shanghai.* Oxford: Oxford University Press.

Sun Bing, chief ed. 1996. *Zhongguo xiqu zhi: Shanghai juan.* Beijing: Zhongguo ISBN zhongxin.

Wang Pei, Chen Jianyun, and Lan Liu, chief eds. 1999. *Shanghai huju zhi.* Shanghai: Shanghai wenyi chubanshe.

Yang Feifei, narrator, transcribed and ed. Zhang Jianqing. 1986. "Xiang qianbei laoshi yu chuantong yishu xuexi." *Shanghai xiqu shi liao huicui* 2:108–12.

Zhu Jiesheng and Xu Yinping, eds. 1988. *Huju yinyue jian shu.* Shanghai: Shanghai yinyue chubanshe.

CHAPTER 9

Architectonic Composition in South Indian Classical Music

The "Navaragamalika Varnam"

ROBERT MORRIS

In this chapter, we shall study "Valachi Vacchi," a famous and beautiful composition of South Indian classical music by the nineteenth-century composer Kottavasal Venkatarama Iyer, more generally known as the "Navaragamalika Varnam" because it is based on a sequence of nine ragas. Nava means nine, raga is melodic mode, malika means garland, and varnam refers to the musical form, commonly translated as etude. "Valachi" is quite popular and has been commercially recorded at least seven times. Using transcriptions of "Valachi," we will illustrate the varnam form in detail and show how the composition is uniquely structured by the sequence of ragas, their differences and similarities, the composition's contour, rhythmic, and motivic development, and the music's relation to the sung text.

Indian Classical Music and Carnatic Music

The term "classical music" has many connotations and meanings; in India it denotes music that is serious, rigorous, connected with Indian religious and secular traditions, and publicly presented to an audience in a concert setting. Indians make a distinction between their use of the term *classical* to denote their early written literature, which derives from about 1000 B.C.E. to 1000 C.E., and their art music, which, while reaching back about four hundred years, is current and still being created and performed. There are, however, many kinds of Indian music—pop, film, devotional, folk, classical—so a concentration on the classical traditions only provides one aspect of the extraordinary diversity of music in South Asia. And the classical traditions themselves are diverse, divided into many strains and lineages of vocal and instrumental music that sometimes vie for being the most authentic or traditional. Yet Indian classical music can be roughly divided into two large practices, Hindustani and Karnatak (Carnatic). Hindustani music is practiced in North India, Pakistan, and Bangladesh, whereas Carnatic music flourishes on the South Indian peninsula. In this chapter, we will concentrate on Carnatic music.[1]

The religious context of Carnatic music is almost completely Hindu, whereas Hindustani music has both Hindu and Islamic connections. Historically, Carnatic music was less prone to influence from other forms of music, as South India was not the seat of invasions from the West or North. Despite some claims to the contrary, this does not make Carnatic music "more" classical or traditional than Hindustani music, for South India is populated by Dravidian people, whose language and customs are not homologous with the Aryan, Sanskrit culture of North India, even if South India has been influenced by it. In fact, some South Indians prefer to trace their music to a different classical culture, the classical Tamil civilization that flourished in South India fifteen hundred years ago. In any case, Carnatic and Hindustani music, although they share basic melodic and rhythmic concepts, are sufficiently different in many important ways. Presumably because of these differences, South Indians generally prefer their own classical music to that of the North Indians, and vice versa. It also should be recognized that Indian music is also practiced outside of India, including many North American cities where Indians have migrated and settled. Almost all the major Indian musicians frequently tour and give concerts in these pockets of Indian culture embedded throughout the world.

In the nineteenth century, Carnatic music and dance was performed in South Indian courts, villages, and temples, but as the twentieth century progressed and South Indian cities grew and eventually became independent of Western rule and control, the music migrated to the cities. Today, the centers of South Indian classical music are in cities such as Chennai (formally Madras), Mysore, Tajavour, Madurai, and Kochin.

Despite the urbanization of South Indian music, it is still largely taught in the traditional manner.[2] An accomplished musician accepts young students

1. Perhaps the most detailed technical exposition of Carnatic music written for the Westerner is Pesch (1999). For a more ethnomusicological approach, see Viswanathan and Allen (2004).

2. Music is also taught in universities and music schools, where students are sometimes taught in (large) classes.

Vocalist Trivandrum R. S. Mani Iyer in performance, December 1956, Madras, with: violin, Kumbakonam P. Krishnaswamy; mrdangam; Srirangam R. Kannan; ghatam, Vikku Vinayakaram. Photo from Sri Rangarajan Krishnaswamy (Kannan), used with permission.

into his musical *parampara* or lineage. Students are first taught vocal music even if the parampara is instrumental, because the musical ideal of Indian music is vocal music, and the corpus of Carnatic music is vocal composition, which is then adapted for instruments. Music is usually taught one-on-one or in small groups by rote, without notation, phrase by phrase. After the student has learned a number of compositions, improvisation is taught, again by musical exchanges between the teacher and pupil. At this stage, students may accompany their teacher in concert, and sometimes, at the teacher's discretion during a performance, perform a part of a composition or improvise a bit.

Performance Contexts for Carnatic Music

Carnatic Music is presented by music organizations called *sabhas*. In Chennai, for instance, each sabha's board of directors selects musicians to invite to play concerts and present lectures. Only a few sabhas own a concert hall, so most rent local lecture, municipal, and school halls. Many of the concerts are free to the public, especially those given in daylight hours. The sabhas have differing degrees of prestige, but all are considered bone fide. The first among them is the Music Academy, which is not usually referred to as a sabha, but is organized in the same ways as the others. The Music Academy is centrally located and has its own buildings, including a large concert hall that seats about fourteen hundred; it also publishes its own (unrefereed) journal, books, and music (in Indian notation), produces recordings, and dispenses honors and prizes.

A typical concert of Carnatic music has some affinity with classical concerts in the West, but with notable differences. Perhaps the most important difference is that Indian music is improvised to various degrees, unlike Western classical music which presents complete and notated compositions that are "interpreted" by the performers. The venues for Indian concerts are not always elegant or intended for music performance. However, all Carnatic music is amplified so any venue is only as good as the amplification system and house speakers, which sometimes leave much to be desired.[3] Typically, large paintings of the three composer-saints of Carnatic music[4] with offerings to them and Hindu deities are placed prominently on or near the stage. The stage usually has a curtain, which is opened just before the musicians play. Thus, the musicians warm up and tune without being seen by the audience and are in place with their instruments and microphones when the curtain goes up. This reminds one of *darshan* in Hindu temples, where the temple images are displayed in clothing and jewelry only at certain times of day to temple visitors, who assemble at the appointed time.

A concert is usually given by a lead singer or instrumentalist accompanied by another singer or instrument, usually the violin,[5] and one or more percussion instruments, such as the *mrdangam,* a double-headed, barrel-shaped drum, played on both heads by the hands. Other percussion instruments include the *kanjira,* a tambourine with one jingle made of lizard skin, and the *ghatam,* a clay pot. The playing techniques of these instruments are intricate, involving a great many timbres and a vast repertoire of well-known patterns and compositions. A drone instrument is also played in concerts, usually by a student of the main performer. A chordophone lute called a *tampura* was formally used

---

3. Since the 1950s, concert amplification has been adopted so that the voice and instruments can project to large audiences without forcing or otherwise degrading the subtle ornamentation that is at the heart of Indian music.

4. These are Thyagaraja (1767–1847), Muthusvami Diksitar (1775–1835), and Syama Sastri (1762?–1827).

5. Baluswami Diksitar, one of Muthusvami Diksitar's brothers, imported the Western violin into Carnatic music in the nineteenth century. The instrument has not been changed (except for the tuning G,D,G,D) but the performer plays it sitting down supporting it by both the chin and the foot, so as to permit the complex and manifold features of Carnatic melodic ornamentation.

for this purpose, with its strings tuned to the tonic and secondary note of the raga, stroked over and over; nowadays the tampura is going out of fashion and a simple, hand-held harmonium called a *sruti box* is played, or various electronic drones imitating the tampura and sruti box are employed instead. The use of electronic drones is especially common when performances take place in other countries, because the tampura does not keep in tune outside of India's climate; in addition, the instrument is one more bulky but delicate instrument to carry and transport.

Carnatic concerts follow a standard format. They start with the rendition of complete compositions with minimal improvisation, gradually introducing improvisation, first as introductions and addenda to the pieces, then in a more central role involving special types of improvisation that challenge the performer. This culminates in the centerpiece of the concert, *ragam-tanam-pallavi* (or in acronym, RTP). Almost all of the RTP involves improvisation and it can last half an hour or more.[6] After the RTP, the concert winds down with several items from a lighter repertoire of dance compositions and regional folk and devotional songs.

Concerts are not moderated and have no program or program notes. There are no breaks or intermissions, and a typical concert lasts about three hours or longer. The concert items are immediately concatenated with only slight applause between them, if any. Thus, someone who does not know much about the music will be lost. During the performance many listeners show their appreciation by crying out words of joy and encouragement. At the end, if the concert was excellent, all audience members will stand in ovation. The most knowledgeable listeners, called *rasikas,* sit up front and keep the *tala* rhythmic cycles (explained later) by a system of waves, claps, and finger counts. They will always know what is going on and appreciate all the nuances and technical feats the musicians play and improvise.

Raga, Tala, and Musical Form in Carnatic Music

Indian music is based on two fundamental principles: raga and tala. Ragas are melodic modes, each based on one of seventy-two basic scales, often having a different ascending and descending movement of tones, and a set of defining characteristics such as special phrases, ornaments, beginning, stressed, and final tones, and the like. Each raga projects a special mood and is often associated

6. The ragam-tanam-pallavi resembles the *alap, jor, jhala, gat* of instrumental Hindustani music, and a similar format in *Dhrupad,* an older, almost defunct—but recently revived—form of North Indian vocal music.

with a time of day, season, or Hindu deity. There are hundreds of ragas in general use. We will postpone further discussion of ragas since it figures prominently in the musical analysis below. Talas are rhythmic cycles lasting from 2 to 128 beats, divided into parts called *angas*. In South India, there are thirty-five basic *Suladi* talas and many more, but for this paper we need only know the tala of the composition we will study; this tala is Adi, a cycle of eight beats divided into angas of four, two, and two beats, perhaps the most ubiquitous tala in Carnatic music. South Indian musicians "keep tala" by a system of claps, waves, and finger taps called *kriya*. The right hand does these actions on the palm of the left. In Adi tala, the first beat of each anga is shown by a clap, while beats 2 to 4 are shown by finger taps, and beats 6 and 8 have are shown by a wave or a back-clap, a "clap" using the back of the right hand (instead of the palm) on the palm of the left hand. Thus, the entire tala is counted: beat 1 = clap, beat 2 = pinky finger tap, beat 3 = ring finger tap, beat 4 = middle finger tap, beat 5 = clap, beat 6 = wave or back-clap, beat 7 = clap, beat 8 = wave or back-clap.

It is not generally known that Indian music is replete with long and complex fixed compositions. This may be because most listeners are more generally aware of the practice of Hindustani music where improvisation is featured in concerts and complete compositions are rarely performed. But, as we have seen in Carnatic concerts, a performer will sing or play compositions as well as improvise in various formats and styles. The repertoire of Carnatic music is divided into music for practice (part of the pedagogy of aspiring musicians and amateurs) and concert music. Practice music is called *abinaya sangita,* and is said to have been codified by Purandara Dasa (1484–1564), who is known as the "father" of South Indian music. Abinaya sangita consists of elementary pieces composed in the raga Mayamalavagaula,[7] and uses many of the classical Suladi talas. More advanced compositions including *svarajati*s and *varnam*s are composed in various ragas, and are often played in concerts. As we will see, the varnam has an important role in teaching and preserving the characteristics of their ragas. The most prevalent form of concert music is the *kriti,* a three-part form[8] that may include complex relations among its sections, including development and climax.[9]

---

7. Mayamalavagaula is based on a scale that is roughly equivalent to the Western major scale, but with a flat second and sixth. It is used as an introductory raga because it instructively contains all three different sizes of diatonic adjacencies (minor, major, and augmented seconds, in Western terminology).

8. There are, however, a few two-part kritis, mainly written by Muthusvami Diksitar, such as "Vallabha Naayakasya" in Begada raga and Rupakam tala.

9. See Morris (2001) for an exposition of the kriti form.

The varnam is probably the most complex musical form of Carnatic Music.[10] Compositions in this form are often performed at the beginning of a concert because they provide a means of warming up in the course of playing an old, formal, and traditional piece composed by a venerated composer. This corresponds to the Western practice of playing a Prelude and Fugue from the *Well-Tempered Clavier* by J. S. Bach at the beginning of a piano recital. "Valachi" is a *tana* varnam, which is to be rendered in a vocal style called tanam, in which each note is sung with a strong and regular pulsation. This lends an august and weighty air to the performance. Unlike the kriti form mentioned above, the varnam is a binary form.

Introduction to "Valachi Vacchi"

Figure 9.1 outlines the form of a typical varnam, the first part of which—called *purvanga*—has three subsections, the *pallavi, anupallavi,* and *muktayi svara,* and the latter part—called *uttaranga*—is a series of passages called *citti svara* interspersed with a refrain (called *ettugada pallavi,* or *carana*). In performance, any section of the form may be repeated. In addition, the uttaranga is often performed at one and half times the tempo of the first part, and both the purvanga and uttaranga may be performed in double-time on optional repetition. Other more technical aspects of the varnam form will be taken up shortly.

Figure 9.1.2 presents the varnam form as articulated by "Valachi." As indicated, not all sections are texted. The pallavi, anupallavi, and carana are set to words, but the text tends to be formulaic, with the carana often setting an incomplete sentence. The svara sections are sung in sargam (Indian solfège), using the Indian note names, sa, ri, ga, ma, pa, dha, ni (which correspond to the Western do, re, mi, fa, sol, la, ti). A translation of the text (in Telegu) of "Valachi," given in figure 9.2, appears to be a prayer by the composer to the deity Sree Venkatesa. The name of this deity is also the "pen-name" or mudra, of the composer. The mudra is included in the text of the second section of the purvanga, the anupallavi, of a composition, which is how a composition's composer is identified. Sometimes different composers share the same mudra, as in this case, which has led to "Valachi" being identified with a more famous composer, Pattanam Subrahmanya Ayyer (1845–1902), who lived a generation later than Kottavasal Venkatarama Iyer.

Most varnams are set in a single raga and tala. It is important that a varnam present a concise and exhaustive repertoire of the most important features and

---

10. See Ramakrishna (1991) for a definitive study of the varnam.

FIGURE 9.1.1. *General form of the varnam.*

A: Purvanga (first part)
  pallavi (with text, two or more cycles of tala)
  anupallavi (with text, two or more cycles of tala)
  muktayi svara (sargam, two or more cycles of tala)
  pallavi (opening phrase)

B: Uttaranga (latter part)
  ettugada pallavi (carana) (with text)
  citti svara 1 (sargam [Indian solfege])
  ettugada pallavi
  citti svara 2 (sargam)
  ettugada pallavi
  citti svara 3 (sargam)
  . . .
  citti svara n (sargam)
  ettugada pallavi

phrases of its raga. In this way, the varnam serves as musical "dictionary" that authoritatively illustrates the salient traits of its raga within the context of a musical composition. Because "Valachi" is composed in nine ragas—the scales of which are shown in figure 9.3—it provides a sharp and distinctive illustration of each raga and puts the differences among them in relief. The ragas involved are in order: Kedaram, Sankarabharanam, Kalyani, Begada, Kambhoji, Yadukulakambhoji, Bilahari, Mohanam, and Sree. We will examine these ragas in greater detail presently. As I mentioned earlier, the tala for "Valachi" is the eight-beat Adi, with angas of 4 2 2.

You can hear "Valachi" in CD track 15.[11] The singer Trivandrum R. S. Mani Iyer performs the composition, accompanied by mrdangam and a sruti box, the hand-held harmonium that sustains the drone. The vocal quality is typical of South Indian music. It is open throated, even if it may initially sound "nasal" to ears unaccustomed to this music. It is often difficult to pin down the pitch of the voice to an exact note as the music is subject to a great amount of ornamentation. The types and degree of this ornamentation comprise one of the main differences between Carnatic and Hindustani music, the latter employing slower pitch modulation more like the Western glissando, and more sparingly than in Carnatic music. The drummer is improvising his part but is constrained by the tala, his role as accompanist, and standards of taste exemplified by his

11. The source for the recording is *An Anthology of South Indian Music, Vol. 2,* Ocora C 590002 (CD).

FIGURE 9.1.b. *Form of* "Valachi" *Navaragamalika Varnam.*

A: *Purvanga*

    pallavi (raga Kedaram two cycles of tala)
    anupallavi (raga Sankarabharanam, two cycles of tala)
    muktayi svara 1 (raga Kalyani, two cycles)
    muktayi svara 2 (raga Begada, two cycles)
    pallavi (raga Kedaram, opening phrase only)

B: *Uttaranga*

    ettugada pallavi (raga Kambhoji, one cycle of tala)
    citti svara 1 (raga Yadukula Kambhoji, one cycle, slow gait)
    ettugada pallavi (raga Kambhoji, one cycle)
    citti svara 2 (raga Bilahari, two cycles)
    ettugada pallavi (raga Kambhoji, one cycle)
    citti svara 3 (raga Mohanam, two cycles)
    ettugada pallavi (raga Kambhoji, one cycle)
    citti svara 4 (raga Sree, four cycles)
    ettugada pallavi (raga Kambhoji, one cycle

particular parampara. Because he, too, knows this composition, probably having been taught to sing it when he was a student, his improvisation fits the composition like hand in glove.

The entire performance is transcribed in figure 9.4, but without the mrdangam part. It is not given since, as indicated earlier, it is improvised; furthermore, as "Valachi" is a teaching piece, it would be often learned and performed without accompaniment. But even without the drum part, the transcription is undoubtedly difficult to read on first hearing, because it attempts to notate every nuance of melodic ornamentation. These nuances are integral to the composition and the ragas on which it is based, not improvisations on—or per-

FIGURE 9.2. *Text of* "Navaragamalika Varnam."

Pallavi: Valachi vacchi yunna naapai Chalamu seeya meeraa saami.
Anupallavi: Cheluvudaina Sree Venkateesaa Kalasi melasi kougalimcha.
Carana: Pada saroja mula ney nammidhi.

Rough Translation:

Pallavi: Lovingly I have come to you, why don't you glance and show your grace on me.
Anupallavi: O beloved SreeVenkatesa, let us embrace.
Carana: I have always believed in your lotus feet.

FIGURE 9.3. *The ascending and descending scales of the nine ragas in* Valachi Vacchi. *The scales of these ragas conform to the ones given in Ludwig Pesch,* The Illustrated Companion to South Indian Music, *New Delhi: Oxford University Press, 1999, and S. Bhagyalekshmy,* Ragas in Carnatic Music, *Madras: CBH Publications, 1990.*

formance deviations from—a simpler compositional scheme. In fact, I chose to transcribe this recording because it is a definitive representation of the composition, without additional melodic and rhythmic elaboration, which occurs in certain contexts, especially when the composition is played on Indian instruments. What the transcription notates is what is passed down from teacher to pupil in all of its complexity and rigor. For even though Carnatic music is

FIGURE 9.4. *Author's hand transcription of* Valachi Vacchi.

FIGURE 9.4. *Continued*

FIGURE 9.4. *Continued*

Muktya swara.

MS1a
Kalyani   S N S R - G S R G M PD DM GR NG R N G N S   S R G M P

9.

10.

MS1b   D M G R S - D N S R R G - G M P D G - M P D D N P D   M P D N S

Muktya swara 2

MS2a
Bejada   N D D P M - G R G (R) M - G R G N   P S N R S G R G M P P S R S

11.

MS2b   S R G M G M R - S R - S N D P M M - G R S S   M G G R R S N

12.

Return $
Pallavi
(Kalaan)   Ja la   chi -

13.

315

FIGURE 9.4. Continued

316

FIGURE 9.4. *Continued*

317

FIGURE 9.4. *Continued*

318

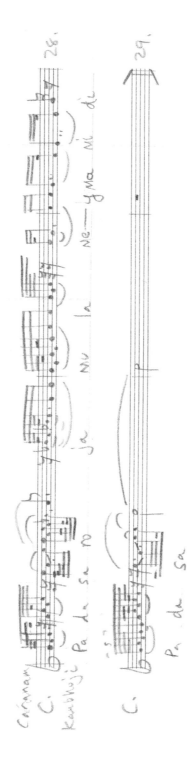

FIGURE 9.4. *Continued*

often given a kind of skeletal notation, a composition's identity is not located there, but in its aural form, which is much more resistant to change or degradation because of the exacting way in which music is taught and learned. There are however different versions of the same composition, but these are not considered variations but recensions. I hasten to add that a simple but adequate notation system is employed for various purposes including pedagogy, but it is only useful if one already has internalized the structural details and performance practices of Carnatic music. Moreover, collections of compositions written in Indian notation often contain errors, which are obvious to those who use the notation mainly as a memory aid. For instance, one source for an Indian notation of "Valachi," Panchapakesa Iyer (1997:37–38), frequently deviates from my transcription.

The transcription is written so the tonic note of the ragas is C. Each line of the transcription is exactly one tala cycle long with the quarter note notating a beat in measures of four, two, and two beats, corresponding to the angas of the tala. I have not given a time signature. Adi tala would sensibly fit an 8/4 signature, but, in the case of many varnams, each beat may be subdivided into half beats, what is called "rettai kalai." Then the time signature would be 16/8. In this case, it is likely the performers are dividing each beat, but the tempo is fast enough so that it might have been performed without division. A videotape would make this clear. In any case, varnams are usually taught in rettai kalai. In the transcription, lines are aligned beat for beat with subsequent lines for comparison and are numbered at the right. Each section of the composition is labeled on the left including the name of the raga used.

Analysis of "Valachi Vacchi"

Let us now examine "Valachi" in more detail. First, I will discuss the varnam's first large section, the purvanga, then the second section, the uttaranga. Figure 9.5 provides simplified transcription for the opening pallavi section of "Valachi," illustrating only the notes and basic rhythm of the composition, without ornamentation or details of timing. It shows the pallavi's two subsections, each lasting one cycle of the tala and repeated once in this performance. The contrast between the lower tessitura and the rhythmic regularity given by the melismas in the first subsection and the higher range and irregularity of the second is typical of a pallavi section. The rhythmic structure of the second subsection projects a pattern of $3 + 3 + 2$ sixteenths followed by 4×3 sixteenths, ending with $5 + 7$ sixteenths. Collecting these three groups of sixteenths, we have a $2 + 3 + 3$ beat structure that cuts across the $4 + 2 + 2$ beat structure of the tala. These kinds of rhythmic designs are typical and pervade this composition.

FIGURE 9.5. *Pallavi of* Valachi Vacchi.

As for the melodic aspects of the pallavi, listen to CD track 16, a portion of a lecture on Kedaram raga by Dr. S. Bhagyalekshmy. This talk is available in India on cassette and consists of Bhagyalekshmy reading from her book, *Ragas in Carnatic Music.* In figure 9.6, I provide a transcription of this aural excerpt because the cassette's sound quality is poor, the talk is laden with technical terms, and the author's accented English will be unfamiliar to many listeners. I have written the text on the left, with commentary on the right. I have not transcribed the music she sings, but included the Indian notation as it appears in her book.

The talk provides a few reasons why the composer of "Valachi" chose Kedaram as the first raga of the composition. Kedaran is auspicious and asso-ciated with opening a concert just as varnams are. Because Kedaram is a *ghana raga* it should be sung during the first part of a concert, followed later by more purely melodic, *naya* (literally, sweet) and *ratki* (literally, full-blooded) ragas that occupy the center of a concert. All the other ragas in "Valachi" are naya or ratki, except for the last, Sree, which is a ghana raga. Kedaram's wider in-tervals and striding, heroic quality provides an august beginning to the piece. As Bhagyalekshmy says, Kedaram "shines" at medium tempo and varnams are sung at medium speed.

I mentioned earlier that varnams display the most salient features of their ragas. To show this listen to CD track 17 in which Dr. Bhagyalekshmy sings the *sancharis*, the most characteristic phrases, of Kedaram. I have notated these in Indian and Western notation in figure 9.7. These sancharis provide a quick survey of the raga. We hear that the scale-degrees $\hat{1}$, $\hat{3}$, and $\hat{5}$ are the most preva-lent notes, with degrees $\hat{4}$ and $\hat{7}$ in much less conspicuous positions in the phrases. These two notes are chaya and tend to approximate the pitch of $\hat{3}$ and $\hat{1}$. This is so close in the case of the motion pa ni ni pa ($\hat{5}\,\hat{7}\,\hat{7}\,\hat{5}$) that the pitches might well be notated pa sa′ sa′ pa ($\hat{5}\,\hat{8}\,\hat{8}\,\hat{5}$). In fact, I have observed no differ-ence at all between ni and sa ($\hat{7}$ and $\hat{8}$) in some performances, and different

FIGURE 9.6. *Transcription of Dr. S. Bhagyalekshmy's talk on raga Kedaram.*

text: sentence by sentence	*commentary*
This is a vakra audava shadava janya raga.	This raga has six notes, five in ascent and six in descent, a crooked ascending scale, and is derived from a parent scale (called Sankarabharanam) equivalent to the Western major scale.
Arohana and avarohana of Kedaram raga is: s m g m p n S' - s' n p m G r s. In the arohana, only one swara is vakra.	The ascent and descent of this raga is (in solfege) do fa mi fa so ti do; do ti so fa mi re do. One of the notes (Ma, $\hat{4}$) is out of order in the ascent.
The swaras taken by this raga are: Shadja, Chatusruti Rishabha, Antara Gandhara Sudha Madhyama, Panchama, and Kakali Nishada.	The scale degrees taken by the raga are $\hat{1}, \hat{2}, \hat{3}, \hat{4}, \hat{5}, \hat{7}$ (no chromatic notes).
A Dhaivata varjya raga.	Scale degree $\hat{6}$ is not used in the raga
An upanga raga and belongs to the Dvitiya Ghana Panchakas group.	All notes are from the parent scale; the raga is one of the "ghana" ragas (literally dense, that is, serious). There are two quintets of Ghana ragas; Kedaram is from the second.
Madhyama and Nishada are the raga chaya svaras.	Scales degrees $\hat{4}$ and $\hat{7}$ "shadow" the degrees $\hat{3}$ and $\hat{1}$, respectively to the point of sometimes sounding the same.
The following raga sancharas sgmp-ps's'np-mGr-s'r'r'G's' figure as visesha sancharas.	These are melodic phrases, which characterize this raga, but are used sparingly.
Morning time is the most appropriate time for singing this raga.	An auspicious raga used for singing invocatory pieces for dance, opera, and religious discourses.
A tristhayi raga that invokes vira rasa	A raga used in all registers and will permit phrases of a wide compass; the raga invokes a sense of heroism and valor.
Kedaram is a minor raga with limited scope for alapana and swara prastara.	This raga is not often used in improvisation as its tone material does not permit extensive elaboration.
The raga shines well in madhyamakala sancharas.	The raga sounds best in medium tempo
At the commencement of a concert singing this raga creates a musical atmosphere.	

FIGURE 9.6. *Continued*

text: sentence by sentence	*commentary*
Kedara of Hindhusthani music is different from this raga since it belongs to Kalyan That.	A different raga with the same name is used in North Indian music; it also has a different parent scale equivalent to the Lydian mode.
Natbihag of Hindusthani music has some resemblance to Kedaram of Carnatic music.	Another North Indian raga, Natbihag, has some similarity to Kedaram.

sources of the Indian notation for specific compositions in Kedaram often differ in notation for this motion. Scale-degree 2, only in the descent of the raga, often takes a special ornament, but the ornament is not obligatory. The brackets in figure 9.7 show one of the raga's visesha sancharis; these are characteristic phrases that are used only sparingly in performance, often cadentially.

The pallavi of "Valachi" derives from these sancharis. In figure 9.8, I have notated the pallavi again, this time indicating from which sancharis it is generated. As you can see, sanchari 2 is responsible for the most material. Interestingly, visesha sancharis are not used.

Before progressing on to the next section of the purvanga, I want to note a few global characteristics of the pallavi. The contour of the first subsection starts on the low fifth degree, touches high C, and returns to the low C, producing a <021> contour.[12] The second subsection[13] has the same type of contour with the same boundary pitches up to the next to the last syllable "sa." The last two syllables "sa-mi," are set by a <120> contour, the retrograde of the first. The members of the *contour-class* of <021> continue to proliferate through the rest of the composition.[14] As for the frequency counts of the notes in the two subsections, the range of the two is the same, but one senses an upward trend in the second subsection as a result of the greater frequency of higher pitches as compared with the first, which has half of its duration spent on middle C.

12. Musical pitch contour has been notated in the music theoretic literature as sets of numbers; 0 is the lowest pitch, 1 next lowest, and so forth. Thus, <021> indicates a three note figure where the lowest note (0) comes first, the highest (2) second, and the middle (1). The three-note figure gives the most salient notes spanning the musical phrase from which it is derived. See Morris (1994).

13. I segment subsection two before the syllable "sa" because the line returns to middle C on the previous syllable "ra" after a long departure.

14. A contour class is the set of contours related by identity, retrograde, inversion, and retrograde-inversion. Thus the contour class of <021> includes the contours <021>, <120> (retrograde), <201> (inversion), and <102> (retrograde-inversion).

FIGURE 9.7. *Sancharis of Raga Kedaram sung by S. Bhagyalekshmy.*

1.

g mp n p, m G   r   s r r g S

2.

s mg mp nn p p m m g r

3.

g mp n n p p s' n s'

4.

n s' m' m' g' r' S'

5.

r' s', n p   m g,   r

6.

g mp n n p p m G r-   s n . p . n . s r r   g S

* asterisks mark chaya notes
that approximate the pitch of
the note a semitone above or
below.

** The bracket indicates a
vesesha sanchari to be used
sparingly in performance.

The next section of the purvanga, the anupallavi, features raga Sankarabharanam, a major ratki raga. In both varnams and kritis, the anupallavi tend
to complement the pallavi. The pallavi starts out in the low or middle range of
the voice, while the anupallavi is higher, more intense, and eventually descends
as it returns to the pallavi's opening phrase. In "Valachi" the contrast is heightened since the raga of the anupallavi is new.

Sankarabharanam is a major raga, one of the jewels of Carnatic music,
with a multitude of compositions written in it. It has subtle and quick ornaments with niceties of intonation and melodic shape. The visual complexity of
the transcription of the anupallavi (lines 5–8) indicates this. Nevertheless, the
contrast with Kedaram is stabilized because all of the notes of Kedaram are included in Sankarabharanam and the most frequent notes of both are the tonic,

FIGURE 9.8. *Derivation of Pallavi of* Valachi Vacchi
from Sancharis of Kedaran.

FIGURE 9.9. *An ornament on the fourth degree of Raga Sankarabharanam, beat 3 of line 6 of the transcription of* "Valachi."

ornamented notes:

dai _____

underlying notes:

third, and fifth, with the fourth and seventh having many special ornaments that disguise their pitch identity. For instance, the third beat of line 6 of the transcription, shown in figure 9.9, sets the syllable "dai," and is composed of two ornamented notes, degree's $\hat{3}$ and $\hat{4}$, an eighth-note each. Note that the fourth degree does not occur in the transcription, as the ornament flows around the fourth touching the third and fifth in a special rhythmic pattern. This is a typical ornament in Sankarabharanam. In any case, many of Kedaram's sancharis are also performable in Sankarabharanam. In fact, Kedaram's sanchari number 4 occurs at the climax of the anupallavi. (See line 7 and 8, beat 3 of figure 9.4.)

The next part of the purvanga is the muktayi svara sections, which are sung without text in sargam, Indian solfege. In "Valachi" there are two of these sections. The first muktayi svara is in raga Kalyani in lines 9 and 10; the second is in raga Begada in 11 to 12. These ragas contrast with Kedaram and Sankarabharanam since they introduce new pitch-classes, $\sharp\hat{4}$ and $\flat\hat{7}$. However, this change is not so obvious. In the case of Kalyani, although the sharp fourth is essential to the raga's identity, it often functions as a chaya svara below the fifth degree, or features an ornament like that in figure 9.9, that slides around the underlying pitch. Furthermore, many of the other notes in Kalyani have ornaments that touch the natural fourth. There is no ambiguity however since the Indian solfege syllable clearly identifies what scale-degree is being sung regardless of the note content of the ornament. All of these inflections of the fourth can be found on lines 9 and 10 of the transcription; and so it is perhaps not until the first beat of line 10 that one hears a clear sharp fourth, in a descending Kalyani sanchari that skips over the fifth degree.

Like the sharp fourth of Kalyani, the flat seventh in Begada is an important characteristic. However, both the natural seventh and the flat seventh occur in Begada, and there has been some disagreement in the scholarly literature whether Begada should be associated with a parent scale that includes the natural or flat seventh. My transcription doesn't show any flat seventh, but the very first sixteenth of line 11 is often rendered in other performances of

"Valachi" as a clear flat-seventh as is the second sixteenth of beat 3 of line 12. Because the music is going to return to the opening of the pallavi in Kedaram next, the absence of a clear flat seventh clears the way to the return.

The two ragas of the muktayi svara sections contrast similarly to Kedaram and Sankarabharanam. Kalyani is a major and ancient raga, with a great amount of ornamentation. Begada is a less complicated raga, but has great appeal. The junction at line 11 of the two ragas brings out their differences in another way. The end of each line of Kalyani ends with an upward gesture, whereas the entrance of Begada at line 11 descends with the potential flat seventh. Furthermore, whereas the passages of Kalyani are in low-middle range, Begada's music eventually ascends to the high fourth, connecting the passage to the climax of the anupallavi in Sankarabharanam, which also alluded to a sanchari of Kedaram.

The uttaranga section of the varnam begins with line 14 and contrasts with the purvanga in a number of ways. First, its form is different; it is not unlike the Western baroque rondeau, with the ettugada pallavi or carana section serving as the refrain. In "Valachi" the carana is set to raga Kambhoji, another deep and complex raga, featuring a flat-seventh. We see in retrospect that Begada, the last raga of the purvanga, helps make the transition to the uttaranga as it also has a flat seventh. The carana section is texted while the other sections of the uttaranga, called citti svara, are sung in sargam. But note that the first three syllables of the carana's text are pa, da, sa, from "pada saroja." These syllables are set by the notes pa dha and sa of Kambhoji raga so that they sound like sargam, which ingeniously links the carana refrain with the citti svara sections that precede it. Another revealing feature of the carana is the very clear sixth-degree, dha, on beat 3, a relatively long, unornamented note on the syllable "ro." This clear articulation of the sixth complements the lack of this pitch-class in the raga Kedaram in the pallavi.

Now we turn to the most salient aspects of the uttaranga. The choice of some of the ragas for the citti svara sections relates to Kambhoji. Look back at figure 9.3 to see the scales of the ragas in "Valachi." The first citti svara section (line 16) is in Yadukula Kambhoji, a naya raga whose name links it to Kambhoji. It is quiet and subtle, sharing Kambhoji's parent scale and some sancharis. It is often rendered at a slow tempo, which is reflected in the longer note values in the passage. This section then represents a virtual tempo contrast with the rest of the composition but is balanced by the fact that it is so clearly related to Kambhoji. The second citti svara (lines 18–19) is two cycles long and in the raga Bilahari. This raga has no flat seventh and therefore connects to the parent scale of ragas in the purvanga. Its scale allows only five notes in ascent, whereas all the notes are permitted in the descent. The five ascending notes look forward to the next raga, Mohanam, as they are the notes of that raga. This connection is brought out in line 19, where except for the first and last beats of the cycle, the notes are those of Mohanam. The look of the music in Mohanam in the third citti svara section (lines 21–22) shows that this raga is not so heavily ornamented as Bilahari or most of the other ragas in the composition. However, it is marked by prominent slides between its notes, particularly between the third and the fifth and the sixth and tonic.

The last raga of "Valachi" is Sree, a ghana raga, which frames the entire composition with the opening ghana raga, Kedaram. Moreover, both Sree and Kedaram have vakra (zigzag) scales. Sree's citti svara section is four cycles long. This continues a trend of lengthening the citti svara sections from one to two, and now four cycles. An important reason for this expansion is that the tonal material for Sree is different from the other ragas, in that it has both a clear flat seventh and flat third. This difference is a delightful surprise and given weight by the longer duration of its section. Of course, the move to two flats from none is motivated by the move from Kedaram, through Begada, and Kambhoji, which brought the flat seventh into prominence in the uttaranga, and perhaps prepares the addition of a second flat. But the reduction of Bilahari's notes to Mohanam's, without a seventh or fourth—also the weak notes in Kedaram— makes the entrance of Sree striking.

Stepping back to see more global issues of design and balance over the whole composition, consider figure 9.10. It provides a chart of the basic features of each section, including the tone material of the ragas, the *maxima* (highest notes), *minima* (lowest notes), and salient tones, and the basic contours of each section's subsections.

The tone material of the ragas is given in stacks of fifths rather than as scales because the entrance of new notes follows a pattern of adding or subtracting fifths. For instance there is a pattern of adding "lower" fifths from Kalyani to Sree, and the move from Bilahari to Mohanam is symmetric by deleting a fifth from each end of the stack of fifths in Bilahari.

The ranges for each section show that these rise and expand over the course of subsections. This reflects in microcosm the pattern of the relation between the pallavi and anupallavi. It is also noteworthy that the carana refrain in the uttaranga has the smallest range and contrasts with the other sections with which it alternates.

The dominant pitches are simply those with the greatest frequency, white notes being most frequent and black notes less so. Notes not notated are infrequent or absent. We see that frequency is not always associated with extremes of range or with the major tones in a raga. We can also trace the degree to which a pitch is emphasized throughout the composition. For instance, as I mentioned earlier, dha, notated as A on the chart, is absent from the pallavi because it is not sung in raga Kedaram. And it continues only in a weak role in the purvanga except for the second subsection of the muktayi svara passage

FIGURE 9.10. *Basic features of each section of* Valachi Vacchi.

Purvanga:

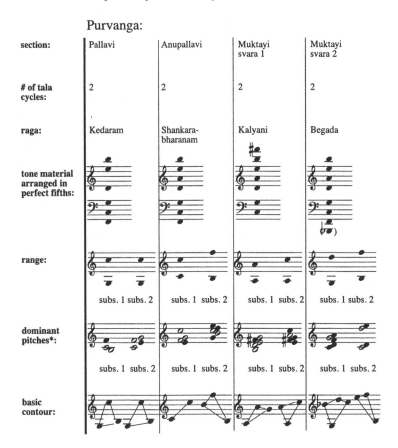

section:	Pallavi	Anupallavi	Muktayi svara 1	Muktayi svara 2
# of tala cycles:	2	2	2	2
raga:	Kedaram	Shankara-bharanam	Kalyani	Begada
tone material arranged in perfect fifths:				
range:				
	subs. 1 subs. 2	subs. 1 subs. 2	subs. 1 subs. 2	subs. 1 subs. 2
dominant pitches*:				
	subs. 1 subs. 2	subs. 1 subs. 2	subs. 1 subs. 2	subs. 1 subs. 2
basic contour:				
comments:	Both cycles have same contour; only tone material that is not a set of stacked fifths.	Includes tonal material of Pallavi; higher register; contrasting contours; last contour is R of first of Pallavi.	Minimally different tonal material from last sections; Muktayi svara 1 and 2 are parallel to Pallavi and Anupallavi.	Highly contrasting tonal material from Muktayi svara 1; has only four-part contour of first half of varnam; last contour is R of first of Muktya svara 1.

* Half-note heads indicate the most prevalent pitches in a section; quarter-note heads mark tones of secondary frequency.

FIGURE 9.10. *Continued*

Uttaranga:

Carana	Citti svara 1	Citti svara 2	Citti svara 3	Citti svara 4
1	1	2	2	4
Kambhoji	Yadukula Kambhoji	Bilahari	Mohanam	Sree

(repetitions of Carana)

| Smallest range but four-part contour; functions as refrain. | Virtural half-tempo; low range; same tonal material as in Carana. | Minimally different tonal material as last two sections; four part contours; last contour same as in Carana. | Tonal material subset of all other sections; Mohanam is also a subset of Bilahari; last contour R of Carana. | Highly constrasting tonal material from all other sections; use of Eb makes it unique (in analogy to the unique tonal features of the opening Pallavi), hence this is the longest section; last contour same as Carana; other contours are I, RI, and P of first contour of (opening) Pallavi. |

in raga Kalyani. In the uttaranga, dha has much greater role in the repeated carana and in all of the other ragas until the last raga Sree, where it makes a very slight contribution because of the nature of that raga's pitch movement. This highlights once again Sree's special role in "Valachi."

These basic contours are members of the set of contour primes.[15] All of the contours are either repetitions of the contour of the pallavi or carana, or are serial transforms of these contours.

The comments below the chart summarize some of the parallel and contrasting forms and process that hold the composition together.

As we have seen, "Valachi" is highly structured, concerned with issues of balance and contrast, something we might associate largely with the aesthetics of Western music. But the theme of unity within difference runs through a good deal of Indian philosophy. And as a composition with more than one raga is not an ordinary feature of Indian classical music, a need for unity might be all the more keenly felt by an Indian listener. It is particularly interesting that Valachi achieves this unity in part by ordering its ragas in analogy to the roles of ragas in a Carnatic concert. But speculations aside, our study of "Valachi" has shed some light on the nature of Indian music, its musical forms and processes, and its underlying forms and practices.

Commercial Recordings of "Valachi"

S. Balachander; Veena Maestro of South India, Odeon MOCE 1026 (LP).
An Anthology of South Indian Music, Vol. 2, Ocora C 590002 (CD).
Kadhri Gopalnath, Saxophone, Sony Nad AV 9249 2 (CD.)
Gottu Vadyam Master Ravikiran, Magnasound CD-CSC15022 (CD).
Golden Melodies; M. L. Vasanta Kumari, Shankar CDSV 1021 (CD.
Popular Varnams; Bombay Sisters, Pyramid CD PYR 7023 (CD).
Moments of Ecstasy (Vol 1); Maestro Shashank, INRECO 2701 C-583 (cassette).

References

Morris, Robert. 2001. "Variation and Process in South Indian Music: Some *Kritis* and their *Sangatis." Music Theory Spectrum* 23(1):74–89.
———. 1993. "New Directions in the Theory and Analysis of Musical Contour." *Music Theory Spectrum* 15(2):205–228.

15. By taking any contour's, highest, lowest, first, and last pitch as a contour in and of itself, we form the prime of the contour. Since the four determinants of a prime may not be distinct, a prime may have from two to four pitches. While there is no upper limit on the number of different contours there are only twenty-five basic primes. Complex contours can be reduced in stages through intermediate contours by an algorithm given in Morris (1993).

Panchapakesa Iyer, A. S. 1997. *Ganamrutham Varna Malika*. Madras: Ganamrutha Pra-
churan.

Pesch, Ludwig. 1999. *The Illustrated Companion to South Indian Classical Music*. New
Delhi: Oxford University Press.

Ramakrishna, Lalita. 1991. *The Varnam: A Special Form in Karnatak Music*. New Delhi:
Harmon Publishing House.

Viswanathan, T., and Mathew Harp Allen. 2004. *Music in South India: Experiencing
Music, Expressing Culture*. New York: Oxford University Press.

CHAPTER 10

Mozart

Piano Concerto No. 17 in G Major, *K. 453, Movement I*

William Benjamin

In contrast to the other chapters in this volume, this one discusses a kind of music that will be familiar to many, perhaps even most readers, and that some will have studied in depth. As well, many of the tools of contemporary music analysis used throughout this volume were developed to study the sort of music I will be treating, music from the European classical canon. As a result, there is an abundance of well-made and aesthetically illuminating analyses of such music. Both of these considerations raise the question as to why my contribution fits or might be needed in this context. Perhaps some answers will emerge as readers make their ways through what follows, but I think it best to begin with a brief statement of conviction and purpose.

Some recent analysts of European tonal music have aspired to the perspective of the scientific observer. Although often versed in the practice of this music, and personally attuned to its values and connotations, these analysts see themselves as generating abstract descriptions of musical passages that are well formed in some theory, descriptions that aim at something importantly true about those passages even if they tell us only so much about how the music is perceived by composers, players, or listeners, and much less about its meanings for segments of the society in which it arose.[1] Were I to adopt this stance,

---

For suggested recordings of the Mozart work discussed in this chapter, refer to the bottom of page 353.

1. For a general discussion of the relevance of analysis to the aesthetic appreciation of music, see Benjamin (2001).

Malcolm Bilson, fortepiano, John Eliot Gardiner, conductor, with members of the English Baroque Soloists. Photo by Clive Barda, used with permission.

this analysis might be as etic, in its own way, as any other in this collection. But the scientific pose is not one I care to adopt. Instead, I usually try, as an analyst, to describe aspects of music as I believe they can be heard and, indeed will likely be heard by a sufficiently sensitive and informed listener. That is hardly a scientific perspective, but neither is it what one might call an insider's perspective pure and simple. In any case, what I believe may be of value in what I do here is not to be measured along the emic–etic axis, but in terms of whether it points to centrally important features of European tonal music that reveal its distinctiveness but, at the same time, suggest drawing fruitful connections with other kinds of music. I have tried to do this in terms of two aspects of structure, both of which I think are absolutely fundamental: the manner in which the music attains rhythmic complexity, and the ways its most sophisticated pitch structures are rooted in a vernacular substrate.

I speak here of rhythm in a broad sense, as including durational patterning and meter on various time scales, different qualities of motion, and relations of expansion and contraction; rhythm as applying to all the dimensions of music—harmonic progression, melody, motivic organization, dynamics, instrumentation, and so on—none of which is without its manifold rhythms, of which those lying beneath the surface, and therefore slower moving, determine the musical experience as much as others that can be clapped.[2] Glib dismissals of European music as rhythmically uninteresting are easily countered with this concept of rhythm in mind. Still, it may be instructive to show how, in a context that presents no wrinkles at the rhythmic surface, such as might be apparent from the notation or might soon become obvious to the aspiring sight-reader, there may yet reside—below the surface—an intensity of rhythmic intrigue that may help to explain why the music remains so endlessly absorbing to its admirers.

It scarcely can be denied, however, that the glory of European art music lies in its pitch structures. These are anchored in memorable tunes that both accommodate and imply a complex of coexisting melodic strands. Such complexes, heard as polyphonic webs, give rise in the mind to the impression of slower-moving successions of harmonies, the patterns of which are then deployed to create form on various levels. To be sure, I don't propose to offer a thorough account of counterpoint and harmony in an important tonal piece. As I've explained, anyone interested in such an account is easily provided with a thousand references to the literature. Besides, it is clear that such an account would do little to persuade the reader that European tonal music is of a piece with the world's art music, not to mention its music in general. An opportunity resides here rather in attempting to relate a sophisticated tonal work, in regard to its harmonic and melodic organization, to some musical object in its associated musical vernacular, the folk or popular music traditions from which it took nourishment. By apprising oneself of the tie that binds a singular work of genius—I use the word unabashedly—first to a song that just about everyone knows, and second to art-musical transformations of the song that are themselves conventional, one acquires a standpoint from which to see just how and how far the artwork represents a singular departure, to see more clearly in

2. Many music theorists would trace contemporary developments in the study of rhythm in European tonal music to Cooper and Meyer (1960). Although their method of applying the feet (combinations of stressed and unstressed syllables) of classical poetic meter to music has not been widely accepted, their imaginative extension of this method to longer spans of music, whereby phrases, periods, and whole sections are grouped in a manner analogous to single notes at the surface, has had a lasting impact. An early, deeply impressive, argument for seeing all of the content of musical experience as irreducibly rhythmic is Boretz (1971).

what way it is deviant, exceptional, and possibly subversive of the circumstances in which it was born and subsequently cultivated. Important tonal artworks have come down to us because they were cherished by generations of players and listeners. What better path do we have to the social interpretation of some music, to sympathetically or critically engaging the collective psyche of a culture that celebrates a specific work, than by way of understanding the musical and ideological challenges the work presents, in light of its audience's common fund of received and assumed musical knowledge, musical-vernacular base, and superstructure of art-musical conventions?

Choosing the Work at Hand: An Account

My decision to analyze the first movement of Mozart's Piano Concerto No. 17, in G Major, K. 453, took shape in descent through a hierarchy—style-period, genre, composer, movement, work—that is less a matter of logic than a response to history. European music of the eighteenth and nineteenth centuries is often divided into three periods: the late Baroque (c.1690–1750), the Classical (c.1740–1830), and the Romantic (c.1820–1890). These articulate a progressive change in what it means for something to be a musical work. For the late Baroque, a work was a kind of trace of the application of conventional technique to the problem of providing music for a particular social purpose. Such an application may have been especially imaginative, or else routine, but in either case the primary criteria of success at the time of composition centered on the composer's adeptness at deploying standard materials in accepted ways and at making music to fit a social context.[3] By contrast, for the Romantic era, a work was an expression of the composer's individuality at a particular stage of development. Hence, it was valued for its uniqueness and, to an extent, in direct proportion to the degree it deviated from conventions of whatever sort. Its functionality, rather than being explicit and concrete, became implicit, general, even transcendental: instead of meeting the demands of some occasion or activity, it was intended to engage, inspire, and uplift an idealized audience of well-intentioned acolytes, in the manner of a vision of metaphysical truth.[4] The music of the Classical period lies between these extremes. Claims can be

---

3. Included among the social contexts of the late Baroque are some that are purely personal, but socially legitimated, for example, the solitary singing of devotional songs or the playing of keyboard pieces written to develop the skills of aspiring musicians.

4. This attitude, which persists even to the present among concertgoers, finds its extreme expression in Schopenhauer's philosophy, which confers on music the power to convey an experience of the nuomenal world, the reality that lies behind all transient phenomena, and to cancel the subjective suffering that is proper to transience.

made for its Romantic qualities, and indeed it is during this period that the unique work (e.g., Beethoven's "Eroica") asserts itself over and against conventions as a primary source for future composers. At the same time, all Classical works are strongly connected to each other by convention, and all use common funds of musical devices and materials. It is this balance between the standard and the unique that has made the best Classical music so inviting to analysts and that makes it especially suited to my approach, which, as explained earlier, assumes some interplay between masterworks and the layers of a conventional musical knowledge base.

Once the decision is made to look at Classical-period music, the choice of composer limits itself quasi-automatically to Haydn, Mozart, and Beethoven. To put it another way, one would have to be following some contrary instinct, or grinding some unusual axe, not to choose one from among this triumvirate. Having put my revisionist impulses and grinding tool aside for this project, I gave no thought to anyone else, but at the same time, I had to move to the level of genre be able to pick one in clear preference to the others.

In explaining my choice of genre, I should say first off that I did not consider writing about vocal music, whether lyric, dramatic or narrative in tone. This decision bespeaks a desire to reflect the dominant and distinctive achievements of music in the Classical period, which are surely of composing textless music, the intrigue of which is deeply engaging while lying essentially outside language.[5]

From a structural standpoint, the choice among the instrumental-music genres of the Classical period is not crucial, as sonatas, quartets, symphonies, and concertos—names that correspond to specific instrumentation—are based on similar successions of movements written more or less in the same forms. (Well, not quite the same in the case of the concerto, as we shall see.) Although the Classical concerto is normally in three movements, as against four in symphonies, sonatas, and quartets, its distinctiveness lies mainly elsewhere. More than any other instrumental genre, the concerto is public music, intended for a relatively broad, informed but inexpert audience. Critics have argued about whether concertos movements are dramatic,[6] but no one doubts that they share with opera arias an appeal to a wider audience of music lovers. Hollywood great Joan Crawford said it this way in a line from a movie quoted by Joseph Kerman: "I like some symphonies, but I like all concertos" (Kerman 1994: 162).

In response to the genre's broad appeal, commentators have tended to see the concerto as being about the relationship of the one to the many, and have

5. Postmodernists such as Lawrence Kramer (1995, 2002) have done a lot to undermine this claim, and to show that "pure" music is shot through with language-situated ideology.

6. See Webster (1996).

understood this relationship as antithetical.[7] Of course, symphonies, too, have their individuals and groups, their soli and tutti, but in the concerto the individualistic impulse is personified in a solo part that begins by elbowing in on themes first given to the orchestra, overlaying or elaborating them in an atmosphere of play, and moves on to transform or transcend those themes with a music of display that expresses independence, willful strength, even courage.[8] Yet the Classical concerto is misrepresented if described as some sustained allegory of the quest for individual freedom. Its prevailing atmosphere, the purely orchestral sections and solo perorations aside, is one of dialogic interplay, laced with occasional conflict, but essentially cooperative.[9]

Sensitivity to this cooperative interaction is conveyed in these words by Mozart's and Haydn's contemporary, the theorist Heinrich Koch:

> There is a passionate dialogue between the concerto player and the accompanying orchestra. He expresses his feelings to the orchestra . . . Now in the allegro it tries to stimulate his noble feelings still more; now it commiserates, now it comforts him in the adagio. In short, by a concerto I imagine something similar to the tragedy of the ancients, where the actor expressed his feelings . . . to the chorus. The chorus was involved most closely with the action and was at the same time justified in participating in the expression of feelings. (Koch 1793:119)[10]

Because Koch's analogy is easily falsified in many particulars,[11] it may be that his strategy was, in part, to lend prestige to the concerto of his time through association with a particularly venerable model. And yet there are passages in many Classical concertos that seem to validate the reference he is making.

---

7. The English critic Tovey writes, "Nothing in human life . . . is more thrilling . . . than the antithesis of the individual and the crowd; an antithesis which is familiar in every degree, from flat opposition to harmonious reconciliation, and with every contrast and blending of emotion . . . the concerto forms express this antithesis with all possible force and delicacy" (1936:6–7).

8. Critics have understood this dynamic in differing ways. For Joseph Kerman (1994: 151–168) it reveals the changing relationship of Mozart to his actual audience. For Susan McClary (1986:156), it "articulates a society/individual problematic."

9. For a detailed study of concertos in the light of eighteenth-century concepts of dramatic dialog, see Keefe (2001).

10. This translation is from Nancy Kovaleff Baker's edition and partial translation of the *Versuch* (1983:209).

11. Chorus and actor in Greek tragedy do not speak simultaneously, and do not repeat large chunks of common material in alternation. In general, too, one does not complete the other's thoughts, and the chorus's more static, reflective tone typically contrasts with the more labile attitudes of the protagonists, a contrast reflected in their different poetic meters.

In figure 10.1, from the movement I will be analyzing, the solo tumbles via a long, rather tortuous succession of arpeggios (mm. 184–202) into a place from which its own resources provide no escape (203–206). It falls then to the orchestra (= chorus) to suggest a way out, which it does with a certain joyous concision in measures 207–210. But the soloist, seeming unable to hear what the orchestra is telling it, departs from where the latter leaves off (mm. 211 ff) with a new, exceedingly plaintive expression of its own, as if still reeling from what it experienced a few measures earlier. This is truly the stuff of drama, and plausibly, of tragedy; and it is thus that the concerto is brought close to opera, ironically, in this case, by music that is not at all vocal in character.

As well as being a public genre of relatively clear overall symbolic significance, the Classical concerto lends itself to cross-cultural comparison because it incorporates improvised music, which is generally absent from symphonies, sonatas, and the like. Most concerto movements provide space for a more or less lengthy solo passage just before the orchestral conclusion. This *cadenza*, which serves as a final comment on important themes and a final delay of the movement's most important cadence, is supposed to be improvised, and thus represents the acme of the soloist's display of independence by way of intellectual and technical control.[12] A second level of improvised content, pertaining specifically to the piano concerto, has only come fully to light in recent years, as a result of research into the performance practices of the eighteenth century. It consists in the fact that the soloist is expected to improvise a continuous accompaniment to the orchestra whenever the latter is playing on its own for any extended period of time.[13] Space limitations prevent me from discussing these (and other) possibilities for improvised content in a specific movement, but they clearly open up the concerto to comparison with culturally diverse musical productions (see, further, Levin [1989]).

Having chosen my genre, I decided to analyze a concerto movement by Mozart because the most dazzling excursions are embedded in the conven-

12. Today, most players play memorized cadenzas, many of which date from a much later time than the concerto they are performing. Even in the eighteenth century, cadenzas were often prepared in advance by players who did not want to chance making them up on the spot. Whereas Mozart composed cadenzas (sometimes more than one) to a large selection of his concerto movements, documentary evidence shows that *he* was quite capable of improvising one equivalent to those he published.

13. Consisting of the bass line and chords which together clarify aspects of both the pitch and the rhythmic structures of the orchestra's music, this kind of accompaniment is becoming a feature of historically informed performances, one that significantly transforms the effect of the genre by causing the solo part to emerge, as it were, out of the orchestra rather than *ex nihilo* and, therefore, as a member of rather than in quasi-natural opposition to the large group. See Derr (1996).

FIGURE 10.1. *Mozart,* Piano Concerto in G Major, *K. 453. I, mm. 184–227 (orchestral part reduced for second piano).*

tional designs of his best work. The second movements of his concertos include some of the most compelling lyricism in all of music, but they are basically interludes, accompanied songs for the piano. The third movements are games of accommodation and reconciliation, representing the happy endings of all good comedy.[14] It is in the first movements that that the full extent of his achievement in the genre is evident: negotiation, opposition, provocation, rejec-

14. Passages from a number of piano concerto finales, including K. 453, are discussed in Jamison (1996).

FIGURE 10.1. *Continued*

tion, and other problematic states are invoked—along with those less fraught—by way of textural and harmonic, rhythmic, and formal complexity. Thus, the importance of the genre for its culture rests primarily on these movements, which are most filled with content that substantiates the aesthetic independence that music had newly won in Europe.

The seventeenth concerto, in G major, was written in Vienna in the spring of 1784, when Mozart was twenty-eight. The second of two concertos written for one of the composer's piano students, the daughter of a wealthy government official, it is not especially well known, and the literature about it deals mainly

FIGURE 10.1. *Continued*

with the last two movements: the second, notable for its unusual tonal plan,[15] and the last, a set of variations, for its coda, which overtly mimics the closing ensembles of the composer's comic operas.[16] The absence of extended commentary on the first movement may reflect the polished but conventional "galant"

15. This is described in detail in Schachter (1996). A tonal analysis of this movement is also found in McClary (1986).

16. Wye Allanbrook (1996:98 and 105) cites a list of well-known critics who characterize this final movement as being in comic-opera style.

FIGURE 10.1. *Continued*

style—dominated by graceful melody and symmetrically arrayed phrases—of its themes. For much of its course, this movement is robust but genially conversational in tone, and untroubled by the orchestra and piano being at cross-purposes. Of the coruscating passion of the great minor-key concertos (K. 466 and K. 491) there is scant trace, and the orchestral sections lack the symphonic weight of those in, say, the C major concerto, K. 503. By contrast, there are some wonderful subtleties of rhythmic design in the themes, and one large section of the movement (the development, excerpted in figure 10.1[17]) follows a harmonic trajectory that, in its relationship to the historical evolution of European tonality, may be described as truly visionary. For my purposes, this juxtaposition of music that is routinely polished (if adorned with subtleties) and music that is singular in expression and technique seemed just right, as exemplifying the ideal balance sought by the great Classical composers in their attempt to engage both expert and naïve listeners, and to express a world in which the painted silk of the thematic surface can at any time be brusquely stripped away to reveal a turbulent inner life.

The Concerto Genre and Its First-Movement Form

As already noted, the Classical concerto is a three-movement work. The first movement is a lengthy, complex construct, which presents a number of full-fledged themes—self-contained musical statements comprising several interrelated phrases (musical groups of several bars that close in the last of those bars)—and a variety of other segments that are repeated over the course of the movement in varied forms, and that link together to connect, introduce, extend, delay, or conclude themes. First movements are generally in a fast tempo, in common (4/4) time. Typically, they are cast in a form that is understood, but the relationship of which to other formal models has been much debated. A synthesis of current views about this form, illustrated with reference to K. 453, follows a brief discussion of Mozart's instrumental resources.

Mozart's concertos were written for the fortepiano, the eighteenth-century precursor of the modern grand piano, and a string orchestra of some twenty players complemented by a small group of wind instruments. The wind band may be as small as four or as large as twelve. Always present are two oboes and two natural (in modern times, French) horns. Found most often, in addition, are two bassoons and a single flute. A number of concertos employ two trumpets and a pair of kettledrums (played by one person) for the purpose of adding weight to the sound of the complete orchestra at strategic points. Finally, a number of the later concertos use two clarinets. The Concerto No. 17 occupies a midway position in terms of this range of wind-band size, employing the standard group of seven: a flute, and two each of oboes, bassoons, and horns. This is just a large enough group to be able to enjoy a modicum of independence from the strings, without being large enough to dominate the

---

17. As regards the placement of this section in the movement, see the discussion of form in the next part of this chapter.

music for any length of time. As a result, there are no full-fledged themes introduced here by the winds, as happens in a number of the later concertos, and little more than incidental use of the winds in counterpoint to the strings.

Space limitations preclude any discussion of dialogic relationships among the wind band, the string group, and the soloist, a fascinating topic that suggests opportunities for cross-cultural comparison. I turn, instead, to an outline of first-movement form in the Classical concerto (henceforth: concerto form) as worked out in K. 453.

Concerto form was elaborated by Mozart in the 1770s, shortly after it had emerged in the work of other composers, and he applied it consistently thereafter.[18] Oddly, it is only since the 1980s that a viable consensus has emerged about this form and its relationship to other forms. The most basic point of agreement is that there are strong parallels between concerto form and sonata form, the most important form in Classical instrumental music. Readers uncertain of the principles of sonata form will infer a good deal from the following (see especially the discussion of the movement's harmonic design later), but may want to consult a textbook on musical form or a survey of the historical period. Other elements of consensus are (1) that, compared to sonata form, concerto form proliferates more thematic material, is more modular in its design, and is less involved with the progressive development of its themes in its development section (one of the main sections of a sonata form); (2) that the solo part concludes with a cadenza, which is missing from plain sonata-form movements; and (3) that the contrast between orchestra and soloist is form-defining and results in an aspect of large-scale organization that complements the sonata-form aspect, namely that of an orchestral frame around, and one major orchestral insert within, the quasi-sonata form. In conformity with recent critical work,[19] concerto form can be listed in six sections, as follows:

1. First orchestral presentation of thematic material.
2. Solo sonata exposition, with orchestral participation.
3. Second orchestral presentation of excerpts of the thematic material first presented in 1.
4. Fantasy for solo with orchestral accompaniment, having the tonal (more rarely the motivic) character and phrase structure of a sonata development.
5. Sonata recapitulation (a varied repeat of section 2) with the piano and orchestra more nearly equal than in section 2.

---

18. The analytical overviews of Classical concerto form that I drew upon for the synopsis that follows are found in Dennis (1971:11–90 and 185–187); Leeson and Levin (1976/77); Rosen (1980:69–95); Kuster (1991:3–15); and Caplin (1998:243–251).

19. The listing follows closely the model suggested in Kuster (1991:7).

6. Concluding orchestral presentation of thematic material, interrupted by the solo cadenza.

Sections 2, 4, and 5 constitute a kind of sonata form, which is complemented by sections 1 and 6, a weighty thematic frame for orchestra, with strong thematic and motivic connections to 2 and 5, and by section 3, an orchestral insert based on fragments of section 1. Sections 2, 4, and 5 are solo dominated, but each may contain purely orchestral passages, particularly section 5, which can begin with a lengthy orchestral passage that might be taken for yet another insert if it did not function as an essential element in the sonata reprise. Much of this is likely to be confusing, but I trust it will become clear to the reader who follows the detailed formal analysis of K. 453, I, which I present in the following table (figure 10.2). Readers are advised to study this table with the score in hand. After going through this material, they should compare it with the general outline just given, to verify that the latter applies. The table employs some terms in general use, whether of harmonic analysis (e.g., "V (harmony)," and "full cadence") or formal design (e.g., "theme," "transition," and "recapitulation"). Other terms ("sentence," "presentation phrase," and "codetta"), certainly less familiar, are taken over from William Caplin's *Classical Form,* which readers may wish to consult. I have explained many terms found in the table in what follows.

Aspects of Rhythmic Structure in Selected Passages

Subtleties of Measure Grouping in a Theme

A glance at the rightmost column of figure 10.2 reveals manifold use of the label "sentence" to describe various subsections. The first such use occurs at A1, the first theme in the first orchestral presentation, shown in figure 10.3.

A sentence, following Caplin (1998: 35–48), is an arrangement of melodic and harmonic material in time—a rhythmic arrangement—within the confines of a single theme (here, sixteen bars). A sentence begins with a short melodic idea that elaborates tonic harmony. Here, the basic idea is most easily grasped as the violin melody in measures 1–4, which centers on the fifth of the tonic chord (G,B,**D**) until measure 4, in which a motion to E5[20]—on beat 2—

20. I use the now conventional Acoustical Society of America (ASA) pitch nomenclature, based in the piano keyboard. The lowest C on the piano is C1, the highest C8. Middle C is thus C4. All pitches within an octave share a number with the C below them. E5 is thus the E directly above C5, the note an octave above middle C.

FIGURE 10.2. *Formal organization in K. 453. I. Asterisks refer to notes on page 353.*

Sections and sub-sections:

name, character, dynamic(s), and orchestration	Meas. (with timing on four CDs)*	Basic grouping structure (of sub-sections)**	Tonal direction (of sub-sections)	Formal types and functions (of sub-sections)
A. First Orchestral Presentation	**1–74**			
1. Principal theme; placid, *piano* strings and horn with some wind dialogue	1–16	(4+4) + ((2+2) + 4 = 3 by elision)	Establishes tonic key, → full cadence, elided	Sentence, thematic presentation
2. Conclusion to theme becoming transition; active, *forte* tutti; then *piano*, solo winds	16–34 MP: 0:28 RG: 0:27 MJP: 0:32 MB: 0:28	(3+3) + (1+1 + 2 = 1 by elision) + ((2+2) + (1+1) +4)	Confirms I then leads to V, where a potential half cadence is elided by a standing on V, which passes back to I	Two three-bar waves acting as codettas followed by four-bar phrase transitioning to half cadence; cadential extension, joined to link to new theme
3a. Subordinate theme; initial pathos-tinged lyricism, with mood lightening at cadences; *piano* strings, then winds with string interjections	35–49 MP: 1:00 RG: 1:03 MJP: 1:06 MB: 1:01	((2+2) + 4 = 3 by elision) + ((2+2) + 4 = 3 by evasion)	Tonally mobile, stepwise descending bass, → elided full cadence; all repeated to second cadence (evaded by bVI)	Sentence: mobile presentation phrase over stepwise-descending bass, followed by continuation-to-cadence phrase; all repeated

346

3b. Active concluding part to second theme; tutti, *forte*	49–57 MP: 1:25 RG: 1:29 MJP: 1:32 MB: 1:26	(2+2) + ((1+1) + 3 = 2 inflated to 3 so that m. 57 overlaps with next sub-section)	Elaboration of bVI → full cadence in tonic key	Sentence-like preparation for and statement of principal cadence of Section 1
4. Codetta section, beginning much like music at m. 16; strings, then tutti, *piano* then *forte*	57–74 MP: 1:40 RG: 1:44 MJP: 1:47 MB: 1:40	(4+4) + (2+2) + (2+2) + (1+1)	Confirmation of arrival on I	Progressively shorter waves, dissipating energy of principal cadence
B. Solo sonata exposition	**75–171**			
1. Principal theme; *piano*, largely as in Section A, but for solo with wind accomp. (strings in 87–90).	75–94 MP: 2:10 RG: 2:18 MJP: 2:20 MB: 2:10	(4+4) + ((2+2) + (4+4 = 3 by elision))	Confirms tonic key in solo part, → elided full cadence	Sentence with cadential segment (last four bars) repeated; solo presentation of first theme
2. Transition beginning with codettas to first theme; *piano*, str. + fl., followed by solo elaboration; leading to solo passage work with str. and wind accompaniment	94–109 MP: 2:44 RG: 2:53 MJP: 2:54 MB: 2:45	(3+3) + ((2+2+1+1) + 4)	Tonic arrival at end of theme is confirmed; then, six bars of modulation to D+ major. (VI of G+ = II of D+) → half cadence in D+ followed by four bars of standing on dominant	Two 3-bar waves followed by six-bar sequential passage effecting modulation. Four-bar cadential extension at m.106 may be heard as expansion of normative two-bar completion of preceding six.

FIGURE 10.2. *Continued*

347

FIGURE 10.2. *Continued*

Sections and sub-sections: name, character, dynamic(s), and orchestration	Meas. (with timing on four CDs)*	Basic grouping structure (of sub-sections)**	Tonal direction (of sub-sections)	Formal types and functions (of sub-sections)
3. New subordinate theme, in two parts, fused into one continuity; *piano*, solo dominated, with accomp. first of str., then of winds, then of winds + str.; ending as in A2	110–138 *MP*: 3:11 *RG*: 3:22 *MJP*: 3:23 *MB*: 3:12	((2+2) + ((1+1) + 2)) + ((2+2) + ((1+1) + (1+1), . . . abandoned and fused to new group: (2 + 2) + ((1+1) + 2)	Music in dominant key. Antecedent → half cadence; consequent implies motion to I, which is aborted in favor of a switch to minor mode and a motion to another half cadence, where there is a standing on V	Period: eight-bar antecedent with sentence-like segmentation; consequent aborted after 6 bars, with bars 5 and 6 repeated; fused to sequential eight-bar phrase with sentence-like segmentation
4. Original subord. theme (A3a), in dominant; *piano*, given by solo with str. accomp., then by winds with str. accomp. and solo interjections	139–153 *MP*: 4:01 *RG*: 4:14 *MJP*: 4:15 *MB*: 4:03	((2+2) + 4 = 3 by elision) + ((2+2) + 4 = 3 by elision)	As in A3a, but leading twice to elided full cadences in the dominant key	As in A3a

348

5. Concluding themelets: a. solo with string accomp., *piano*; b. solo with wind accomp. *piano*, followed by solo with thickening accomp., crescendo	a. 153–160 MP: 4:25 RG: 4:40 MJP: 4:40 MB: 4:27 b. 160–171 MP: 4:37 RG: 4:52 MJP: 4:53 MB: 4:38	a. (2+2) + ((1+1) + 2 = 1 by elision) b. (2+2) + (5 + 2 + 1 = 0 by elision)	a. closing themelet, ending in elided full cadence b. second closing themelet, ending with expanded progression to main cadence of section, elided	a. sentence, of motivically neutral character b. sentence, also of motivically neutral character, with expanded second phrase
C. Second orchestral presentation (excerpts from A), acting as a coda to B	**171–183**			
1. Transposition of A2, tutti, *forte*, followed, after a link, by a cadential segment taken from A3b tutti, tutti, *forte*	171–178 MP: 4:55 RG: 5:12 MJP: 5:12 MB: 4:57	3 + (2 + 3 = 2 by elision)	Canonical harmonic progressions over a tonic pedal → elided full cadence (in dominant key)	A three-bar wave is followed by a two-bar link, rising an octave to a three-bar cadential segment, elided at the cadence point
2. Transposition of third group in A4, tutti, *forte*, lengthened and modified with a cadential segment, *piano*, str.	178–183 MP: 5:07 RG: 5:25 MJP: 5:25 MB: 5:09	(2 + (2) + 3 = 2 by evasion); meas. 180–181 group both with preceding 2 and following 3 bars	One full cadence dovetails into a second, which is evaded by a motion to bVI of D+	A two-bar wave is followed by its repetition, which turns into a five-bar phrase, the last bar of which is replaced by the start of the next major section

FIGURE 10.2. *Continued*

Figure 10.2. *Continued*

Sections and sub-sections: name, character, dynamic(s), and orchestration	Meas. (with timing on four CDs)*	Basic grouping structure (of sub-sections)**	Tonal direction (of sub-sections)	Formal types and functions (of sub-sections)
D. Fantasy for solo with orch. accompaniment (tonally: sonata development)	**184–226**			
1. Developmental core passage; solo, in fast arpeggios, accomp. by winds in slower arpeggios and str. harmony, *piano*; followed by point of arrival and stretch of stasis	184–207 MP: 5:18 RG: 5:37 MJP: 5:38 MB: 5:20	((2+2) + 4) + ((2+2) + 7) + 5 = 4 by elision	Large-scale sequence: model departing from Bb+ (bVI of D+ = bII of A-); restatement departing from A- (I of A- = IV of E-) and leading to standing on the V of E-	A two-bar basic idea is repeated and followed by four bars of modulation. Pattern is then restated a half-step lower, with the modulating segment expanded to seven bars; passage concludes with two two-bar waves and the elided start of a third.
2. Short link in strings, *piano*	207–210 MP: 5:59 RG: 6:21 MJP: 6:19 MB: 6:00	4	V of e- transforms into V of C+ (= V of C-)	Linkage function underlined by singular syncopated surface rhythm

3. Transition-like passage for solo, melody with Alberti bass and punctuating strings; followed by lead-in to reprise, all *piano*	211–226 MP: 6:06 RG: 6:29 MJP: 6:26 MB: 6:07	(2 + 2 + 2 + 2) + (2 + 2 + 2 + 2)	Quasi-sequence: model begins on C- (= IV of G-) and restatement on G- (= I of G-) leading to a standing on the V of G+	Continuous music of two-bar waves
E. Sonata recapitulation	**227–319**			
1. First theme, as in A1; with solo elaboration replacing or complementing str. lines in concluding bars, *piano*	227–242 MP: 6:34 RG: 6:57 MJP: 6:54 MB: 6:35	(4+4) ((2+2) + 4 =3 by elision)	As in A1	As in A1
2. Conclusion becoming transition; as in A2, *forte*, with solo replacing winds in last four bars, which must be presumed to revert to *piano*	242–260 MP: 7:00 RG: 7:24 MJP: 7:20 MB: 7:01	As in A2	As in A2	As in A2
3. Second theme from B; exactly as in B3, with some piano-wind dialogue in last four bars	261–289 MP: 7:32 RG: 7:58 MJP: 7:53 MB: 7:33	As in B3	As in B3, but in tonic key	As in B3

FIGURE 10.2. *Continued*

FIGURE 10.2. *Continued*

Sections and sub-sections:

Sections and sub-sections: name, character, dynamic(s), and orchestration	Meas. (with timing on four CDs)*	Basic grouping structure (of sub-sections)**	Tonal direction (of sub-sections)	Formal types and functions (of sub-sections)
4. Original second theme, from A, as in B4	290–304 MP: 8:23 RG: 8:51 MJP: 8:44 MB: 8:22	As in B4	As in B4, but in tonic key	As in B4
5. Concluding themelets, as in B5	304–319 MP: 8:46 RG: 9:16 MJP: 9:09 MB: 8:46	As in B5	As in B5, but in tonic key	As in B5
F. Concluding orchestral presentation, interrupted by cadenza	**319–349**			
1. Concluding music from A3b; tutti, generally *forte*, with ending modified to prepare cadenza	319–327 MP: 9:11 RG: 9:42 MJP: 9:35 MB: 9:11	As in A3b	As in A3b, but leading to a cadential six-four chord	As in A3b

			Prolonged final cadence	
cadenza	*MP:* 9:28 *RG:* 10:00 *MJP:* 9:52 *MB:* 9:27			
2. Codetta section, as in A4, closing with added bass-wind dialogue derived from ending of A2, B3, and E2; at first *piano*, str. with some wind counterpoint, then *forte*, tutti	328–349 *MP:* 10:44 *RG:* 11:16 *MJP:* 11:16 *MB:* 10:43	As in A4, with four extra bars- (1+1) + (1+1)- before final (1+1)	As in A4, with added bars resolving to I a motive previously on V, thereby adding stability to final tonic	As in A4, with expansion responding to importance of cadence at end of cadenza

*Four recordings, all in print at the time of writing, were consulted. MP is from Sony Classical SX4K 46443 (1991), Vol. II of the complete concertos, with the English Chamber Orchestra, Murray Perahia, soloist and conductor. RG is on Elektra/Asylum/Nonesuch 79042-2 (1982), with the Orpheus Chamber Orchestra, Richard Goode, soloist and conductor. MJP is on Deutsche Grammophon 439 941-2 (1995), with the Chamber Orchestra of Europe under Claudio Abbado, Maria João Pires, soloist. And MB is on Archiv 463-111-2 (1986), the complete concertos, with the English Baroque Soloists under John Eliot Gardiner, Malcolm Bilson, soloist.

**Groups are designated by the number of measure downbeats they subsume. Thus, "4" stands for a group that traverses four measure downbeats. A "4" group may of course begin before a downbeat (with an anacrusis) and may continue in its fourth bar, after the fourth downbeat.

FIGURE 10.3. *Mm. 1–17, the principal (first) theme in the first orchestral presentation.*

implies a change to (C,**E**,G), fully realized in the accompanying parts. This is the chord on the fourth scale-degree of G major (= IV). The next event of the sentence is a complementary idea, which exactly balances the first. In this instance, one has the melody of measures 5–8, which exactly conforms to that of 1–4, except in reverse, moving from E5 (mm. 5–7) to D5 (m. 8, beat 2), and from (C,**E**,G) to (G,B,**D**). These complementary ideas form a self-contained whole, a phrase, which constitutes the first half of the sentence. It has the function of presenting a locus of thematic activity and is thus aptly named a "presentation" phrase.

The second half (or phrase) of the sentence likewise has two parts, but their functions are not one and the same, as with the two parts of the presentation phrase. The first part serves to continue, develop, and intensify the melodic and harmonic activity exposed in the presentation. Here it consists of two groups of two measures each (9–10 and 11–12), the second being almost a repetition of the first. The melodic gist of each of these two groups is, like that of the two four-bar presentation groups, a step motion, G5 (9, beat 4) to F#5 (10, beat 3), and this implies, in turn, a simple harmonic move, from (**G**,B,D) to (D,F#,A). The second of these chords has D, the fifth scale-degree of G major, as its root and is thus labeled "V." The complementary relationship of the two harmonic moves thus far executed can be seen by ordering the three major chords involved as follows: <C,E,G>, <G,B,D>, <D,F#,A> = <IV, I, V>. As is readily seen, each successive chord in this ordering is built on the last ("top") note of its predecessor.

Collectively, the three chords present all seven tones of the G major scale. The musical syntax makes clear that (G,B,D) is the main (central) chord and that motions to the two others are complementary elaborations of, or deviations from that main chord. As we shall see, the elaboration in the upward (rightward) direction, to (D,F#,A) is privileged, leading to V being called the dominant (= D) and IV the subdominant (or dominant from below = S), I being the tonic (= T). The aspects of continuation and development in measures 9–10 and 11–12 are obvious by virtue of the same kinds of relations being pursued as were first explored in the presentation phrase; that of intensification is a result of the generally higher melodic register, the use of wind–string dialog, the strongly accented chords in measures 10 and 12, and, most of all, of the acceleration that comes about because the same kind of melodic and harmonic move that took four bars in measures 1–4 and 5–8 here takes only two.

The second and last part of the concluding phrase of the sentence is called the cadence, and its function is to bring the theme as a whole to a close. The cadence stretches in this instance over measures 13–16, and consists of a stepwise descending melody (E5 down to G4) over a harmonic progression that uses, in melodically disguised forms, the three basic harmonies discussed above. The (C,E,G) harmony is represented here by a variant (C,E,A), in the first half of measure 15, and the basic cadential progression of harmonies is thus (G,B,D) in measure 14—prefixed by an elaborating chord in m. 13—(C,E,A) and (D,F#,A) in measure 15, and (G,B,D) once again in measure 16. A thick chord with top note G5 overwrites the expected melodic G4 of measure 16. This kind of overwriting of an expected concluding event by the first event of a new group represents a type of rhythmic compression that is often called *elision*. It gives the impression that one bar of music (sometimes more) has been folded back over on to a preceding bar. Here, it is as if measure 16 represented two bars, one concluding the first theme, and the second beginning a new subsection.[21]

Measures 9–16 as a whole, despite executing a continuation of the presentation phrase followed by a cadence, is labeled by Caplin as a *continuation phrase.*

What I have described thus far is perfectly standard, and would tend to substantiate the view that music of the Classical period is rhythmically square in the extreme. And yet the impression arises, and persists as one listens repeatedly to this theme, that some important aspect of its rhythmic vitality has been overlooked in this description. What this might be is perhaps suggested when it is noticed that the accompaniment to the theme, in the strings and the solo part, begins only in measure 2, and seems clearly to group the bars in twos beginning at that point and, what amounts to the same thing, to place accents at the onsets of even numbered bars. The melody, by contrast, groups the bars in two beginning in measure 1, and thus to accent, if in a less overt way, the downbeats of odd-numbered bars. The grouping of bars in the accompaniment is largely a function of where the harmonies change (at mm. 4, 9, 11, etc.) and that in the melody is largely a function of rhythmic detail and contour in the melody itself, which clearly groups measure 2 with measure 1, measure 4 with measure 3, measure 6 with measure 5, and so on. The grouping conflict is particularly subtle in the continuation segment (mm. 9–12). Melodic activity, as just noted, groups 10 with 9 and 12 with 11. But if one reads the harmony as shifting with each bar, as follows: I (G,B,D), V7 (D,F♯,A,C), I, V, there would seem to be nothing to argue for grouping measure 11, contrarily, with measure 10, thus preserving the conflict. A closer look reveals, however, that measure 11, rather strangely, does not repeat measure 9, because it is lacking the G root of the I harmony on its first beat. The result is that measure 11 sounds much weaker than measure 9, and can even be heard as continuing the D root (or the V harmony) initiated in measure 10, and thus as in fact grouped with measure 10. The intended ambiguity (is the harmony of m. 11 a I or a V and does this bar group with the preceding or the following bar?) is intensified when the theme is repeated as E1, in the solo sonata recapitulation. The corresponding measures, 235–238, may be seen in figure 10.4. The piano part in these measures are so fashioned that the impression in measure 237 is of a continuation of the V7 chord from the preceding bar. In other words, measure 237, rather than sounding as a repetition of measure 235, and thus grouping exclusively with measure 238, groups as well with measure 236, to which it acts as a harmonic continuation.

21. For a formal treatment of elision and related phenomena, see Lerdahl and Jackendoff (1983:55–62).

FIGURE 10.4. *Intensified ambiguity of measure grouping in mm. 235–238.*

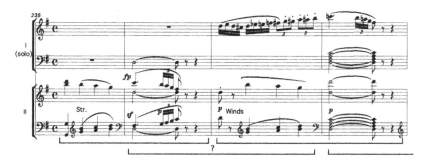

Careful consideration of this opening theme has shown us an instance of polymeter in Classical music, where we perhaps least thought to find one. If the whole note length of the notated bar is the beat, the two meters in play are both 2/1, but one begins on odd-measured downbeats, the other on even-measured downbeats. Music theorists describe this kind of subsurface polymeter as a hypermetric conflict.[22] Such conflicts are widespread in Mozart's music (the reader may recall the opening of his Symphony No. 40, in G minor) and they contribute to the music's fabled grace, to a lightness that avoids any hint of superficiality.

Nonthematic Rhythmic Continuity

A fundamental rhythmic distinction obtains, in this music, between thematic and nonthematic sections. Themes are composed of phrases, and although many phrases lack cadences (e.g., presentation phrases), a group of measures is conceivable as a phrase primarily because it sounds self-contained. To put it another way, a phrase starts, goes along and, at some point comes to a stop, even if that stop does not have the conclusiveness of a cadence. So, in figure 10.3, the harmonic-rhythmic circumstances preceding measure 8 do not permit speaking of a cadence in that bar, but there is surely some effect of closure there, allowing one to say of mm. 1–8 that they contain a presentation phrase. The music presented in figure 10.5, however, is differently organized in rhythmic terms.

Here we have most of section A2 (mm. 28–34 are omitted), in which the arrival point of the first theme (the tonic harmony) is first confirmed and this concluding activity then merges into a transition to A3, the second theme.

22. Hypermeter is a term used in music theory for subsurface meter in which the beats are downbeats of successive notated bars, grouped into hyperbars (normally of uniform length, for example, two, three, or four notated bars long).

FIGURE 10.5. *Wave-like segments in section A2. mm. 16–27.*

The music of A2, typical of nonthematic sections, is more processive than that of A1. It has no internal stopping points and sounds, therefore, as if bounding ahead to some distant point of stability, located, as it turns out, at measure 35, the start of A3. Another way of saying this is that the segments of A2 are not phrases, for the most part. Measures 16–18 and 19–21, which are almost identical, are cases in point. They have beginnings, but no points of termination. Of course the beginnings at measures 19 and 22 might be heard as the end-points of these segments, making each of them into a four-bar phrase the cadence of which has been elided, but this roundabout explanation serves to obscure a distinction that is better brought out in the open: we should rather speak here of concatenated segments that flow into one another, and think of them as successive waves rather than as separate phrases. (Figure 10.2 makes repeated use of the term "waves," to capture this distinction.) Measures 22–25, by contrast, are a phrase. They point clearly toward a half-cadence (on the chord [D, F♯, A]) at the downbeat of measure 25, at which point forward motion is preserved by the intrusion of a new segment, hence, by elision. This new segment, which does not deviate harmonically from its starting point for ten bars (25–34), serves to prepare for the entrance of a second theme. In effect, then, rhythmic flow is a very important variable in this music, working as it does to shape the character and, thereby, define the formal function of a subsection.

Expansion and Contraction

The rhythmic phenomena discussed thus far, of conflicting pulsation/accentuation and different types of flow, are apparent at the musical surface, provided the listener is sensitive to them. Not so the phenomena to be discussed now, in reference to figures 10.6.a, 10.6.b, and 10.7. These point to an extreme richness and flexibility of rhythm, involving effects of expansion/retardation and contraction/acceleration that are the norm in well-made tonal music, although no less important for being ubiquitous.

In figures 10.6.a and 10.6.b, a simple underlying continuity (10.6.a) is subject to a process of elaboration that adds extra notes in such a way as to expand the underlying pattern to exactly twice its original length (10.6.b).

Figure 10.6.a presents, in bare outline, a pair of phrases in a question-answer (usually called an antecedent-consequent) relationship. The break between the two phrases is shown by the vertical double stroke at the end of bar 4. The two phrases begin exactly the same way but whereas the first ends incompletely on scale-degree 2 (the key here is D major, the subordinate key of the B section, and thus of B3, B4, and B5) in the melody over scale-degree 5 in the bass, implying the cadence chord (A,C♯,E), the second ends conclusively on the tonic in both melody and bass, implying the harmony (D,F♯,A). Such a pairing of phrases is called a *period.*

Sentence and period are the two most important thematic archetypes of music in the Classical style. In subsection B3, where the soloist introduces a new second or subordinate theme, one never given out by the orchestra in A, these two archetypes are deployed hierarchically in a most interesting way. The conceptual foundation of this theme is the simple period just discussed, but its actual surface is outlined in figure 10.6.b. The example, which represents measures 110–133 in a reduced sketch, should be compared with the score or used as a guide in listening to the complete passage.

The relation of 10.6.a to 10.6.b should be readily apparent if only the larger note-heads in 10.6.b are attended to, as these correspond exactly to the notes in 10.6.a. The smaller note-heads represent events that elaborate and expand the underlying content of the music. In the transformed (elaborated) version, the fourth event of 10.6.a—A5 over C♯4—appears a beat early in 10.6.b, but carries through for two bars until it reappears as C♯5 over A3 in bar 4. The fifth event of 10.6.a appears on the downbeat of measure 114 in 10.6.b, but is then repeated on the downbeats of measures 115 and 116, whereupon the phrase closes as in 10.6.a. In effect, a four-bar phrase has been expanded to eight bars. But something else is afoot: the bracket over the top staff in measures 110–111 covers a succession of pitch classes that reappears in the bass in measures 112–113, two octaves lower, similarly bracketed. Thus, measures 112–113 can be heard as a disguised repetition, with change of register and revised counterpoint, of measures 110–111. But measure 115 is a repetition of measure 114 and measures 116–117 are clearly a cadential segment. In effect, then, measures 110–117 are not only a four-bar antecedent (in expanded form) but also an eight-bar sentence. The two basic archetypes of the style are thus brought into simultaneous play, on two different levels.

The theme concludes by expanding the consequent phrase. This expansion begins in parallel fashion: measures 118–123 correspond exactly to measures 100–115. Measures 124–125 then duplicate measures 122–123, shifting material from the solo to the winds so it remains fresh. At this point we expect a full cadence corresponding to measures 7–8 of figure 10.6a, but such a one is denied. A sudden shift to minor tonality at measure 126 indicates the abandonment of the cadence and the fusing of a new phrase to the incomplete consequent. This

FIGURE 10.6.a. *A simple period.*

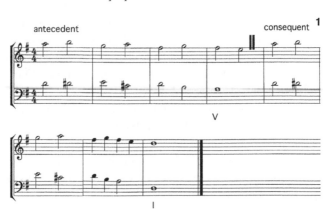

phrase is itself sentencelike: eight bars long, it is based in large part on an accelerating series of transpositions of a two-chord pattern, first heard in measures 126–127. Such a series is called a sequence. In the last two bars of this phrase, 132–133, the sequence gives way to a progression that forms another half-cadence. The music in this part of the movement, as noted earlier, is engaged in a series of tactics, of which this is the first, for delaying a really strong (full) cadence in the dominant key. In this movement, that cadence arrives only at measure 171, although it is preceded by weaker (elided) full cadences at measures 146, 153, and 160.

If the last two examples show a very particular rhythmic relationship (of expansion) between an underlying pattern and the musical surface, the next one displays relationships of both expansion and contraction that are so characteristic of European tonality as to be virtually endemic to it. Figure 10.7 shows

FIGURE 10.6.b. *Sketch of the soloist's new subordinate theme,*
mm. 110–133.

FIGURE 10.7. *Mm. 139–146, the opening of subsection B4.*

the opening sentence of B4, the solo statement of the subordinate (second) theme first presented as A3.

This illustration contains all the notes of the passage (with the orchestra part reduced for piano, as always), but adds some analytical symbols. The point of the analysis is to show that, while the surface rhythm presents steady eighth-note motion marked by a half-note pulse more or less throughout, and is thus scarcely of aesthetic interest, underlying, slower-moving melodies exhibit a great variety and plasticity of rhythm.

An underlying melody, in tonal music, is usually some kind of line pro-ceeding by step motion. So, for example, the bass line proceeds entirely in de-scending step motion beginning in measure 139 (some of the descending steps are transformed into rising sevenths, for example, the opening <D3, C♯4> may be understood as a transformation of <D3, C♯3>). At the same time, though, this stepwise descent is in the service of a much slower underlying descent from D3 in m. 139 to C♯4 in measure 143. Over this large-scale motion, the upper line (the tune) executes a parallel descent, from F♯5 in measure 139 to E5 in measure 143. Large-beamed note-heads point out these motions. From this point, the music first returns to its tonal starting point of a top-voice F♯ over a bass D, in measure 145, first beat. But the F♯ is an octave lower than at the start, which gives the upper voice a chance to move down from E5 in measure 143 to F♯4 in measure 145, and to fill in this descending seventh with a scale (indicated with longer-stemmed notes). This scale is of course a close relative of the scale with which the bass connected its opening D3 to C♯4 (m. 143), but, whereas the scale in the bass occupied four bars, the subsequent one in the upper voice occupies only two. The effect is one of a reversal of linear motion—back to the opening interval of F♯ over D—occurring twice as fast. This acceleration pushes the music toward the sentential cadence, in measures 145–146. This involves a structurally important descent in the upper voice, from F♯4 to D4, through E4, all within two bars, and thus representing a further speeding up of underlying melody. All in all, a surface that, at first blush, may appear rhythmically unchanging, reveals a strongly purposeful deployment of accelerating patterns, used to clarify certain points as goals.

It is impossible to generalize about how the endless rhythmic subtlety of music in the Classical style may relate to its social functions. Complexities of the kinds revealed in figures 10.5 and 10.7, which may be termed "systemic" because they are omnipresent in the style, are connected with the teleological or end-directed nature of this music. Play with archetypes, and specifically with archetypal lengths, as in figures 10.6.a and 10.6.b, seems to function mainly as a challenge to our cognitive capacities, and thus as a way of giving experienced listeners interesting things to do with patterns they know very well. This is a basis whereon important works in the Classical style reward almost endless rehearing, in an effort to absorb patterns made elusive through rhythmic transformation. Finally, conflict of subsurface pulsation revealed in the discussion of figure 10.4 is more of a personal trait than a style feature. In other words, it is less a matter of musical style than one of personal style, of Mozart's style, and it charms us with its beautiful economy, rather in the way that we are gripped by the way some people gesture or move.

Any of these ways in which our imaginations are engaged by the rhythmic subtleties of Classical music may be ideologically interpreted, and probably must be if the social importance of this music is to be understood. But my aims, which are more modest, will have been served if the notion that European tonal music lacks rhythmic interest has been, in some measure, dispelled.

Harmonic Design: Visionary Transformations of Vernacular and Conventional Sources

In this final analytical foray I sketch out the tonal form of the concerto movement, with particular emphasis on its succinct, but closely packed fantasy section (**D**). I will begin with a digression, treating first a very familiar folk song, and then a short model composition, which I have contrived as a sort of link between the song and the concerto movement. The three pieces of music are connected by sharing a particular form, one with a middle section that creates a specific type of tonal tension with the surrounding principal sections. The folk song I picked is one that Mozart knew well. As for the model composition, I have used it in preference to an authentic Classical composition for its heuristic value in relating very explicitly both to the folk song and the concerto, which it does without introducing too many extraneous features.

The tune written out in figure 10.8.a is probably familiar to every reader. Mozart, too, was familiar with "Twinkle, twinkle, little star," except that he knew it as "Ah! vous dirai-je maman," a popular French children's song on which he based a set of keyboard variations. It is hard to think of a tune more archetypal with respect to European tonality. Its form is typical of European folk songs: an ABA, or ternary design. The first phrase (mm. 1–4) establishes the tonality (G major) with its opening leap of a fifth and subsequent stepwise descent back to the tonic. Measures 5–8 are a contrasting middle that proceeds (twice) stepwise from the fifth scale-degree to the second, ending on a half-cadence; and measures 9–12, a closing phrase that reprises the opening one, bring the tune as a whole to a balanced, satisfying close.

When Mozart used this tune for his variations, he adapted it to a different formal scheme, one conforming to the Classical ideal of binary symmetry. He did this by the simple expedient of repeating the first phrase, as in figure 10.8.b. The new measures 5–8 create literal two-part symmetry with measures 1–4, and measures 1–8 now balance measures 9–16 in length.[23] This AABA design is also encountered frequently in European (and American) songs, often in slightly more complex variants. For example, instead of beginning with a repeated phrase, such tunes sometimes open with a period of the type discussed earlier, or with a pairing of phrases in which the second modulates to a secondary key. The extent and literalness of repetition in the closing phrase is another variable. But the third phrase, the contrasting or digressing move to a half-cadence, is a virtual constant within a large body of vernacular song which, by virtue of its relation to surrounding phrases, is the form's single most defining global feature.[24]

---

23. Of course, the original symmetry of the two A sections around the B sections now disappears, but this is, in a sense, more of a visual or spatial type of symmetry, in that it requires a grasp of the whole for its appreciation. The new binary symmetries can be appreciated more locally, on the fly, as equivalent stretches of time (as hypermeter—see footnote 22).

24. Theorists who emphasize the contrasting qualities of this third phrase call this form "small ternary," notwithstanding its binary symmetry, whereas others who focus on the balance between pairs of phrases are more inclined to the name "rounded binary."

FIGURE 10.8.a. *"Twinkle, twinkle, little star" (= "Ah! vous dirai-je maman").*

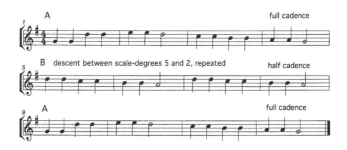

The fundamental structure of this third phrase, a descent from scale-degree 5 to scale-degree 2 (occurring twice at the surface in "Twinkle . . . "), is also important as the model for the middle section in sonata form, the most important conventional form in European art music. This section, known as the *development,* serves to extend the cadential harmony of the first section, the *exposition.* It does this in a very simple way. This harmonic end-point is the chord on the fifth scale-degree—(D, F♯, A) in G major—made into a temporary tonic. Because the skeletal melody of the third phrase is a stepwise descent from the fifth scale-degree (D) to the second (A), it is a motion from the root of this chord to its fifth. As such, it carries the chord's imprint throughout its course, and serves to build up a desire for, or expectation of, the return of tonic harmony—(G,B,D) in G major—at the start of the reprise, the final phrase in simple tunes like "Twinkle . . . "

How the folk song form just discussed relates to sonata form may be seen by considering figure 10.9 in relation to figure 10.8.b.

FIGURE 10.8.b. *Mozart's adaptation of "Ah! vous dirai-je maman."*

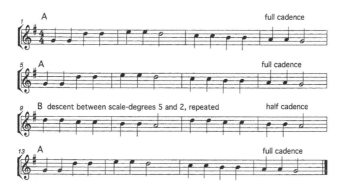

Figure 10.9 presents a minimal movement in sonata form, created for this occasion for the reason set out above (CD track 18). The texture is two-part, consisting throughout of an upper voice and a bass. Such a framework might be regarded as a kind of draft for a movement in early Classical style that, with thickening inner voices, doublings, and more rhythmic differentiation, could be turned into a final version.[25]

The first phrase of figure 10.9 (mm. 1–4) is a harmonization of the corresponding phrase of figure 10.8.b (or 10.8.a). It ends in a full cadence—on a G in both voices, implying the chord (G, B, D), with the bass G preceded by a leap from D (m. 4, b. 2). In the standard terminology of sonata form, this is a principal theme. The second phrase (mm. 5–9) begins like its counterpart in figure 10.8.b, except that the first note is an octave higher. (Please follow the larger asterisked notes in figure 10.9, beginning in m. 5.) At measures 7–8, the corresponding bars of figure 10.8.b are transposed up a fourth to D major, signaled by the presence of C♯ in measures 7 and 9. The instability introduced in measures 7–9 by C♯, and secondarily by ornamental pitches foreign to both G major and the local key of D major, is further promoted by the five-measure length of this phrase, which undermines any easy internal (binary) symmetry of length. The phrase ends inconclusively on the dominant chord of the new key (A, C♯, E), with a melodic cadence tone absent from the folk-song model, the highly unstable seventh scale-degree (C♯) of D major. Measures 5–9 constitute a minimal transition, leading to a subordinate theme (mm. 10–20). Beginning as an approximate melodic mirror (inversion) of the principal theme—<A5, D5, E5, F♯5> inverts <D4, A5, (B5, A5), G5, F♯5>—this theme is more loosely spun out, largely because it approaches a possible full cadence in D major in measures 16 (even so, it would be seven bars long), evading this cadence by substituting F♯ for D in the bass on the downbeat of bar 16, and finding its way back to the desired cadence in measure 20. Note that the large note-heads in the melody of measures 12–16 are an expansion of the melody of measures 3–4 (second half of the first Twinkle phrase) transposed to D major, whereas the melody of measures 16–20 restates the whole first Twinkle phrase (still in D) in varied form.

The whole exposition section of this little piece (mm. 1–20) is best understood as being in two (unequal) halves, measures 1–9 and measures 10–20. Each half contains two melodic statements of the first Twinkle phrase in some form (mm. 1–4, 5–9; 10–16, 16–20). The two halves may be heard as formal counterparts, in expanded form, to the first two phrases of figure 10.8.b.

The development section of this movement is a mere nine bars long, but its relationship to the archetypal descent of phrase 3 in figure 10.8.b (phrase 2

---

25. Mozart's frequent practice, for complex textures, was to first write out the two principal voices of large stretches of music, before returning at a later stage to add inner voices.

FIGURE 10.9. *A short, model composition based on "Twinkle . . . ," in sonata form (CD track 18).*

in figure 10.8.a) is clear. Instead of descending uninterruptedly, by step from D5 to A4, the melody of this section breaks this motion into two stages, each traversing the interval of a third. These thirds are shown with large note heads in the upper voice. The first <D, C, B> occupies measures 21–24, the second <C, B, A>, measures 25–28. Measure 29 provides an extra buffer between this section and the next, helping to delineate them. Each of the two melodic thirds is accompanied by the bass in such a way as to suggest its own key, the first implying A minor, the second the tonic key (G major), and both ending in half cadences in their respective keys. But despite this added richness of tonal content, the underlying sense of the upper voice, as a descent from D5 to A4, is preserved.

A recapitulation begins in measure 30. Like the exposition this contains three phrases. The first (30–33) simply restates the principal theme. The second (34–38) recomposes the transition so that it ends in relation to the tonic key where the original transition (5–9) ended with respect to the dominant key, that is, on F♯ over D instead of C♯ over A. The music then concludes by transposing the subordinate theme to the tonic key, introducing changes of octave to promote a better sense of continuity with what precedes and convincing closure for the movement as a whole.

All of this is meant to pave the way for detailed discussion of some of the melodic and harmonic complexities of the concerto movement. If I had the space, I could show how the whole of the movement's B and E sections, its sonata exposition and recapitulation, may be heard as extended elaborations of the corresponding sections in figure 10.9, but I will concentrate on the more limited task of showing how the development section of figure 10.9 (mm. 21–29) serves as a model for the remarkable music in figure 10.1, the fantasy for solo with orchestral accompaniment (section D), which I have already discussed from a dramatic standpoint. This is among Mozart's most visionary passages from the point of view of harmonic technique, prefiguring as it does many harmonic innovations of the nineteenth century. I will show that underlying the sophisticated emotional interplay of figure 10.1, symbolized by changing tonalities and textures, can be found a simple melodic line, descending in step-motion, that has the same tonal function as the contrasting phrase of "Ah! vous dirai-je maman."

Before determining if this is indeed the case, a short harmony lesson is in order. In my discussion of the sentence I had occasion to propose an ordering of the notes of a major or a minor scale that forms a succession of chords: <<C,E,G>,<G,B,D>, <D,F♯,A>> in G major; <<C,E♭,G>, <G,B♭,D>, <D,F♯,A>> in G minor (using the raised seventh scale-degree, F♯). Just as there is an underlying progression of melody—generally of stepwise descent connecting two tones of the same triad—that governs the upper voice of passages in a tonal movement, there is an underlying progression of triad roots that governs the bass. Let us call the three chords in our abstract ordering by their standard names: subdominant, tonic, and dominant. So, in G major, (C,E,G) is the subdominant harmony, (G,B,D) the tonic, and (D,F♯,A) the dominant harmony, or S, T, and D, for short.[26] The underlying root-series that govern bass lines of tonal passages are segments from a cyclic (periodically repeating) series of the form <T,S,D . . . >. In other words, progressions of harmonies (and, thus, guiding series of roots in the bass line) are segments from this series, such as <T,S,D,T>, <S,D,T,S,D>, <D,T,S,D,T>, and so on. Figure 10.10 makes this clear using standard notation.

System 1 shows the cyclic series <T,S,D . . . > expanded to ten terms. Three (ordered) segments are bracketed and labeled x, y, z. These segments are presented on system 2. On system 3, the same segments are modified, dissonant tones being added to selected S and D chords.[27] Specifically, pitch-classes a sixth or seventh above the S-chord roots are added, along with some a seventh above the D-chord roots. These additions are reflected in the addition of superscripts to the corresponding S and D labels. The purpose of the added tones is to destabilize S and D chords relative to the T (and some D) chords, which are not tampered with. On the last system, the same harmonic progressions are arranged to produce upper voices that move by step and bass motions that express, in their contours, the hierarchical primacy of the T–D connection (and subordinate status of S events). Specifically, the bass notes of S events are always left by step (a sign of dependency on the D that follows), whereas those of T and D event are normally left by leap.

This excursus on harmony prepares the reader to read figure 10.11, an analysis of figure 10.1, the D section of the concerto movement. Here we have three systems, labeled Rem. (for remote), Med. (for medial), and Sur. (for surface). System Rem. presents an underlying level of structure that is archetypal for sections of this kind, while system Med. presents a modification of the content of Rem. that underlies the content of this fantasy section in particular. Finally, system Sur. presents all the harmonies of the actual music in a rhythmic simplification that is also a metric reduction: one ♩ on this system represents one 𝅝 (one bar) in the score. All events on Med. reappear as surface-level harmonies on Sur., where they are elaborated with other events. Most events on Rem. reappear on Med., but two are replaced with more distinctive events and one new event is added on the latter. The systems are aligned so that

26. This terminology goes back to the eighteenth-century theorist and composer Jean-Philippe Rameau. The S, D, T labeling became standard by way of the writings of the late-nineteenth-century theorist and historian, Hugo Riemann.

27. Dissonant because they are step-related to a triad tone, to the root in the case of a seventh, to the fifth in the case of a sixth.

FIGURE 10.10. *The derivation of harmonic progressions from the*
<T,S,D . . . > cycle.

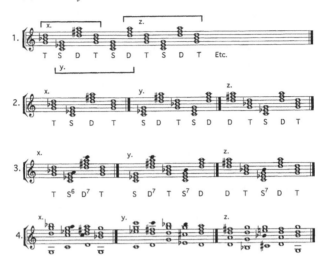

representations of the same event at different levels appear directly over one
another.

Level Rem. begins with a D major chord that represents the goal of the
exposition (section B in figure 10.2), the tonic chord of the key of D major in
its most stable form (with outer-voice Ds). This chord is also the goal of orchestral section C. The next ten events on this level are a standard way of harmonizing the "Twinkle" stepwise descent. Based on pattern y on system 4 of
figure 10.10, the structure of these events is exactly that of the mini-develop-
ment in figure 10.9. Here, too, the descent is broken up into two thirds: <D5,
C5, B> followed by <C5, B♭4, A4>. Thus, the scale-degree series <5,4,3,2> in G
is broken up into two shorter series: <4,3,2> in A minor followed by <4,3,2> in
G minor. The use of B♭ (from G minor) rather than B (G major) is a departure from figure 10.9's model structure, brought about the desire for the second
half of the descent to more exactly reproduce the first half, which is "naturally"
minor. In other words, the ten central events on Rem. form a *sequence*, in
which a five-chord model (pattern y) is stated and then transposed. Sequences
are generally understood to form the backbone of sonata developments, functioning rather like vertebrae, but here (and in many other cases) the whole section is composed, at an archetypal level, of a model and its single repetition in
another key. Each of the two chord strings in this sequence is an <S,D,T,S,D>
string, ending in a half cadence in its respective key. The special symbol $S^{P\rightarrow}$
that replaces the second S in each five-chord string (the P stands for "prepara-

FIGURE 10.11. *Hierarchical analysis of the D (fantasy) section.*

371

tion") denotes a chromaticized form of the S6 chord (e.g., with D# replacing D in the first chord) normally found in half cadences in development sections.

Level Med. introduces three changes, affecting four events. The first change is a transformation of the first S chord, D minor at measure 184, to a B♭ major chord. Thus transformed, this event serves not only as an S in A minor, but as a new tonic (of B♭ major) in its own right, thus continuing the T function of the preceding D major chord while providing a sharper contrast than D minor would have, had it been given tonic status at the musical surface. The second transformation is more far reaching. The A minor T chord at measure 192 is reinterpreted as an S in E minor, and leads to a $S^{P→}$ chord in that key, which duly progresses to a dominant (D). A fundamental characteristic of development sections thus emerges: their quality of tonal fluctuation and, at many points, of degrees of tonal indeterminability. These sections present far-ranging successions of keys, often in rapid succession, but the junctures between these keys, unlike those of the harmonies that articulate them, are not points in time, but durationally imprecise regions that may be heard to begin and end at quite different times of the musical surface by different listeners.

One reason for introducing E minor at level Med. is to solve a compositional problem at level Rem., the awkwardness of the juncture between the first and second <S,D,T,S,D> strings of its basic sequence. The D at the end of the first string connects somewhat roughly to the S at the start of the second. This shift, from an E major to a C minor (labeled an "M" shift in the example[28]) is papered over on Med., where a transposition of the first string's last two chords to E minor brings that string to a close on a B major chord. An M-shift now connects this dominant chord to a D-function chord (G major) in C minor, at measure 209, this being the third new chord on Med. This leads in turn to the T-function C minor chord at measure 211, which is promptly reinterpreted as an S-chord in G minor, leading to the second string of the large-scale sequence, as at Rem. Med., then, retains the use of M-shift from Rem., but uses it to link chords of identical function in different keys, thus connecting the strings more securely. It also enhances the parallelism between strings by beginning both with T = S reinterpretations, and it introduces a cadence in a new key (E minor). At the same time, the upper voice at Med. is largely the same as that at Rem. and preserves its underlying structural descent.

This brings us to Sur., a stage of further elaboration that is truly visionary in its transformational qualities. If the reader plays through the harmonies on this level, singing the top voice, he or she will notice that, whereas the overall melodic profile remains the same, the harmonic and tonal flow has become

---

28. Using the label "M" to name the shift from a major triad to another (major or minor) triad with a root a major third below is based on Kopp (2002:166–169).

extraordinarily rich. In particular, a profusion of keys has emerged at the surface, five new ones in addition to the six already there (including destination and goal keys) at Med. At the same time, the high adventure of the surface flow of chords is, if anything, more coherent than that at underlying levels. How is this possible? Because the harmonic flow is entirely directed by the <T,S,D . . . > cyclic paradigm, as can be seen by reading the relevant symbols in the middle of Sur. beginning at measures 184ff and continuing at measure 196, under the system. The technique Mozart developed to combine extreme harmonic coherence with radical tonal instability is one of functional compression: repeatedly, particular events are called upon to occupy two or even three successive slots in the cyclic pattern. So, for example, the B minor chord at measure 190 is first a D (in B-) in relation to the preceding $S^{P\rightarrow}$ (functioning in this way because its bass note F♯ is the root of the dominant harmony (F♯, A♯, C♯) in the key), and must then be quickly reimagined as a T (still in B-) and, finally, reconceptualized as an S (in A minor) in relation to the succeeding D (m. 191). Such reinterpretation is implied many times in the section as a whole, and makes for an extraordinary density of tonal content despite the limited number of harmonic events.

Mozart's Legacy and the Naturalization of Tonality

Many contemporary students of culture have noted how traditions tend to naturalize their conventional rules, regarding them as if they were natural laws. This has certainly been the case with the basic principles of tonality. The scales, the melodic formulae, the metric conventions, and the cadential harmonic progressions of tonal music have all seemed to the European mind to arise out of the very nature of tone itself.[29] We now believe, for the most part, that tones as such have no will, and impose nothing upon us. What instead determines the music we write and play are the interests of our culture as these come up against the evolving limits of human perceptual and cognitive capacity. Tonal music

29. Heinrich Schenker, the most important music theorist of the twentieth century, titled a series of ten analytical pamphlets he published in 1921–1924 *Der Tonwille* [The Will of Tones], subtitling them as "for the purpose of witnessing the immutable laws of music, thereby conveyed to a new generation." His idealistic conception seems rather narrow today, but the view that there are elements of European tonality to which humans are cognitively predisposed (for example, octave equivalence and the consonance of the perfect fifth) is not necessarily ethnocentric, or wrong. Any successful musical tradition undoubtedly respects (and makes imaginative use of) a particular set of cognitive requirements or constraints.

has enjoyed enormous success because it satisfied the cultural need for a music that listeners could remember in detail despite its complexity, that gifted musicians could improvise, that would privilege the individual voice (melody) but adequately symbolize collective contexts (polyphony), that would project clear goals and reach them, and, above all, that might stand totally on its own as a medium of expression.[30]

Because the resources of tonal music were developed to meet the needs of European culture in the domain of musical expression, one is scarcely surprised, given the culture's dynamic and progressive character, to find that its music has undergone successive waves of style change. Yet the impression persists that, for over two hundred years, something real and essential persisted, underlying the shifting appearances of European music itself. Hypostasized in this way is something known as "common-practice tonality," or, in music theoretical circles, as "the tonal system," the positing of which can lead to the belief that tonal composers shared a set of rules—conscious or not—for generating coherent pieces. This is mistaken. Instead, I think, a few composers working at the earlier stages of one of modern Europe's most successful cultural ventures (fully comparable to its development of science) invented techniques for generating local continuity—for example, filling in the spaces between the chords on Med., in figure 10.11, to produce the chords at Sur.— that were then explored productively for more than 150 years.[31] J. S. Bach, Mozart, and Haydn were preeminent in this achievement. In particular, the modes of harmonic continuity first proposed in the D section of this concerto and in comparable works by Mozart continued to occupy the best minds of music through several generations. They operate in music by composers as historically separate as Beethoven, Schubert, Chopin, Wagner, Debussy, Schoenberg, Stravinsky, and Ellington, who apply them subject to very different aesthetic considerations. To have been among the first to excavate channels of connection and continuity (or labyrinths of delay) that provided enduring fascination and intrigue for the returning ears of countless creative musicians over nearly two centuries is, perhaps, the soundest definition of musical genius, in the European context at least. In this sense, Mozart was among the supreme geniuses of European music.

---

30. Was there actually a cultural need for music to stand on its own, or was this a by-product of serving other needs? One might argue that an ostensibly nonrepresentational music, and one unconnected to explicit ritual or ceremony served the claims (pretensions?) of the European Enlightenment to be speaking universally, for all of humanity.

31. The distinction I am making is between the work of music as a whole, which cannot be made according to rule, and the specific procedures involved in generating continuity, for which rules (generalizations) can be formulated. Works of music are as much about discontinuity (necessarily rule-free) as continuity (possibly rule-bound).

References

Allanbrook, Wye Jamison. 1996. "Comic Issues in Mozart's Piano Concertos," in *Mozart's Piano Concertos: Text Context, Interpretation,* ed. Neal Zaslaw. Ann Arbor: University of Michigan Press, 75–105.

Baker, Nancy Kovaleff. 1983. *Introductory Essay on Composition: The Mechanical Rules of Melody, Sections 3 and 4.* New Haven: Yale University Press.

Benjamin, William. 2001. "When Are Musical Structures of Aesthetic Relevance?" *Tidschrift voor Musiktheorie,* 8.2 (2003):95–101.

Boretz, Benjamin. 1971. "In Quest of Rhythmic Genius," *Perspectives of New Music* 9.2 and 10.1: 149–155.

Caplin, William E. 1998. *Classical Form: A Theory of Formal Functions for the Instrumental Music of Haydn Mozart and Beethoven.* New York: Oxford University Press.

Cooper, Grosvenor, and Leonard Meyer. 1960. *The Rhythmic Structure of Music.* Chicago: University of Chicago Press.

Derr, Elwood, 1996. "*Basso Continuo* in Mozart's Piano Concertos: Dimensions of Compositional Completion and Performance Practice," in *Mozart's Piano Concertos: Text Context, Interpretation,* ed. Neal Zaslaw. Ann Arbor: University of Michigan Press, 393–410.

Forman, Dennis. 1971. *Mozart's Concerto Form: The First Movements of the Piano Concertos.* London: Hart-Davis.

Irving, John. 2003. *Mozart's Piano Concertos.* Aldershot, UK, and Burlington, Vt.: Ashgate.

Keefe, Simon P. 2001. *Mozart's Piano Concertos: Dramatic Dialogue in the Age of Enlightenment.* Woodbridge, UK: The Boydell Press.

Kerman, Joseph. 1994. "Mozart's Piano Concertos and their Audience," in *On Mozart,* ed. James M. Morris. Washington: Woodrow Wilson Center Press, and Cambridge: Cambridge University Press.

Koch, Heinrich Cristoph. 1793, *Versuch einer Anleitung zur Composition,* vol. 3. Rudolstadt, 1793.

Kopp, David. 2002. *Chromatic Transformations in Nineteenth-Century Music.* Cambridge: Cambridge University Press, 2002.

Kramer, Lawrence. 1995. *Classical Music and Postmodern Knowledge.* Berkeley: University of California Press.

———. 2002. *Musical Meaning: Toward a Critical History.* Berkeley: University of California Press.

Kuster, Konrad. 1991. *Formale Apekte des ersten Allegros in Mozarts Konzerten.* Kassel: Bärenreiter.

Leeson, Daniel, and Robert Levin. 1978. "On the Authenticity of K. Anh. C 14.01 (297b), a Symphonia Concertante for Four Winds and Orchestra," in *Mozart-Jahrbuch.* Austria, 70–96.

Lehrdal, Fred, and Ray Lackendoff. 1983. *A Generative Theory of Tonal Music.* Cambridge Mass.: MIT Press.

Levin, Robert. 1989. "Instrumental Ornamentation, Instrumentation, and Cadenzas," in *Performance Practice: Music after 1600,* ed. Howard Mayer Brown and Stanley Sadie. Basingstoke, UK: Macmillan, 267–291.

McClary, Susan. 1986. "A Musical Dialectic from the Enlightenment: Mozart's Piano Concerto in G Major, K.453, Movement 2," *Cultural Critique* 4:129–170.

Rosen, Charles. 1980. *Sonata Forms.* New York: Norton.

Schachter, Carl. 1996. "Idiosyncratic Features of Three Mozart Slow Movements: The Piano Concertos K. 449, K. 453, and K. 467," in *Mozart's Piano Concertos: Text Context, Interpretation,* ed. Neal Zaslaw. Ann Arbor: University of Michigan Press, 321–326.

Tovey, Donald F. 1936. "The Classical Concerto," in *Essays in Musical Analysis, Vol. 3: Concertos.* Oxford: Oxford University Press.

Webster, James. 1996. "Are Mozart's Concerto's 'Dramatic'? Concerto Ritornellos versus Aria Introductions in the 1780's," in *Mozart's Piano Concertos: Text Context, Interpretation,* ed. Neal Zaslaw. Ann Arbor: University of Michigan Press, 107–137.

CHAPTER II

Autonomy and Dialog in Elliott Carter's
Enchanted Preludes

JOHN ROEDER

Social and Artistic Context

Chamber music (written out exactly for a few instruments, one on a part) has long occupied a special position in Western culture. From its origins in the sixteenth century (Bashford 2001) the genre has emphasized both the distinctive identities of the individual players and their changeable roles—playing solo or together, alternating ideas, accompanying, and imitating each other. Yet it also spotlights the identity of the composer more than improvisational genres do; its performers function less as co-creators than as actors of scripted, interacting roles in the composer's imagined play of pitch and rhythm.

Such art invites interpretation through analogy with everyday experience. Indeed, early chamber music mirrored the culture that made it. Much of it was intended for amateurs, members of society, who experienced the music by performing it. The importance it placed on every player reflected one of the distinguishing themes of Western culture, individualism, with which it emerged (Barzun 2000). Its focus on individuals' relationships matched that of home, coffeehouse, and salon in a regimenting, industrializing world.[1] The critic Theo-

Licensing and permissions for this chapter were underwritten by a Publication Subvention Grant from the Society for Music Theory.

1. Habermas (1962) shows that in the 1700s new types of public venues developed that fostered social intercourse freed from distinctions of social status. Chamber music, which bloomed during that century, manifests a similarly egalitarian association of voices.

*Elliott Carter in his studio. Photo © Meredith
Heuer 2000, used with permission.*

dor Adorno (1962:87, 92) even attributed "social virtue" to the genre, referring
to the "ephemeral concordance of participants" it creates that "anticipates a
state of things in which competition would be cured of aggression and evil."
Accordingly, verbal accounts of chamber music often describe it in terms of
social intercourse.

As explanations, however, such metaphors are compelling only as far as they
can be imputed to specific, audible musical patterns.[2] For chamber music into
the nineteenth century, a set of generally accepted compositional principles, a
"common practice," facilitated a social interpretation that was widely shared
by musicians and audiences. For instance, a hearing of "voices" in chamber-
music parts was plausible not only because they were played by distinct performers on distinct instruments, but because they changed pitch in different
directions with different rhythms, following the rules of counterpoint. "Conversation" involved varied repetition of specific musical motives and themes.
And "argument" could be attributed to contrasts, or audible divergences from
established patterns.

2. The "conceptual mapping" of musical objects and relations to textual descriptions
of human actors has been theorized in Zbikowski (2002:243–286).

Eventually, however, the socially accessible nature of chamber music was transformed as Western culture increasingly rewarded independence, initiative, and productivity with money or fame. The composer has now become a sort of entrepreneur who specializes in creating musical scores, leaving their performance to other professionals. By making memorization unnecessary, scores enable performers to play more newly composed, technically and interpretatively challenging pieces. Scores also establish intellectual property rights, so that composers can "brand" their works, in order to foster more demand. Musicians seeking novel, distinctive identities naturally gravitate toward chamber music, since virtuosity and coordination are best achieved by well-rehearsed small groups of highly skilled players. Written compositions need not have a standard form, nor rely on stock gestures or repeated patterns, as do most musics that are unwritten or improvised. Variety and density of ideas can abound, ideally with every detail crafted to produce effects that cannot be achieved otherwise. Indeed, in order to appreciate fully the art of these compositions, audiences need repeatedly to listen to them in concert or on recordings, and study the scores. These habits further encourage composers to write music too complex or rapid to be grasped without such contemplation. Such specialization limits market appeal, to the extent that many composers now teach in universities without expectation that their music can sustain them financially. Professional prestige has replaced monetary gain as compensation.

"It is here, in the field of chamber music, that as a creator and human being [the composer] fully achieves his freedom" (Bujic 1982:124). But such freedom entailed the abandonment of the common practice and amateur performance that facilitated understanding music through metaphors of social intercourse. In its most extreme manifestations—seeking novelty, and cut off from dance, ritual, religion, and other social contexts that make less exact music so profound in other cultures—contemporary chamber music teeters on the edge of solipsism. It embodies the tensions in Western society between the individual and the community, narcissism and intimacy, autonomy and interdependence, demagoguery and dialog.

One Composer's Response

These tensions are vividly manifested in *Enchanted Preludes*, a brief duet for flute and cello composed in 1988 by Elliott Carter (b. 1908). The first page of the score is reproduced as figure 11.1, and a complete recording is provided on track 19 of the CD accompanying this volume.

Carter, an American who lived through most of the tumultuous twentieth century, is often characterized as a modernist—a seeker of new musical

FIGURE 11.1. *Elliott Carter,* Enchanted Preludes, *score page 1 (mm. 1–9).*

language. Certainly he strives for novelty. He has said that each of his works has a "special vision" that "give[s] it its own identity and differentiate[s] it from others" (Carter 1997:257). His technical self-sufficiency manifests itself in the rigorous, idiosyncratic systems he has developed for organizing rhythm and pitch, which are evident in his writings, sketches, and scores (Schiff [1998], Bernard [1988]). Rhythms in *Enchanted Preludes* are composed around a "long-range polyrhythm": throughout the piece each instrument moves independently to its own, extremely slow beat.[3] Carter also carefully organized pitch. He catalogued all the types of chords that can be constructed from the twelve-tone scale, and used them to create both consistency and variety of harmony within and among the parts.[4] At the beginning of the piece he also seems to have encoded in pitch both the name of the dedicatee and her date of birth.[5]

On first consideration, such organization does not offer much hope of hearing the work in terms of social intercourse. It is difficult to hear such slow beats—about every 6.7 seconds in one instrument and about every 5.4 seconds in the other. Not is it easy to infer them from the score, which notates the parts at a common, faster tempo, especially as they do not account for most of the aurally immediate rhythmic details. Similarly, few listeners would claim to hear Carter's *recherché* techniques of note-combination.

That a social interpretation is viable, however, is suggested by the composer's descriptions of the parts in his chamber music as autonomous agents. For example, he wrote about one piece that the performers "are each given music idiomatic to their instruments, meant to appeal to the[ir] imaginations . . . , and cast them into clearly identifiable, independent roles" (Carter 1997:261). Concerning *Enchanted Preludes* he was reported to say that he "tried to mirror some of [the dedicatee's] brightness, charm, and irresistible enthusiasm" (Porter 1988:92). Carter also professes attention to the interaction of these highly in-

---

3. Link (1994). Schiff (1998:46–47 *et passim*) uses the term "structural polyrhythm" to refer to the same technique. The composer himself first described it in "The Time Dimension in Music (1965)" (Carter 1997:224–228). In *Enchanted Preludes,* the cello's basic tempo is 11.2 beats per minute (MM) and the flute's is MM 9. The beats are often articulated by loud or otherwise marked events, or by changes of material. In figure 11.1, the slow beats of the flute are articulated by the attack of the **mf** D♯4 at the beginning of measure 3, the attack of the long E4 (after silence) in measure 5, and the attack of the long D♯4 (after silence) in measure 7—every fifty-sixth triplet ♪. The slow beats of the cello are articulated by the **mf** attack in measure 3, the attack of the bowed tremolo at the end of measure 4, the attack of the low notes in measure 6, and (weakly) by the attack of the F4 in the middle of measure 8—every thirtieth ♪.

4. Carter's system of chords has recently been published (Carter 2002). His classification scheme closely resembles those proposed by theorists for analyzing post-tonal music, for example, Forte 1973. In *Enchanted Preludes* "Carter emphasizes the use of four four-note chords (Nos. 3, 13 and 15) [*sic:* the fourth chord is not listed]": Schiff (1998:141–142).

5. Porter (1988:92). According to van Dyck-Hemming (2002: 195–196), the dedicatee's name, Ann Santen, is encrypted following a system used by Ravel in *Menuet sur le nom d'Haydn,* in which the letter sequence A–N–N–S becomes the flute's opening series of notes A–G–[ignoring the A♭]–G–E. This scholar also claims that the month and year, May 1938, of Mrs. Santen's birthday are encoded by Carter's numbers for the collections formed by cello's first three notes (trichord type 5) and by the flute's first six notes (hexachord 38), respectively.

dividuated parts. He describes his scores as "scenarios, auditory scenarios, for performers to act out with their instruments, dramatizing the players as individuals *and participants in the ensemble*" (Carter 1997:221). For some works he has even outlined the entire form in terms of the players' social interactions.[6] In a work contemporaneous with this one, he described "giving each member of the performing group its own musical identity . . . thus mirroring the democratic attitude in which each member of a society maintains his or her own identity while cooperating in a common effort."[7]

His brief program note for *Enchanted Preludes* is similarly evocative: "the two instruments combine their different characters and musical materials into statements of varying moods." The circumstances of its commission ("a birthday present for Ann Santen, commissioned by her husband, Harry") together with the fact that cello and flute were played in the Santen household, suggest approaching the piece specifically as a portrait of a marital relationship (van Dyck-Hemming 2002:203). Indeed a review of the first performance makes this interpretation explicit, reading it "as, among other things, a musical representation of a contented, complementary, mutually supportive, fruitful couple" (Porter 1988:92).

But what is the couple talking about? How is the relationship portrayed? Does it change during the piece? Without grounding in the specific details of the piece, as with tonal music, metaphors are no more helpful than are tempo ratios and pitch-class sets. To analyze the music in these social terms it is necessary to find accessible, audible musical materials and processes that can be directly associated with social identity and interaction. They also should be consistent with the more abstract, non-tonal structures that Carter is known to employ.[8]

---

6. Probably the most remarkable example is his description of the Brass Quintet as "a meeting of five brass players who have come together to play slow, solemn music. As they start to do so . . . the weak member of the group, the horn, interjects irrelevant, disruptive ideas that momentarily upset the plan. Given the atmosphere of discord that arises between the players, each begins to assert himself, joining partners in small groups while the excluded ones try to bring back the slow music. . . . Midway through, the horn deplores its alienation in a long unaccompanied solo, which arouses the others to a menacing duo for trumpets and an angry trio for trombones and horn. All this leads to a violent altercation that finally is settled by an agreement to continue the slow music of the beginning , , , " (Carter 1997:258).

7. Cited in Eisenlohr (1999:238), which elsewhere reproduces numerous similar comments by the composer.

8. My analysis is inspired in part by the accounts of the Introduction to Carter's String Quartet No. 2, in Cogan and Escot (1976:59–71, 206–207, 284–289). They focus on basic features of the music, including registral process, distinctive pulses, interval repertoires, imitation, "beat" modulation. They also remark on more abstract structure, observing, for instance, how the same type of chord is produced by different intervals.

Sources of Autonomy: Definitions

> Each of my works has sprung from a consideration of the instruments used in it. The special sound character of the instrumental combination has usually dictated to me all the ideas and their methods of development. In each case I have tried to find the type of music which would be the most idiomatic for the combination, for I am more concerned with sound than with abstract procedure. (Carter 1997:209)

The sound world of *Enchanted Preludes* is defined primarily by the pitch-range, timbral, and articulative capabilities of two strongly contrasting orchestral instruments. The flute is played by blowing into the instrument, which is held horizontally to the mouth, and by using both hands to finger the keys that produce changes in pitch. (During short chamber pieces the player often stands.) Normally playing just one pitch at a time, it ranges from full-sounding tones in a woman's vocal range to shrill high pitches. Because its energy source is breath, it can produce subtle shadings of loudness and timbre, and its notes can be smoothly connected (by fingering) or detached (by tonguing each attack), but the length of its gestures is limited. The cello, in contrast, is played sitting down, by holding the instrument vertically between the knees and by bowing (*arco*) or plucking (*pizzicato*) its strings with the right hand while fingering with the left. It is primarily a bass instrument, ranging two octaves below the flute, but it also has striking, intense high tessitura—overlapping the flute's lower range—and is capable, though harmonics, of reaching very high pitches as well. It can play two, three, or even four pitches at the same time (double-, triple-, and quadruple-stops), and it can sustain indefinitely.

Carter enhances the instruments' identities, projected by their contrasting timbres and ranges, with obvious contrasts of the most elemental musical percepts—pitch, interval, and meter. To describe these contrasts some basic technical definitions will be helpful. I will label *pitch* by diatonic letter-class (possibly modified by an accidental) followed by a number that indicates the octave, which changes at each C, starting with the lowest C on the piano. (Thus "middle C" is called C4, the pitch a semitone below is called B3, A♯3, or C♭4, and the cello's open strings are C2, G2, D3, and A3.) Because *Enchanted Preludes* constantly circulates all twelve notes of the chromatic scale but does not arrange them into diatonic scales or consonant triads, I will name *intervals* between pitches by the number of semitones they span, and assume enharmonic equivalence. (This assumption will be justified by the analysis to follow, which shows that differently spelled intervals function equivalently.)

The clear contrasts of pitch and rhythm between flute and cello can be specified accordingly. Most noticeably, they use completely disjoint repertoires of intervals. Whenever the flute connects two pitches melodically (without a long silence), the interval is always 1, 3, 5, 8, or 10, whereas every interval between connected or (registrally adjacent) simultaneous pitches in the cello is 2, 4, 7, 9, or 11.[9] (Neither features the only remaining pitch interval, 6.) Although the pitch structures are not diatonic, the distribution of intervals in these repertoires is easy to hear with reference to that familiar scale: each instrument has a "second" and a "seventh" (minor in the flute, major in the cello), a "third" and a "sixth" (minor in the flute, major in the cello), and a "perfect" interval (fourth in the flute, fifth in the cello). Interval 7 is natural to the cello in the sense that it spans adjacent open strings; we shall see that Carter exploits this property at some important moments.

The autonomy of the instruments, so evident in their disjoint interval repertoires, is also manifested in temporal features more audible than the long-range polyrhythms mentioned earlier. The published score obscures their independence, since it shows both parts in a single tempo with coordinated meter signatures and bar lines. Although this written tempo is useful for the performers, it is not apparent to listeners because the instruments rarely attack on the notated beat, and because they subdivide it differently. However, one can hear other regularities within each part by listening to *accent*—the emphasis of moments by loudness, high pitch, change of texture, or duration of events that begin then. When a series of accents marks off a series of equal durations, it creates a *pulse stream*, with a characteristic tempo, that gives momentum and continuity to the materials (Roeder 1994). Depending on context, I will refer to a specific pulse stream either by the way its characteristic duration is written on the score (such as "seven triplet ♪s"), or by its tempo, in beats per minutes (MM). In figure 11.1, the tempo of regular accent is different in the flute (MM72) than it is in the cello (MM67.2), that is, each instrument proceeds at its own pace. Although these pulse streams are not visually obvious on the score, I will show later in this chapter that they are easy to hear. We also shall see that each instrument often presents a distinctive *meter*, which I define simply as the persistent grouping of a relatively fast beat into either twos (duply) or threes (triply) by regular accent.

The instruments also differ in their moment-to-moment rhythmic behavior. Each plays short series of events, called *groups*, that exhibit certain con-

---

9. Schiff (1998:141–142) sources the intervals in the two hexachords of an all-interval twelve-note chord, like those Carter uses in other compositions. Indeed, in measures 6–7, the cello plays six different pitches {C2,G2,B2,C♯3,A♯3,A4} spanning the interval series <7,4,2,9,11>, and the flute plays six different pitches {D♯4,G♯4,E5,D6,F6,F♯6} spanning the interval series <5,8,10,3,1>. Together, these collections contain every note of the chromatic scale.

sistencies of loudness, attack density, contour, and register. Certain types of gestures recur: *trills,* by which I mean any rapid, even alternation of two pitches, not always close together (flute, m. 1; cello, m. 5); *tremolos,* by which I mean the rapid reiteration of a single pitch (flute, m. 1; cello, m. 6); *sustained* sounds (flute, mm. 5–6; cello, mm. 2–3); and *lines,* or series of connected pitches (flute and cello, m. 8). At any given moment, however, their groups usually contrast; they variegate their groups mercurially; and they start and stop their groups at different times.

These systematic oppositions of timbre, pitch, tempo, and grouping that Carter designed to maximize the autonomy of the instruments are particularly well suited to the genre of chamber music, because they facilitate a familiar distinction between individual actors. Obviously, such categories of discourse as "disagreement" and "talking at cross purposes" map conceptually to passages in which the two instruments strongly project their characteristic materials. However, these consistent characters also create the potential for the instruments to be heard as "cooperating" or engaging in "dialog," much as common-practice textures and contrapuntal procedures could in early chamber music.

Consider that, despite all the autonomy arising from the constraints of this piece's sound world, the instruments can be heard to "respond positively" to each other if:

- One repeats the type of group just played by the other.
- One changes its register to play near the other.
- One repeats a pitch just stated by the other. The instrumentation of the work creates asymmetries in this respect. The cello is most capable of reacting in register and pitch. It can duplicate all the flute's pitches, the highest ones "artificially," by playing harmonics of its normal notes. The timbre of these harmonics even mimics the purer tone of the flute, although they are quieter. Conversely part of the cello's range is inaccessible to the flute, a private territory.
- One repeats a diatonic type of interval (such as a "seventh") just stated by the other. A single brief repetition may not be very significant, but the more pitches or interval-types that are repeated, and the longer their durations, the stronger the interaction. Note, however, that one instrument can never repeat two or more pitches of the other *in the same order,* because it must maintain its distinctive interval repertoire.

An instrument can be heard to "respond negatively" if it responds positively in some ways, but strongly contrasts in others. I mean no value judgment by the word "negative"; it simply indicates variation in the place of expected repetition.

Furthermore, instruments can be heard to "cooperate" if:

- They simultaneously present similar textural, dynamic, or registral changes, for example, both gradually become faster, louder, and higher in parallel, even without otherwise interacting.
- They attack at the same time. This is most effective if the attacks are both accented in other ways, and if the instruments clearly mark their beats leading up to the attack, so that the listener can anticipate the moment of coincidence. If the instruments consistently articulated the beats of their distinctive pulse streams, they would attack together at least every 12.5 seconds—about every four measures. They could also attack together whenever their beat subdivisions coincide, which they could do every eighth note in figure 11.1. Remarkably, almost all such potential coincidences are avoided. In figure 11.1 they attack together only twice, at measure 3, beat 1 and at measure 8, beat 4.5, and the latter is not accented or prepared in any way. This avoidance makes the few coincidences that occur more significant.
- One instrument provides a foil for the other, for example, a relatively regular, inconspicuous, and characterless stream of sound (or even silence) against which the other instrument can set itself in relief.
- The timbres of the instruments blend. Although normally quite distinct, they blend well when the cello plays high soft harmonics, and when they both trill.
- They restrict their relations to only a few, or very distinctive intervals. Most of the time, as the instruments proceed, many different intervals form between them. The result can be a bewildering excess of information. Passages that limit the interinstrument intervals to three or four sizes give the impression of cooperation. Certain intervals that are used sparingly can also help associate different passages; one potential candidate is the tritone, 6, which is the only interval that does not belong to either instrument's repertoire.

One might imagine other modes of cooperation as well. Indeed, the extent to which we hear "response" and "cooperation" depends not only on the relatively objective structure of the piece's sound universe but also on how we conceive what we are listening to.

Even these very general consequences of the precompositional design accommodate a social reading of the piece as a portrait of a couple's relationship. The cello moves at a more deliberate tempo than the flute, and is more suited to react positively (as it can play nearly all the flute's pitches), but less inclined to evoke positive reaction (as the flute cannot play many of its pitches). Each naturally respects the other's rights to play, side-stepping the other's toes, so to speak. Separately they possess completely different repertoires; but their repertoires complement each other, omitting only an interval that appears when they are together.

But this reading still lacks specificity, in that it does not treat actual events or interactions in the order that they appear in the composition. Nor does it suggest any particular musical shape or goals. So in the remainder of this essay I will describe the form of the instruments' dialog through a series of analyses. The first will characterize the changing interactions of the instruments and the overall form of the piece in terms of its most easily perceived musical properties. The following analyses will nuance this overview by examining the pitch and rhythmic details—still readily perceptible—of certain passages, thus characterizing the interactions much more specifically. We will see that to the extent that the piece can be heard as a portrait of a couple's relationship, it is rich, subtle, and trenchant. A listener who remains open and alert to the basic and readily perceptible features of the instrumental parts will observe the instruments responding to each other and progressively deepening their cooperation throughout the piece.

Textural Overview

> What counts in listening to music is following the grand line, its forward motion, its reversals and dramatic and expressive moments. . . .
> For music is primarily flow in time, and its unity parallels the various kinds of flow of events about which we have feelings and thoughts.
> (Carter 1997:207)

The instruments' relationship develops in a series of episodes, each of which presents consistent, continuous activity, marked at its beginning by substantial change. Although these activities and changes involve very specific pitch and rhythmic processes, the form is very clear even if one attends simply to texture, dynamics, register, general types of gestures and the relative prominence of the instruments. The following narrative, keyed to timings on the recording, delineates the episodes as I hear them.[10] A good way to follow it is to read its description of each section, then play the associated segment of the record-

---

10. Van Dyck-Hemming (2002:203) presents a timeline that identifies formal divisions of the piece according to changes of loudness and "types of motion." Because she does not attend to all of the features I mention, some of her divisions differ from mine. For example, she hears an important division at 4'46", when both instruments have their loudest attacks (*sff*), but I hear this moment as part of an alternation of loud attacks that begins at 4'40".

ing, listening for the features it describes and pausing playback before the next section begins.

A. 0′00″–0′21″. Quick, isolated bursts of activity begin. The instruments' gestures are so diverse, and they change direction and loudness so frequently, that focus and connection are thwarted. Yet the gestures fall into three types that will recur throughout the piece: a rapid alternation between two pitches (*trill*), sustained sounds, and sharply articulated events scattered widely in pitch. At first the instruments alternate their groups, but soon they start to play concurrently, each stringing pitches together into longer lines, which suddenly crescendo and splay apart in register. This is a *climax*—a strongly emphasized moment to which the music builds, and from which it relaxes.

B. 0′22″–0′46″. The first significant change follows the dynamic and registral climax just mentioned. Both instruments revert to quiet, scattered, middle-register pitches. When the cello pauses, the flute settles into constant quiet murmuring. Its pitches are so brief, various, and separate that none of them comes into focus. But it gives the first sense of direction to the music, by gradually changing from isolated attacks to connected events to almost continuous rapid playing. As its *density* (rapidity of attack) rises, so do its pitch and loudness. Meanwhile the cello, after a few trills, switches to a scattered pizzicato. This change coincides with the highest pitch of the flute, whose register and density subsequently relax. When the flute has backed off (at 0′36″) the cello begins another new gesture—a sustained arch-shaped line. As it peaks, the flute suddenly counterpoises its own sustained line, to which the cello reacts with a noisy, agitated descent to a loud quadruple-stop. The flute counters with loud pairs of notes, but then both instruments rapidly trail off in a fading ascent.

C. 0′46″–1′15″. Long, high, sustained pitches in the cello preface a return to a rapid alternation of gestures, as at the beginning of the piece. Initially the instruments seem more responsive, as a trill in the flute elicits a high trill in the cello. But then they diverge: the cello cascades quickly to another loud chord, while the flute twitters. Thereafter the alternation of activities and types of playing intensifies, with little response. Abruptly the cello drops out, and the flute plays its first regular rhythm, coloring the pitches with a fluttertongue. As it stretches its line out, accelerating to a pitch climax, the cello reenters and settles into a regular quick pizzicato.

D. 1′15″–1′53″. After the whirlwind variety of the first seventy-five seconds the music now relaxes into longer sections of consistent and cooperative behavior. The flute dominates the texture, first stringing together a warm-toned arabesque, then changing to a light chattering of quickly repeated pitches, then dwelling on long, wide, sustained lines. In the background the cello segues from its energetic pizzicato to long pitches that soar languidly to a great height. While both instruments sustain pitches together, one experiences the first sense of focus, cooperation and harmony.

E. 1′53″–2′46″. As the cello achieves its highest pitch, the flute retakes its lowest register, where it resumes playing sustained melodic fragments, interspersed as earlier with some brief chatter. The cello responds to these fragments with its own lines, in the same register and with many of the same pitches, interspersing them with trills. Some of the pitches crescendo strongly, and both instruments peak slightly in loudness (although not in other respects). Then, as the flute insinuates its own trills, the dynamics slacken until the instruments alternate soft rapid trills in the middle register.

F. 2′46″–3′19″. The cello now unfolds a sustained melody, descending to its lowest pitch then rising back up. The flute responds by extending the rise to a high peak. As it falls back, the cello similarly takes over and extends the downward motion. The seesawing intensifies quickly until both instruments bump repeatedly and loudly against fixed high pitches. From this climax a rapid falloff in pitch and loudness prepares for the next section, which is anticipated by the cello's changing to a spacious pizzicato.

G. 3′19″–3′53″. A relaxed flute solo, the longest so far, gives pause to the proceedings, whereupon the cello accelerates its bounding pizzicato. Once it sets this faster tempo, it bows its longest melody so far, another arabesque that rises to focus, by insistent repetition, on pitches in the intense tenor register. The flute relegates itself to a less focused but independent role, interspersing scurrying middle-register gestures with crescendo fluttertongues.

H. 3′53″-4′40″. The increasing momentum is broken by a series of loud, disconnected declamatory gestures in both instruments. The intensity gradually diminishes, and the instruments begin to imitate each other's gestures and to recall earlier materials. But then a particularly obnoxious outburst from the cello (at 4′24″), answered by an equally vigorous swoop of the flute, provokes the quickest buildup so far. The cello saws agitatedly, and the flute plays an accelerating series of ascending swoops, ending piercingly on its highest pitch so far.

I. 4′40″–4′58″. This latest climax breaks up the continuity even more than at the previous sectional division. The flute and cello stutter single, starkly disconnected events. Eventually but in very different ways they restore momentum: the cello rises twice from a low trill to a high, sustained pitch, while the flute increases its attack density into rapid middle-register murmuring. Suddenly, however, both instruments pause on nearby pitches, crescendo, and break off.

J. 4′58″–end. There follows a quiet but striking new texture in which the instruments rapidly alternate and imitate each other's pitches within a tight range. After the preceding disagreements, this intense interaction heightens tension. Suddenly the instruments break out to climax again loudly on their respective extremes—the flute on a very high long pitch, the cello on its lowest open strings. Then they quickly reconverge to a welter of middle-register gestures, and fade away.

This overview indicates the most important divisions in the composition, and begins to indicate how processes of texture, register, and loudness can be conceived as descriptive of the instruments' relationship. At first, the alternation of brief contrasting gestures emphasizes their separateness. In section B, this autonomy strengthens as their contrasting gestures lengthen, but each instrument begins to acknowledge the other by changing its gestures at important points in the other's processes. The interaction intensifies as each responds explicitly to the other by imitating a gesture; but such responses lead at first to more intense opposition. Starting at section D, however, the instruments find several different ways to cooperate. First the cello recedes to the background, letting the flute play a sustained melody. Then both instruments sustain pitches together. In section E, they respond to each other's melodic fragments slowly and deliberately, and then gradually change together to concurrent trills. This cooperation prepares for the positive responses in section F, the most sustained so far, where the instruments take turns contributing to a single melodic shape. Although they soon become distinct, they progress in parallel toward a mutual peak, and then they relax together. The beginning of section G marks a reversal in the trend of increased dialog. First each instrument presents its longest sustained gesture, a kind of monolog foregrounded by indistinct, independent activity in the other. Then in section H the gestures become briefer and reminiscent of previous interaction; the listener senses continued responsiveness but increased tension, which culminates when both instruments suddenly flare to a concurrent loud peak. After a brief period of disintegration, they respond to each other most intensely, in section J, leading mutually to a final peak and relaxation.

As musical analysis, however, the overview still leaves some basic questions unaddressed. Do the specific interval- and tempo-distinctions between the instruments contribute to the development of the relationship, and if so, how? And how do they engage in more specifically musical processes of the piece? For instance, the sectional structure of the piece shown by this overview is not a standard form involving reprise—it is not strophic or otherwise recapitulatory. So it cannot create convincing closure in the most common way, by repeating a passage it has established as an ending. This compositional problem is heightened by the absence of traditional harmonic, contrapuntal, and melodic cadence formulas. The following discussion begins to address these specific issues.

Pitch-Interval Dialog

> In a way [musical patterns] are comparable to words and their grammatical interconnections. One word follows another, the second expanding or more often limiting the first, the third or fourth putting the previous ones in a new light. Then as whole groups of words, phrases, sentences, and paragraphs are heard these big groups react with each other, giving new meanings to what has gone before and suggesting what is to come. (Carter 1997:208)

Considering only grouping, density, and register, as we did in the overview, there appears to be little connection between the instruments at the beginning of the piece. However, although their rhythmic gestures are diverse, the instruments are already engaging in a dialog, a two-sided interaction in which both parties initiate ideas and respond to each other. To hear this, we have to recognize recurring intervals and pitches, which, of all the things we can aurally distinguish, we can describe most precisely.

The give-and-take of this dialog is sketched on figure 11.2, which presents the pitches of measures 1–5 in order but omits their durations. As indicated by the key in the left corner, solid and open notes respectively represent flute and cello pitches, and slurs denote trills (construed loosely as any quick alternation between two pitches). Numbers over brackets and lines indicate the magni-

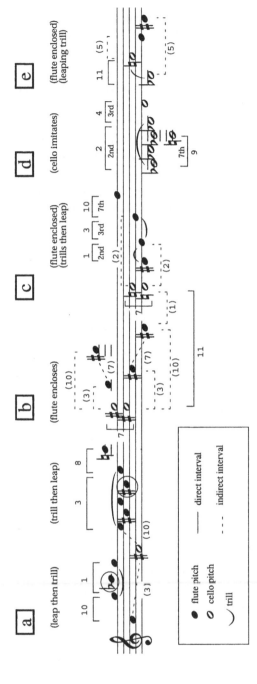

FIGURE II.2. *Pitch-interval interactions between flute and cello in mm. 1–5.*

392

tude of significant intervals, measured in semitones; solid lines connect pitches that are directly successive in one instrument, while dashed lines indicate some significant "indirect" intervals between pitches that are not successive, or that are played by different instruments.[11] In the following analytical commentary, the alphabetical label on each paragraph keys it to the moment indicated by at the same letter on the example.

a. The flute's opening gesture connects a large ascending interval, 10, to a short high trill on a small interval, 1. The cello's response, a plucked F♯4, comes as a complete *non sequitur,* because it introduces a new instrument, a new timbre, a new articulation, and a new pitch that is a new interval, 3, below the flute's first pitch. The flute's continuation can be heard as an attempt to assimilate the cello's disruption into its own discourse. The E5 that it plays is the same interval above the cello's F♯4, 10, that it played from its first pitch A4, and by falling 3 from the E5 to C♯5 it echoes the interval from that A4 to the cello's F♯4. From these reconciliatory pitches it then proceeds to execute a gesture very similar to its first: a low trill on a small interval, connected to a large ascending interval.

b. Uncompromisingly, the cello presents another new interval, 7, in a way that the flute cannot imitate—as two simultaneous, greatly extended pitches. We have heard these pitches before; in fact they had similar prominent functions, as suggested by circles on the example: the G♯5 was (as A♭5) the highest pitch of the flute's high trill, and the C♯5 was the lowest pitch of its low trill. But to recombine them in such a new way makes it seem as if the cellist was only half-listening to the flute, and is attempting to change the subject with a *pro forma* acknowledgement of the flute's highlights. The flute responds to this digression by symmetrically enclosing the cello's 7 with its characteristic intervals 3 and 10: that is, the flute's B5 and A♯5 are 3—the first interval of its second gesture—and its F♯6 and D♯4 are 10— its very first interval—above the cello's high and low pitches, respectively. The containment is not an entirely negative response; it acknowledges the cello's idea by replicating its interval, 7, indirectly between successive pitches in the same register.

c. Just as the flute's enclosing strategy becomes clear at the D♭4, the cello appears to resist confinement by shifting down 11 to another 7 double-stop, {D4, A4}, close to the bottom of the flute's range. In response the flute re-

11. Processes of interval deployment in Carter's music have been treated by Bernard (1983:5–34, esp. pp. 30–33) and Cogan and Escot (1976:64–71). Harvey (1989) similarly advocates close attention to specific intervals rather than to pitch-class sets.

mains accommodating, gradually insinuating {E4 ,G4} trills whose pitches are again equidistant from, but now *contained by* the pitches in the cello. Thus the encloser becomes enclosed. Once this symmetrical arrangement has stabilized, the flute appends to the trill a light leap upward by 10, recalling its original gestures.

d. The cello maintains its curiously defiant attitude. It forestalls further enclosure by moving out of the flute's range and reverting to a quickly decaying soft pizzicato. But it also tentatively echoes the flute for the first time, answering the ascending staccato <D♯, E, G> with a rising pizzicato <A♭, B♭, D>, and adding a note a large leap away. Measured diatonically, all the cello's intervals have the same size (second followed by third, plus a leap of a seventh) as those of the flute, but different qualities, so the cello's imitation introduces more new intervals to the dialog. Unlike previously, the flute makes no new response.

e. Seemingly mollified by the flute's forebearance, the cello now offers a remarkable reconciliation. For the first time it plays a sustained trill, clearly recalling the same gesture in the flute. Indeed, since its pitches are 11 apart, this gesture unites the trill and leap that the flute has repeatedly tried to establish. Moreover its pitches invite the flute into symmetrical enclosure— all the flute has to do is repeat the D♯4 and E4 that so prominently led to its first enclosure (described at (c) above). The sustained trill energizes the invitation, which the flute accepts deliberately and resonantly. The enclosure involves the only interval in the instruments' combined repertoires, 5, that has not yet been heard, so cooperation also brings completion.

The dense detail of this pitch-interval dialog is perhaps best appreciated by slowly playing figure 11.2 on a piano. Clearly it would be impossible to sustain it as the music proceeds, because no new intervals can be introduced, and the accumulation of new pitches overwhelms memory. But the analysis does show that the opening already presents active interactions, made audible and meaningful by the strict intervallic autonomy that the composer has given to the instruments.

Initial Rhythmic Interactions

Analogously the rhythmic autonomy of the instruments, manifested by the different tempi at which they play, provides a clearly structured environment for them to interact. To recognize both the pulse streams and their interactions, it is helpful to renotate the original score. Figure 11.3 does so for the beginning

FIGURE 11.3. *Mm. 1–9, renotated according to the instruments' distinct tempi.*

of the piece, explicitly showing the parts at different tempi.[12] Specifically it notates the triplets of the flute part in the original score more simply as regular duple durations at a faster tempo. Bar lines (and beaming) within each part indicate pulse streams and meter, as will be explained presently. Each system of figure 11.3 matches the corresponding system of figure 11.1, and measure numbers are also placed at corresponding points. Approximate timings, keyed to the recording, are also shown at the beginning of each system. Because figure 11.3 provides a clearer metrical orientation to the rhythmic groupings and important moments in the piece, it is easier to follow than the score when listening to the recording (try it).[13]

Simply identifying tempo ratios as a source of the instruments' autonomy (a common strategy in analyzing Carter's music) neglects the more important, changeable aspects of the piece: the varying presence of each pulse stream; the varying degree to which it creates meter; and the interaction of the instruments with respect to the metrical expectations they set up. With reference to the renotated score, it is possible concisely to narrate the instruments' rhythmic interactions, and to relate them to the pitch-interval interactions already observed.

- The flute leads off by introducing its characteristic duration, notated as ♩.. in figure 11.3, as the time span from its initial attack to the end (and climax) of its first gesture. To repeat this duration, and so to initiate a pulse stream, the flute needs to accent the moment indicated by the subsequent dotted bar line on figure 11.3. However, the cello distracts attention from that moment by attacking its {C♯,G♯} fifth just before it. As we heard the cello's initial pitch as a *non sequitur,* we might as well hear this attack to prevent the flute from establishing its beat (such a reading matches our hearing of this event as "changing the subject"); or the flute might be understood to postpone its agenda momentarily out of respect or curiosity.
- In any case, as the cello sustains, the flute resumes setting the tempo. It replays its characteristic duration, this time from the group-initiating B5 to

12. Link (1994:76–78) shows the different tempi in measures 71–76 by similarly renotating the parts. The instruments' tempi are derived as follows. In the original score, the flute's accents appear every seventh triplet-♪, the tempo of which, at the notated tempo of ♩ = 84, is $84*6/7 = 72$. The cello's accents are five ♪s (or multiples thereof) apart, the tempo of which is $84*4/5 = 67.2$.

13. The intervals and tempi in each part are so consistent that it is possible to identify errors in the printed score, because they violate (without other motivation) the consistent behavior. I indicate such errors with asterisks on the following figures, and explain them in the appendix.

the high F♯6, as shown by the location of the latter at the next bar line. (The flute's metrical persistence matches the initiative it is showing by enclosing the cello.) These attacks set up definite metrical expectations that are symbolized by the solid bar line at the end of the system, expectations that an attack at that point (that is, at the beginning of the second system of figure 11.3) would articulate *both* the ♩·· from the earlier F♯6 *and* the ♪·· from the C6 (which ended the first group) to the B5 (which stated the second group). Indeed, the flute attacks an accented event when expected. Surprisingly, the cello attacks at the same instant. It sounds as if the cello is measuring the flute's timing, and reacting to it, consistent with our understanding of the interval dialog at this point.

- As explained in figure 11.2(c), the flute now reverses its role with respect to the cello; however, closer attention to rhythm nuances that interpretation. As the flute places its pitches symmetrically within the cello's fifth, it becomes more continuous and irregular, alternating duple, triple and more rapid divisions, and changing pitch unpredictably. This seems to disorient the cello, for it no longer plays on or before the flute's beats. Still, the flute does maintain its tempo by regular peaks of loudness, at which gestures (often after rests) also change.[14] Bar lines on figure 11.3 show that these accents appear every ♩··. By the end of the second system, then, the flute has strongly established a MM72 beat. While listening to the recording, one can entrain this beat by clapping with the flute's first accented onsets; and for the next two systems (ignoring the cello) one can maintain it with reference to the accents shown at the bar lines.

- Another level of rhythmic organization in the flute's music is signified by the distinction between solid and dashed bar lines on figure 11.3. Starting with the onset of the C6, every second MM72 beat has a stronger accent, indicated by a solid bar line, and so these slower beats group the faster ones into a duple meter. I will call such beats *strong*. The presence of this meter helps explain why the flute sounds so deliberate on the third system: its long notes and dynamic peaks appear on the strong beats, so satisfying the listener's expectation of metric continuation.

- Figure 11.3 continues to show the bar lines extending into the fourth system, but none of the flute's accents support the duple meter it established. Perhaps the cello enables the flute's freedom by gradually establishing its own distinctive pulse stream and meter. Starting with its first double-stop,

---

14. Van Dyck-Hemming (2002:202) demonstrates the regularity of measures 5–6. In the original score (figure 11.1), some of the flute's dynamics and accent marks are parenthesized, possibly signifying relatively mild stress.

many of the cello's important accents mark the beats of a MM67.2 pulse
stream, which are indicated by bar lines every five ♪s in the cello part (as
no meter is evident before the first double-stop, figure 11.3 shows no bar
lines prior to it). At first, because the accents rarely mark successive beats,
this pulse stream cannot be heard. However a longer duration does immediately repeat. The thirty ♪s from the onset of the loud {D4,A4} double-
stop to the onset of the long {B♭3,A4} trill recur from the trill to the onset
of the cello's next event, the stuttering {C2,B2} double-stops. This duration is exactly twice the time from the first double-stop to the second. On
the figure, solid bar lines indicate this regularity. By the end of the passage, when the five-♪s pulse is also clear, the cello's pulse combination produces a triple meter, in contrast to the flute's duple. Its presence explains
why the cello now sounds so deliberate on the third system: the {C2,B2}
double-stops begin on the cello's strong beat. This imitates the flute's recent action of placing long notes on *its* strong beat.

- The flute's response to the cello's metrical achievement can be recognized
  by continued attention to pulse-stream interactions. Once established, the
  instruments' respective beats should coincide every 15 flute-measures;[15]
  these points are indicated on the figure by bar lines that connect the staves.
  After the shared attack in measure 3, the next shared beat possible in this
  scheme occurs near the end of the third system. Although the cello gives
  this moment token emphasis, the flute gives it none at all. Considering
  how volubly and consistently it has provided accent so far, its silence here
  could hardly be taken as serendipitous.

- Indeed the flute's subsequent actions reinforce the impression that it is responding to coalescing of the cello's meter. First, it recalls the cello's disruptive opening gambit: it attacks a long note (on its strong beat) just before the cello's next anticipated strong beat. Soon after, as the cello starts
  to provide accent every five ♪s, the flute starts to neglect articulating its
  own beat.

This narrative suggests that rhythmic interactions, in the context of the
instruments' distinct pulse continuities, account for important aspects of the
character of this introductory passage. During their rapid-fire intervallic repar-
tee, the flute and cello maintain metrical composure, each emphasizing its materials at its own characteristic pace. Their autonomy is further evident in the
different ways that they organize their respective measures: the flute produces

---

15. Fourteen cello-measures of five ♪s last 70 ♪s, or 35 ♪s, which equals 105 triplet ♪s,
the duration of 15 flute-measures of seven triplet ♪s.

more frequent accents, and emphasizes every second one, whereas the cello's places fewer accents farther apart but gives each one more weight. Each also seems to anticipate the other's strong beats, and to take the other's keeping of strict time as an opportunity for relative rhythmic freedom.

Such a detailed account of interactions also makes it possible to answer some fundamental questions about the piece's form. So far, we have described how it divides texturally into distinct sections. We have also taken on faith the existence of a long-range polyrhythm, according to which the instruments' strong beats will occasionally coincide. But neither of these descriptions engages the developing pitch and rhythmic relationship of the instruments, nor explains how the ending provides satisfying closure. Let us therefore examine other sections, remaining focused on the basic musical processes—of pitch, interval, meter, and pulse—that animate the piece's sound world.

Deepening Engagements

In the manner of figure 11.3, figure 11.4 renotates measures 30–58 to show the distinct tempi of the instruments. During this passage these tempi are easier to follow, either by clapping along with the flute' accents (ignoring the cello) starting in measure 30, or (ignoring the flute) clapping along with the cello's accents starting in measure 32. Moreover, as shown by the solid bar lines, the pulse streams are organized hierarchically within each part into a meter—again duply in the flute and triply in the cello—more clearly than were the pulse streams in figure 11.3. The persistence of pulse streams and meter gives this passage, over a quarter of the entire piece, a rhythmic coherence that the preceding and following sections lack.

Clear cooperative behavior also unifies this section. Moments at which the instruments' beats coincide (shown again by bar lines that connect the staves) are rarely marked strongly, but the behavior of the instruments tends to change immediately after them. For instance, after the coincident beats in measure 32, the instruments shift to long sustained notes; after measure 41, the cello peaks in pitch and the flute retakes a low register; and after measure 54, both instruments switch to trilling dyads. Meter also changes subtly after this last coincident beat: the cello effectively doubles its tempo, placing accents on multiples of five thirty-seconds—as shown by the bar lines drawn through half the cello staff—instead of multiples of five ♪'s.

Abstractly, at least, the reappearance of these particular tempi starting at measure 33 recalls the beginning of the composition. Pitch processes strengthen this association. The instruments resume their enclosing behavior, and they recall specific intervallic ideas of the opening measures. Figure 11.5, in a format

FIGURE 11.4. *Continued*

FIGURE 11.4. *Continued*

similar to figure 11.2, summarizes these reprises during the sustained-note passage, measures 33–41.

   a. In measure 33, the flute and cello repeat series of interval from measure 1:
      the semitone returning-note figure and a succession <3,8> in the flute,
      with a double-stop 7 in cello harmonics.
   b. Soon thereafter the instruments resume the enclosure behavior of measures
      2–5, featuring the flute's characteristic interval 3. The cello's {D5,C#6} double-
      stop symmetrically encloses the flute's Bb5 and F5.
   c. Then the flute plays two 3s, {A4,C4} and {A#5,C#6}, that symmetrically
      enclose the cello's next double-stop, {E5,F#5}. The cello's two pitch-dyads
      exactly recall measures 18–19 [0'46"-0'52"].

FIGURE 11.5. *How mm. 33–4 reprise the opening music.*

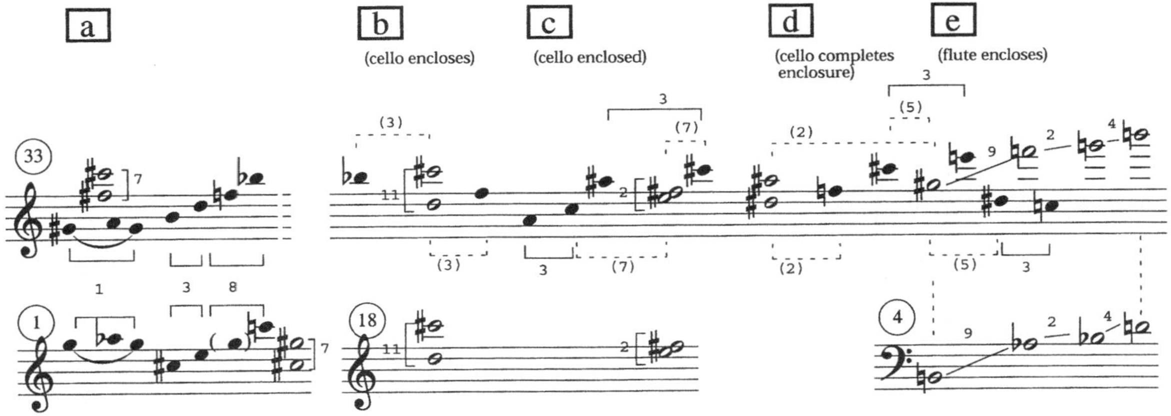

403

d. As the cello changes to {D♯5,A♯5}, the flute plays an F5 that is 2 above the lowest note. The cello completes the symmetry by abandoning double-stops to play G♯5, 2 below the {D♯5,A♯5}'s highest note.

e. The flute again plays two 3s, {C♯6,E6} and {C5,D♯5}, which now symmetrically enclose the cello's G♯5. As the cello floats higher it reprises the distinctive series of intervals, <9,2,4>, that it played pizzicato in measure 4.

This renewed cooperation seems to open the door to new modes of inter-action. For instance, starting at measure 42, as they shift down to a lower reg-ister, they begin a dialog of contradiction. The flute plays a long C4 then A♭4. As it sustains the latter pitch, the cello enters with C4, recalling the last flute pitch, and crescendos to heighten the expectation of change. However, it can-not continue to imitate the flute without playing an interval 8 that belongs to the flute, so it changes instead by 9 to A4, emphasizing its difference and its independence. Similarly, in measures 46–47, the cello answers the flute's <D4,F4> 3 with {D4, F♯4} 4, sharing one pitch but clinging to its own interval.

Closer cooperation develops further into this quiet long section. To illus-trate, figure 11.6 abstracts the pitches of measures 54–58, labeling the direct in-tervals within each instrument with solid brackets and larger numbers, and the indirect intervals with dotted brackets and smaller parenthesized numbers, as in earlier figures. It shows that the instruments engage in similar behavior: each presents two of its small intervals (mostly in trills) then two of its large intervals. Across the passage, then, both flute and cello gradually expand their intervals. At the point of transition from small to large (in the middle of the figure) the instruments exchange pitches, recombining those that made small intervals, {D♭4, E♭4} and {A4,B♭4}, into large intervals {C♯4, A4} and {E♭4,B♭4}. Another striking coordination becomes evident by considering interval *classes,* that is, by considering 1s and 11s to be the same type of interval, 2s and 10s, 3s and 9s, and so on. Under this scheme, one can hear the instruments exchang-ing materials: in the second half of the passage, the flute plays the same classes of interval that the cello played in the first half, and vice versa. Another col-laboration is clarified by the dotted brackets, which for each pair of dyads show the four intervals between flute and cello. Considering these intervals along with the dyads themselves, one can hear every pair of dyads presenting exactly one of each of the six interval classes.[16] The resulting harmonic stasis helps to create a cadence.

16. This particular "all-interval tetrachord" is practically ubiquitous in Carter's music. Passages in *String Quartet No. 1* and *Night Fantasies* similarly organize a variety of dyads into chords of this type; see Carter (1997:219–220), and Link (1994:105–108).

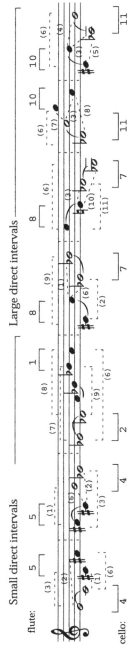

FIGURE 11.6. *Cooperation in mm. 54–58.*

Closure

To understand how these varying engagements come to a satisfying conclusion, let us examine, with attention to by-now familiar processes of pitch and rhythm, the music from the climax at measure 105 to the end. Figure 11.7 notates the instruments in two different tempi, as did figures 11.3 and 11.4. Its solid bar lines show that the instruments resume their independent but strictly metrical behavior, which is the main source of continuity during the abrupt changes, intensifications, and reprises of the closing passage. These all occur on the flute's or cello's beat, so clapping along with one or the other is especially gratifying. However, the presence of these meters varies substantially. This indicates continued rhythmic interaction, which coordinates with some other significant interactions:

- For instance, from measures 108–111, the flute's rapid runs do not clearly support its meter. This helps foreground the cello, which accents each of its strong beats with its open-string C2 or with high, sustained pitches.
- When the cello concludes its brief solo on a blaring A♭4, the flute suddenly halts its runs on a loud B♭4. The interval 2 between them, which is agitated by the cello's intensity and the flute's fluttertongue, is noteworthy. Because it is a member of the cello's repertoire, the flute cannot produce it except collaboratively. In the entire piece this has happened rarely but always emphatically: in measure 3, when the flute enclosed its {E4,G4} within the cello's {D4,A4}(see (c) in figure 11.2); in measure 36, during an analogous enclosure (see (d) in figure 11.5); in measures 45 and 52, during close imitation (figure 11.4); and at the crux of the highly cooperative passage in measures 54–57 (see figure 11.6). Its presence here, then, may be taken as a signal of the flute's willingness to resume closer interaction with the cello. Both instruments crescendo expectantly as they hold this interval, but the cello suddenly "blinks," shifting to another pitch, and then playing a confused tritone (6), which belongs to neither of their repertoires.
- Undeterred, the flute proceeds to initiate the closest engagement of the piece. A brief review of previous rapprochements is helpful for appreciating its significance. In measures 43–47 (figure 11.4, [1'57"]), the instruments shared single pitches, but disagreed on intervals. In measures 54–57 (figure 11.4, [2'34"]), they maintained a constant set of interval classes but (mostly) avoided sharing pitches. Now, in measures 111–114, they both construct brief fragments, using their own intervals, from the same six pitches {F4,G♭4,A4,B♭4,C5,D♭5}. In other words, they have found a way

FIGURE 11.7. *Mm. 105–121 renotated according to the instruments' distinct tempi.*

to maximize contact while still maintaining their distinctive intervallic identities.

• During this contact their rhythms are also very similar. Especially starting in measure 113, the cello mimics the flute's rapid melodic fragments. However they also hold strongly to their metric identities. Figure 11.7 shows that all the flute's group-beginnings, long notes, and dynamic accents occur on

FIGURE II.7. *Continued*

its MM72 beats. The cello, despite some new fast subdivisions to be discussed below, maintains a slow pulse, producing accent at each solid bar
line in the figure.

• After measure 114, the cooperation breaks down. The flute breaks first out
  of the pitch collection. The cello responds with a loud E5, which it leads
  to C5 by its characteristic interval 4. The flute contradicts this gesture in

the same way the cello contradicted the flute in measures 43–47 (figure 11.4): it also plays E5, but then changes to C♯5 by its own characteristic interval 3. Along with the intensifying dynamics, this contradiction gives the entire pitch-sharing episode an affect of competition, rather than harmony. Indeed the instruments instantly proceed to climax once more in their extreme registers.

- Meanwhile, the cello has been complicating its metrical behavior, as explicated in figure 11.8. The top staff of each system shows the pitches and dynamics of the part's most accented events. The lower staves rewrite the rhythm using as the basic beat a ♩ at MM67.2 (rather than the actual five-♪s). This rhythm shows that during measures 105–110 the meter is clearly quadruple. For the first three measures, it is quite easy to beat along with the recording; the fourth measure is muddled, but the long A♭4 in the fifth measure clearly appears on the beat. When instruments change to their intense pitch engagements of section J, the cello's meter undergoes several shifts. As shown on the bottom system of figure 11.8, it keeps the beat, but groups it into a triple meter (the strong beats are signaled by long notes). It then doubles the slow ♩. beat, producing what is notated on the figure as two measures of 6/8. At measure 117, however, it reverts to a clear quadruple meter again, signaling the strong beat with the loud open-string C2 that has appeared so frequently at other strong beats since measure 105. As shown on the bottom staff, this strong beat is exactly four 4/4 measures from the start of the section, so if one beats time to the original meter, this event will sound strong.

- In the last few measures after these climaxes, the opposition is mollified by a variety of cadential processes. The return of the cello's low C2, which has often marked section boundaries, is the first sign of ending. Thereafter, both instruments reduce their loudness and retreat to a less extreme register. As detailed by figure 11.9, they also make numerous allusions to their opening music. The flute's quick descent in measure 118 to a sustained D♮4 is nearly the retrograde of its rapid flourish in measure 6, and its final pitches allude to its trills in measures 3–4. The cello arpeggiates the same pitches in measure 118 as it did in measure 7; in measure 119 its trembling {B♭3, A4} double-stops recall the trill on the same pitches in measure 4; it includes a left-hand pizzicato on its open C string, as did measure 7; it exactly replays the pizzicato pitches of measure 4; and it ends with a sustained double-stop in harmonics that recalls measure 3. Although these diverse gestures sounded disruptive at first, they now seem relatively stable both in context of what we have since experienced, and because they proceed more consistently with the established meters.

FIGURE 11.8. *The cello's changing meter in mm. 108–120.*

- The hard-won conciliation is confirmed by the final event of the piece at measure 120, when the instruments' respective strong beats coincide *and* they attack together for the first time since measure 3.[17] The significance of this moment in the larger narrative of the piece is that the instruments have found ways to reassert their independence but still direct it towards a predictable and unifying goal. The effect depends on the instruments making their pulses clear enough to follow so that the listener can anticipate their coincidence. Indeed, they are clear: regular beats in the flute can easily be entrained from 5′09″, and in the cello from 5′14″. The final pitch-state of the instruments also projects a union of equals: they share G4 but maintain their identity, the cello sustaining it calmly with A4, as part of the "cooperative" interval 2, and the flute fading from a flutter-tongue (recalling its invitation to cooperate in mm. 111) to a slowing stutter.

17. Both Link (1994) and van Dyck-Hemming (2002) remark on this shared attack as a consequence of the large-scale polyrhythmic design, but don't discuss how it is prepared by pulse clarity and pitch reprises.

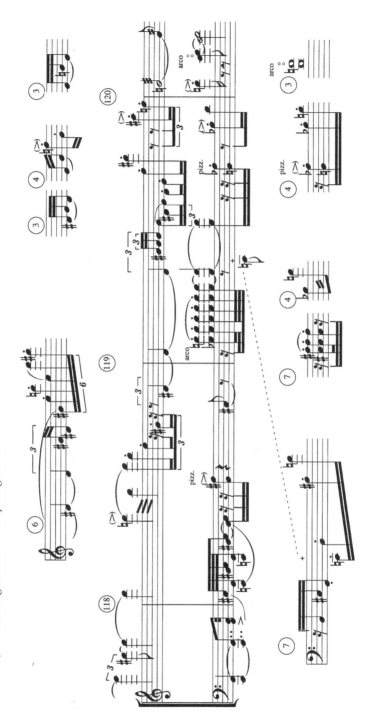

FIGURE II.9. *Concluding allusions to the opening music.*

Summary

Taking a broad view of the musical details discussed in figures 11.2–11.9, we can now see how, as the piece progresses, the interactions between the instruments deepen, first as manifested in their sharing of pitches. Initially the instruments acknowledge each other's pitch territories, through symmetrical positioning, sharing no pitches except to make contrasting gestures. The symmetrical posturing persists for a while, but then the instruments begin to share many more pitches within similar sustained gestures. Starting at measure 43, they deliberately match some pitches but contradict others.[18] Near the end of the piece, they share a large number of pitches, but end up competing to brand the shared collection with their distinct intervallic identities. Finally, they resolve to share a single pitch and an interval that has been featured earlier during their most cooperative episodes.

In parallel, metrical dialog also develops across the piece. At first the instruments react negatively to each other's regularity by distracting attention from each other's anticipated beats. In the central cooperative sections, there is less conflict, but they resolutely maintain their metrical independence. At the end, however, these distinct pulses are instrumental—indeed, essential—in directing them to a shared attack.

Enchanted Preludes thus reconciles the tension between autonomy and dialogue on several levels. As a token of Carter's composition practice, it strongly presents that composer's distinctive, sophisticated, and novel musical language, but it employs that language in an elemental enough way to be accessible to attentive audiences. The interactions of the highly differentiated instruments can be read as a narrative of conciliation, in which they find ways to respect and highlight each other's differences, and even to share materials. Such a reading also appeals to audiences' historical understanding of chamber music as an abstract representation of social intercourse, placing the work squarely in the traditions of the genre. The richness of the dialog that is made possible by its highly refined autonomies may be taken as symbolic of a close marital relationship, or perhaps more generally as an affirmation of the democratic ideals of the composer's society. In any event, the piece exemplifies how contemporary musicians who reject traditional modes of coordination and continuity can invent special sound worlds in which elemental, expressive processes are formed and perceived.

---

18. See Link (1994:78) for a description of another intermediate, rhythmic stage in the developing relationship between the instruments.

Appendix: Errata in the Published Score of *Enchanted Preludes*

CLEAR ERRORS:

- m. 14, beat 1, cello: the beamed group should be ♪ ♪ ♪, not ♪ ♪ ♪
- m. 39, beat 1, flute: there should be a triplet bracket over the first (tied) ♩ and the following ♪.
- m. 65, beat 1, cello: the first note should be an ♪, not a dotted ♪.
- m. 72, beats 3–4, flute: a quintuplet bracket is missing over the ♪ ♩ here.
- m. 111, beat 3, cello: this beamed group is a ♪ too short; the last note head should probably be a ♪, and the following rest a dotted sixteenth.
- m. 113: the time signature should change to 3/4.
- m. 119, beat 2, cello: the C2 should have a + over it, indicating left-hand pizzicato.

PROBABLE RHYTHMIC ERRORS

In each case the corrections involve a simple reversal of order, and will maintain the established pulse streams, which the uncorrected versions do not.

- m. 38, beat 4, cello: the beamed group should be ♪ then dotted ♪, not vice versa.
- m. 43, beat 4, flute: the triplet group should be ♩ then ♪, not vice versa.
- m. 115, beat 6, flute: the beamed triplet group should be ♪ then ♪, not vice versa.

POSSIBLE PITCH ERRORS

- m. 23, beat 1, flute: the first pitch, F5, forms intervals, 7 and 4, with the preceding and following pitches, but these intervals are not characteristic of the flute. Should it be E5?
- m. 109, beat 4, flute: the A4s should be natural, not sharp as they are earlier in the long measure, in order to form the characteristic intervals 3 from the preceding F♯4 and 5 to the following D5.

References

Adorno, Theodor W. 1962. *Introduction to the Sociology of Music.* Trans. E. B. Ashton, 1976. New York: The Seabury Press.

Barzun, Jacques. 2000. *From Dawn to Decadence.* New York: HarperCollins.

Bashford, Christina. 2001. "Chamber Music." In *The New Grove Dictionary of Music and Musicians,* ed. S. Sadie and J. Tyrrell. London: Macmillan, vol. 5, 434–448.

Bernard, Jonathan. 1983. "Spatial Sets in Recent Music of Elliott Carter." *Music Analysis* 2/1:5–34.

———. 1988. "The Evolution of Elliott Carter's Rhythmic Practice." *Perspectives of New Music* 26/2: 164–203.

Bujic, Bojan. 1982. "Chamber Music in the Twentieth Century: Cultural and Compositional Crisis of a Genre." *British Journal of Aesthetics* 22:115–125.

Carter, Elliott. 1997. *Collected Essays and Lectures, 1937–1995.* Ed. Jonathan Bernard. Rochester, N.Y.: University of Rochester Press.

———. 2002. *Harmony Book.* Ed. Nicholas Hopkins and John F. Link. New York: Carl Fischer.

Cogan, Robert, and Pozzi Escot. 1976. *Sonic Design.* Englewood Cliffs, N.J.: Prentice Hall.

Eisenlohr, Henning. 1999. *Komponieren als Entscheidungsprozeß: Studien zur Problematik von Form und Gehalt, dargestellt am Beispiel von Elliott Carters "Trilogy for oboe and harp" (1992)*. Kassel: Gustav Bosse Verlag.

Forte, Allen. 1973. *The Structure of Atonal Music*. New Haven, Conn.: Yale University Press.

Habermas, Jürgen. 1962. *The Structural Transformation of the Public Sphere: An Inquiry into a Category of Bourgeois Society*. Trans. Thomas Burger, 1989. London: Polity.

Harvey, David I. H. 1989. *The Later Music of Elliott Carter: A Study in Music Theory and Analysis*. New York: Garland.

Link, John F. 1994. "Long-Range Polyrhythms in Elliott Carter's Recent Music." Ph.D. dissertation, City University of New York.

Porter, Andrew. 1988. "Preludes to Felicity." *The New Yorker,* June 13:92–94.

Roeder, John. 1994. "Interacting Pulse Streams in Schoenberg's Atonal Polyphony." *Music Theory Spectrum* 16/2:231–249.

Schiff, David. 1998. *The Music of Elliott Carter*. 2nd ed. Ithaca, N.Y.: Cornell University Press.

van Dyck-Hemming, Annette. 2002. "Diskurse zur 'Musik Elliott Carters'. Versuch einer dekonstruktiven Hermeneutik 'Moderner Musik'." Ph.D. dissertation, Rheinischen Friedrich-Wilhelms-Universität zu Bonn.

Zbikowski, Lawrence. 2002. *Conceptualizing Music*. New York: Oxford University Press.

Contents of the Companion Website www.oup.com/us/aswm

Track	Time	Title	Performers/Composers
12	5:22	*Oleg Tumulilingan* (first part)	Musicians of STSI Academy, Denpasar, Bali. Recorded in Denpasar by the author, 1991.
13	8:38	*Ladrang Pangkur*	Condhong Raos Group, Ki Nartosabdho, director. From P. T. Wisanda/Lokananta cassette *Aneka Pangkur* (WD-508), recorded 1976.
14	8:29	*Jin Yuan Seeks Her Son,* sections 4–6.	Yang Feifei. The recording comes from the singer's own archives. Used with permission.
15	5:35	*Valachi Vacchi*	Trivandrum R. S. Mani (vocal), T. H. Subaschandran, (mrdangam). From *An Anthology of South Indian Classical Music,* 4-CD album, C 590001/2/3/4, Ocora Radio France. Used with permission.
16	1:46	Lecture	Dr. S. Bhagyalekshmy. From the cassette series *Raghadara: Encyclopedia on Carnatic Mela and Janya Ragas* (CBH Audio, Chennai, Tamil Nadu, India).
17	0:48	Sung examples	Dr. S. Bhagyalekshmy
18	1:54	A short model composition based on "Twinkle . . . ," in sonata form	William Benjamin, piano. Recording corresponds to the author's figure 10.9. Including a recording of Mozart K.453/I proved impractical, but the author suggests several widely available ones on p. 353.
19	5:33	*Enchanted Preludes* (Elliott Carter)	Dorothy Stone, flute; Erika Doke, cello. Courtesy New Albion Records Inc., www.newalbion.com. The California EAR Unit—NA019CD.

Numbers in boldface direct the reader to definitions or initial descriptions.

(a) ask Irani / Javanese etc musicians
to describe / analyse
a piece of western music

(b) to discuss our (ie western)
concepts of music
ie emotion
role of rhythm
melody / harmony / accompaniment etc.
pitch / tuning

(c) mistakes r
(how do the players respond?
what is a mistake?)

Lightning Source UK Ltd.
Milton Keynes UK
UKOW06f1536280615

254250UK00001B/28/P